The Philosophical Foundations of Early German Romanticism

SUNY series, Intersections: Philosophy and Critical Theory
Rodolphe Gasché, Editor

The Philosophical Foundations of
Early German Romanticism

Manfred Frank

Translated by Elizabeth Millán-Zaibert

State University of New York Press

Published by
State University of New York Press, Albany

© 2004 State University of New York

All rights reserved

Printed in the United States of America

For information, contact State University of New York Press, Albany, NY
www.sunypress.edu

Production by Judith Block
Marketing by Fran Keneston

Library of Congress Cataloging-in-Publication Data

Frank Manfred, 1945–
    [Unendliche Annäherung. Part 3. English]
    The philosophical foundations of early German romanticism / Manfred Frank ; translated
by Elizabeth Millán-Zaubert.
      p. cm. — (SUNY series, Intersections)
    Includes bibliographical references (p.) and index.
    Contents: On early German romanticism as an essentially skeptical movement — On the
historical origins of Novalis' critique of Fichte — On the unknowability of the absolute —
On the search for the unconditioned — On Hölderlin's disagreement with Schelling's
Ich-Schrift — On Hölderlin's critique of Fichte — On Isaac von Sinclair — On Jakob
Zwilling's Über das Alles — On Novalis' pivotal role in early German romanticism — On
Friedrich Schlegel's place in the Jena constellation — On the origins of Schlegel's talk of a
Wechselerweis and his move away from a philosophy of first principles — On Schlegel's
role in the genesis of early German romantic theory of art.
    ISBN 978-0-7914-5947-8 (alk. paper) — 978-0-7914-5948-5 (pbk. : alk. paper)
    1. Romanticism—Germany. 2. Philosophy, German—18th century. 3. Philosophy,
German—19th century. I. Title. II. Intersections (Albany, N.Y.)

B2748.R64F74213   2003
141'.6'0943—dc22
                                  2003059023

10 9 8 7 6 5 4 3 2 1

Contents

Acknowledgments   vii

Frequently Cited Texts and Abbreviations   ix

Introduction: "What Is Early German Romanticism?"   1

Lecture 1   On Early German Romanticism as an Essentially Skeptical Movement: The Reinhold-Fichte Connection   23

Lecture 2   On the Historical Origins of Novalis' Critique of Fichte   39

Lecture 3   On the Unknowability of the Absolute: Historical Background and Romantic Reactions   55

Lecture 4   On the Search for the Unconditioned: From Jacobi's 'Feeling' to Schelling and Hölderlin's 'Intellectual Intuition'   77

Lecture 5   On Hölderlin's Disagreement with Schelling's *Ich-Schrift*   97

Lecture 6   On Hölderlin's Critique of Fichte   113

Lecture 7   On Isaac von Sinclair   127

Lecture 8   On Jakob Zwilling's *Über das Alles*   141

Lecture 9   On Novalis' Pivotal Role in Early German Romanticism   151

Lecture 10   On Friedrich Schlegel's Place in the Jena Constellation   177

Lecture 11   On the Origins of Schlegel's Talk of a *Wechselerweis* and His Move Away from a Philosophy of First Principles   191

Lecture 12   On Schlegel's Role in the Genesis of Early German
              Romantic Theory of Art   201

Notes   221
Glossary   251
Bibliography   255
Index   277

Acknowledgments

This translation has been a kind of infinite approximation all of its own, and its completion is due in part to the support and assistance of many people. First of all, to Manfred Frank who, through his written work and in generous conversation, helped me to see the contemporary philosophical relevance of early German Romanticism. Professor Frank also helped me to develop my own interpretation of Friedrich Schlegel's views and, as the antithesis of the stuffy Herr Professor Doktor, provided a marvelous atmosphere of *Symphilosophie* during the two years I spent in Tübingen working with him (and in the philosophically rich company of my fellow Romanticists, Marion Schmaus, Heather Sullivan, Eva Corino, and Birgit Rehme-Iffert). The seed of this project was planted by Dagmar Mirbach, and I am grateful to her for her friendship and support. I would also like to express gratitude to the series editor, Rodolphe Gasché, who has been supportive of the project from the start and patiently understanding throughout the process. Many thanks are owed to the production editor, Judith Block, for her efficiency and kind support during the final stages of this project. The Department of Philosophy at DePaul University helped by providing two graduate research assistants to help with the project. Joanie Benno helped with the preparation of the bibliography and Christina Gschwandtner meticulously proofread the entire manuscript and translated some of the passages in Lectures Three and Eight. I consulted versions of Lecture Four and Lecture Five that were translated by Michelle Koch, my thanks to her for sharing that material with me. A version of the second part of Lecture Nine was translated by Günther Zöller, and I have consulted his excellent translation.[1] Recently, during an NEH summer institute on early German Romanticism under the direction of Karl Ameriks and Jane Kneller,

I had the good fortune of having the opportunity to discuss some final translation decisions with fellow participants. Michael Vater and Yvonne Unna were particularly generous and helpful, many thanks are owed to them. Bob Richards read the entire manuscript, and his comments were of great value. To my husband, Leo, I owe an infinite amount of gratitude for his unwavering encouragement and patience through my long engagement with this project.

Frequently Cited Texts
and Abbreviations

AA   *Kants gesammelte Schriften* (Akademie-Ausgabe). Published
            by the Königliche Preußische Akademie der Wissenschaften,
            Berlin (Reimer), later by the Deutsche Akademie der
            Wissenschaften in Berlin and Leipzig, de Gruyter. 29 vol-
            umes, 1900 ff.

Aenesidemus [Gottlob Ernst Schulze]: *Aenesidemus oder über die Funda-
            mente der von dem Herrn Professor Reinhold in Jena gelieferten
            Elementar-Philosophie. Nebst einer Vertheidigung gegen die
            Anmassungen der Vernunftkritik*, 1792. New edition, edited
            with an introduction by Manfred Frank. Hamburg: Meiner,
            1996.

Beyträge   Karl Leonhard Reinhold, *Beyträge zur Berichtigung bisheriger
            Mißverständnisse der Philosophen*. Jena: Widtmann and
            Mauke, 1790, 1794.

CPR   Immanuel Kant, *Critique of Pure Reason*, translated by
            Norman Kemp Smith. New York: Modern Library, 1958.

FHA   Friedrich Hölderlin, *Sämtliche Werke* (Historisch-Kritische
            Ausgabe), edited by Dietrich E. Sattler. Frankfurt/M.-Basel:
            Verlag Roter Stern, 1975 ff.

GA   Johann Gottlieb Fichte, Gesamtausgabe der Bayerischen
            Akademie der Wissenschaften, edition by Reinhard Lauth
            and Hans Jacob. Stuttgart-Bad Canstadt: Fromann, 1962 ff.

GW   Salomon Maimon, *Gesammelte Werke*, edited by Valerio
              Vera, 6 volumes. Hildesheim: Olms, 1965–76.

KA   Friedrich Schlegel, *Kritische Ausgabe seiner Werke*, edited by
              Ernst Behler, et al. Paderborn: Schöningh, 1958 ff.

KTA   Friedrich Hölderlin, *Sämtliche Werke, Kritische Textausgabe*,
              edited by D. E. Sattler. Darmstadt and Neuwied: Luchter-
              land, 1982.

Mat.   *Materialien zu Schellings philosophischen Anfängen*, edited by
              Manfred Frank and Gerhard Kurz. Frankfurt/M: Suhrkamp,
              1975.

NS   Novalis, *Schriften*, edited by Paul Kluckhohn and Richard
              Samuel. Stuttgart: Kohlhammer, 1960 ff.

Plitt   *Aus Schellings Leben. In Briefen*, edited by Gustav Leopold
              Plitt, 3 volumes. Leipzig: Herzel, 1869/70.

Raisonnements *Philosophische Raisonnements von Issak von Sinclair*, in
              Hannelore Hegel, *Issak von Sinclair zwischen Fichte, Hölderlin
              und Hegel: Ein Beitrag zur Entstehungsgeschichte der ideal-
              istischen Philosophie*. Frankfurt/M: V. Klostermann, 1971.

Spin.2   Friedrich Heinrich Jacobi, *Über die Lehre des Spinoza in
              Briefen an Herrn Moses Mendelssohn*. Breslau: Löwe, 1789.

StA   Friedrich Hölderlin, *Sämtliche Werke* (Stuttgart Edition),
              edited by Friedrich Beißner and Adolf Beck. Stuttgart:
              Cottanachfolger, 1943–85.

SW   Friedrich Wilhelm Joseph Schelling, *Sämtliche Werke*,
              edited by K. F. A. Schelling. Stuttgart: Cotta, 1856–61.

TS   Ludwig Tieck, *Schriften*. Berlin: G. Reimer, 1828–1854.

Versuch   Karl Leonhard Reinhold, *Versuch einer neuen Theorie des
              menschlichen Vorstellungsvermögen*. Prague and Jena:
              Widtmann and Mauke, 1789.

WW   Johann Gottlieb Fichte, *Werke*, edited by Immanuel Her-
              mann Fichte. Berlin: Veit, 1846–46.

Introduction
"What is Early German Romanticism?"

Elizabeth Millán-Zaibert

I n introducing these lectures on early German Romantic philosophy to Anglophones, I face a similar problem to that which captivated early German Romantic philosophers: the problem of where to begin. Theirs was the problem of philosophy's starting point; the problem of what the foundations of our knowledge claims are.[1] Mine is the problem of introducing the early German Romantic thinkers as philosophers, given that they are pervasively viewed as merely, or predominantly, literary figures. My beginning point is in part determined by the widespread misconceptions and caricatures concerning the nature of early German Romanticism, factors which impede an accurate understanding of the movement.

Early German Romanticism or *Frühromantik* is a movement heralded for its poetic achievements, scorned for its nationalistic leanings, and characterized as a celebration of the imagination in its most creative freedom. Moreover, the movement is also seen as having sowed the seeds of fascism, Nazism, and many other evils.[2] The early German Romantics themselves are typically described, therefore, as thinkers lost in swells of passion and with a will guided by nothing more than the indulgences and excesses of the individual creative spirit, and so bent on the path of the destruction of reason and science. Yet, they are at times also described as thinkers who helped to promote liberalism, toleration, and decency in society.[3] What is the true nature of this seemingly Janus-faced movement and of these thinkers who seem at once not only to be poetic, progressive social leaders, but also dark villains set on unsettling the very structures of a just and decent society?

Answering questions such as "*What is early German Romanticism?*" or "*Who counts as an early German Romantic and why?*" is not as easy as it might seem. The very term "early German Romanticism" limits our answers from the start in rather obvious ways. Anyone outside the sphere of influence of the German language (central Europe), could not count as a German Romantic. And one would also have to consider the specific chronological assessment of Romanticism in general which divides it (rightly, for reasons that shall become clear immediately) into early, middle (or high), and late Romanticism. Early German Romanticism was centered alternatively in Jena and Berlin between the years of 1794 and 1808. This geographical/chronological demarcation is important in distinguishing the movement from what was indeed a more literary movement, middle Romanticism (1808–1815), which was shaped by the work of poets and artists such as Achim von Arnim, Clemens Brentano, Caspar David Friedrich, and Adam Müller. Moreover, it provides a way to distinguish early German Romanticism from what was a more conservative movement, late Romanticism (1816–1830), whose leading figures included Franz Baader, E. T. A. Hoffmann, Johann von Eichendorff, Friedrich J. Schelling, and the elder Friedrich Schlegel who himself underwent a major philosophical transformation.

Rather than simply giving names and dates, in these lectures, Manfred Frank tackles the difficult problem of how to characterize the early German Romantics by attending to their philosophical positions and achievements. Frank analyzes several key texts of the early Romantic period, beginning with the first reactions to Immanuel Kant's critical philosophy that were voiced by Karl Leonhard Reinhold and Johann Gottlieb Fichte, because it was around these two figures in Jena between the years 1790 and 1794, that a circle of students forged a philosophical path radically different from the path of their teachers, a path that eventually led them to break new ground in the analysis of the very definition of philosophy. In Jena and Berlin, a strong community formed around August Wilhelm Schlegel and his brother Friedrich, as well as Friedrich Daniel Ernst Schleiermacher, Friedrich von Hardenberg (Novalis), Ludwig and Sophie Tieck, Dorothea Veit Schlegel, and Caroline Schlegel Schelling.

While these geographical and chronological details are important, and to pay some attention to these factors at first is almost a perfunctory duty, they leave the philosophical substance of this movement obscure. Manfred Frank is well aware that one does not arrive at the philosophical meaning of any movement merely by finding a group of thinkers who overlapped in the same place at the same time. If this were the case, G. W. F. Hegel, J. G. Fichte, Friedrich Schiller and J. W. Goethe would have to be considered Romantics, and as Frank shows in the lectures, we see that most of them were not members of the early German Romantic movement (even if some of them, most notably, Goethe and Fichte, had a great influence upon some of the members of the movement): not every German thinker working in Berlin and Jena between 1794 and 1808 was an early German Romantic. Who then, of the collection of luminaries that happened to come together in what has been called "the wonder year of Jena" (1794–95) and the period shaped by this "wonder year," are we to count as an early German Romantic?[4]

Frank's lectures provide a compelling way of characterizing the early German Romantics, and thus of answering our question. Frank improves greatly upon the standard ways of grouping these thinkers together with the figures in Germany (or more particularly in Jena and Berlin) with whom they merely overlapped chronologically or geographically—Frank provides a *philosophical* way of characterizing these figures through a central philosophical commitment that they shared—their epistemological anti-foundationalism: that is, their skepticism regarding first principles in philosophy; that is, skepticism regarding self-justifying propositions, to use the parlance of contemporary epistemology.

Frank's lectures inject the movement with new philosophical life. Frank characterizes the early German Romantics by focusing upon a common philosophical position that they shared and were dedicated to developing, which clearly set them apart from other thinkers who wrote and thought during the same period and in the same geographical area. Frank focuses in particular upon the work of Friedrich Schlegel, Novalis, and Friedrich Hölderlin (a Romantic in his own right, though not belonging to the Jena or Berlin circles). His analysis convincingly shows why major figures who worked in Jena during this period do not count as Romantics.

To many philosophers, it will come as a surprise that there are any philosophical dimensions of note to be found in Romanticism. The very notion of "Romantic philosophy" in the minds of these thinkers is a sort of oxymoron, and hence any sort of philosophical legacy nonexistent. Indeed, most scholars who write on early German Romanticism are more interested in the literary legacy of the early German Romantics than in any philosophical legacy.[5] There has also been significant historical work done on the period–work that seeks to reconstruct the movement by carefully giving an account of the various relations between the major figures. So the period has received attention *as* a literary movement, but works such as Frank's, which seeks to help us appreciate the movement *as* a philosophical movement, are rare. This is due in large part to the uncritical prejudice according to which it just does not make sense to put the terms "romantic" and "philosophy" together in the same proposition (unless to generate contradictions). Along these lines, the term "romantic," it might be argued, is an adjective used to modify poetry or art, or even the temperament (and not an analytic or clear-minded one at that) of a person, but it cannot be used to describe a kind of philosophy, if philosophy is to be seen as a *systematic* approach to the "big" questions of life, to wit, questions about what there is, what we can know, how we should live, and the like.

But what could the Romantics tell us? They offer no traditional system, in fact, they present much of their work in fragments, in the pages of a journal that was intended to shock and raise more questions than it settled.[6] But that there exists a prejudice of sorts against Romanticism in general should be clear if we keep in mind that the Romantics were not the only philosophers who embraced nontraditional ways of expressing their views. Plato, Nietszche, and many other thinkers whose philosophical credentials are unquestionable come to mind. But, above all, Ludwig Wittgenstein, a cult figure amongst positivists, comes to mind in this connection. The unconventional literary form used by Wittgenstein has not led to his dismissal by even the most intolerant of philosophers (intolerant vis-à-vis the sorts of questions that philosophy should ask), yet it has been a perennial problem in the reception of Early-German Romantic thought.

The work of the Romantics is filled with appeals to art and to history and to what is a seemingly cryptic "longing for the infinite." One might then justifiably ask: how are we to get answers to any important questions from the Romantics if they seem to pull us in a direction away from the strict arguments of the philosophers? After all, it is likely that in order to develop a position on anything, one needs a "serious" system (not a playful one composed of fragments and dialogues). Were the early German Romantics, with many of their ideas expressed in fragments and essays, just a group of poets who might have offered much in the way of enriching aesthetic culture, but not much in the way of giving us a philosophical legacy from which we could come closer to the truth? Below I shall explore why this question can be answered with a resounding no. My strategy in this introduction will be to present two clusters of arguments. First, I shall present some remarks about the general historical aspects of early German Romanticism aiming to reveal how many strictly philosophical concerns the thinkers of this movement had. Second, as I sketch the nature and structure of the lectures themselves, other more specific philosophical aspects of early German Romanticism shall be discussed.

Philosophy and Related Fields

Nowadays, in English-speaking circles, if Romanticism is appreciated at all, then it is usually insofar and inasmuch as it is a literary movement, while attention to its philosophical dimensions remains neglected. Because many of the central texts are not yet translated into English, this neglect is, while by no means exclusive to it, especially widespread in the English-speaking world.[7] The early German Romantics did produce much of literary value. A large part of their efforts was devoted to questioning the role of art for society and for *philosophy*. It is perfectly legitimate, and indeed necessary if one wishes to present a comprehensive account of the movement, to focus upon the literary dimensions of the movement. To consider early German Romanticism as a literary movement is *one* valid way to interpret it, but it is by no means *the only* one, and it is certainly an erroneous way, if this interpretation entails that literature was *all* the early German romantics were about. If we treat early German Romanticism merely as a literary movement, Friedrich Schlegel, Friedrich von Hardenberg (Novalis), and Friedrich Hölderlin emerge at best as gifted writers and poets, but their contributions to philosophy go unrecognized, as Frank compellingly shows.

The contributions to philosophy by early German Romantics were significant; they have influenced important philosophers. Wilhelm Dilthey's work, for example, was informed considerably by the romantic view of philosophy as an essentially historical enterprise.[8] Walter Benjamin's dissertation on the concept of art criticism in German Romanticism is primarily a study of Friedrich Schlegel's views.[9] It is important also to keep in mind that the early German Romantics were, in fact, the first generation of Kant readers. Within this first generation of Kant readers, we find, naturally, important challenges to the universal claims of reason and a move towards incorporating history and political issues into philosophy. In German philosophy through Kant, moreover, history and politics were not considered primary areas of concern for the philosopher. Early German Romantic philosophy was groundbreaking, also, in incorporating these concerns into philosophy, and in the development of the field we know today as the human sciences (*Geisteswissenschaften*).[10] Furthermore, as Manfred Frank's lectures illustrate, the romantic skepticism, regarding the possibility of a philosophy based on first principles, sought to constitute an alternative to both Kant and Fichte's transcendental idealism and so to re-definition of the very goals and methods of philosophy itself. These contributions often go unrecognized and cannot be fully appreciated if we are unaware of the philosophical underpinnings of the early German Romantic movement.

The early German Romantics did produce much of literary value and a large part of their enterprise was committed to questioning the role of art for society and for philosophy. But the view that limits early German Romanticism to a mere literary movement does not do justice to the very conception the early German Romantics had of their own project. The members of this movement did not see their work merely as part of a literary movement; they saw themselves as philosophers, and thus, they had a philosophical project in mind, one which in many ways challenged the traditional boundaries between philosophy and literature, and also between philosophy and other related fields. It is perfectly legitimate, and indeed necessary if one wishes to present a comprehensive account of the movement, to understand its literary dimensions, but to leave it at that is to mutilate at least the self-understanding that its founders had of it. The early German Romantics were seeking to redefine the categories of poetry and philosophy; hence, they employed unconventional forms for the expression of their ideas. Most characteristic was the use of the fragment, a literary form that lends itself to creative interpretation. Yet, while this literary form might make conceptual analysis difficult, surely it does not preclude its possibility. I believe that it is precisely this difficulty that has hindered philosophical investigations of the contributions from these thinkers.

Manfred Frank's lectures offer a comprehensive and detailed analysis of the philosophical underpinnings of early German Romanticism, and given that this is a movement shrouded in misunderstandings that have led to its neglect by Anglo-American philosophers, a translation of these lectures into English will be a valuable addition to some of the recent scholarship done by North American and English philosophers in this field.

Recent Work on Early German Romanticism

Recent work in English on early German Romanticism has helped to bring more attention to the philosophical dimensions of this movement. Frederick Beiser has produced some of the best work on the early German Romantics; he is one of the leading authorities on early German Romantic scholarship in the United States. Beiser presents the historical backdrop of the movement, carefully presenting the philosophical controversies which engaged the early German Romantics and served to open the path of their own philosophical development. He has shown how early German Romanticism is related to the Enlightenment, challenging the view that Romanticism represented a break from the ideals of the Enlightenment. Beiser convincingly shows us where to place the early German Romantics on the *philosophical* map.[11] Andrew Bowie, who currently works in England, has done a great service to the field through his first-rate translations of Schleiermacher and Schelling. Moreover, he has demonstrated fascinating connections between the view of the early German Romantics and the work of some contemporary analytic philosophers.[12] Richard Eldridge has drawn important connections between naturalism and Romanticism.[13] Robert Richards has presented a portrait of the Romantics that highlights their serious interest in science, allowing their relations to the work of Johann Friedrich Blumenbach and Kant to unfold.[14] Slowly, early German Romanticism is emerging as a philosophically rich movement that addresses issues very much on the minds of contemporary philosophers of both the Anglo-American and the Continental traditions, for example, anti-foundationalism, coherence theories of truth, and naturalism.

This work in English joins a collection of work carried out by scholars in Germany that has helped to correct the distorted view resulting from an excessive emphasis on the literary character of early German Romanticism. In Germany, Dieter Henrich's work has contributed to this end. Henrich focuses primarily on the importance of Hölderlin's Homburg Circle to the development of early German Romantic theory, but he also gives a reconstruction of the constellation of thinkers who comprised the group known as early German Romantics, showing their relations to the major philosophical currents of the time.[15] Working with Henrich on this project has been Marcelo Stamm, and his forthcoming work, *"Mit der Überzeugung der Entbehrlichkeit eines höchsten und einzigen Grundsatzes . . ." Ein Konstellationsporträt um Fr. I. Niethammers Philosohisches Journal einer Gesellschaft Teutscher Gelehrten* [With the conviction of the dispensability of a highest and single first principle . . .] A constellation portrait of Friedrich I. Niethammer's *Philosophisches Journal of a Society of German Scholars*), does much to substantiate the claim that the early German Romantic project constituted a move away from a view (like Reinhold's and Fichte's) that philosophy must depart from a single absolute first principle. Stamm shows that the early German Romantics adopt a view according to which our search for knowledge is guided by a principle of approximation. Meanwhile, Manfred Frank and others (Wilhelm Baum, Jürgen Stolzenberg, Violetta Waibel) have done work to bring the particular contributions of the Jena Circle into clearer focus. Baum, for example, brought together for publication the hitherto unknown correspondence between Reinhold's Jena students, such as Erhard, Forberg, von Herbert, Niethammer, and Novalis. Manfred Frank's prolific work in this area has done much to reveal the philosophical foundations of this movement.[16] He recently edited a special volume of the *Revue Internationale de Philosophie* entitled, *Les fondements philosophiques du premier romantisme allemande.*[17]

Both Henrich and Frank have done much historical, philological, and philosophical work in this area. They have been most influential in building a body of literature that treats the figures of this movement as serious philosophers, and their example has been followed by other scholars in Germany and in the United States.[18] The work of philosophers like Henrich, Frank, Eldridge, Bowie, Beiser, and others is serving to open early German Romanticism to the philosophical community at large.

We have come a long way from the situation Stanley Cavell described in *This New Yet Unapproachable America: Lectures after Emerson and Wittgenstein,* (Albuquerque, NM: Living Batch Press, 1989).[19] In this book,

Cavell informs us that he was first made aware of various writings from the journal *Das Athenäum* (1798–1800) in the translation and interpretation offered by Phillipe Lacoue-Labarthe and Jean-Luc Nancy in *The Literary Absolute: The Theory of Literature in German Romanticism.*[20] In particular, Cavell is impressed by Schlegel's call for a new relation between philosophy and literature, and reflects upon the relevance and acceptance that such a call finds in the philosophical climate of today.

> I guess such remarks as "poetry and philosophy should be made one" would not in themselves have been enough even in my day to have gotten one thrown out of most graduate programs in philosophy, but their presence, if used seriously, as a present ambition, would not have been permitted to contribute to a Ph.D. study either; and like vestigial organs, such ideas may become inflamed and life-threatening.[21]

We may finally be in a position to realize that calls to bring philosophy closer to poetry, far from being calls that threaten the life of philosophy, may actually help to enhance it, and so the Romantics should be welcomed as participants in contemporary philosophical debates. Cavell's work is, in a certain way, "romantic" in its own right, that is, regarding the sort of skepticism to which it leads. This skepticism is well-described by Richard Eldridge as one that generates questions like: "What is a philosophical result? What is philosophical activity?" Eldridge goes on to make a connection between Cavell's view of philosophy as "neither empirical generalization nor legislation, but rather reading, or criticism, or understanding from the inside" and Romanticism.[22]

"Reading, or criticism, or understanding from the inside," are related to a concern that Schlegel and Cavell share—a philosophical concern for mediality, something Frank discusses at length in lectures 10 and 11. Schlegel rejects a deductive method in philosophy, for he does not believe that we can locate a first principle. He claims that:

> Our philosophy does not begin like the others with a first principle—where the first proposition is like the center or first ring of a comet—with the rest a long tail of mist—we depart from a small but living seed—our center lies in the middle.[23]

A philosophy based on first principles would provide a perspective from the outside, that is, from a point that established all that followed from it. Such a position is foundational, and the first principle or foundation stands outside of the matter that it serves to explain. Fichte's philosophy is foundational through and through; he was certain that philosophy must begin with the subject and even proved this. For Fichte, the structure of the I and its sufficiency to posit the Non-I generated a system of knowledge that was the result of certainty regarding primitives. Fichte's primitive I does not depend in any way upon what follows or is deduced from it. Hence, we can understand the whole scope of knowledge through an analysis of its parts. Schlegel gives up the attempt to establish anything in this way, he begins in the middle, within the flow of reality, taking history into account. Indeed, Schlegel argues that philosophy is in need of a comparative history.[24] He describes his method as genetic or synthetic as opposed to deductive or syllogistic.[25] A recent defender of such a "middle" position, eloquently sums up the common view shared by those who defend it:

> We are never "prior to" communities. We find ourselves *in* them, at least in virtue of being involved in particular practices and more generally in virtue of our ability to use language and to manipulate symbol systems at all. Here we do not start in the beginning; we start in the middle.[26]

Reading, criticism, and understanding which begins "from the inside," begins in the middle, with our involvement in the reality that philosophy seeks to understand. With this move to the inside or the middle, history takes on a greater role for philosophy, and so it should come as no great surprise that the Romantics call for philosophy to be historical. Now we shall examine the details of the move that gave rise to romantic mediality.

The Rejection of First Principles

According to Friedrich Schlegel, the leading thinker of early German Romanticism, philosophy does not begin from a first principle. In *Athenäum* Fragment 84, he claims that, "philosophy, like epic poetry, always begins in *media res*." As such a claim joins others like "poetry and philosophy should be made one," it is tempting to read Schlegel as calling for a collapse of the distinction between philosophy and poetry. But removing boundaries in order to merge disciplines is not Schlegel's concern at all. His emphasis on mediality and the relation between philosophy and poetry are part of his concern with the nature of knowledge.

Claims calling for the union of philosophy and poetry and comparisons between the methods of philosophy and those of poetry lead some to dismiss the Romantics as anti-Enlightenment thinkers, more interested in feelings and art than with reason and rigor. While the early German Romantics do not abandon reason as the ultimate touchstone of knowledge, they do abandon the idea that philosophy begins with any first principle whatsoever.

Once we understand this aspect of early German Romanticism, we can begin to understand the concerns that underlie Schlegel's interest in mediality.

Romanticism was anti-foundationalist through and through; and it was so in an attempt to capture the inherent incompleteness of philosophy and knowledge. In the first book of the lectures on the history of philosophy, which he delivered in Cologne, Schlegel stresses this point. In this book, entitled *The Historical Characteristics of Philosophy according to its Successive Development,* Schlegel addresses the problem of where we begin when we philosophize:

> To desire to provisionally prove what the beginning point of philosophy is, concerns separating out the first principle of philosophy (if there is such a principle), as is actually attempted in some scientific introductions. One can admit, that in a tentative treatment the point from which one must begin to philosophize will be searched for and proved.[27]

Of course, if there is no such principle, it will only be searched for and never found. Schlegel's position is that we never begin with the certain knowledge that there is such a principle; instead we must begin with what we have— a history of what has been thought by other philosophers before. According to Schlegel, an introduction to philosophy can only be a critique of all earlier philosophy. His first lecture concerns the problem of introducing philosophy, and this is ultimately the problem of the beginning of philosophy, which was understood as the question of the foundations of human knowledge. According to Schlegel, any attempt to begin with a pure point of certainty is impossible:

> To abstract entirely from all previous systems and throw all of this away as Descartes attempted to do is absolutely impossible. Such an entirely new creation from one's own mind, a complete forgetting of all which has been thought before, was also attempted by Fichte and he too failed in this.[28]

For Schlegel and the early German Romantic philosophers in general, philosophy is more than a deductive science and cannot be evaluated solely on the basis of the rules of logic (even if it cannot violate these laws). Knowledge of what came before is necessary, because any given philosophical system is just one among many, and in order to fully understand each part, some view of the whole must be present.[29] Philosophy is historical, but is not thereby reduced to history, because it concerns the analysis and investigation of ideas, opinions, and thoughts; philosophy is best understood via a historical critique of these ideas, opinions, and thoughts.[30]

This recognition of the importance of history for philosophy represents an important shift in the development of post-Kantian philosophy. In spite of a close connection with Fichte's work, the Romantics cannot be classified as Fichteans. Indeed, in the course of Frank's lectures, it becomes clear that although the early Romantics were influenced by Fichte, they departed from him in important ways, and hence, it is a mistake to consider early German Romantic philosophy as just another form of absolute German idealism. Fichte held that in order to be a science of knowledge, philosophy must be based upon an absolute first principle and the *Wissenschaftslehre* is his attempt to secure this principle and thereby solve the problem of philosophy's starting point

The reaction of the romantic philosophers to their contemporaries can be fully understood only if we come to an understanding of their anti-foundationalism, the central root of Romanticism.[31] Take, for example, Schlegel's critique of Fichte, which is essentially a critique of Fichte's arch-foundationalism.[32] In a fragment from 1796, Schlegel announces:

> Philosophy in its proper sense has neither a first principle, nor an object, nor a definite task. The *Wissenschaftslehre* has a definite object (I and Non-I and their relationships), a definite principle [*Wechselgrund*] and therefore a definite task.[33]

It is only when we begin to understand the skeptical underpinnings of the movement that we are in a position to understand the philosophical significance of Schlegel's claim. And until this happens, the term "romantic" will continue to enchant and draw poetic associations, but will not receive the attention it deserves from philosophers. An important contribution made by Frank's lectures is that they provide a nuanced way in which to appreciate the philosophical contributions of the members of the early German Romantic movement, in part by giving us a deeper sense of the meaning of "romantic."

While one central key for unraveling the mystery of the philosophical significance of early German Romanticism is an understanding of the anti-foundationalism that its members endorsed, it is not the only one. Having made the case that in order to fully appreciate the meaning of "romantic," we must look to more than merely the literary dimensions of the early German Romantic movement and begin to pay more attention to the philosophical dimensions, we can now consider these two dimensions together in order to achieve a comprehensive view of the meaning of the adjective "romantic" for the early German Romantics.

"Romanticism" as a Comparative Tool

The early German Romantics' use of fragments and dialogues was in keeping with their desire to call the traditional roles of poetry and philosophy into question. It is within the context of this challenge that the term "romantic" first became significant in the philosophical work of the early German Romantics. In the very early phases of this movement, this term did appear, but only as, in the case of Friedrich Schlegel's work, a term of literary criticism, to denote a certain class of writings or a certain period of the history of literature: romantic poetry was opposed to classical poetry, it was subjective and artificial *(künstlich)* whereas classical poetry was objective and natural.[34] In his classical phase, Schlegel viewed the limitlessness of modern poetry as negative. This changed around 1795 as did his use of the adjective *"romantisch"* which took on a much broader meaning, becoming an aesthetic ideal and indeed the catchword of a philosophical movement. Schlegel's Hellenism or *Gräkomanie* was guided by the belief that only objective principles could lead to the creation of beautiful art, that only within certain limits could aesthetic experience be realized, and as the ancient civilizations worked within these limits, that is, within a limited range of themes and methods, art attained its perfection in these classical examples. After 1795, this position evolved into an appreciation for the subjective elements of art, for the presence of the individual in the art. The early Romantics no longer viewed the ideal of art as an accomplished state of perfection but an eternal process of becoming. This evolution is consistent with the early German Romantics' developing interest in viewing and understanding art in terms of its history.

According to A. O. Lovejoy, the Romantic doctrine of art can be traced to Kant and to a debate concerning the ancients and the moderns that took shape in the 1790s.[35] Following Ernst Behler, we can understand the meaning of the term "romantic" in two ways, chronologically and typologically.[36] Chronologically, "romantic" "referred to a tradition of literature originating in the Middle Ages and pervading literary writing in modern Europe, but which was held in low esteem by neoclassicists and even excluded from the literary canon."[37] Schlegel himself puts this in the following way:

> This is where I look for and find the Romantic—in the older moderns, in Shakespeare, Cervantes, in Italian poetry, in that age of knights, love, and fairy-tales where the thing and the word originated.[38]

The "romantic" then belonged to an earlier period, but was a tradition that Schlegel and others (A. W. Schlegel, Schleiermacher, Novalis, etc.) hoped to revive as a means of understanding modern politics, aesthetics, and philosophy. The reason they looked to this period in order to address these issues becomes clear when we understand the typological meaning of the term. According to Behler:

The typological referred to certain exotic traits in literature, including compositional and structural ones, which were originally expressed in Romanesque literature, but which were now found everywhere.[39]

Yet, we must not limit this term to traits in literature. Schlegel writes:

> According to my point of view and my use of the term, romantic is that which presents us with sentimental material in a fantastic form (that is, in a form determined by the fantasy).[40]

Hence, Schlegel's use of the term "romantic" added an important new perspective to the debate of this period concerning the relation between the ancients and the moderns. Instead of carrying out the debate only in terms of chronological categories, the Romantics shifted the foundation of the discussion to a conceptual one, that is, to a discussion concerning the meaning of the classical and the romantic, yet not merely as adjectives to describe literature. Certainly, the term "romantic" became a tool for classifying poetry, but more precisely, it became a way of comparing the past with the present in a way which superseded literary categories: it became a way of comparing the past with the present in a philosophical way. In Fragment 116, we find Schlegel's announcement that "romantic poetry is a progressive, universal poetry."[41] Romantic poetry is an ideal, a poetry that is progressive because it is always in a state of becoming, never reaching completion.[42] This view of the inherent incompleteness of poetry holds also for the romantic view of philosophy, and of knowledge itself. It is in this sense that we may speak of a philosophy that is romantic.

The group of thinkers that contributed to *Das Athenäum* were introducing, via the term "romantic," a new, revolutionary description of an ideal not only of poetry, but also of reality in its boundlessness: an ideal which committed them to a certain philosophical method. However, this term was not, in their time, used to describe the thinkers themselves. According to Behler, "new school" or "Schlegelian school" was the most frequent designation.[43] One of the most important contributions of this "Schlegelian school," was the historical turn that they carried out. Their method, in breaking with the deductive method that informed the work of Fichte, carved out a new space for the role of history in philosophy. The early German Romantics followed Kant in characterizing their age as the "Age of Criticism," yet they did not believe that Kant's "critique" went far enough.[44] In one fragment, Schlegel calls Kant a "half critic," later explaining that:

> [A] critique of philosophizing reason cannot succeed without a history of philosophy. [This] is proved to us by Kant himself. His work as a critique

of philosophizing reason is not at all historical enough even though it is filled with historical relations and he attempts to construct various systems.[45]

The romantic method served to infuse the meaning of critique with history. A critique of philosophy that is historical enables the critic to compare a given philosophical contribution to others. When history is incorporated into the very method of philosophy itself, we can assess a given contribution of a philosopher not only by *classifying* her arguments as valid or invalid, sound or unsound, but also by *comparing* the merits of the contribution to other contributions made by other philosophers from different periods.[46]

Structure of the Lectures

This translation is a version of the third part of Manfred Frank's larger volume entitled, *Unendliche Annäherung. Die Anfänge der philosophischen Frühromantik* (Infinite Approximation: The Beginnings of philosophical Early Romanticism). The German version that was published by Suhrkamp contains three parts and a total of thirty-six lectures. The first part deals with Kant's legacy and how it was assimilated and criticized by figures such as Salomon Maimon and Johann G. Fichte, setting the stage for a set of issues that were to be passed onto the Romantics. Naturally, the early Romantics had unique and original solutions to the problems left by Kant's critical philosophy. Part two of the German version introduces the issues that arose in response to Reinhold's solution to the problems posed by Kant's transcendental deduction. Frank's presentation of the critiques to Reinhold's principle of consciousness (*Satz des Bewusstseins*), introduces the philosophically rich contributions of figures that remain almost unknown to English-reading philosophers. The work of figures such as Aenesidemus (pen name of G. E. Schulze), Johann Benjamin Erhard, P. J. A. Feuerbach, Friedrich Karl Forberg, Franz Paul von Herbert, Friedrich Immanuel Niethammer, August Wilhelm Rehberg, Johann Christoph Schwab, and Friedrich August Weißhuhn, with few exceptions, have yet to be translated into English.[47] (Many of these figures have, until recently, received very little attention even in Germany.)[48] It is only in part three of the lectures that we come to figures that are relatively well-known (even if sorely misunderstood) to the English-reading public. The figures highlighted in this part of Frank's lectures, and in the following translation, include, Friedrich Heinrich Jacobi, Friedrich Hölderlin, Friedrich J. Schelling, Friedrich von Hardenberg (Novalis), and Friedrich Schlegel. Only a few of the thinkers featured in the lectures, such as Isaac von Sinclair and Jakob Zwilling, will be new to many readers. Hence, it made most sense to publish the lectures from part three in English, for there is enough of the primary material already translated to make a secondary source relevant to an English-reading public. This translation is based on a manuscript that actually preceded the version of the lectures published by Suhrkamp in 1997. Furthermore, some restructuring was done to enable the lectures to stand as an independent whole.

The lectures begin against the backdrop of controversies surrounding Reinhold and Fichte's attempts to revise Kant's philosophy.[49] Hence, a few words surrounding these controversies are in order. Following Frederick Beiser, we may describe the philosophical mood in Germany between 1781 and 1794 as largely set by the following three events: the publication of Kant's *Critique of Pure Reason* (A version 1781, and B version 1787), the Pantheism Controversy between Mendelssohn and Jacobi, which reached its peak in 1785, and the publication of Fichte's *Wissenschaftslehre* in 1794. The main problem discussed in the aftermath of these three events was the authority of reason and its "self-evident first principles."[50] What Frank's lectures illustrate is that the group of thinkers that became known as the early German Romantics developed a kind of skepticism in response to these events. They are not the irrational poets lost in swells of passion that many have (mis-) characterized them to be.

In lecture one, Frank defends the claim that to understand the philosophical underpinnings of early German Romanticism one must understand the reactions that the thinkers who constituted the Jena Constellation (1789–92) had to the philosophical positions of both K. L. Reinhold and J. G. Fichte. In his defense of this claim, it becomes clear why it is a grave mistake to read the work of this group of thinkers as falling under the umbrella of the tradition of German idealism (à la Fichte). Frank also indicates that the early German Romantics reject Reinhold's attempts to secure a first principle for philosophy. Hence, the *Frühromantiker*, can best be characterized as skeptics vis-à-vis the possibility of securing a foundation for our knowledge claims. That which is characteristically "romantic" is a kind of skepticism regarding the efforts of Reinhold and Fichte to secure a first principle for philosophy. Further, Frank clearly shows that the goals of the Jena Circle (whose most prominent philosophers were Friedrich Schlegel and Novalis) were not at odds with the Homburg Circle (whose most important member was Hölderlin) but that both groups shared a kind of romantic skepticism. This view of the movements stands in contrast with some claims that Dieter Henrich has made regarding these movements.

Henrich, for example, has argued that the Homburg Circle was more important than the Jena Circle in overcoming a philosophy of reflection. Throughout the lectures, Frank makes a strong case for the claim that the Jena Circle was no less important than the Homburg Circle in revealing the priority of Being over consciousness. In lecture two, Frank provides the historical background for an understanding of Novalis' *Fichte-Studien* as any-thing *but* songs of praise for Fichte's philosophy, and so as an important contribution to a break with a philosophy of first principles, and from the view that with self-consciousness one could posit a principle of deduction for philosophy. In this lecture, Frank introduces a group of thinkers that are largely unknown in the English-speaking world, but whose role in the devel-opment of early German Romanticism was central because of their criticism of Reinhold's philosophy. Frank discusses the work of Friedrich Immanuel Niethammer, Franz Paul von Herbert, Friedrich Carl Forberg, Johann Ben-jamin Erhard, and Carl Christian Erhard Schmid, focusing in particular upon the latter two. Schmid was Novalis' tutor and remained his lifelong friend and mentor. Erhard was a close friend of Novalis and is described by Frank as "the most intellectually outstanding figure" amongst Reinhold's students. Both Erhard and Schmid grew increasingly critical of their teacher's views, in particular of Reinhold's attempt to go beyond the results of Kant's *Critique of Pure Reason* through appealing to the concept of representation. Frank then shows how some of these criticisms influenced the development of Novalis' views. Henrich has claimed that Novalis was merely a philosopher of secondary importance, who followed in the larger footsteps of Hölderlin. The views of Novalis that Frank presents in these lectures pose a serious challenge to such a reading of Novalis.

Lecture three provides the reader with a detailed historical and philo-sophical account of why the unknowability of the Absolute became a prob-lem for early German Romantics and how they dealt with this problem. Frank traces this theme of the relation between the finite and infinite back to Crusius, Kant, and Jacobi—highlighting the influence that their thought had upon Schlegel, Novalis, and Hölderlin. By the end of the lecture, one can see why Frank can claim that, "one simply cannot read early German Romanticism as an appendage to so-called German Idealism." Frank argues that early German Romanticism is not an appendage to German idealism, that it is not even a breed of idealism at all. Frank supports this position by analyzing Fichte's relation to the early German Romantic philosophers, for even if it is a mistake to read the early German Romantics as Fichteans, Fichte's influence upon the development of their thought is indisputable.

In lectures four–eight, Frank discusses the dependence of Schelling and Hölderlin's work on Fichte, and introduces Issac von Sinclair and Jakob Zwilling, two rather obscure figures who were an important part of the con-stellation of thinkers developing responses and alternatives to Fichte's abso-lute idealism. Much of what Frank is doing in lectures four through eight involves the preparation of a "constellation portrait" of Hölderlin's *Urtheil und Seyn*. That is, he carefully introduces and analyzes the positions and figures that shaped Hölderlin's work and the influence that *Urtheil und Seyn* had upon Hölderlin's contemporaries. We are introduced to the philosophical backdrop that influenced the development of Hölderlin's thought and also to the particular relationships with thinkers of the period that were no less important in shaping his thought. The friendships that ebbed and flowed between Hegel, Schelling, Hölderlin, Sinclair, and Zwilling were philosophically significant insofar as these thinkers developed many of their ideas in response to each other.

We learn, for example, that Schelling's enduring attachment to Fichte's philosophy of the I was a major point of contention between him and Hölderlin. Frank convincingly shows that several passages of Hölderlin's *Urtheil und Seyn* are only comprehensible if they are read as reactions to Schelling's *Vom Ich* text, for both thinkers were struggling with the same issues and shared their ideas liberally with each other. Traces of the personal relation that they shared are found in their published work. Schelling continued to press his claim that consciousness determined Being, while Hölderlin moved to defend the claim that Being determines consciousness. Hölderlin does not dismiss the theme of self-consciousness, but he does relegate it to a status secondary to that of Being. And in this shift from self-consciousness as having the status of a principle of philosophy to the status of self-consciousness as merely one prominent theme amongst others, we have what Frank claims is the "first consummate expression of early German Romanticism." Frank argues that if self-consciousness can no longer be claimed as the principle of deduction for philosophy, then the transcendence of Being forces philosophy along the path of an infinite progression and the search for knowledge becomes an infinite task. The notion of knowledge as infinite progression is a result of the unknowability of Being, its transcendence. Being simply cannot be adequately comprehended by consciousness. This does not mean that Being remains completely unknown to us; the path towards it is opened by aesthetic experience, and Frank spends much time unpacking the role of aesthetic experience in early German Romantic philosophy and what the implications of this role were for the early German Romantics' view of philosophy. With Frank's analysis, the fact that the leaders of the early German Romantic philosophical movement were also talented poets takes on a new and deeper meaning.

Lectures seven and eight fill in the details of Hölderlin's relation to Sinclair and Zwilling by introducing us to Sinclair's *Raisonnements* and Zwilling's, *Über das Alles*. Sinclair was in Jena during the spring of 1794 and listened to the first part of Fichte's *Wissenschaftslehre* and to Schmid's lectures. Sinclair was also a close friend of Hölderlin's and took care of him before Hölderlin, having suffered a mental breakdown, was sent to Tübingen, where he died in complete isolation from the circle of friends over whom his thought had exerted such a strong influence. As Frank tells us in lecture seven, Sinclair drew "aesthetic consequences from the failure of reflection to epistemically secure the Absolute," hence, a look at his work fills out the details of the aesthetic consequences of the overcoming of a philosophy determined by reflection. For his part, Zwilling also emphasizes the role of beauty and aesthetic experience in our cognitive experience, but he, unlike, Hölderlin and Sinclair, did trust reflection to "heal the maladies" created by the separation of the self from the world, or to use Fichte's language, the I and the Non-I. According to Zwilling, reflection is the only medium through which we can make unified Being comprehensible. Frank ends his lecture on Zwilling (lecture eight) with a comparison of Hölderlin, Sinclair, and Zwilling's views of Being and the role of reflection in grasping it. Whereas Zwilling's approach to understanding the nature of Being through reflection leads to a breed of absolute idealism, Hölderlin and Sinclair clearly distance themselves from absolute idealism.

While Frank rejects Henrich's claim that Hölderlin was the primary figure in overcoming the philosophy of reflection, he does not deny that Hölderlin and those figures closely associated with him made great contributions to early German Romantic philosophy. Nonetheless, according to Frank, the greatest contributors to the philosophical foundations of early German Romanticism were Novalis and Friedrich Schlegel, two figures whom Henrich relegates to secondary status and whose work has been neglected by most philosophers.

Part of this neglect can be attributed to a problem that has plagued the work of many thinkers from the period: central texts of Hölderlin, Zwilling, Sinclair, and Novalis first became accessible to the public in the twentieth century. And certain texts are still unrecovered or are rumored to be hidden from public view by those who do not want to loosen them from their possessive grip. There is the additional problem of the editions that do exist being pieced together in incoherent ways. As Frank tells us in lecture nine, it was not until the 1920s that Paul Kluckhohn's efforts yielded the first "half-way" critical edition of Novalis' work. These efforts were added to by Hans-Joachim Mähl in the 1960s, and now we are well on our way to having a truly critical edition of Novalis' work. Without comprehensive editions of the work of the central figures of early German Romanticism, it is nearly impossible to achieve a comprehensive understanding of the movement

In lecture nine, Frank spends much time reconstructing the context in which Novalis first began to develop the thoughts that guided his *Fichte-Studien*. He then turns to the issue of how the *Fichte-Studien* relate to the ideas developed by Hölderlin and his circle. Novalis, unlike Hölderlin, established an explicit connection between the thought that Being is beyond knowledge and the characterization of philosophy as an infinite task. Next, Frank documents, staying quite close to Novalis' texts, that Novalis' view of philosophy did not amount to absolute idealism. Although Fichte is present in the title of Novalis' work, it was not the case that he was a blind follower of Fichte. Novalis concluded that philosophy could never reach the Absolute, and certainly could not be grounded upon it. Novalis wholeheartedly rejected a philosophy based upon first principles.

Frank shows that early German Romanticism was much more skeptical and modern than its reputation would have it seem; yet, as he also points out, its reputation is based on stereotypes and a complete ignorance of some of the fundamental texts that shaped the movement, so once a careful and deep treatment of these texts is provided, Romanticism's reputation is easily redeemed. A crucial step in this redemption is a correct understanding of the difference between absolute idealism and early German Romantic philosophy. Frank understands idealism as "the conviction—made especially compulsory by Hegel—that consciousness is a self-sufficient phenomenon, one which is still able to make the presuppositions of its existence comprehensible by its own means." In contrast, the early German Romantics are convinced that "self-being owes its existence to a transcendent foundation," which cannot be dissolved by consciousness. According to this view of the primacy of Being, the foundation of self-being becomes a puzzle that can no longer be handled by reflection alone, for reflection alone cannot grasp Being—it needs something more. What is this something more? Our experience of the beauty of art.

Friedrich Schlegel is the figure that Frank uses to analyze the role that art came to play in early German Romanticism. Lectures ten, eleven, and twelve present Schlegel's views on this matter and his role in the Jena Constellation. As Frank tells us, Schlegel was a latecomer to the working out and transformation of the sort of philosophy that was being shaped by Fichte and others. Schlegel developed his position chiefly in conversation and written correspondence with Novalis, and eventually came to articulate an original view of philosophy as an infinite activity that could not be grounded upon first principles. Frank highlights the aesthetic consequences that Schlegel drew from the fact that the Absolute transcended reflection and points to the coherence theory of truth that emerged from Schlegel's considerations.

The beauty of art enables us to experience something whose meaning cannot be exhausted by thought and hence helps us to comprehend or grasp Being (although never exhaustively). Because philosophy is a kind of longing for the Absolute and art is an instrument that helps us to approximate the Absolute, Schlegel claims that philosophy is completed in and as art. This is not a silly, unphilosophically "romantic" claim, but one that goes to the heart of the philosophical foundations of early German Romanticism. In order to unpack the role of aesthetic experience in early German Romanticism, Frank discusses the philosophical relevance of allegory, wit, irony, and the use of the fragment in Schlegel's work. Each of these connects to Schlegel's solution to the problem of the limits of our knowledge and the limitless of the Absolute, which in its very limitlessness propels us beyond our finite limits. Frank provides a careful reading of Schlegel's *Lectures on Transcendental Philosophy* (delivered in Jena 1800–01), and a series of private lectures given in Cologne (1804–05) to support the claims he makes concerning Schlegel's view of the relation between art and philosophy. As in most of the preceding lectures, Fichte serves as a point of contrast in Frank's analysis of Schlegel's position. Many of Schlegel's claims regarding the nature of philosophy and its foundations take shape in reaction to the claims put forward in Fichte's *Wissenschaftslehre*.

Most of lecture eleven is dedicated to a discussion of one of Schlegel's most original contributions to the discussion concerning the foundations of philosophy: the *Wechselerweis*. This notion of an alternating or reciprocal proof structure was Schlegel's alternative to Fichte's philosophy based on first principles. Frank gives a comprehensive account of the possible sources of Schlegel's use of the term "*Wechselerweis*" and its variations. The *Wechselerweis* is central to Schlegel's view of philosophy as a historical, comparative science. References to the *Wechselerweis* are found scattered throughout Schlegel's writings, in his fragments, essays, and in his lectures. Perhaps the most compact presentation of this idea is to be found in the second appendix to the fragments which appeared under the title, *Philosophical Apprenticeship*.[51] These are twenty-four fragments concerning the nature of philosophy in general, and Schlegel's view of its starting point in particular. Schlegel's turn toward the *Wechselerweis* is the result of his skepticism regarding the feasibility of a philosophy based on first principles and his conviction that the form and content of philosophy are inexhaustible (*unerschöpflich*).[52] The interplay between at least two principles that is the essence of the *Wechselerweis* is the method that captures reality that is not fixed and static, but in a constant process of change. Frank discusses the role of this *Wechselerweis* in Schlegel's thought and provides a thorough discussion of the origin of this term in Schlegel's work, tracing it to thinkers such as Fichte, Schelling, Johann Friedrich Herbart, Johann Heinrich Abicht, and Novalis.

The final lecture, lecture twelve, is dedicated to a discussion of the role of aesthetic experience in Schlegel's view of philosophy. Schlegel was convinced that the absolute unpresentability of the Absolute could not be overcome religiously, conceptually, or sensibly, but only by alluding to it indirectly. This was precisely what allegory achieved; it was the kind of poetic saying that said more than it seemed to. Allegory and wit are ways of presenting the infinite to the finite mind. Romantic irony is another tool used by Schlegel to transform the tensions between the finite and the infinite in our cognitive experience into a kind of reciprocal play (*Wechselspiel*) between the finite and infinite. Romantic irony is a device that enables Schlegel to capture the tensions, without freezing the eternal movement between that which is without limits and that which is defined in terms of limits. Frank captures the essence of romantic irony thus, "[i]n order to become comprehensible, that which is pure must limit itself; any border contradicts the essential infinity of that which is pure however; therefore, it must always overstep the limits which it sets to itself, and then limit itself again, and then overstep the limits, and so on and on." Romantic irony enables us to engage in this infinite play between the infinite and the finite. Schlegel characterizes the human condition in terms of a feeling of longing for the infinite, a longing for something that we as finite humans, can never possess, but which guides our search for knowledge and leads to the insight that the search is all we can hope for, not the possession.

As Frank clearly shows, early German Romanticism was not an optimistic movement, it was not endowed with the security granted by a God that would reconcile all tensions or the sort that an absolutely grounded metaphysics could give us. The early German Romantics looked straight in the face of the multiple layers of human character—an inconsistent, contradictory, searching nature. After reading Frank's lectures, we reach the final line of the final lecture, Schlegel's claim that, "[w]here philosophy ends, poetry must begin," and are in a position to understand this claim *not* as a giddy, silly call to escape the demands of philosophy with the make-believe world of art, but as the expression of a serious reflection upon the nature of knowledge and of the limitations of our ability to ever reach a final word.

On Early German Romanticism as an Essentially Skeptical Movement

The Reinhold-Fichte Connection

I call these lectures "The Philosophical Foundations of Early German Romanticism." I owe you some explanation for this title. First let me clarify what I mean by the term 'foundations.' I do not mean something like principles or highest fundamental propositions, from which other propositions are deduced. This is worth emphasizing because the post-Kantian mood in Germany was filled with a tendency to view philosophy as an activity which necessarily departed from an absolute principle. Karl Leonhard Reinhold and Johann Gottlieb Fichte fit squarely into this tradition. Fichte was a professor in Jena from 1794–99 and his predecessor had been Reinhold, who had introduced a philosophy of this sort in 1789.[1] Certainly, the group of thinkers who became known as the early German Romantics were influenced by both Reinhold and Fichte, indeed Friedrich von Hardenberg (Novalis) had been Reinhold's student from 1790 to 1791. During this time and also later, Novalis was in contact with a number of fellow students who had also studied under Reinhold and whose names have now been forgotten; among them Johann Benjamin Eberhard, Friedrich Karl Forberg, Franz Paul von Herbert, and Friedrich Immanuel Niethammer stand out. In disputes concerning Reinhold's *Philosophy of Elements* (*Elementarphilosophie*), this group of young thinkers came to the conclusion that a philosophy, which seeks to follow a method of deduction from some highest fundamental principle, is either dispensable or downright impossible.

In the course of these lectures, I will show you that Novalis and Friedrich Schlegel shared this conviction, namely, that it is impossible to establish an absolute foundation for philosophy. Moreover, I shall indicate which arguments this critique of first principles rests upon. Thus, by the title "The Philosophical Foundations of Early German Romanticism," I do not mean to imply that the philosophy of early German Romanticism rested upon a fundamental proposition as did the philosophy of Reinhold (and later that of Fichte). To the contrary, early German Romanticism was oriented against such foundations.

You will now object that I am here parting from the predominant view of early German Romanticism as it is represented in academic research. When early German Romanticism, which included thinkers such as Friedrich Hölderlin, Novalis, and Friedrich Schlegel, has been considered at all as an independent epoch in the development of modern thought, then it has only been in relation to the development of so-called German idealism, that is in relation to thinkers such as J. G. Fichte, F. W. J. Schelling, and G. W. F. Hegel. One can say of Fichte, Schelling, and Hegel, of course, with the appropriate specifications and modifications, that they either assumed a primary and absolute fundamental proposition for all thought, or that they executed a process of thought that led to such a fundamental proposition, to so-called absolute knowledge. The early Romantics also speak often (using the terminology of that time) of the Absolute or the unconditioned, but they were of the opinion that we could not grasp the Absolute or the unconditioned in thought, to say nothing of being able to arrive at it in reality. Consider Novalis' famous first *Blüthenstaub*-fragment: "Everywhere we *seek* the unconditioned (*das Unbedingte*), but *find* only things (*Dinge*)." In some formulations (which sound revolutionary if one modernizes the discursive context in which they were expressed), Novalis finally concluded that there was not an Absolute at all: that the Absolute was only a Kantian idea and that any attempt to pursue it led to "the realm of nonsense." In this statement, the metaphysical conclusions of German idealism were rejected— many years before these metaphysical conclusions were clearly articulated in Hegel's mature system. Because posterity has passed clear judgment upon the possibility (or, more accurately, the impossibility) of this sort of metaphysical thought, early German Romanticism has more affinities with contemporary thought than with the idealism of Fichte and Hegel. In early German Romanticism, respect for the finitude of our potential for knowledge (a respect which Kant had already shown) begins to be taken seriously. But until just recently we did not know what the philosophical dimensions of early German Romanticism really involved.

That this was the case is astounding when one considers that early German Romanticism is generally considered to be the phenomenon that brought the German language into concert with European culture. The general conception of early German Romanticism, a view shared by many scholars as well, is that it attempted to bring the "German Spirit" to world literature. This contribution is viewed both positively and negatively. The negative aspects attributed to early German Romanticism are its anti-Enlightenment ambitions (for example, attempts to reestablish religion, especially Catholicism) and conservative political convictions. Georg Lukács went so far as to invent a history of direct cause and effect that passed "from Schelling to Hitler" (as is explicit in the subtitle of his famous book *The Destruction of Reason*).[2] But this is clearly wrong because Schelling was no Romantic, and the Nazis, as can be shown in detail, hated the protagonists of early German Romanticism.[3] In the authors of early German Romanticism, the Nazis saw— and rightly so—ground breakers of the literary avant-garde, whose irony was biting and whose sincerity was doubted, enemies of the bourgeoisie, friends and spouses of Jews, welcomed guests and discussion partners at the Jewish Berlin salons, aggressive proponents of "the emancipation of the Jewry," and finally "subversive intellectuals" (a slogan which the Nazis used indifferently to refer to members of the political left, to Jews as a group, and to intellectuals). Finally, the early Romantics were the closest friends of committed Democrats and Jacobins who constantly came into conflict with the censors, especially because the young Friedrich Schlegel was a Jacobin. Erhard was the most radical of the group and was Hardenberg's (Novalis') "real friend." Moreover, Erhard was indebted to Novalis for a lifesaving position working for Novalis' uncle, the Prussian minister and later chancellor, Karl August von Hardenberg. And it was Novalis who, when in 1798 he went to a spa in Teplitz for a health cure with von Herbert, a mutual friend of his and of Erhard's, allowed the correspondence between von Herbert and Erhard to occur under his noble name, protecting his two friends' correspondence from the censors.

I suggest that we do not occupy ourselves long with the clichés on either side. These clichés are the result of misconceived prejudices. Though prejudices do play a role in philosophy, they are at odds with the definition of philosophy as a love of knowledge. Even more fatal to us than both of the prejudices I have mentioned (which apply more to the literary dimensions of early German Romanticism than to its philosophical dimensions) is the misconception that early German Romanticism was a fantastic variation of absolute idealism as established by Fichte. This misconception rests upon a misinterpretation of the actual influence that Fichte's work did in fact have upon the central figures of early German Romanticism. Novalis' first independent writings (of 1795–96) show the strong influence of Fichte's *Wissenschaftslehre*. In the case of Hölderlin (whose first independent philosophical reflections were sketched in 1794–95), this influence seems even more evident, especially because he was Fichte's student. And a good case can be made for the influence of Fichte upon Friedrich Schlegel, who came to Jena in 1796 and had close relations with Fichte.

This is, in fact, the way it seems. But I will show you in the following lectures that although Fichte was highly appreciated by those named above, their thought did not follow his, but rather diverged radically from it. Most importantly, their thought had different presuppositions—this is what I meant just now when I spoke of foundations. In imagining the occasion of Fichte's appearances in Jena, you must remember that his audience—which consisted largely of former students of Reinhold or newcomers who had been informed by them—expected new arguments against the philosophy of first principles from their new teacher.[4] But Fichte provided the opposite: he sought to show that a philosophy based upon absolute principles was the right way of going about things, but that Reinhold's fundamental proposition could not be the first and highest proposition, and that it had to be replaced by what Fichte called the "absolute I." Among the group of Reinhold's former students, this thesis then reactivated the reservation concerning the feasibility of a philosophy based on first principles. This reservation had already been expressed between 1790 and 1792 (when Novalis had been Reinhold's student and had had access to the most important circle of thinkers critical of a philosophy based on first principles). But now it was not Reinhold's philosophy, but rather Fichte's, which was the object of critique. Novalis and Friedrich Schlegel's skeptical reactions to a "first philosophy" or a philosophy based on an absolute principle can best be understood within the context of the criticism which grew from Reinhold's *Elementarphilosophie*. Hence, that group of thinkers whose names have been forgotten, becomes more important. Previous research on early German Romanticism has neglected to examine the important relations between the criticism of Reinhold's philosophy and the subsequent criticisms of Fichte's philosophy. In order to fully appreciate the philosophical foundations of early German Romanticism, reactions to both Reinhold and Fichte must be studied and understood.

Why then has the Reinhold-Fichte connection been neglected? The sources that have enabled us to reconstruct this relation were, for many years, unavailable to scholars. These sources did not receive much attention until not more than ten years ago, although the essential ones had already been published two hundred years ago in forgotten collections of letters and in smaller publications. The rediscovery of these sources happened during the course of a substantial research project, to which Dieter Henrich, the initiator and leader of this work, gave the name "constellation-research." By "constellation-research," Henrich meant the scholarly and large-scale philological reconstruction of the discussion that occurred among Reinhold's students between 1792 and 1795 and of the context in which it occurred. This discussion has been gathered from correspondence which had until recently been difficult to access and was sometimes only salvageable from archives. Henrich concentrated his research upon the reconstruction of Hölderlin's early thought (from the period around 1795). Henrich's ongoing research is directed toward the investigation of the thought of a relatively unknown scholar, Carl Immanuel Diez, and of his influence upon the Jena Circle (1792). Diez was at one time *Repetent* (a *Repetent* is more or less equivalent to an assistant professor of today) at the *Tübinger Stift*, the still existing theological seminary which has known world famous students such as; Johannes Kepler, Georg W. Hegel, Friedrich Hölderlin, Friedrich W. J. Schelling, David Strauß, and Eduard Friedrich Mörike. Now, Diez, *Repetent* at the *Stift*, had a decisive influence upon the formation of the thought of Niethammer, Hölderlin, Schelling, and Hegel, and later, in Jena, upon that of Reinhold. My own thesis is that what was specific to early German Romantic philosophy can also be explained through appeal to this constellation, particularly the work of Novalis, who—in contrast to Hölderlin—had actually been Reinhold's student and a friend of the first strong critics of Reinhold's proposed "first philosophy." As a result of the systemic investigation of the discussion amongst Reinhold's former students in Jena between 1792 and 1795, entirely new sources have surfaced, and with them fresh, new insights have emerged. These new sources are so groundbreaking that it is no exaggeration to say that they not only place early German Romanticism scholarship upon an entirely new foundation, but that they also provide it with an entirely new mission. In the following lectures, we shall explore a portion of these new and pathbreaking sources.

The second point of clarification has to do with my use of the term 'Early German Romanticism.' I intentionally take the expression 'early Romanticism' (*Frühromantik*) to have a broader sense than that in which it is commonly used. One commonly understands early Romanticism as meaning the philosophical and literary production of a circle which consisted of friends who found themselves together in Berlin and/or Jena between 1796 and 1800 and which came to be centered around the house of the Schlegel brothers in Jena: that is to say, authors such as Wilhelm Wackenroder and Ludwig Tieck, Novalis, and Friedrich Daniel Ernst Schleiermacher, Friedrich and Wilhelm Schlegel (not to forget Caroline and Dorothea Schlegel, as well as Sophie Tieck). Hölderlin and his circle are usually not included as members of the early German Romantic movement because—despite the meeting between Novalis and Hölderlin in the home of Niethammer at the end of May 1795, and despite the great attention which Tieck, Schlegel, and Franz Brentano paid to Hölderlin's lyrical work—there was no direct relationship between the two circles. When Hölderlin himself was considering plans to found a journal, he alluded only indirectly to *Das Athenäum*, the famous journal of the Jena Circle that was published between 1798 and 1800. We have, in particular, little knowledge of how much Hölderlin knew of Friedrich Schlegel, who was the most productive, theoretical author and especially the best-known classicist of the group. On the other hand, we do know that Hölderlin was familiar with Schleiermacher's lectures of 1799, *On Religion: Speeches Addressed to Its Cultured Despisers*. Emil Petzold has already demonstrated that the influences of this work are to be found in Hölderlin's *Brot und Wein*.[5] But such relations between the two circles are incidental. It is in no way necessary to refer to them in order to demonstrate the unity in structure of thought between the Jena Circle and the Homburg Circle. This unity can, according to the newest research, be largely explained by the fact that the thought of the two circles was built upon the same foundation. Namely, they both develop the results of the constellation of conversations that played out among Reinhold's students starting in 1792.

Much nonsense has been promulgated with the goal of contrasting the basic inspirations of Hölderlin and of the early Romantics, especially in the field of literature. Among this nonsense is the prejudice that, due to his lifelong orientation toward the Greeks, Hölderlin should be more appropriately considered a classicist, while the Romantics were more oriented toward the Middle Ages. First of all, Hölderlin completed the same "turn toward the national" as Novalis and Schlegel, at the latest in his letters to Casimir Ulrich Böhlendorff. And second of all, it was Friedrich Schlegel himself whose thought is especially rooted in the foundational works of the classical epoch generally and in the classical period of art in particular; it was with reference to Schlegel that the satirical term 'Graecomania' was invented by Karl Philipp Moritz, I think. So, when viewed clearly, no essential difference arises here, but rather a strong parallel.

With this I have, of course, not yet said anything about the meaning of early German Romanticism itself. I propose the following ad hoc definition, which I will have to justify in the following lectures, piece by piece. The thought of Hölderlin and that of Hardenberg (Novalis) and Schlegel *cannot* be assimilated to the mainstream of so-called German idealism, although these philosophers developed their thought in close cooperation with the principle figures of German idealism, Fichte and Schelling (Hegel, a latecomer to free speculation, played at that time only a passive role). The thought of Hölderlin, Novalis, and Schlegel implies a tenet of basic realism, which I will provisionally express by the formula, that that which has being—or, we might say, the essence of our reality—cannot be traced back to determinations of our consciousness. If *ontological* realism can be expressed by the thesis that reality exists independently of our consciousness (even if we suppose thought to play a role in structuring reality) and if *epistemological* realism consists in the thesis that we do not possess adequate knowledge of reality, then early German Romanticism can be called a version of ontological and epistemological realism. Early German Romanticism never subscribed to the projects of liquidating the thing in itself (*Ding an sich*), which are characteristic of the beginnings of idealism from Salomon Maimon to Fichte, Schelling, and Hegel. One can object that the early German Romantics adopt, to borrow a term from Michael Devitt, the "fig leaf realism" of Kant and Reinhold, both of whom distinguished a reality independent of our knowledge of it from the a priori conditions of our knowledge, and both of whom described the quest for knowledge of reality as an infinite task, which will therefore never be exhausted. Kant assigned the name 'idea' to the object of this inexhaustible inquiry into reality. An idea is a concept for which no (concrete) intuition can be appropriate—for example, totality. And this means that we finite beings, for obvious reasons, strive toward a completeness of knowledge, but can never arrive at it, since we have a finite number of intuitions available upon which to base our judgments. The early German Romantics, in reference to this infinite project, spoke of the "longing for the infinite" (*Sehnsucht nach dem Unendlichen*). In "longing for the infinite," the early German Romantics believed themselves to have provided an unconventional, but by no means unsuitable translation of the Greek *filosofiva*.

Today, I will not elaborate extensively upon the issues relating to Kant's use of the terms 'thing-in-itself' and 'idea.' They relate to central points in Kant's theory, which were heatedly discussed and forcefully attacked by his contemporaries—particularly by the old-Leibnizians of the Wolff School, but also by Jacobi, Maimon, and Aenesidemus-Schulze.[6] I will mention *one* point of attack, which concerns a contradiction in Kant's explanation of the origin of our sensations. Like many present-day proponents of a causal theory of reference, Kant held that the passivity of our sensations was due to the effect of a thing in itself. He asks: What would an appearance be without something that appears—without an aboutness? If I think of this affecting conceived of as an application of the principle of sufficient reason, then the following contradiction arises: According to Kant, causality is a category (a pure concept of the understanding). The concept of causality cannot be employed to lead beyond the realm of appearances and of the subjective. In particular, it cannot be used to make the world of sensible appearances understandable as the product of a reality existing in itself, as Kant does, thus leading to inconsistency. Here, of course, we have the origin of Kant's dualism: there is a reality existing in itself, of which we know nothing; opposed to this reality there is a consciousness, which must be characterized as "completely without content" or "empty." Kant takes into consideration that there could be a root that is common both to the reality existing in itself and to consciousness, but which is itself unknown. The Kantian system breaks into two parts; this common root would bind these two parts together into a unity. This systematic unity can only be thought of as an idea. Here we have, by the way, a crude, imprecise, and ad hoc definition of the second of Kant's core theses: the unity in which reality and consciousness exist together cannot itself be the object of our knowledge. This unity can only be spoken of in terms of hypothetical concepts. They serve our reason, playing a necessarily regulative role in unifying our knowledge. But the "real pursuit" of them would, as Novalis says, "lead into the realm of nonsense."

My point now (turning back to early German Romanticism) is that Hölderlin and Novalis are in complete agreement concerning the thesis of the priority of Being over the subjective view of Being. From this point of agreement, they progress into other thoughts, according to which the path toward knowledge must be described in terms of a process of infinite approximation or as a necessarily incomplete progression. These thoughts of a priority of existence over the subjective view of it and of the path toward knowledge as infinite approximation are, when taken together, incompatible with the kind of philosophy which Reinhold presents in his *Attempt at a New Theory of the Human Faculty of Representation* and to the sort of method referred to by Fichte in the first paragraphs of the *Foundation of the Wissenschaftslehre*. These are philosophies that start from the certainty of a highest and immediately evident fundamental proposition from which our valid beliefs can be derived as logical implications. For a long time, I thought that Hölderlin's and Novalis' talk of Being stood for a higher fundamental proposition like the ones that they attributed to Reinhold and Fichte. Since then I have realized that this interpretation was wrong. Being does not stand for a principle superior to the so-called absolute I, but rather for the thought that we cannot exhaust our access to reality by mere thought, or that, as Hans Georg Gadamer says, "in all understanding there is more Being than we are aware of." This thought, which moves the finitude of our means of attaining knowledge into the foreground, is entirely compatible with the belief that our knowledge cannot ultimately be grounded in a highest principle. It is also entirely compatible with a basically skeptical disposition toward philosophy, which I would again like to characterize as typically romantic.

Now, in order to make your way easier, I should say a few words about the previously mentioned group which was brought into view by Henrich: the Jena Constellation. Only against the background of this Jena Constellation is it possible to entirely understand the claims I have introduced. The most important point about the intellectual constellation of 1789 to 1792 is that Hölderlin and later Novalis and Friedrich Schlegel were exposed to the Kantian philosophy. In the following lectures, we shall consider this Kantian legacy through two texts, which for the last two hundred years went unnoticed. The first is the second edition (from 1789) of Jacobi's *Spinoza Buechlein*.[7] The second is Reinhold's *Beyträge zur Berichtung bisheriger Missverständnisse der Philosophen* (Contributions to the Rectification of Hitherto Held Misconceptions of Philosophers), which represented his turn in the summer of 1792.[8]

Reinhold's text was only discovered due to a curious event. We shall consider it first.

In response to the so-called Vienna Jacobin Conspiracy of July 1794, the Austrian reactionaries conducted a raid of suspected Jacobins who had been influenced by studying Kant. In this raid, part of the correspondence of Baron Franz Paul von Herbert, owner of the white lead factory in Klagenfurt, was confiscated.[9] The police are usually more thorough than are the philologists. Thus, a letter to the Baron from the Jena professor of philosophy, Friedrich Immanuel Niethammer, was kept in the archive of the Imperial and Royal Ministry of the interior. Baron von Herbert was patron to Niethammer (and also, by the way, to Reinhold, who was of humble means). Niethammer had been Hölderlin's "friend" and "mentor" since their time at the Stift. Their relationship solidified during their time together in Jena.[10] Niethammer's letter to von Herbert is dated June 2. In it he speaks of "the dispensability of a single highest principle of all knowledge," and thus of the failure of Reinhold's and Fichte's attempts to establish our knowledge on a highest proposition, the truth of which could be secured by immediate evidence.[11] During his formative phase, Niethammer was a student of Karl Leonhard Reinhold. Reinhold is known in the history of philosophy as the founder of a philosophy that determines the acceptability of propositions by their derivability from a highest principle that is in itself evident. But, in the summer of 1792, Reinhold himself was troubled by doubts as to whether such a philosophical program could be carried out.

It seems that two personalities played a role in the origin of this philosophical crisis: Novalis' former tutor, Carl Christian Erhard Schmid, and the Tübingen *Repetent* Carl Immanuel Diez. In a letter to Johann Benjamin Erhard (dated July 18, 1792), which Henrich has recently published,[12] Reinhold admits—and this is an admission which is repeated in none of the writings he published at the time—that his philosophy rests upon premises which cannot all be grounded right from the beginning, but which can be grounded only in succession (or by later justification).[13] In the case of Reinhold's *Elementarphilosophie*, the presupposition which is implicitly assumed is that of the self-activity of the subject, which is the only active element in all the relations addressed by the 'principle of consciousness.' So the foundation is not a principle that is laid down right from the beginning, but is rather accomplished through a final idea. This must be an idea in Kant's original sense (namely, a relational category which is expanded for the purpose of systematizing our knowledge into the unconditioned). Now ideas are only hypothetically valid. They regulate our reflections upon the world, but do not constitute objects. If final foundations only follow from ideas, then, paradoxically, they can never be ultimately justified (since they never follow ultimately). And so the program of a deduction from a highest principle is transformed into an infinite approximation towards a principle that can never be reached. In other words, the first principle becomes a regulative idea. Reinhold's former student, Novalis, recapitulates this twist (the result of which should have remained binding for Novalis himself) when he says that "the absolute I" must be transformed into a "principle of approximation."[14]

And now we take a jump forward. In the fall of 1796, another young Jena student of philosophy recorded the following conviction:

> [. . .] Philosophy [must], like the epic poem, begin in the middle, and it is impossible to present philosophy and to add to it piece by piece, so that the first piece would be in itself completely grounded and explained (*KA* XVIII: 518, Nr. 16).

The student was Friedrich Schlegel. Eight years later, in the private Cologne lectures for the Boisserée brothers, he is able to articulate his claim even more clearly:

> Our philosophy does not begin like others with a first principle—where the first proposition is like the center or first ring of a comet—with the rest a long tail of mist—we depart from a small but living seed—our center lies in the middle. From an unlikely and modest beginning—doubt regarding the "thing" which, to some degree shows itself in all thoughtful people and the always present, prevalent probability of the I—our philosophy will develop in a steady progression and become strengthened until it reaches the highest point of human knowledge and shows the breadth and limits of all knowledge (*KA* XII: 328, 3).

And in July, another former student of Reinhold, namely Novalis, notes:

> What do I do by philosophizing? I am searching for a foundation. At the basis of philosophizing there lies a striving toward thought of a foundation. But foundation is not cause in the actual sense—but rather inner nature— connection with the whole [coherence]. All philosophizing must terminate in an absolute foundation. If this were not given, if this concept contained an impossibility—then the urge to philosophize would be an infinite activity. It would be without end, because an eternal need for an absolute foundation would be at hand—and thus it would never stop. Through the voluntary renunciation of the Absolute, infinite free activity arises in us— the only possible Absolute which can be given to us, and which we find only through our incapacity to arrive at and recognize an absolute. This Absolute which is given to us may only be recognized negatively, in that we act and find that through no action do we arrive at that which we seek. This may be called an absolute postulate. All searching for *one principle*

would be an attempt to square the circle. *Perpetuum mobile.* The philosopher's
stone (*NS* II: 269 f., Nr. 566).[15]

Other things that Novalis says are just as decidedly Reinholdian. For example, he claims that the subject, thought of as "cause" (this would be
Reinhold's "absolute subject") is "only a regulatory concept, an idea of reason—it would thus be foolish to attribute real efficacy to it" (l.c., 255, Nr.
476; cf. l.c., Nr. 477). Or: "All search for the first principle is nonsense—it
is a *regulatory idea*" (l.c., 254, Nr. 472; cf. 252, lines 5 ff. and 177, Nr. 234,
lines 15 ff.). "A pure law of association [coherence] seems to me to be the
highest axiom—a hypothetical proposition" (l.c., lines 12 ff.).

Between Reinhold's doubts concerning a first philosophy and Schlegel's
and Novalis' decided departure from it, a history is played out which stands
quite at odds with what the historians have to say to us about the origin of
the so-called absolute idealism. This history has to do with skepticism regarding the possibility that beliefs can be ultimately grounded through a deduction
from a highest principle. When this principle breaks apart under the blows of
such doubt, then the belief in the "relativity of all truth" can spread, as is
assumed in the citation from Schlegel. In Schlegel's *Review of the First Four
Volumes of F. I. Niethammer's Philosophisches Journal* (*KA* VIII: 12–32), which
he himself characterizes as his "debut on the philosophical stage":

> How can there be scientific judgments, where there is not yet a science?
> Indeed, all other sciences must oscillate as long as we lack a positive phi-
> losophy. However, in other sciences there is at least something relatively
> firm and universally valid. Nothing is yet established in philosophy, this is
> shown to us by the present state. All foundation and ground is still missing
> (*KA* VIII: 30 f.).

At the time this conviction was written, Fichte had already been teaching
at Jena for three years, and had already claimed, in principle, that his
Wissenschaftslehre had laid a firm and universally valid foundation. When we
keep this clearly in mind, the boldness of Schlegel's skeptical objection stands
in sharp relief. Inquiry into the history which played out between Reinhold's
philosophy of first principles and Schlegel's and Novalis' reactions to it will
be *one* topic of these lectures. But before developing this theme, I shall first
address another important piece of background information.

The basic skeptical conclusion for which I have presented evidence
and whose effect turned back upon Fichte could be cultivated within the
context of the Jena discussion through a reflection upon the semantics of the
term 'knowledge.' Jacobi discussed the semantics of knowledge in the seventh

Beilage of the second edition of his book on Spinoza (known as the *Spinoza Büchlein*). There Jacobi shows that the definition of knowledge as justified belief leads to an infinite regress. His argument is as follows: Facts become known, and they are formulated in propositions (that is, Kantian judgments). If a state of affairs is a fact (and thus something known), the statement corresponding to the fact must, by definition, be conditioned by something else that serves to justify it. So this statement must be conditioned by another statement, which must itself be conditioned by another statement, which must in turn be conditioned by yet another statement, and so on ad infinitum. If all of our beliefs are conditioned by other beliefs, then we can never attain knowledge of the unconditioned. So, if we stand by this strong definition of knowledge, all propositions are valid only conditionally. Yet if we assert the existence of an Absolute, there must be at least *one* proposition that is not valid conditionally, but unconditionally. An unconditionally valid proposition is one which has validity that is not derived from a condition of being grounded upon another proposition. Jacobi called the knowledge that is expressed in an unconditional proposition, "feeling" (or belief [*Glaube*]). To believe means: to take a fact to be certain without anything further, where no additional light would be shed upon the fact through an additional grounding of it—where a grounding is neither possible nor necessary. Novalis recapitulates this position succinctly with the words: "What I don't know, but I feel [. . .], I believe" (*NS* II: 105, lines 11–13; lines 1–3).

The skepticism of the early German Romantics is targeted precisely against a program of absolute foundations. They question whether there is immediate knowledge and find Jacobi's appeal to faith an untenable solution to the problem of the unknowability of the Absolute. According to the romantic position, our knowledge is situated in an infinite progression and has no firm, absolute foundation. (Because of this, and only because of this, is Schlegel's statement that *"Truth is relative"* valid. [*KA* XII: 92]). And evidence, even in the form of common sense intuition, cannot replace the grounding which is missing (and which is, in an ultimate form, impossible).

We know that Novalis and Friedrich Schlegel not only knew Niethammer well, and were even friends with him, but that they also regularly read the *Philosophisches Journal einer Gesellschaft Teutscher Gelehrten* (Philosophical Journal of a Society of German Scholars), the publication which Niethammer had announced at the beginning of January 1795 and had edited since May of that year (cf, for example, *NS* IV: 200). Schlegel not only reviewed the first three years' issues of the *Journal*, but he also collaborated on several texts that appeared in the *Journal* (cf, *KA* VIII: CLV ff.). Novalis' earliest philosophical notes are not in the literary form of fragments, but rather of a *Brouillon*, and these writings may have been intended for the *Philosophisches Journal*. Support for the hypothesis that Novalis' notes were written for the *Philosophisches Journal* is the fact that there were letters from Novalis to Niethammer in which Novalis speaks of his intentions to contribute to Niethammer's *Journal*. The editor of the critical edition of Novalis' works had access to these letters, but they have since been lost (*NS* II: 32). Clearly, there is strong evidence in favor of the thesis that the early German Romantic philosophers were involved in critiquing a philosophy based on first principles. Niethammer's *Journal* was a literary vehicle that served these purposes and hence became a forum for this discussion.[16] The general tone of criticism is well-illustrated in an article for the journal that Niethammer wrote. The article was entitled, "Concerning the Demands of Common Sense on Philosophy,"[17] and was written as an introduction to the goals of the journal in general and the skeptical response to a philosophy based on first principles in particular. In this article, Niethammer, as the title of the essay suggests, announces his methodological turn away from Reinhold and attempts to substantiate his doubt concerning the possibility of a philosophy based on first principles. In his skeptical response to the *Aenesidemus* issue, Niethammer had already expressed doubt concerning the possibility of a transcendental proof of the so-called fact of experience (which even skeptics did not dispute). In the classical version of the transcendental deduction, such a proof follows *modo tollenti* from a retroactive inference (*Rückschluß*) to a priori laws of our mind, from which the beliefs we take to be true follow as necessary consequences. Niethammer attempted to expose the following circle in this process of derivation: first, experience is established in consciousness; second, going back from experience, principles are arrived at as antecedents; third, these principles are then supposed to confirm the foundation of experience. But it is not only the case that from the consequent, there is no certain inference to one and only one "determined" antecedent, because the same consequent can follow from many different antecedents (Kant himself knew this [*CPR* A368]). Moreover, according to Niethammer, it is the case that there can be no necessary relation between a contingent empirical proposition and an a priori apodictically valid proposition. In the remainder of the essay, Niethammer denies that the grounds of derivation could consist at all in a priori synthetic propositions.

A critique of the procedure of transcendental deduction that is even harsher than the one developed by Niethammer, was the one that was put forth by another of Reinhold's rebellious students, namely, the philosopher (and later famous jurist) Paul Johann Anselm Feuerbach.[18] His argument rests upon the insight that the evidence for the first principle must be immediately evident, hence this first principle must be understood as a mere factual (empirical, a posteriori) truth.[19] If a truth is only factual (as Reinhold consistently tells us of the facts of consciousness), then it lacks the necessity which is demanded of a priori truth. The necessity of a factual truth would result only if the fact were justified by a universal rule of inference (the major premise of the syllogism) and the fact and rule of inference together implied the conclusion—and the first principle of philosophy lacks just this relationship of necessity. Because the adherents of an absolute "first philosophy" make reference to a "first principle" as a piece of evidence (that is, a conscious experience or a belief of healthy human reason), the supposed principle can be formulated *modo ponente* in a classical syllogism only as a minor proposition (that is, as a singular proposition). The validity of a singular proposition can only be empirical (if for the sake of the argument we abstract from mathematical propositions like "two is an even number"—but note we are dealing with facts of consciousness). Feuerbach is positive that grounding can only follow from regulative ideas—thus, it can never follow ultimately.

Feuerbach's conclusion converges with the conclusions reached by Friedrich Karl Forberg, Novalis, Friedrich Schlegel, and many others, namely: Claims to truth can only be understood as an infinite approximation toward knowledge which is never complete (Feuerbach, l. c., 317 ff.). Thus, as Schlegel says, "an absolute understanding" is denied "in the philosophy, which denies an absolute truth." (KA XII: 102; cf. 102). And: "Every system is only an approximation toward its ideal. Skepticism is [thus] eternal [insurmountable, incircumventable]" (KA XVIII: 417, Nr. 1149). I have already mentioned similar formulations by Novalis (the most important example is the note taken over by Forberg; NS II: 269 ff., Nr. 566).

Friedrich Schlegel developed an alternative to approaches like those of Reinhold and Fichte, that is, to approaches which sought to develop a philosophy based upon a single, absolute first principle. His alternative was that of an alternating or reciprocal principle (*Wechselgrundsatz*) or an alternating proof or reciprocal proof structure (*Wechselerweis*) operating in thought.[20] Novalis, on the other hand, took a slightly different path, one which is strikingly close to that of Hölderlin (in May 1795). Novalis shows that the reflexive nature of our self-consciousness (Fichte's "highest point") is incompatible with the thought of an Absolute (that which Novalis, along with Jacobi, calls "original being" [*Urseyn*]). Thus, reflexive self-consciousness, as an I, cannot be taken as the first principle of philosophy. Rather, the foundation for this I is transformed from a piece of evidence immanent in consciousness (which is felt in an intellectual intuition) into a "principle of approximation," that is, into a Kantian idea, which we are supposed to approach in an infinite progression. The thought of conferring reality to this idea leads, says Novalis, "into the realm of nonsense" (NS II: 252, line 6). Or also: "Everywhere we *seek* the unconditioned, but *find* only things" (l.c., 412, Nr. 1).

I have given you, in rather broad brushstrokes, the main lines of the debate that shaped early German Romantic philosophy. Now, I would like to provide you with some details of an important but little known source of inspiration for the development of Novalis' thought: the person and work of Carl Christian Erhard Schmid, author of *Empirische Psychologie* (Empirical Psychology).[21]

Schmid lived from 1761 to 1812. He was the most important orthodox Kantian of his time, and was in correspondence with Kant himself. He became the victim of one of the most evil acts of terrorism in the history of modern philosophy: the *Act of Annihilation*, which Fichte directed against him in the *Philosophisches Journal* in 1795. But the very fact that Fichte got himself into such an uproar about Schmid was naturally motivated by something which should be of great interest to us: the significance of Fichte's *Wissenschaftslehre*. Fichte claimed that the *Wissenschaftslehre* went beyond what Kant had shown in his *Critique of Pure Reason*, however, Schmid denied this. Schmid later garnered Kant's agreement on this point. Schmid did not belong to the circle around Reinhold and Niethammer (to whom he was nevertheless close; so for a time he planned to edit the *Philosophisches Journal* together with Niethammer); rather, he had been the tutor of the young Friedrich von Hardenberg (later known as Novalis) from 1781 to 1782. Schmid maintained contact with Novalis until Novalis' untimely death in 1801. So, the former tutor became a meaningful and central figure for Novalis—as Niethammer was for Hölderlin: teacher, philosophical mentor, and friend. In 1790, Novalis was studying at Jena, and attending Schmid's lectures (he attended, among other things, his lectures on *Empirische Psychologie*). During this decisive phase of Novalis' life, Schmid acted as his philosophical mentor and also as a friend and confidante. Teacher and student were quite close. Conclusions concerning intellectual dependencies between the two may also be drawn. These I will elucidate in the next lecture.

Lecture 2

On the Historical Origins of Novalis' Critique of Fichte

I begin today's lecture with a question that was posed by one of the most important members of the early German Romantic movement: "What do I do by philosophizing?" This question was posed in July 1796 by a twenty-four-year-old man, who soon after had to replace his good family name with a pseudonym as protection from the censors. He had only three hours a day to ask such questions, for his profession was not philosophy, he was trapped in a bureaucratic office as government attorney at the regional government office in Tennstedt.[1] Here is his answer to the question he posed, an answer that is no less captivating today than it was when he first expressed it:

> I am searching for a foundation. [. . .] All philosophizing must terminate in an absolute foundation. Now, if this were not given, if this concept contained an impossibility—then the urge to philosophize would be an infinite activity. It would be without end, because an eternal need for an absolute foundation would be at hand—and thus it would never stop.[2]

The young attorney was Friedrich von Hardenberg who wrote philosophy under the pseudonym of Novalis. He had studied with Reinhold in Jena from October 1790 to October 1791 and had close relations with his teacher.[3] Karl Leonhard Reinhold's achievement in the history of philosophy is considered to be the development of his *Elementarphilosophie*. The core thought of this *Elementarphilosophie* is that the search for knowledge (as he quite aptly translates the Greek word *filosofiva*), which has followed a traditional course of an uncertain groping, can be grounded upon an ultimate foundation. He called the discovery of this foundation "the one thing of which humanity is in need." The problem that inspired this discovery as the solution to the problem of the foundation of all knowledge was described by Jacobi in his *Spinoza Büchlein* (which was the expanded second edition of his book on Spinoza and was published in 1789) as follows: When, in the old and honorable tradition, we describe knowledge as justified belief or supported opinion, we land in an infinite regress.[4] (It is pertinent to note that this old and honorable tradition is still very much alive—for example, in the work of Roderick Chisholm, or even more recently, in the work of Lawrence BonJour.) We base our claims to knowledge upon propositions which can only express knowledge under the condition that they are supported by other propositions which express knowledge, and so on. This regress can only end in a proposition which is "*un*-conditionally valid." "Unconditionally" means: not dependent upon a higher condition. Such a proposition must be intelligible as in itself valid, without anything further: "a foundation for it being neither needed nor possible." Such a proposition would have to be self-evident. For 'self-evident' literally means that which clarifies itself from or by itself.

Reinhold believed that he had found such a proposition. He called it the "principle of consciousness" (*Satz des Bewußtseins*). According to Reinhold, all other propositions that can make a claim to truth can be developed from this "principle of consciousness"—either through logical or analytic derivation. By "analytic" Reinhold meant roughly the same thing which gave contemporary analytic philosophy its name: that which follows from the understanding of the meaning of expressions which are used, including the meaning of the logical particles (*Formwörter*).[5]

This project of establishing a first principle for philosophy seemed to have reached its completion in 1794 with Fichte's philosophy of the absolute I. But doubts soon occured to Reinhold's students. These doubts fell into three basic categories. It was first disputed whether a system of beliefs could be based upon evidence at all; because evidence consists in private conscious experience. One cannot develop intersubjective consensus by appeal to this private evidence, but that which we call knowledge rests upon the development of intersubjective consensus. Second, in addition, upon closer analysis, this private evidence is not clearly distinguishable from "the demands of common sense." We can usually only establish the claims of common sense upon so-called intuition—that is to say, we believe in them. Statements of belief do have a character similar to that of Euclidean axioms. If they could be proven, then they would immediately lose their status as highest axioms—for a proposition that has its foundation in another proposition is not the highest. Thus, the foundation of knowledge becomes a matter of belief. As Novalis will say: "It is a product of the faculty of imagination, in which we believe, without being able to recognize it according to its nature and to our own nature."[6] But the third objection proved to be the most serious and the most fruitful: Reinhold's highest proposition does not actually stand on its own two feet. Rather, its foundation presupposes other propositions which are supposed to follow from it. This is a ruinous result for a philosophy baed on an absolute, first principle, but it is one that Novalis holds to be unavoidable. In so doing, he makes it hard for the crowd of researchers of early German Romanticism who regard his early thought as a somewhat fantastic and mixed-up variety of the foundationalist philosophy to make their case. He creates even more difficulties for the editors of the critical edition of Novalis. To their great merit, they have edited and reconstructed the ordering of Hardenberg's earliest philosophical writings *in toto*. But, through their choice of the title *Fichte-Studien* (*Fichte-Studies*), they have presented an entirely inappropriate picture of the young Hardenberg with respect to his appropriation of Fichte's early idealism, and have thus distorted what in German hermeneutics is called *"Wirkungsgeschichte,"* the history of the public reception of Novalis's work. Now, it is the case that Novalis' basic impulse toward the criticism of idealism was a result of his earlier schooling by Reinhold and by his former tutor (and mentor) Carl Christian Erhard Schmid. Novalis had knowledge, even if only indirect knowledge, of Schmid's criticism of Reinhold and Fichte, as well as the criticisms of his former fellow students at Jena, Friedrich Immanuel Niethammer, Franz Paul von Herbert, Friedrich Carl Forberg, and especially Johann Benjamin Erhard. Because this is so, I must explain this last point in more detail.

I will limit myself to Schmid's and Erhard's critiques. Not only was Novalis able to hear Schmid's *Empirische Psychologie* as a series of lectures at Jena in 1791: he cited it occasionally[7] and owned a copy.[8] Novalis' contact with Erhard was also intense. He referred to Erhard as his "true friend" in 1798.[9] Erhard's uncle, a minister in Berlin and later chancellor of Prussia, was instrumental in Novalis being hired in Ansbach. Morevoer, it was Erhard who, in August 1798, while on vacation in Teplitz with their mutual friend von Herbert, allowed the correspondence between him and von Herbert to be sent under his own noble name in order to protect his Jacobin friend from being spied upon by the censors and the police.[10] Erhard was the most intellectually outstanding figure in the circle of Reinhold's students, even though we must laboriously draw his most ingenious objections out of letters, the most important of which are, to top things off, unpublished, and must be salvaged from archives.

In *Empirische Psychologie*, Schmid had bitterly but pertinently criticized Reinhold's use of the concept of representation as an elementary terminus to be used in philosophy as a starting point (*Erster Theil*, sect. IX ff.). The concept of representation, says Schmid, is unsuitable as a principle of deduction for philosophy, because it is arrived at by means of an abstraction from the multitude of psychic experiences and acts.[11] Schmid claims that it is worthless to undertake a derivation from a genus-concept which orginates in this manner, because the following circle becomes immediately apparent: From individual events I obtain, *via abstractionis*, that from which I then pretend to derive the events themselves.[12] Novalis was also able to become familiar with this objection through his teacher at Leipzig, Karl Heinrich Heydenreich, who had put forth such a critique in a much-noticed critical review of Reinhold in 1790. Reinhold was so deeply impressed by this review that he published it in its entirety in the appendix to the first volume of his *Beyträge* and modified his earlier view of the deduction from the highest principle.[13] Henceforth, Reinhold differentiated between *being-contained-in* and *being-contained-under*, such that the former came to mean an implication *in nuce*, while the latter signified the relation of an object to a class of objects (or better, the relation of the instantiation of a particular under a universal).[14] The former case is a relation between parts to a whole which trivially contains them. The latter relation, on the other hand, is very weak and is unfit to be a principle of derivation. What falls under a concept is by no means included in it (*cf.* Kant *CPR* B40). One who, for example, understands the genus-concept of justice, does not, by means only of this understanding, know anything about the practices of the present English judicial system, although these practices fall under the genus-concept. Or, just by correctly understanding the concept of 'mammal,' one does not know anything about the existence of kangaroos.[15] The a priori specification cannot be constructed out of the genus-concept. Thus, Kant wisely renounced explaining the genus-concept of 'representation' as a principle, much less as a principle of deduction, although he himself had shown that all concepts concerning the ways in which the mind is affected or functions fall under the concept of 'representation' (see *CPR* A320/B376 f.; further *CPR* B676 f.— a passage to which Schmid himself refers in *Empirische Psychologie*: I, sect. X, 161). Unlike mathematics, philosophy works with concepts that are not *made*, but rather with concepts that are *given*. Unlike mathematical constructions, what is contained *under* concepts cannot be developed out of concepts. This is, as you know, the reason why Kant held that philosophy could provide no definitions but only expositions (*CPR* A727/B754 ff.).

A standard objection of the Leibnizians to Reinhold[16] (which was taken up by August Wilhelm Rehberg and can also be found in Erhard[17]) was that Kant had neglected this distinction. Novalis presents a strong formulation of this sort of objection in his *Fichte-Studien*. In note number 438, he says: "Only an *Exposition* of essence is possible. Essence is simply not (re)cognizable" (*NS* II: 238, lines 33 ff.; cf. 239, line 12). And in note 445, he says that philosophy cannot begin with a definition; a definition of the highest can only be thought of *anticipando* (243, lines 7 f.). In note number 466 (*NS* II: 250 ff.), where he discusses the absurdity of comprehending the highest as the highest genus, Novalis criticizes Reinhold with respect to this issue. For Reinhold had said that the expression 'principle' (*Grundsatz*) stood for a genus-concept.[18] He had also demanded from philosophy that it follow the guideline of the species-genre distinctions as long as in, "resolving (*auflösen*) concepts of nearest genus (*genus proximum*) and nearest species (*differentia proxima/specifica*), one did not convince oneself of having arrived at something irresolvable (*unauflösliches*), which as such cannot be a compound concept.[19] Reinhold spoke of a concept which could not be further analysed and which could of course, he said, only be a single one, "as of the only possible highest genus-determining principle."[20]

If this is the theoretical context to which Hardenberg's critique refers, then it is in fact clear that he borrows here from two predecessors: Heydenreich and Schmid. Schmid had distinguished two concepts: He calls the genus of representation either "general faculty" or "general power," depending on whether it comes into play as a foundation of the possibility or as a foundation of the reality of (particular) representations. He then specifies that the genus of representation "comprehends what is left over *under* itself, as the logical gender (that is, the genus] does the kinds, but (that that genus of representation] in no way makes the kinds understandable according to that which differentiates them" (*Empirische Psychologie*, I, sect. XII: 163). Distinct from this, says Schmid, is the "one and only substance" the "*radical* or *absolute fundamental power*," which was put forth by the dogmatists, for example, Spinoza (Ibid., sect. VIII: 159; sect. IX: 160). Schmid then goes on to claim that the "reality of manifold appearances of a certain kind is derived" out of the "one and only substance," which one can, of course, he says, only posit as a Kantian idea (Ibid., sect. IX: 160). For the relation of the fundamental power, if there were one, to that which is derived from it, would be the relation of containing-in or of whole to part. With his proof that the positing of such a fundamental power is only the result of a progressive abstraction from a plurality of irreducible powers of the mind and functions of consciousness (cf. Ibid., sects. XII und XIV: 163 ff., 166 ff.), Schmid not only wanted to strike a blow to Reinholdian philosophy of first principles, but to the Wolffians as well (he mentions Wolff and Platner by name). Naturally, he also wanted to declare his opposition to the Fichte of the first *Wissenschaftslehre*, whom he actually did attack in the pages of the *Philosophisches Journal* (III/2 [1795]: 95–132).[21] There, Schmid offered the following sketch of Fichte's thought: Fichte traces the thought of I-as-self-consciousness back to "the absolute faculty of abstraction."[22] According to Fichte, it is due to this faculty that anything which is not the I, that is, any object, can be observed. As this abstraction is pressed further, "the more empirical self-consciousness nears pure self-consciousness." But, given this account of Fichte's thought, it is clear that Heydenreich's (and Schmid's) reproach of Reinhold's philosophy, in particular, his use of the concept of representation, also applies to Fichte's abstraction. This is nicely summarized in the following assertion:

> The *representation* and the *faculty of representation* are not the *prius*, but rather the *posterius*, and can in no way provide *premises* for science.[23]

Schmid's student Novalis would later take issue with this view in a peculiar sequence of notes that begins with note 466 and continues for several pages. It begins with a consideration concerning whether that "sphere" which contains "essence" and "property" as the highest *relata* (interrelated terms) of the Absolute (*NS* II: 251, lines 14 ff.; as well as Nr. 444, 241, lines 20 ff.) can be conveniently comprehended as "the highest genus—the genus of all genera, or the actual absolute genus" (lines 23–25). The passage closes with the thought that the progressive abstraction to the highest genus, or the search for that which is first in an infinite series of derivation, is nonsense: "it is a *regulative idea*" (254, lines 11 ff.). The passage centers around four distinct arguments. First: That which is supposed to be fit for a definition (or, as Reinhold says, is "*omnimodi* self-determined in it,"[24]) must be demarcated from a lower and from a higher genus; but in the case of the highest genus, the demand that it be demarcated from a higher genus is completely nonsensical: in the highest genus there is not "a common and a distinct characteristic" (Nr. 445, 243, lines 6 ff.).[25] But from this follows, second, that an end of the chain of genera is not to be found:

> In the end, every genus necessarily presupposes a more comprehensive genus[26]—a space—and if that is so, then the highest genus is a *Nonens* [something not existing]. [. . .] the concept of genus, species, and individual has only regulative, classifying use—no reality in itself, for otherwise it would have to be infinite. We must not pursue the idea, for otherwise we land in the realm of nonsense (251 f.).

Third: Novalis goes through several of the contemporary candidates suggested as viable options for the identification of the highest genus; first the concept of 'thing' (251, lines 5 ff.; passim), then that of 'representation' (l. c.), and finally that of the 'I' or the 'subject' (Nr. 470, 253, lines 20 ff.). All are discarded: the concept of the I is rejected, because it is a *relatum*, a part of a sphere, and cannot be thought of as an Absolute (253, lines 28 ff.).[27] The concept of the '(absolute) cause' (meant in the same sense as in Reinhold's *Attempt at a New Theory of the Human Faculty of Representation*)[28] finds no favor with Novalis. Projected into the infinite, the concept 'cause' would again be "only a regulative concept, an idea of reason—it would thus be foolish to attribute real efficacy to it. Thus, we seek an absurdity" (Nr. 476, 255, lines 12–14; cf. Nr. 477, lines 25 ff.). A fourth argument (which enters the text later) hearkens back to Heydenreich and Schmid. In this argument, Novalis maintains that that which would be found in the course of the procedure of progressive abstraction, that is, the "highest genus," lives through the reality of that from which it is abstracted. Not only would it be circular to undertake derivations from a genus-concept that had been discovered in such a fashion; in so doing, one would not explain but would merely presuppose the individual: "I can never come to know the individual through the genus; rather, through the individual [I can come to know] the genus" (Nr. 567, 271, lines 17 ff.). "The peculiar sphere of the genus is the species, or the the individual. It only exists through the latter" (261, Nr. 513).

These four points are clearly not points that Novalis gathered because he supported Fichte's views. Quite the contrary, Novalis' critique of a philosophy based on first principles stands in bold opposition to Fichte's philosophical approach. Fichte had to conceive of his principle—'I am'—as a descriptive truth (even if he would later reinterpret it, in a rather unclear manner, as a postulate). The source of Novalis' insights was clearly not Fichte. Novalis' considerations could well have been inspired by his friend and fellow student, Friedrich Karl Forberg, who uses Kant's argument (*pace* Reinhold and Fichte) against the possibility of definition for fundamental philosophical concepts and repeatedly refers to Erhard.[29]

Returning to Schmid—he attacked Reinhold once more very effectively in a review of Reinhold's *Fundament*-piece. The review appeared at the beginning of April 1792 in the Jena *Allgemeine Literatur-Zeitung*. In it, Schmid shows that Reinhold is mistaken if he believes that the whole of the Kantian faculties can be reduced to *one* principle. According to a step in this proof which Novalis also considers decisive, Schmid claims that Reinhold, instead of deriving corollaries from the principle of consciousness, tacitly presupposes that at least some of the corollaries are valid and indeed "that the principle of consciousness had done the least to demonstrate what needed to be proved, and that what happened in the so-called derivation was that other principles were smuggled in to carry out the deduction" (*Allgememeine Literatur-Zeitung*, pp. 57 f.). Schmid strikingly demonstrates this point through several examples. However, in contrast to the former Tübingen *Repetent* Carl Immanuel Diez's critique of Reinhold, in Schmid's critique the self-activity of consciousness, which is tacitly presupposed in Reinhold's account of the production of form (and of all activities to which the principle of consciousness applies) is not included amongst his examples, but the causal law is.[30] Schmid thinks that Reinhold must presuppose the validity of causal law in his theorem of the supply of matter by the thing in itself. (In addition, Schmid is of the opinion that, as Eberhard, Schwab, and Rehberg had already shown, Reinhold confused the thing in itself with Kant's noumenon, the aspect of the thing in itself that is grasped by the intellect.[31] By no means, says Schmid, did Reinhold prove the validity of causality from the principle of consciousness (Ibid., 58). Emotions and desires, he says, are also not derivable from the genus-concept of representation (Ibid., 52). Finally, Schmid objects, Reinhold did not uncover the premise *from* which subject and object follow, as either "immediate" or "inner," but rather as merely "mediate" and "external" conditions of representation (l. c.). Such a conclusion implies, says Schmid, the following intricate situation: If I wanted to arrive at the external conditions of representation—the real existing subject and object—starting from their manifestations in "mere representation," then this conclusion would have to follow from the schema of a Kantian "inference of reason" (*Vernunftschluß*). According to Schmid: "for [such] a conclusion, at least *one* additional premise would be necessary, which would have to be just as primitive as the principle of consciousness" (Ibid., 58). Now the Kantian "inference of reason" is a mediate conclusion, because, to reach it, in addition to the general rule of inference which serves as the major premise, another (singular) minor premise which is logically independent of the major premise, is required. If this restriction is lifted (so if the minor premise is logically dependent upon the major premise), then we are dealing with an immediate conclusion or a "inference of the understanding" (*Verstandesschluß*). For example, from "All cats have a hide," it immediately follows that "Some cats have a hide," but only mediately does it follow that "Murr has a hide." For "Murr is a cat" is a judgment of observation, and as such it is singular and cannot follow from the universal proposition of the premise. Schmid's objection, which amounted to the claim that the deductive procedure of a philosophy based on a first principle suffers from a logical fallacy, had an exalted career, to which I will later return. The objection, if sound, would be deadly for any philosophy resting upon *one* principle. Consider Reinhold's philosophy: even if Reinhold's procedure of inference back to premises were successful, it would not lead to *one* principle, but rather to *two* (logically) independent principles—similar to the operation which Friedrich Schlegel considers under the name *Wechselerweis* (alternating or reciprocal proof).[32]

Now a quite important consequence follows: If the premises of a philosophy based on first principles are not derived from one absolute principle but are rather presupposed, then Reinhold's procedure cannot be said to have the character of an analytical derivation from premises which are secured by evidence; that is, it cannot have the character of an analysis guided by entailment relations generated by the principle from which one begins. The character of the derivation is rather solely that of a *hypothetical*-deductive procedure of the same sort as Kant's derivation from (regulative) ideas of reason: "That which is only assumed as a hypothesis can make no demand to universality with respect to this property, because it remains open whether one will assume this or another or no explanatory hypothesis at all to be the indubitable fact" (Ibid., 59). So the set of premises from which an *explicandum* (the thing to be explained) follows, according to one or more universal rules, remains open. In other words, this set of premises is not sufficiently determined by the concrete *explicandum*. Kant, Maimon, and Aenesidemus-Schulze had already emphasized this.

But now it is time to hear about Erhard's objections, which are more impressive, because they have greater implications for the advancement of a philosophy carried out in the Kantian spirit. Erhard's objections were devastating to certain students of Reinhold, for they shattered a commonly held belief. We see this developed in Erhard's correspondence with some of these students.

Erhard does not dispute the fact of self-consciousness as a first principle (or starting point) of philosophy. Reinhold did not raise self-consciousness to the position of such a first principle, but was pushed in this direction in the summer of 1792 under the influence of his critics, among them the former Tübingen *Repetent* Carl Immanuel Diez. It is, in the standard formulation of his theory of the faculty of representation (from 1790 on), actually the *subject* which appears as the sole actor in all operations to which the "principle of consciousness" refers: It is, namely, the subject which in consciousness now relates the representation to itself and to the object, and now differentiates it from them. If one spells out the implications of this, one quickly arrives at the insight that all representations must be characterized as conscious relations to the subject, and that (in representation) the subject alone is active. In reference to Reinhold's starting point, Novalis notes: "In all consciousness, the subject is presupposed—it is the absolutely active state of consciousness" (*NS* II: 253, lines 25 f.). Erhard also assumes this. But he does not attribute any special epistemic role to self-consciousness. Indeed Erhard criticized Schelling for just such a move, his sarcastic review of Schelling's work *Vom Ich oder Über das Unbedingte des Menschlichen Wissens* (On the I—or the Unconditioned in Human Knowledge) (1795), rattled and angered Schelling to such an extent that, in an aggressive reply, Schelling even denied that in this work he had aimed at a philosophy from a highest principle.[33] In his review,[34] Erhard reproaches those who speculate about an I which is supposed to be an Absolute, and criticizes those thinkers who describe this I, using expressions which imply a radical distinction between it and a possible object of our (empirical) consciousness. We can only become conscious of that which is determined and thus demarcated from other things. Because such consciousness, according to Erhard, exhausts the sphere of all consciousness (including, of course, that of our moral personality [91]), we are not conscious of the I in its absolute freedom. The supposed absoluteness and purity of the I rest upon its objective indeterminacy (91). For this,

Schelling uses the expression 'intellectual intuition' (90). Erhard closes his review with this biting mockery:

> As far as the [reviewer] can comprehend, the real object of [Schelling's system] is guaranteed by nothing other than an intellectual intuition, which does not even earn this name in so far as nothing is intuited in it, for in its entire interior, the reviewer can find nothing which the predicate of the absolute I fits, if he does not take the absolute I to be the deliberately thoughtless [mental] state, into which one can place oneself, if one completely checks the action of the faculty of imagination, and has no feeling but the feeling of self-determinability. This special feeling, of course, has something very mysterious, because one can differentiate nothing within it, and a philosophy that is founded upon it can turn out to be nothing other than the description of the life of nobody. One can say all possible things about it, without danger of being held answerable, because each time one can claim that he did not mean that which the other refutes. Meanwhile, it is not to be assumed that a philosophy should be established in Germany, which has as its principle and final goal a sinking into the big nothing, which some Indian sects extol as the highest good. Rather, something nobler must necessarily lie at the basis. This can be nothing but the feeling of our personality. [. . .] As moral beings we are [in fact] not the object of knowledge, but rather we should act (90 f.).

By no means does Novalis agree with such a moral-philosophical conclusion. But he does agree with Erhard's belief that there is "just as little [. . .] an absolute subject as [there is] an absolute space" (*NS* II: 253, lines 28 f.). Already in the first section of his *Fichte-Studien*, Novalis had considered the circumstances under which a transcendent being (or "original being") could be made accessible to consciousness. For Novalis, the highest consciousness attainable is not self-positing, but rather the (passive) feeling of a border, beyond which something that is to be believed must be assumed: "The I [is] fundamentally nothing [. . .]—Everything must be *given* to it"; "thus, philosophy always needs *something given*"; "we are born [with empty categories]— that is, with shelves without content. [. . .] They want to be filled—They are nothing without content—They have an urge to be, and consequently to have content, for only in so far as they have content are they real" (*NS* II: 273, lines 31 ff.; 113, line 30; 250, lines 19 ff.). To be sure, this giving of content must comply with the structure of our consciousness. Novalis thinks of this as reflection, and by this he thinks of it as a conversion and a disguising of that which is given. But reflection can also shed light upon its own "con/inverted being" and thereby correct it. (An object reflected twice in two subsequent mirrors, is restored to its original relations: left is anew left and right is right.) In the first few pages, Novalis operates with the assumption of an 'intellectual intuition,' which he naturally presents differently than does Schelling—he presents it not as a plenitude of existence, or *plenitudo realitatis;* rather, he views it as our incapacity to recognize such a *plenitudo realitatis:* "The spirit of feeling has vanished out there"; "the borders of feeling are the borders of philosophy"; "The human feels the border of everything enclosing him. He must believe in *original action* (*Urhandlung*), though certainly as he may know anything else" (114, lines 8 ff., lines 1 ff.); 107, lines 1–3). During the course of the *Fichte-Studien,* intellectual intuition loses its function more and more. Finally it is abandoned in favor of a return to the Kantian system of ideas and postulates, somewhat in the spirit of Schmid and Erhard.

Erhard's methodological doubt shook the belief that many of his contemporaries had in the possibility of a philosophy from a highest principle:

> Philosophy [he says] that starts from a principle and presumptuously derives everything out of it always remains a sophisticated piece of art. Philosophy [on the contrary] that climbs to the highest principle and portrays everything else in complete harmony with this highest principle, not derived from it, is alone true.[35]

In his letters to Reinhold and Niethammer (from July 1792 to May 1794), Erhard calls this method "analysis."[36] This method—oriented around the language of the Wolffian school, to which Kant adhered—proceeds from that which is established to the foundation itself. In contrast, Reinhold's and Fichte's deductions were synthetic. They start from the principle and develop its implications. But their philosophy cannot advance synthetically, because the principle of consciousness, or that through which Fichte's I is stated, is not yet justified: it does not stand on its own two feet. Rather, the truth of the principle of consciousness stands in need of other assumptions. The truth of the principle of consciousness can only be reached through an abductive[37] ascent from the conditioned to its consequent condition, and it can only be reached as a hypothetical claim. If, in addition, one believes that this leads to the infinite—that the final certainty fails to appear at all—then one must entirely give up the thought of a definitive foundation. Accordingly, the (romantic) "longing" moves to the place of the infinite, and an evidential theory of truth is replaced by a theory which must demonstrate all relations of the world and of consciousness in as strict a "harmony" as possible (as Erhard says). This new theory is a kind of coherence theory. Novalis commits himself to such a coherence theory when he characterizes the foundations with which philosophy justifies its convictions, not as foundations that are given, but rather as foundations that appear in the "connection of [all particular things] with the whole"

(*NS* II: 269 line 27). This foundation of coherence, Novalis continues, is the only remaining option for making his own convictions plausible to those who have given up the pretension to an absolute foundation and thus make "claim to the actual absolute foundation by connecting together that which remains to be explained (*making it whole*)" (270, lines 16 f.). As you just heard, Novalis calls this process a "making whole." For the Romantics, the unconditioned is replaced by the *search* for the unconditioned. As Novalis tells us: "We *seek* everywhere the unconditioned (*das Unbedingte*), and *find* only things (Dinge)" (*NS* II: 412, Nr. 1).

A detailed treatment would be necessary to show how Reinhold's and Fichte's philosophy of first principles would fare in light of such skeptical objections. But we have already anticipated the objections of one of Reinhold's students, and have encountered it again in addressing Schmid's critique of Reinhold (this objection is most intelligently stated in Paul Johann Anselm Feuerbach's 1795 essay "On the Impossibility of a First Absolute Principle of Philosophy," in the *Philosophisches Journal* II/2 (1795): 306–322). Evidence of a highest principle is an unjustified pretension, which, according to fate, agrees with the intuition of common sense. It is in need of a justification from philosophizing reason. But this justification is drawn out of ideas, and ideas are hypotheses or inferences offering the best explanation but not self-evidence. Besides, pieces of evidence are facts. Facts are particular, and can at best be the minor, or second, premises in a formally valid procedure of derivation *modo ponente* (Kant views what he calls the "inferences of reason" as minor premises [*CPR* A103]; they have the structure: If M, then P, S = M, hence, S ∧ P, for example, All cats have hides, Murr is a cat, Therefore, Murr has a hide.). The major premise, on the other hand, must be a universal conditional ("For all x, if x is F, then x is G"). But such an if-then proposition has no implication of existence, which would be necessary for a real principle. Finally, we already saw that Erhard disputed the epistemic accessibility, the intelligibility of Fichte's and Schelling's absolute I. Novalis, along with his Jena friends, concluded that the issue at hand yielded implications which reached much further—as far as Feuerbach's (and, as we shall see, Forberg's) far-reaching conclusion that "the unconditioned in human knowledge" is a *non-sens*, literally a "non-thing" (*Unding*)—an "absurdity" or an "impossible thing" (nothing of note regarding this daring conclusion is to be found in the literature on Novalis). In the literature, Novalis is still styled as the ever-youthful simpleton immersed in a silvery radiance, who is seated to the right side of God himself as his favorite darling and who, unlike us, knew paradise from inside—as in, for example, the writings of Emil Staiger, where this expression originates.

Reinhold, by the way, admitted on June 18, 1792, in a letter to Erhard (which has first now been published by Henrich),[38] that it was Schmid and

Diez who first induced him to completely transform his foundational philosophy. But Diez had simply brought out what was essential in Erhard's objection, which, as Henrich shows, became known to him through Niethammer.

Through this objection, once again, because it is so important, the process of the establishment of premises from a first principle turns into the process of the search for such a first principle. It is unforeseeable if and where this search will end. And it is in view of precisely this consequence that Novalis defines philosophy (as cited at the beginning) as an infinite, open search for a foundation.

Kantian philosophy called these first principles or foundations for our convictions "ideas." Under "ideas" Kant understood concepts which we *must* assume in order to bring unity into our system of assumptions, but to which we may not attribute any objective reality at all. If the foundation of philosophy becomes a mere idea, then this foundation is only a hypothesis. Were we in fact to "pursue" its realization, says Novalis, we would land "in the realm of nonsense." We were able to notice above how emphatically he must have written these words when we saw that he repeated the characterization of this as "nonsense" or an "absurdity" (*Unding*) several more times. As he says: "All search for the first [genus] is nonsense—it is a *regulative idea*." Or: "[what we seek] is only a regulative concept, an idea of reason—it is thus foolish to attribute real efficacy to it. Thus, we are looking for an absurdity."[39] Novalis considers whether Fichte's I is not, "like all ideas of reason, of merely regulative, classifying use—not at all related to reality" (*NS* II: 258, lines 18 ff.). One does not consistently come to determinations of empirical reality from such an idea. Also, factual control over the termination of arguments cannot be excercised by one idea. One hundred and fifty years later, Ludwig Wittgenstein was to note that, "the chain of reasons has an end." But not because we would be pushed into accepting an intersubjectively enlightening piece of evidence, "but rather because, in *this* system, there is no foundation."[40]

But Novalis goes much farther when he speaks of concepts that guarantee the unity of the system of beliefs as "necessary fictions."[41] A fiction is not a discovery (*Findung*), but rather an invention (*Erfindung*):

> The highest principle must absolutely not be something given, but rather something freely made, something *invented*, something *devised*, in order to ground a universal metaphysical system [. . .].[42]

This is a very strong conclusion that in the context of absolute idealism, with its emphasis on foundations, is also truly astonishing. Through this conclusion, the circle to which Erhard's method of the analysis of the faculty of representation leads back is indeed closed. This method was occasionally characterized as one of "invention"—for example, by the young Reimarus

(Johann Albrecht Heinrich, son of the famous Hermann Samuel), who was at that time a well-known physician and logician. Reimarus was in correspondence with Erhard, and Novalis could have known of him through a logic manual of Johann Christoph Hoffbauer, which Novalis refers to in *Fichte-Studien* (*NS* II: 191, line 21).[43]

Given the nature of invention, moments of uncertainty sneak into the process of philosophical analysis.[44] Christian von Freiherr Wolff already saw this. But, says Hoffbauer, the young Reimarus was the first to draw definite conclusions from it:[45]

> To invent, he [Reimarus] says, means to arrive at knowledge of something previously unknown through one's own consideration. [. . .] The inventor arrives at that which he finds, not through the mechanical application of a rule by which that which is sought can already be ensured, and secondly we do not invent [. . .] that which we obtain through the mechanical application of a rule. Thus one can say: to invent means to find that which was previously unknown to us from that which was known to us, and in so doing not to merely follow a rule which was already known to us.[46]

So the process of the analytical search for a first principle approaches invention; it is a procedure of positing rules but not of following them, a procedure that is bound together with the practice of fiction (and, more generally, art). As Walther von Stolzing asks in the *Meistersinger:* "How do I begin according to the rule?" And as Hans Sachs answers: "You set it yourself, and then follow it."[47] Naturally, this conclusion was appealing to the jurist, minerologist, and poet Novalis, who with time developed a taste for leaving "this mountain peak (*Spitzbergen*) of pure reason" behind him "and living with body and soul in the colorful and refreshing land of sense."[48] For Novalis, philosophy was but one branch of learning amongst others:

> One can highly treasure philosophy without having it as a housekeeper and living only from it. Mathematics alone will not just make a mechanic or a soldier, philosophy alone will not make a human.[49]

For a universal genius such as Novalis, this is of course only correct on the assumption (which Kant does not accept) that the process of science demands genius, or artistic gifts.[50]

One should note here that we are not dealing with inventions of just any sort. That which is not given to a discovery (*Findung*) but is given *up* to an invention (*Erfindung*) is (in Novalis's words) an "absolute foundation." Only an [absolute foundation] could provide support for our frail lives and our uncertain beliefs. But such a [foundation] is fiction and invention.

Now let me complete my sketch with some quick strokes. With the definition of the search for foundations as a process of invention, a key role in this search falls to the arts. They have the mandate to represent indirectly to us something final which, by means of rational foundation, is intangible. And the arts maintained this high vocation long before Arthur C. Danto proclaimed the end of invention and the sellout of innovation. We forget too quickly what the expression "religion of art" actually meant in its time, and with what priestly self-presumption not only the Symbolists (through George), but also the provocative Expressionists and Surrealists and even Joseph Beuys understood their work. For the authors of critical theory, above all Adorno, it is in the fictional world of art where the last and only claims suitable for universality of an altogether hopelessly blinded humanity have rescued themselves from their blindness. Martin Heidegger and Jacques Derrida attempt to expand philosophy itself around the language of art, to let philosophy flow into the language of art. Even Wittgenstein wanted the *Tractatus* to be regarded as a work of literary art, in which what is said spares the realm of the unsayable in which the actual message of the work is represented.

And Novalis was already a philosopher who wanted art to be understood as the "presentation of the *unpresentable*," as the actual foundation of our conscious life.[51] Elsewhere he notes:

> According to its character, one can think of no arrival to a place that is unreachable. It is, as it were, only the ideal expression of the sum of the entire succession, and thus, [only seemingly, the last member—the type of every member, indicated by every member. [. . .]
> [Thus] the highest works of art are simply disobliging—There are ideals, which can—and should—only appear to us *approximando*—as aesthetic imperatives.[52]

Or:

> If the character of the given problem is irresolution, then we resolve it when portraying its irresolution [as such].[53]

Novalis believes that through the inexplicable richness of sense in a work of art, that which we cannot approach via the light of a concept or unambiguously, speaks to us allegorically (allegory means understanding something different from that which is superficially said). It is the "puzzle of our existence"; the artwork, he says, is "inexhaustible": "like a human."[54] Art comes to the aid of truth such that the essential thing that is to be said about us as humans, that which would stabilize our wobbly convictions, cannot be possessed. Thus, the early German Romantics are troubled by a "longing"—longing is, after all, a state of not-having, of not-possessing.[55] We can only work toward that which we long for in "infinite approximation" (*approximando*). Who would not see here a certain affinity with Popper's polemic against Sir Isaac Newton's "*Hypotheses non fingo*," especially since Popper's main work carries the following lines from Novalis' *Dialogues* as its motto: *Hypothesen sind Netze; nur der wird fangen, der auswirft. / War nicht Amerika selbst durch Hypothese gefunden?* [. . .] (Hypotheses are nets; only he who casts will make a catch. / Was not America itself discovered through a hypothesis? / [. . .]).[56] Artwork gives us the promise that it will be imperatively demanding, in that it does not place a result in our hands, it does not settle our minds, but rather agitates us: in an undetermined striving toward a foundation like Agathe in Robert Musil's *Man without Qualities*, who searches, doubtingly and skeptically for such a foundation, but does not find one.[57]

At the time when Novalis noted his thoughts concerning the infinite, that is, concerning the impossibility of philosophy as a search for absolute knowledge, he received a visit from Forberg in Jena, who, says Novalis, "even after a long interruption in our friendship, showed a heart full of tenderness to me." Forberg had, as I said, studied with Novalis under Reinhold. Apparently, Forberg was so excited by Novalis' formulation (the one with which I began my lecture today), that, one year later, he wrote in his *Briefe über die neuste Philosophie* (Letters on the Newest Philosophy):

> I will have to seek something like a last "therefore," an [original foundation], in order to fulfill the demand of my reason.
>
> But what then if such an [original foundation] was [. . .] impossible to find? . . .
>
> Then nothing further would follow from this, than that the demand of my reason could never be entirely fulfilled—than that reason [would have to] [. . .] advance its inquiry into the infinite without ever bringing it to an end. The Absolute would then be nothing other than the idea of an impossibility [. . .].
>
> [But] is an unreachable goal any less of a goal? Is the view of the heavens any less enchanting, because it always remains only a view?[58]

On the Unknowability of the Absolute

Historical Background and Romantic Reactions

These lectures are an exploration of the philosophical foundations of early German Romanticism. This overwhelming range of ideas can only be understood by one who is well-acquainted with the Jena Constellation, that is, with the discussion which played itself out between the witnesses to the crisis of Reinhold's philosophy of first principles and those who experienced Fichte's arrival and teaching activities in Jena. Nevertheless, with early German Romanticism we find a shift in thinking which goes beyond these preliminary attempts to question the feasibility of a philosophy based on first principles. Above all, it is important to correct a widely held misconception that early German Romanticism is a movement concerned with a fragmentary and somewhat separate form of speculative idealism—shaped, more or less, by Schelling. As we shall see, Schelling was, in many ways, merely a traveling companion of the romantic generation. This is not to say that we do not find a certain kinship between Schelling's work and the work of some of the Romantics. There is in Schelling's work a fundamental realistic intuition that Friedrich Schlegel and Novalis share and which distinguishes all three from Fichte as well as from Hegel. In a letter to Ludwig Feuerbach, dated October 3, 1843, Marx writes of Schelling's "candid young thought" (*aufrichtige[n] Jugendgedanken*). He was, of course, referring to Schelling's philosophy of nature, in which nature is not, as is the case with Fichte's Non-I, taken over by the I, but rather emerges originally and on equal footing (equiprimodially) with the I from the Absolute, this means that consciousness has no privileged position with respect to the objects of nature. In spite of these affinities with early German Romantic thought, Schelling's thought diverges from it in important ways. Schelling remained tied to a philosophy of first principles and its deductive method; his Absolute is not a mere idea, whose pursuance, according to Novalis, leads to the realm of nonsense. Schelling in fact held the Absolute to be a true being and his philosophy of identity, in its most mature form, showed only scorn and mockery for the notion of an infinite approximation toward the Absolute (cf. *SW* I/4: 358,2). In his early writings, Schelling remains admittedly indecisive regarding whether or not consciousness is capable of taking hold of the Absolute. Still in 1800 in his *System of Transcendental Idealism*, he allows aesthetic intuition to intervene in order to take hold of an object that exceeds the conditions of reflection. But in the *Identitätsphilosophie* (Philosophy of Identity) of 1801, much in keeping with Hegel's philosophy, the Absolute is posited as one with reason; and only in Schelling's late philosophy does the view of his friend Hölderlin first win some ground. According to this view, Being precedes consciousness so that no understanding can exhaust the content of what is meant by Being. With this view, we find once again a space created for the notion of an infinite progression; but this notion has a decisively realistic foundation, which it did not have in the writings of the Kantians.

Now, we must be clear that the term 'Being' in early German Romanticism implies a monistic program of explanation. It presupposes the object of the Kantian idea of a "supersensible ground of unity between theory and practice" as existing (*als bestehend*). At the same time, and this in contrast to the proponents of classical German idealism, it contests the claim that we possess the possibility of securing this ontological presupposition through cognitive means. Here we are dealing with a combination of ontological monism and epistemological realism. That which I call "*Frühromantik*" shares the same object and determination with the project of absolute idealism. But in the work of the early German Romantics, "absolute knowledge" becomes replaced by an absolute "not-knowing" and the result is a skeptical basis for philosophizing. For example, Friedrich Schlegel notes that, "Knowledge (*Erkennen*) already denotes conditioned knowledge. The unknowability of the Absolute is, therefore, an identical triviality" (*KA* XVIII: 511, Nr., 64; cf. 512, Nr., 71). As can be expected, such a negative diagnosis regarding the knowability of the Absolute invites the following question: How may one speak of the Absolute at all? Hölderlin and Novalis were each dedicated to answering this question. To appreciate their responses to this question, we must—once more—turn our attention to the work of one of their predecessors, Friedrich Heinrich Jacobi.

Jacobi critically questioned transcendental idealism. He was particularly interested in the issues of how one can, on the one hand, save some reference to reality in philosophy without acknowledging a thing-in-itself and how, on the other hand, one can be a realist if one explains the reference to the thing-in-itself in terms of causal reference and this in turn, is explained as something non-physical, that is subjective. Jacobi also showed that we can assume a strong concept of knowledge only if we, at the same time, allow for some "unconditioned." For if knowledge were nothing other than justified true belief, then we would find ourselves stuck in an infinite regress; knowledge would always be dependent upon another established assumption, which would have been established or would have to be established, and so on ad infinitum. If there is knowledge, then, according to Jacobi, there must be at least one premise whose validity holds independently of any further grounding, a premise that we would have to hold as true without further reference, that is to say, immediately. Such an immediate "holding to be true" (*für-wahr-halten*), is what Jacobi calls feeling (*Gefühl*) or belief (*Glaube*). Fichte summarizes the main idea briefly and pointedly: "All that is proved proceeds from something unproved" (GA IV: 2, 28). Novalis, too, like most representatives of his generation, was familiar with the second version of Jacobi's *Spinozabüchlein* and follows Jacobi even into the details of his terminology (cf. NS II: 105, lines, 11–13; p. 107, lines, 1–4). In Novalis' work, we find reference to a notion through which Jacobi, once again, significantly influenced the formation of early German Romantic thought and which we will have to study more carefully in what follows. It is developed in a threefold way. In the first way, the unconditioned in human knowledge is associated with the idea of Being—not as something that can be reduced to a condition of knowability, but certainly as something that must be thought of as the foundation for these conditions. That which cannot be known but which must be presupposed as a condition of knowledge is believed. This way of understanding original Being puts it in close company with Spinoza's notion of substance, and brings us to the second development of this notion of the unconditioned; in other words, that it is understood as an *omnitudo realitatis*. Finally and thirdly, this notion of the unconditioned is thought of as the seed or foundation of that experience which has to do with self-consciousness.

Now I must show that and how the early German Romantic reception of these diverse ideas related to one another and could be collected into one unified notion; namely, the proof that we assume something unconditioned in human thought and that this must, at the same time, be explained as the consciousness of a transcendent being. The notion of something unconditioned which was expressed by Jacobi as "original Being" and which he had shown could not be reduced to a relation with self-consciousness impacted the romantic generation which followed him. Influenced by Jacobi's views, the notion of the unconditioned was understood by Hölderlin, and in autumn of the same year, by Novalis and then by Isaac von Sinclair, and a year later also by Friedrich Schlegel, not in the sense of a higher shifting (*Höherverlegung*) of the first principle of philosophy, but rather it was treated as a motive for overcoming a philosophy based upon first principles. Being is not simply the name of a higher principle, like Reinhold's principle of consciousness or Fichte's Absolute I. The expression, 'Being,' stands much more for the experience that a consciousness independent reality must be presupposed if one wants to make certain relations of our consciousness, especially, the elementary factum of self-consciousness, comprehensible.

I shall now begin with a sketch of Jacobi's main ideas and focus, in particular, on those which he introduced in the second edition of his *Spinozabüchlein*. As we know, when Jacobi returned to Geneva, he studied Kant's precritical writings, especially Kant's short piece from 1763, *The One Possible Basis for a Demonstration of the Existence of God.*[1] In this text, Jacobi presented the thesis that Being is not a real predicate and therewith introduced the general theme of "Being in the true sense of the word." This was obviously in tune with Jacobi's growing, albeit critical, interest in the writings of Spinoza. Jacobi's primary intuition seems to have been that the primary meaning of Being is completely singular and hence is to be understood in a unitary sense. Kant had already claimed that the well-understood concept 'Being' is "very simple." This simplicity or single meaning of Being seemed to lead Jacobi back to Spinoza's monistic central notion according to which there can only be *one* substance of which we must say that—at least in the transitive sense of the word—"all individuals *are*" (*alles einzelne ist [oder durchwaltet]*). We find a hint of this in Kant's early writings. For in these early writings, Kant begins with the proof that thought (as an outline of possibilities) presupposes an independent actuality that cannot be conceived merely as a determination of thought (a "real predicate"). But he ends—as the young Johann Gottfried von Herder had already shown—with a variation of an ontological proof for the existence of God. According to this proof, that which exists independently of thought is in turn a necessary being of the same sort as a divine spirit. Jacobi's arguments take a quite similar turn.

Clearly, several motives join here. First, Jacobi wants to secure a clear meaning for the concept of Being—this has been the central theme of metaphysics since the Greeks. From this primary, clear meaning, insight into the various secondary meanings of this term can be made clear. One could question whether this search for the fundamental meaning of Being is sensible at all, whether the term can be made clear in the first place. According to the contemporary German philosopher, Ernst Tugendhat, such a search is futile. And this comes from a thinker who was, not so long ago, convinced, with Heidegger, that such a primary, clear meaning for Being could be found. Now, in contrast, Tugendhat claims the following:

One can only say, that in most Indo-European languages there is a word—"*einai*" in Greek, "sein" in German etc.—in which several modes of usage have been joined—existence, predication, identity, assertive power—which stand for the different fundamental structures of assertoric speaking, and are interdependent.[2]

Amongst these secondary meanings of 'Being,' one of the most important for Kant's contemporaries was the copulative 'is' (or predicative 'being') as is found in what was referred to by a judgment. Judgment was usually understood in the Aristotelian tradition as a subject-predicate connection. Of course, propositions of existence are also judgments, although there is no copulative 'is' involved. Jacobi wanted predicate statements to be understood as a derivative form of Being in the sense of existence, and he believed, not unjustifiably, that he could relate this to an idea of Kant's that had not been worked out in much detail. In conclusion, the clarity of the central meaning of Being and Spinoza's central intuition that everything of which we say "it is" can only refer to one substance, should also be made clear so that the expression of a multiplicity of beings can be explained as an illusion, which has nothing to do with Being itself but rather with the conditions of our knowledge.

Here we can isolate three subtheses of Jacobi's main thesis regarding Being. First, we can distinguish a thesis concerning the uniform and original meaning of the terms 'Being' and 'existence.' Second, copulative or predicative Being must be understood as a kind of "derivative form" of existential Being. And third, Being is something unique because in all beings it is essentially the same.

To what degree could Jacobi have believed that with these highly speculative theses, he could appeal to Kant as a predecessor? Now, Kant had shown in his short, but pathbreaking work, *The One Possible Basis for a Demonstration of the Existence of God*, whose main thesis is taken up with some modifications in the *Critique of Pure Reason*, that "existence (Being) is no real predicate" (*CPR* A598–9/B626–7). This proof was not only meaningful within an idealistic context; it has had consequences that reach into our century. For example, Bertrand Russell, without making explicit reference to Kant, repeats the Kantian thesis that in propositions like "Unicorns exist," or "The author of the *Iliad* exists," or "Homer exists," the word "exists" is to be understood semantically not as a predicate but rather as an operator of existence. According to Russell:

> There is a great deal of philosophy which departs from the presupposition that the concept of existence is a property which one can attribute to things, and that things which exist have this property and things which

do not exist do not have this property. This is nonsense, whether one is thinking of types of objects or individual objects. If I say, for example, "Homer existed," by "Homer" I mean a description, e. g. "the author of the Homeric poems," and I contend that these poems have been written by a particular man, which is a quite dubious contention; but if it were possible to get hold of the person who has actually written these poems (provided there is such a person), then it would be nonsense to say of this person that he existed; not wrong, but nonsense, given that you can say only of persons under a description that they exist.[3]

Kant held a quite similar view. We observe this in the following remark from his work, *The One Possible Basis for a Demonstration of the Existence of God*:

> It is thus not a fully correct expression to say, "A sea unicorn is an existent animal" but rather conversely: "The predicates that I think together as a sea unicorn belong to certain existent sea creatures." Not: "Regular hexagons exist in nature," but rather: "The predicates that are thought together in a hexagon belong to certain things in nature, such as honeycombs or rock crystals."[4]

Hence, Kant anticipates the modern view, that the expression 'to exist' is not, from a semantic viewpoint, a predicate at all, but rather can be replaced by an existence operator. Propositions like, "Sea unicorns exist" (something that Kant and his contemporaries actually believed) are therefore misleading, because they suggest (or give the impression) that we add to the possible sea unicorns, existence as well. Kant himself claims that this way of speaking is misleading: "Existence belongs to a sea unicorn, but not to a land unicorn."[5] What we really mean is: Certain objects of nature really have the predicates that form the presupposition that can indicate something like sea unicorns. Hence, Kant here indicates that propositions of existence are ultimately to be apprehended as particular propositions. And, according to Kant, a proposition like "Existence belongs to a sea unicorn, but not to a land unicorn," says nothing other than that the notion of a sea unicorn is a concept of experience, that is, a notion of an existent thing. Thus, in order to demonstrate the truth of this proposition about the existence of such a thing, one does not look in the concept of the subject, for here only the predicates of possibility can be found, but rather in the origin of the knowledge I have of the subject. One says, "I have seen it," or "I have accepted it from those who have seen it."[6] With this account of existence, Kant not only draws a sharp boundary between existence and predication, but also establishes a connection between both. He holds the position that the proposition "Sea unicorns exist" must be interpreted so that it is indeed the case that some objects meet the condition of being sea unicorns. It is this connection between existence and predication that Kant's speculative colleagues would exploit to the best of their ability.

Now, we should not precipitate our conclusions, but rather orient ourselves more closely to Kant's text. What does the expression 'real' (in the phrase, "Being is no real predicate") mean within the context of the thesis regarding Being? The property 'reality' constitutes—as we all know—one of three subcategories or moments of the main category quality. Through this category, the what-ness (quality) of the given object can be judged, that is, its reality, its *Sachheit* or mode of being.[7] The affirmation, "Existence is no real predicate" means then: With judgments of existence nothing regarding the mode of Being (quality, reality, quiddity) is judged: Being is not a property in this sense. If I say "I exist as an intelligence," the predicate "intelligence" is a real predicate (belonging to the quality of the *cogito*) and the judgment itself is analytic (immediately tautological). Whether such a *cogito* also exists as thinking independently of its properties is not therewith settled. Nonetheless, according to Kant, the proposition 'I think' is already an empirical proposition and contains within itself the proposition 'I exist' (B 422 f.). Where else but there would be found that excess to which the judgment of existence is entitled over and against the judgment of reality?

In his short text from 1763, *The One Possible Basis for a Demonstration of God* (the one which had been so important for Jacobi), Kant, for the first time, presented in a coherent way his thesis concerning the two meanings of the indefinite verbal expression 'Being.' According to this text, Being is the object of a relative positing, existence (*Dasein*) is the result of an absolute positing. Instead of using the term 'positing,' one may also speak of the Latin equivalent—*position*. A positing or position of something is relative, if and only if the something posited is posited in relation to something else (relative to this), for example, when we say "A is B," A *is* only relative to the being of B, it is not absolutely posited. So I can say something like, "Unicorns are white and can be tamed only by virgins," without thereby claiming anything about their existence. This is the sort of positing of the I involved in the claim, "I am as intelligence." In this case, the I is not, as Fichte would claim, absolutely posited (through a thetical judgment), rather the I is merely placed within the class of intelligent beings. The proposition must be read as hypothetical: "If there were an A, then it would belong in the class of B." If we were to speak of an absolute positing of A, it could not be of A in relation to B, but of A in relation to itself; in the latter we would (as Kant claimed) be speaking of the existence of A. If I say "This A exists," I refer not to any other thing or quality belonging to A, I simply posit A without relation to anything as existent. Relative and absolute positing are executed in the form of judgments. Usually, judgments join representations of different classes. In singular, simple statements, the content of an intuition is joined with one concept or, more precisely, the content of the intuition is asserted as it is interpreted by its corresponding concept ("A is B"). In Kant's terminology, both are real determinations. In the judgment "A exists," the content of intuition is not covered over with a concept, but is rather granted Being: the subject is posited as such without any characterizing additions.

Before we take another step, we must be clear that Kant held existential and predicative Being to be specifications of a uniform and original meaning of Being. He called this original meaning "position." In order to eliminate any doubt he writes: "The concept of position or positing is totally simple and on the whole identical with the concept of Being in general."[8] Kant then continues with the claim that a thing can merely be posited in relation to a characteristic of a thing (therefore its concepts), and then we are speaking of the predicative sense of Being; or it can be posited without any relation, then it is posited absolutely. This second sense of position is what we call the "existence" (*Existenz*), "*Dasein*," or "actuality" (*Wirklichkeit*) of an object. What is important is that Kant holds the original concept to be simple and repeats this often. This brings us close to the consequence of Jacobi's argument, namely, that Being in the sense of predication is a deviation of the original sense of Being qua existence. We also saw that Kant anticipated Russell's explanation of the meaning of propositions of existence, namely, that we should not understand the meaning of a proposition of existence in such a way that we would be led to ask of possible unicorns, whether they exist (whether beliefs have the predicate of existence); but rather, we should investigate the animals in the real world and see whether some of them actually meet the description of being unicorns. Hence, Kant draws a distinction not only between the terms 'existence' and 'predication,' but also shows that the original meaning of Being is first fulfilled within the context of predication.

With this interpretation of Kant, a path is opened which leads directly to the early speculations of Hardenberg and Hölderlin. That which I have rather crudely referred to as a "deviation" could also be understood in the following way: the relational (or predicative) sense of Being is a weakening—or disintegration of that sense of Being present in existence. Put another way: predicative Being breaks up (or divides [*ur-teilt*]) Being which is originally undivided and unified; on the other hand, the predicative relation can only be understood from relationless existence. If, however, that is the case, this schema acquires an additional attraction for the early Romantics. For this schema allows a bridge to be built which connects the issue of predicative Being with a central problem for the members of this group—the problem of self-consciousness. We also think ourselves as unified, but as soon as we attempt to represent this unity in consciousness, it disappears and makes room for a relation between subject and object that one can see as something analogous to a judgment. Novalis expressed this in the following way: "We leave the identical in order to represent it" (*NS* II: 104, Nr. 1). In such a speculation, two theses join: the first holds claim to the irreducibility of original Being, to all that is something and has relations to other beings— including self-consciousness which is explained by Hölderlin and Novalis as the epistemic relation of a subject term to itself as the object term. Of course, they had to add a critique of Fichte to this, for Fichte allowed the notion of Being to merge without a break with the epistemic self-relation of a subject transparent to itself. On the other hand, and this is the second thesis, the relation in which the subject I stands to itself as an objectified I must be understood in terms of an irreducible unity, as that which represents to us the notion of Being (in the sense of existence). Just as self-relation must be explained in terms of an undivided unity of a prereflexive self, so analogously, the judgment-like (*urteilsmäßige*) relation of a subject to a predicate is explained in terms of the simple unity of absolute position or existence.

Let's linger a moment with the existential sense of Being which Jacobi, with Kant, explains as the most primitive sense. One could ask: What are the criteria that allow us to really take up an absolute position regarding a thing represented in a concept? Kant's response to this question is quite clear. The granting of existence, through which purely conceptual determinateness is exceeded, is the result of sense perception. Only sense experience can determine whether a concept really has an existential (*daseienden*) content or whether I merely think so. According to Kant, the categories of modality (under which existence falls) "have the peculiarity that, in determining an object, they do not in the least enlarge the concept to which they are attached as predicates. They only express the relation of the concept to the faculty of knowledge" (A219=B266). *Dasein*, *Wirklichkeit* [actuality], or *Existenz* (expressions which Kant often uses as synonyms) refer exclusively to "the question whether such a thing be so given us that the perception of it can, if need be, precede the concept. For that the concept precedes the perception signifies the concept's mere possibility; the perception which supplies the content to the concept is the sole mark of actuality" (A225/B272–3; cf. A374 f: "Perception is the representation of an actuality [*Wirklichkeit*]"; "what is represented through perception is also actual [*wirklich*] in it"; Refl. 5710 [AA XVIII: 332]: "I recognize existence [only] through experience"). If this is the case, then it follows that the characteristic of being absolutely posited falls into the same group with that of the Being of sense impressions (for only through the latter does the faculty of knowledge take material from a source independent of it). Kant also speaks of actuality (*Wirklichkeit*) as "the position of the thing in relation to perception" (A235/B87 note). The "relation" is, of course, different from any other "relative" position exhibited in predicative judgment. For through the relation to perception, the perceived is at the same time "absolutely posited." Perception (which Kant also defines as conscious sensation (*CPR* A225/B272, passim) belongs to the class of intuitions. Here we have our first way of supporting the thesis that Novalis took over from Jacobi, namely, that it is not thought but rather "feeling" which Being is given to. Like perceptions, feelings belong to the class of intuitions. The fact that the notion of Being, in the true sense of the word, does not have anything sensible as its object means, in Hölderlin's way of expressing the matter, that there is an "intellectual intuition" which corresponds to it (Jacobi spoke of 'feeling,' an expression which refers even more directly to the semantic realm of the sensibly given; Novalis and Friedrich Schlegel adopted this expression as well). Jacobi says, in a letter to Hemsterhuis, that the French language has given him the expression '*le sentiment de l'être*' which he finds much "purer and better" than the German term '*Bewußtsein*' (consciousness) (Cf. *Spin.* 2: 193 f.). In fact, this way of speaking is no discovery of Jacobi's. Jean-Jacques Rousseau had made use of this term repeatedly in order to indicate the same state of affairs of the primitive Being of consciousness not mediated by concepts. In the *Profession de foi du Vicair Savoyard*, he asks whether there is a specific feeling of my own existence (*Dasein*) that is independent of the senses.[9] And he answers: "*Exister pour nous, c'est sentir.*" As we know, the "*sentiment de l'existence*" also plays another role in Rousseau's work. What is pertinent for us here, however, is the essential correlation between Being and a type of sense consciousness—all expressions like '*Empfindung*' (sensation), '*Wahrnehmen*' (perceiving), '*Anschauen*' (intuiting), and '*Fühlen*' (feeling) belong to the sphere of sense representation. And the reason for this, according to the thesis common to Rousseau, Kant, and Jacobi is that Being can only be made accessible by sense consciousness. Jacobi explains the unmediated feeling of Being (*sentiment de l'être*) which we cited above, by making a reference to Kant's notions of "transcendental apperception" (*CPR* A107; *Spin.* 2: 194 note). Jacobi expresses this in the following way: "Of our existence (*Dasein*), we have only a feeling, but no concept" (l.c., 420, note). Schelling goes a step further and indicates Kant's admission that we have only a "feeling" or an "indeterminate inner-perception" of the Being of the "I think" itself, that is, of the "sense" of the "cogito" (*CPR* B422 f., note). And we have this "feeling" as license for the rehabilitation of its reference to an object of "intellectual intuition" which—as intuition—is sensible even when its object, the *actus purus* of pure spontaneity, is something intellectual (*SW* I/1: 400 f.). If something did not underlie that which is unveiled by feeling, then thought would literally have no object. Therefore, according to Jacobi, with Being, a notion is grasped which is closer and more intimate to us than the notion of "*cogito*." And it is for this reason that Fichte, Novalis, and Schelling hold that the "*sum*" rather than the "*cogito*" is the highest principle of philosophy. Novalis notes laconically that: "The foundation of thought—*sum*" (*NS* II: 268, Nr. 551). And, in this remark, we again see that the theme of the relation which existential Being has to predicative Being suddenly shifts to the theme of the relation which identity has to conscious self-relation.

Why was Kant's thesis concerning Being—as absolute and relative position—so important to his followers? To show why, you must allow me another short excursion. This will lead us to the beginnings of Fichte's mature philosophy. In 1794, Fichte spoke of his first principle, the I, as something that posited itself. This expression (*sich-selbst-setzen*) makes its way into the *Wissenschaftslehre* slowly, replacing the previous terminology which involved expressions like '*Darstellen*' (presenting) (in contrast to '*Vorstellen*' [representing]) and '*Dasein*,' which Fichte used in his work, *Eigene Meditationen*, and the Zürich private lectures. The meaning of the expression '*setzen*' (to posit) within the context of these texts has seldom been investigated, especially because neither Kant nor his followers used the expression in reference to the spontaneity of selfconsciousness. For the most part, scholars paid attention to the connotation of '*setzen*' with activity. (Fichte presents the term '*setzen*' as synonymous with original activity (*ursprüngliche Handlung*) and couples this with Kant's definition of the intellect as something "whose concept is a deed (*ein Tun*)"; of course, one may also keep in mind Reinhold's translation of spontaneity as "self-activity.") But with this, only one aspect of the reference to a self-positing I is grasped. Fichte wanted to justify his use of this term by reference, in the celebrated first section of the *Wissenschaftslehre* of 1794, not to the phrase 'I think,' but rather by reference to the phrase 'I am' (*WW* I: 84 ff). The same holds already and strikingly in his Zürich Lectures. Jens Immanuel Baggesens reports in his journal that Fichte had said to him: "The principle of all philosophy, its first proposition is: 'I am.'" Indeed, like Johann Georg Hamann and Jacobi, Fichte goes so far as to place absolutely posited Being beneath the notion of the I. "*Pono me existentem*—: *Sum, sum—ergo cogito*." From 'I am' and from no other proposition, "everything else is deduced, the I is the highest reality, Being pure and simple (*das Sein schlechthin*)."

"I am" expresses the pure affirmation of the existence (*Bestehens*) of I-ness (*Ichheit*)—without anything additional. Instead of working with epistemological versions of *ponere* and *setzen*, Fichte prefers to work with the Greek equivalents of these terms, as in the third section of the *Wissenschaftslehre* where the proposition 'I am' is also grasped as "thetical judgment." What does this mean? This question is not difficult to answer if one keeps in mind the Kantian tradition according to which "*Dasein*" (in the sense of "to exist") has the character of absolute "positing" (or "position" or even "thesis"). Here something is posited absolutely, not merely in relation to its corresponding predicate. And such a judgment is precisely a "thesis": "a positing in general, through which an A (the I) is unlike any other thing and is, moreover, not opposed to anything else, but is rather posited absolutely" (WW I: 115). The thetical judgment is not predicatively grasped (even if all potential predicates are to be found within it); its structure is not something-as-something or something-as-not-something. Fichte expresses this insofar as he distinguishes thetical judgments from synthetic or antithetical judgments. In thetical judgments, the subject term is not related to a predicate and synthesized with it (or distinguished from it "anti-thetically"); no, a subject is "posited" as such and without further ado.

Much follows as a consequence of this: If "Being" (qua positing) can no longer be understood as something which (as something transcendental, as category or quasi-predicate) is a determination of thought or a "logical form," then it must be understood as a "singular tantum"—as "a blessed unity, [as] Being in the true sense of the word," as Hölderlin affirms in the prologue of the penultimate edition of *Hyperion* (KTA 10: 163). Being must be thought as one and as something unique, something to which all else would stand in relation, and which, due to its power, would be a being (*Seienden*), next to others. Schelling will later speak of a "transitive" sense of "Being," so that all being (*Seiende*), insofar as it is, has been of absolute Being in this unique sense, that is, it would be contained within Being. One representative example of this is the following claim:

> In the proposition: A is B, nothing other is stated than that: A is the *Esse* (the essence) of B (which, in turn would not be in itself; B is only insofar as its is connected with A). Indeed, this is the sense of the proposition: God is all things, which in Latin must be expressed not so much through *est res cunctae*, as through (*invita latinitate*) *est res cunctas* (SW I/7: 205, note, 1; cf. II/3: 217 ff.; II/1: 293).

The thesis, recognizable in Kant's followers as well, claims that the meaning of Being is simple, that is, there is only one central meaning of Being, and that is Being in the sense of existing. Even predicative Being is comprehensible from this central meaning. Hence, as Schelling already showed, the simple judgment 'A is B' is to be explained in the following way; the predicate B consists only relatively in the Absolute position, that is, it would dissolve the moment that A would withdraw from it. The properties of substance *are* merely, insofar as they are supported by substance in Being and always in an identical, that is to say, "unique" way. In this conceptual switch (*Weichenstellung*), it is of course tempting to understand "Being in the true sense of the word" as analogous to Spinoza's unique substance in the manner stated by Schelling, according to which its mode of appearing is transitive.

And so it seems that from Kant's thesis concerning the relation between relative and absolute positions, there is a direct, even if very speculative path to a monistic world view, clearly directed by Spinoza's theory of the one and all. Dieter Henrich was of the opinion that Jacobi himself had already opened this path for his followers.[10] For the singularity of Being, which was so important to him, is easily joined to Spinoza's fundamental concept *substantia*. According to Spinoza's definition, substance is that which can never arise as the property of something else, hence, it is something which can, if necessary, be attributed to itself (cf. the first definitions, principles and theorems of Spinoza's *Ethics*). From this it follows that if substance exists at all, there is only one substance. This sole and unique substance is, as such, self-sufficient and infinite (whereby "infinite" means that it contains within it all individuals without exception; it is *omnitudo realitatis*). Hence, substance contains within itself these individuals as that which substance itself is not, that is as its own determinations (as its attributes or *modi*). And substance contains these attributes in the same way, as a being amongst other beings, that is, as "having been" a part of Being in some way or another (without the intervention of an external cause). Furthermore, according to Spinoza, it is the case that substance, because it is an *omnitudo realitatis*, must be thought of as that which can only be in being (*nur seiend sein kann*): *id quod cogitari non potest nisi existens*. (Kant would, of course, sharply criticize this ontological proof of substance; according to him, Being is not a real predicate and so no *sachhaltiges* predicate.) For Spinoza, absolute substance is qua absolute, Being pure and simple or absolute Being. (There he reaches, through recourse to the ontological proof of God, the following: God is that whose Being necessarily exists: the famous misunderstanding of the meaning of the expression 'Being' in the sense of 'existence.')

Now, the consequences of Spinoza's arguments, arguments that claimed mathematical evidence for his system, were soon challenged and often refuted by Gottfried Wilhelm Leibniz and Christian von Freiherr Wolff. So Jacobi, who did not plan to advertise for Spinoza, was no longer free to repeat Spinoza's *Ethics* in order to join the uniqueness of the sense of Being with substance. He had first to show that Spinoza's system, regardless of the fact that it was the most consequential of its type (that was Jacobi's thesis at least) rested upon unacceptable presuppositions. At the same time, however, he wanted to assess the motives that led Spinoza's purely rational explanation of the world to its relative dominance. And so, according to Henrich, Jacobi attempted to develop Spinoza's misguided truth of the one-in-all, placing the unity of the sense of Being (*Seins-Sinn*) in all existing things (*Existierenden*) in place of the unity of substance in all of its ways of appearing. This took place in two steps.

Decisive for the first step is Kant's thesis concerning Being, which Jacobi was acquainted with from Kant's essay of 1763. There, Kant not only drew a distinction between absolute and relative positing, a distinction that is, by now, familiar to us. He also defended the thesis that something existent (*ein Dasein*) lies at the basis of every thought of something possible. This claim had important consequences for Hölderlin's reflections on modality in *Urtheil und Seyn*. Kant expresses this is the following way:

> If [. . .] all existence were lifted, then absolutely nothing is posited, there is nothing at all given, no material for any thought at all, and all possibility would be gone. True, there is no inner contradiction involved in the negation of all existence. An inner contradiction would consist in a simultaneous position and sublation of something; but where nothing is posited at all, there no contradiction is committed. However, to claim a possibility without recognizing anything to be actual/real, is contradictory since, if nothing exists, nothing is given either which could make up the stuff for a possible thought; and he who nevertheless wants it to be real, would contradict himself. In analyzing the concept of existence [*Dasein*], we have understood that Being or Absolute position mean just the same thing as existence, provided these terms are not misused to express the logical relation of predicates to subjects, So we have to conclude: the phrase "nothing exists" is synonymous with "there is not anything at all"; and it would be pretty contradictory to add in spite of this that something would be possible (*AA* II: 78).

Kant calls upon Christian August Crusius for support, because Crusius had already presented a similar thesis within the context of the distinction between real and ideal foundations (on the occasion of the discussion of Reinhold's *Elementarphilosophie*). Crusius not only explained, as Kant would after him, sensation as the measure of the actual, but also claimed that the concept of the actual is "prior to the concept of the possible" and with this thesis launched a massive critique of the rationalistic method of most mathematics. Because this prima facie insignificant thesis had such a strong effect on the formation of early German Romantic thought and in particular on its tendency towards realism, I shall give you, unabridged, the crucial passage in which Crusius articulates the thesis:

> It is worth noting that both according to nature and to our knowledge [. . .], *the concept of the actual is prior to the concept of the possible.* I say firstly, that it is prior according to nature. For if there were nothing actual, then there would be nothing possible, for all possibility of something not-yet-existing involves a causal connection between an existing thing and a not-yet-existing thing. Furthermore, according to our knowledge, the concept of

the actual is prior to our concept of the possible. For our first concepts are of existing things, namely, sense impressions, through which we later come to concepts of the possible. Indeed, if one wants to meditate a priori in order to come to the point: the concept of existence is prior to the concept of possibility, because, for the concept of *existence*, I need the simple concepts of *subsistence, co-existence* (*Nebeneinander*), and *succession*. In contrast, for the concept of *possibility*, I am in need of the concept of *causality, subsistence*.[11]

From this it follows for Kant, that being (*Dasein*) is entitled to the modal-determination of necessity. This necessary being (*Dasein*) must further be unique, for it is the ground of every thought of the possible (cf. the third observation of the first part of *The One Possible Basis for a Demonstration of the Existence of God*). Later, Kant distanced himself from this thesis, for at its basis lies the claim that Being is a real predicate. But Jacobi embraced the thesis in this form: for Jacobi Being is completely beyond doubt. He claims of Being that it is, "the pure principle of reality, the Being in all being (*Daseyn*) completely, without individuality and absolutely infinite" (*Spin.* 2: 61, 398). One can call Being a principle because we are dealing with an absolutely insurmountable (*unhintergehbar*) notion. Further, like Spinoza's substance, it is unique: the only ground of all that is possible, regardless of any diversity found in its manifestations. What really is, *is* in one and the same sense, wherever and in whichever form we meet it. Hence, Jacobi can, similar to what Spinoza did for substance, assume an immanence of all single beingness (*Daseienden*) in Being—and with this assumption he again, just like Spinzoa, avoids the unintelligible notion of the transition from the infinite to the finite. The finite does not exist independently of or separately from Being, but rather insofar as it *is* at all, it *is* absolute Being itself (and insofar as this infinite Being is *not*, that is, insofar as it is merely finite, it *is* not at all) (cf. *Spin.* 2: 168 f).

Spinoza claimed that the "transition" from the infinite to the finite was a completely rational consequence and illustrated this by reference to the relationships of implications. For example, the relationships of implication in the case of a triangle and the sum of its interior angles tells us that the sum of these angles will necessarily be 180 degrees, even if I do not see this immediately. It is precisely the rationality of this claim that Jacobi contests. It is, according to Jacobi, not a logical reason which establishes the knowledge of this "transition," but rather experience itself; this means, in other words, that we know about causality, or the law of effect, only from the consciousness of our own ability to practically effect (*bewirken*) or to be affected (*erleiden*) (l.c., 415, cf. 430). As you see, Jacobi here follows Hume's skepticism regarding the a priori nature of the law of causality and he traces the knowledge of the conditioned world, in which the unconditioned has been relinquished, not to something logical but rather to an original experience (*Ur-erfahrung*), which he (like Schelling in his late philosophical realism) refers to as a "revelation." According to Jacobi, Spinoza can lay claim to a strong, rational science, only by resorting to a false theory which holds causal effecting to be something logical (that is, one which confuses a cause with a logical reason).

In spite of the important differences we discussed above, some prominent ties remain intact between Jacobi's critical reconstruction of Spinoza and his own use of the figure of the thorough-reaching (*durchwaltende*) relationships between Being and individual existence (*Dasein*). However, according to Jacobi's view, our knowledge of this relationship is not based upon rational demonstration, it is a knowledge which is revealed to us and is dependent upon experience (what Kant and Crusius claim for the experience of Being). This reliance upon experience does not rob any evidence from the notion of Being—as little as we would doubt the reality of a shrill tone just because we had heard it. This relation between Being and the evident feeling of Being (*Seinsgefühl*) (Rousseau's "*sentiment de l'existence*") is not a relation that would be capable of or in need of a proof: It is a type of immemorial truth of fact whose factuality is indisputable. (Just as Leibnizian "apperception" means a perception which stands on its own, and is hence based a posteriori upon experience and is accordingly infallible; even Kant held the "cogito" not as a conceptual truth or truth of reason, but rather as an "undetermined inner perception" which has, nonetheless, Cartesian certainty.)

Now, we must add some information concerning Jacobi's own theory—that part of it which goes against Spinoza's view: this is the notion of the insurmountable (*unhintergehbar*) presupposition of that which is unconditioned and unmediated and the information concerning the status of certainty which follows therefrom. Once again, I shall follow Henrich's reconstruction as we find it in *Grund im Bewußtsein*.[12]

Jacobi created an impression on his younger contemporaries, in large part due to the following claim: "According to my view, the greatest service an investigator can do is to uncover and to reveal being (*Daseyn*) [. . .]; explanation is only a means, a way to the goal, never the ultimate goal" (*Spin.* 2: p. 42). In this claim, we find the language of rational justification, even of explanation, moved away from the center of the formation of philosophical knowledge—one could even say that such a way of seeing philosophy is shunned. Insight born of revelation is always a priori insight and it is always unmediated in the sense that it is not mediated by reasons. Now, *Dasein* is, as both Crusius and Kant also saw, along with the British empiricists, precisely that which cannot be made clear by explanation, but rather can only be illuminated by experience. We have a particular inner experience of *Dasein* by a feeling of our own *Dasein*. Let me remind you once more that even Kant claimed that the *cogito* must be seen as an "empirical proposition," insofar as according to his information, all knowledge of *Dasein* rested upon perception and that self-consciousness contains the certainty of its own *Dasein* (*cogito ergo sum*). From this, Schelling, making reference to Kant's footnote at B422, establishes the necessity of acknowledging an "intellectual intuition" (*SW* I/1: 401 f.).[13]

Now we must ask ourselves about the sort of conceptual relationship which exists between the experience we have of our *Dasein*—which is an experience of something primitively known (*urbekannte*) and also of a self-feeling (*Selbstgefühl*) and the non-deducible concept of 'Being.' Regarding this issue, Henrich writes:

> If the true content of that which Spinoza sought to grasp as singular "substance" is to be explained by "Being," then "Being" must be understood as a notion which has its logical place in pure thinking, and thus beyond all experience. If one then claims in respect to this, that it does not originate out of reflection or some discourse of justification and that it is, at the same time, necessarily world-containing [. . .], then it follows from this that even that thinking which neither proceeds nor is tied to experience, is in itself dependent on a first principle which at the same time and necessarily develops itself in this thinking. If one now speaks instead of a "Being" that is interpreted as "original Being," of a manifold "being" [*Dasein*] which can only reveal itself, then it seems that a completely different determination of place even of the notion "Being" is implied or comes into play. An argumentation like the following could now be set in motion: The generality of the notion of Being, which cannot be further specified, now causes the notion of thought that is dissociated from all experience to be attributed to Being. It does this by virtue of an illusion [*Schein*] which must be resolved in a critical investigation. In truth, one is to comprehend with the expression "Being" only the general character of the certainty of experience itself—indeed a character that is not further resolvable or specifiable: All experiencing is based on this side of its transition to true knowledge of experience on the assurance that "there is something there" with which we as knowers enter into a relation by means of perceptions. If this were the case, the notion "Being" which is seemingly pure and insurmountable, would have to be interpreted as the general character of the mode of given-ness of all existence [*Dasein*] which is revealed. With this, however, it would have been taken out of the area of rational metaphysics and transferred to the area of a conceptual analysis based upon empirical knowledge [*Erkenntnis*].[14]

One can (and probably must) contest whether the explanation of the certainty we have regarding our own *Dasein* can be indicated in the same empirical way as David Hume's sense data. In this account of Jacobi's position, we need not decide one way or the other. What is relevant for our purposes is to be aware that Jacobi's theory is developed within a theological framework (the expression 'revelation' which Jacobi uses in his account of *Dasein* is evidence for this claim). This explains his distaste for Spinoza's atheism as that of a system realized purely rationally (without any higher revelation). This distaste for Spinoza's rationalism thwarted any chance that Jacobi could, as Spinoza had, conceptualize the transition from the infinite to the finite as a mere modification within a medium of similars (limits and that which is contained by determination and negation are one and the same). Nonetheless, Jacobi wanted to claim that in the finite there is something of the same kind as is found in absolute Being (*Allwill* [= WW I: 134 f.]; *Spin.* 2: 253). Our question now is: what is the nature, according to Jacobi's view of the matter, of this similarity, of this relationship between the finite and the infinite?

It is, its emphasis on revelation notwithstanding, based upon Cartesian certainty. It is the certainty of an "absolute dependence" (as Schleiermacher would call it beginning first in 1822) of the finite on the infinite. This certainty implies—and this is a more interesting and also a more important notion—that we cannot uncover the true nature of the conditioning, itself unconditioned, with the explanatory apparatus of finite foundations (*Begründungen*) and this incapacity is seen as essential. All of our attempts to explain remain within the realm of the conditioned. For to know something "mediately" means to know it by means of a concept or another piece of knowledge, but not from the object of knowledge itself. So, any view of the unconditioned remains always merely "mediated" (*Spin. 2: XXII*). Once again, in Kantian fashion, Jacobi calls the whole of that in which mediate knowledge consists, nature. The expression stands for the dimension within which every conditioned *Dasein* "rests upon an infinitude of mediations" (l.c., 424). Now we have three terms; 'conditioned' (*bedingt*), 'mediated' (*mittelbar*), and 'natural' (*natürlich*) which, according to Jacobi, explain each other reciprocally and can make the basic intuition (*Grundintuition*) of the *Spinozabuchlein* plausible.

We can, according to Jacobi, lend only one meaning to the decisive concepts like 'conditioned' and 'mediated,' if we conceive of them as the negations which they are: they negate the terms 'unconditioned' and 'unmediated' as the ways in which our natural *Dasein* and knowledge is denied. Just as Kant had done in *The One Possible Basis for a Demonstration of the Existence of God*, Jacobi searches in the semantics of the terms 'conditioned' and 'mediated' for a hidden demonstration of negation and ties this to the thesis that negations are always parasitic upon the positions whose negation (or limitation) they execute (cf. AA II: 87,2). I can think of something as "conditioned" only if something whose predicate is "unconditioned" is already thought (*Grund im Bewußtsein*, 64). The same holds for that which is "mediated." To think of something as mediated means to first think of something un-mediated. If the terms 'conditioned,' 'mediated,' and 'natural' have the same conceptual range, then it also holds for the term 'natural' that it cannot be thought without a presupposition of something "supernatural" (*übernatürlich*), for according to Jacobi, 'unnatural' is not a suitable term of opposition for 'natural,' even when 'unconditioned' is the term of opposition for 'conditioned' and 'unmediated' for 'mediated.'[15]

Now these negations and relations of presuppositions hold only when we have also received an indicated epistemic possibility—and this had already been hinted at by the Jacobi's theory of revelation (i.e., that Being is revealed). It is obvious that unmediated consciousness would be necessary, and would be such that it would be essentially different from mediated consciousness. Only such an unmediated knowing would be one whose truth would necessarily enlighten us. And without such an unmediated seeing-into, we would never have any independent, self-contained knowledge. This is because the indefinitely, open chain of reasoning (*Begründungskette*), which is part of mediated knowledge, would make us so dizzy that we would no longer be able to see anything as certain. We know that Jacobi thought that he could stop this regress. He found the way to stop this in feeling, for feeling is a source of unmediated certainty and hence does not involve us in any further attempts to secure it. Recall that for Jacobi, feeling is that organ of knowledge that reveals reality (*Wirklichkeit*), an organ that transcends consciousness and that is, at the same time, a type of self-consciousness. For this reason, we don't need to look for the unconditioned: "We have a greater certainty of its *Dasein* than we have of our own conditioned *Dasein*" (*Spin.* 2: 423 f).

Henrich summarizes this in the following way:

> In this, his grand conclusion, Jacobi connected the advantage of two positions which could appear at first to be utterly irreconcilable. Against Spinozism, he guarded the transcendence of the unconditioned over and against nature. And he simultaneously connected the certainty of the existence (*Dasein*) of the unconditioned with the knowledge (*Wissen*) of conditioned existence in such a way that they are not inferences (*Schlüsse*) which result in the conclusion of the existence of the unconditioned. He who knows of any conditioned as such, already knows *eo ipso* of the existence of the unconditioned which precedes knowledge of the conditioned, not only in the conceptual order, but also in the epistemic order (*Grund im Bewußtsein*, 67).

You will certainly be thinking of the following objection: If my knowledge is merely finite, and if I must think the concept of the non-finite as its contrast, it does not follow that I know anything of the infinite. But to put the objection in this way is to have misunderstood Jacobi. The thrust of his argument does not go so much towards the unconditioned as it does towards our knowledge. And so his thesis is the following: if all knowledge were eternally conditioned throughout by something else, so that knowledge itself would only be insofar as it was conditioned, then we would not know anything at all. If, however, there is knowledge at all, then there must be knowledge that comes to be un-conditionally, that is, knowledge that is not conditioned by anything else. And in this version of the thesis, we can take Jacobi's point quite seriously. We began to see this when we looked at the effect of Jacobi's thought on both Reinhold's and Fichte's philosophy—in particular, their emphasis on securing a first principle for philosophy.

Now we should say a few words about the status of that consciousness in which, according to Jacobi, the knowledge-regress comes to an end. Jacobi calls this consciousness "feeling" and further specifies that this is a type of knowledge of our self. Although all "natural" knowledge is conditioned (and also known to us as conditioned), it holds nonetheless that, "we must not first search for the unconditioned but rather that we have more certainty of its existence (*Dasein*) than we have of our own conditioned existence (*Dasein*)" (*Spin.* 2: 423 f.). You will soon see that this notion has important affinities with Hölderlin's position in *Urtheil und Seyn*, where the knowing self-relation is suffused by a completely relation-less knowledge, which Hölderlin calls "intellectual intuition" and which is evident in Being itself. Jacobi writes: "Of our own *Dasein* we have only a feeling but no concept":—for we know of ourselves (and *that* we are) not through the fact that we are beings of a class of beings (what would be the concept, the experience, which would classify the Being of an I?) nor through deducing the "self," indicated by a "thing" from "its nearest cause" (l.c., 419, footnote)—for then it would be mediated by this cause and would lose its unmediated evidence.

Jacobi expresses this in the following way:

> I take the whole person without dividing him, and find, that his consciousness is composed of two original representations; the representation of the conditioned and the representation of the unconditioned. Both are indivisibly joined to each other, indeed so, that the representation of the conditioned presupposes the representation of the unconditioned, and can only be given in the latter. (l.c., 423).

Here Jacobi claims that the experience of the conditioned can only be given within the representation of the unconditioned—and this can easily be explained from what we have already said. If the conditioned is to contain knowledge, then it is in need of certainty as a witness, and this can only be attained by unconditioned consciousness. And this is the most primitive component of all consciousness; moreover, it first makes the consciousness that we have of ourselves (our own existence [*Dasein*]) possible. As we shall see, Hölderlin and Friedrich von Hardenberg (Novalis) have positions quite similar to this one. They have, however, slightly different ways of expressing this position. According to them, and in keeping with the spirit of Jacobi's position, they claim that the relation of self-consciousness indicates conditioned knowledge, which obtains its Cartesian certainty (literally, then, its unconditioned-ness) only under the presupposition that is not presentable in knowledge. This presupposition is unconditioned Being. This is closely tied to a basic position of realism, which from its very roots, lies in opposition to absolute idealism. Hence, one simply cannot read early German Romanticism as an appendage to so-called German idealism.

Lecture 4

On the Search for the Unconditioned

From Jacobi's 'Feeling' to
Schelling and Hölderlin's 'Intellectual Intuition'

W hen Novalis writes, in the first fragment of his *Vermischten Bemerkungen* (Miscellaneous Remarks) (presumably from 1797) that, "[w]e search everywhere for the unconditioned (*Unbedingte*) and find always only things (*Dinge*)" (*NS* II: 412, No. 1), he formulates the basic problem of his considerations in terminology initiated by Jacobi. But in April or May of 1795, Hölderlin, too, distinguished between possibility and actuality, "as mediated and unmediated consciousness," and gave precedence to actuality over possibility (*FHA* 17: 156, lines 28 ff.). This is done, again following the trail of Jacobi's thought. And, as we have seen, Jacobi, in turn, was influenced by the thought of Crusius and Kant. Actuality, the second modal category, was defined by Kant as having the character of "absolute positing," therefore, the as-existent-positing (*als-existent-Setzung*) of an object (e.g., an intuition) as such—be the corresponding predicate what it may be. Hence, actuality is synonymous with *Dasein* (already in Kant this was the case). We have already seen that Jacobi was likewise struck by Kant's thesis regarding absolute Being, speaking of Being as that which is made evident by (or better, revealed by) "feeling" (which he calls "unmediated consciousness"). Because Hölderlin understood by "Being pure and simple" (*Seyn schlechthin*) the original, still preidentitical unity of subject and object—original in the sense that both are really "the same" (l.c., line 15), hence not through the binding of the one to the other is the synthesis first created—as is the case in the predicative judgment 'A is B,' or even as is given in the judgment of identity 'I am I' (l.c., pp.

17–19). Because Hölderlin understands Being to be a simple (prejudgment stage) unity, it is quite clear that his thought follows in Jacobi's footsteps. That which Jacobi called "feeling" is what Hölderlin (with Fichte and Schelling) calls "intellectual intuition" (l.c., p. 6). It is that consciousness, which immediately understands seamless and unified original Being (*fugenlos-einige Ursein*). Hölderlin describes this in the following way:

> If subject and object are absolutely unified, not merely relatively [as in Kant's "relative positing"], that is, unified in such a way that no division at all can be assumed without thereby injuring the essence of that which is to be separated, then and only then can we speak of absolute Being as is the case with intellectual intuition (lines 2–6).

This nicely illustrates the influence of Jacobi upon Hölderlin's thinking. Nonetheless, this line of Jacobi's thought is most clearly seen in Schelling's early writings. It is worthwhile to take a look at these writings because Hölderlin (and, by the way, Novalis in a similar way as well) deviates in a significant way from two of Schelling's main theses. The first one is Schelling's equation of the terms 'Being' and 'Identity'; the second, his deduction of the modal category possibility from thetical judgment. Schelling's text, *Vom Ich* (*On the I*), had the subtitle, "oder über das Unbedingte im menschlichen Wissen" (*or Concerning the Unconditioned in Human Knowledge*).[1] This text was distributed before *Urtheil und Seyn*, that is, before the Easter holiday on April 5, 1795, and Hölderlin took account of this in his own work. Schelling wrote to Hegel during the period he was working on the *Vom Ich* text. Specifically, on February 4, we find the following passage:

> Philosophy must depart from the unconditioned. Now the question is: where is this unconditioned to be found—in the I or the Non-I. If we can answer this, all is decided (*Mat.* 127).

If the unconditioned is found in the I, we come to (critical) idealism. If the unconditioned is found in the Non-I, we come to dogmatism. It is of no interest to us to here that Schelling rejects both positions through the elevation of his principle (and then naturally, in what follows, is forced to see that he can no longer speak of his unconditioned as the I, for the I, as it is conditioned by the Non-I, is, in virtue of this conditioning, certainly no candidate for any talk of the unconditioned). What is important for our purposes is to look more carefully at Schelling's justification for his claim that one must begin with (or that philosophy must depart from) the unconditioned. And it is here that we find the most striking dependence on Jacobi,[2] not only in the emphatic citations, indeed homages,[3] but also in the argumentation itself. For the following discussion, it is important to keep in mind that and how Schelling appropriated Jacobi's notion that all cognitive mediation presupposes the certainty of something unmediated. Unfortunately, we cannot dwell on the matter now. Schelling focussed upon Jacobi's insistence that there was knowledge (*Kenntnis*), which was valid not only under the condition of something else, but valid without any other condition, that is, knowledge which was unconditioned. Schelling interpreted this—in preparation for his philosophy of identity—as a type of knowledge in which no opposition between the grounded (*Begründeten*) and the ground (*Grund*) or the knowing (*Erkennenden*) and the known (*Erkannten*) was found. This knowledge, notwithstanding its evidence, is not conceptual, but rather rests upon a type of unmediated intuition, which is, to be sure, not sensible but rather intellectual, for it is the intuition of intelligence itself (*SW* I/1: 181, 182). Seen in terms of the terminology, we see Jacobi summoned once again, for he had claimed: "If a concept of the unconditioned and unconnected (*Unverknüpften*) and so of the 'extra-natural' (*Aussernatürliche*) becomes possible, then the unconditioned must cease to be unconditioned" (*Spin.* 2: 425 ff.). In this respect, the unconditioned is the incomprehensible itself (*das Unbegreifliche selbst*) (for I can never grasp it in conceptual thought). But it is not therefore unknown, quite the contrary, it reveals itself as "an unmediated certainty which not only is in no need of any foundations, but also excludes all foundations" (p. 215). This certainty is what Jacobi, as we have seen, calls belief (*Glaube*) or revelation.

Now we want to look more closely at what Schelling makes of this situation. Already in letters to Hegel from January 6, and March 2, 1795, Schelling had introduced the main lines of his new thought. The text which resulted is merely the working-out of a central notion already present in these letters and which was to be written during the first quarter of 1795, thus appearing before Hölderlin's *Urtheil und Seyn*. Schelling begins his argumentation with the observation that every claim to knowledge claims its *reality*. His line of reasoning leads him to make the further claim that there must be "a final point of reality on which everything hangs, from which all understanding, all form of our knowledge, departs" (*SW* I/ 1: 162). So, in a few steps Schelling proceeds from the concept of *real* (this means valid) knowledge to the notion of a highest first principle, which establishes the validity of our knowledge. In this way, he simply follows Jacobi's references to the vicious circle (*Begründungsregreß*) that would be set into motion if there were no such principle. Schelling writes:

> If there is to be any knowledge (*Wissen*) at all, then there has to be a knowledge not acquired through another knowledge that is in its turn acquired through still another knowledge by virtue of which all other

knowledge would be knowledge. In order to attain this proposition, we don't have to presuppose a peculiar kind of knowledge. If only we know anything at all, we at least have to know one thing not known by any additional knowledge and which contains the real ground (*Realgrund*) of all our knowledge.

This ultimate (or highest) knowledge cannot have to seek its real ground in something else. Not only is it *in itself* independent of something higher, but, since our knowledge proceeds from *consequens* to *antecedens* or vice versa, that which is the highest and for us the principle of all knowledge (*Erkennens*), must not be *knowable* (*erkennbar*) through another principle, that is to say that the principle of its being and the principle of its being-known have to coincide, be one and the same, given that it cannot be known but precisely because it is *itself* not something different. So it has to be thought just because of its being, and it must be not because something else is thought, but because it is itself thought. Its affirmation (*Bejahen*) must be contained in its thinking, it has to produce itself through its thinking. If in order to attain one's thought, one would have to think of something else, then this something else would be higher than the highest (*das Höchste*), and this is self-contradictory; in order to attain the highest, I don't need anything other than this highest itself—the Absolute can only be given through the Absolute (l.c., 162 f.).

Schelling continues, claiming that such knowledge must be called "unconditioned," because,

Knowledge, which I can only reach through other knowledge, I call a *conditioned* knowledge. The chain of our knowledge passes from one condition to another; now either the whole of it must be without any support or one must be ready to think that the chain proceeds this way into the infinite, or there has to be a last point from which the entire chain is suspended but which therefore, as regards the principle of its being, is directly *opposed* to everything which is contained in the sphere of conditions, that is to say: it is not only unconditioned but Absolutely *unconditionable*.

[. . .]

As soon as philosophy begins to become science, it at least has to *presuppose* a highest principle and together with it something unconditioned (l. c. , 164).

Schelling analyzes the expression 'unconditioned' in exactly the same way as Jacobi had before him (and as Novalis would after him). It stands for that which cannot be any "thing." If there should be knowledge of this, this knowledge cannot be knowledge of a thing or of an object. The unconditioned must be thought of as objectless or without objectivity.

Does this mean that the unconditioned is therefore subjective? No, it is neither subjective nor objective. For just as every thing is that which it is only insofar as it is something determined, that is, through its delimitation from all other things that it is not, the concept of a subject is only a term of opposition with respect to an object. It is—to speak in Jacobi's words— "conditioned" through the concept of an object. That is enough to exclude it from being a principle of philosophy: "Precisely," says Schelling, "because the subject is thinkable only in relation to an object, and the object only in relation to a subject, can neither contain the Absolute, for both are reciprocally conditioned by each other, both are posited equally to each other" (l.c., 165). The unconditioned real-foundation of our knowledge must therefore be found on this side of the division between subjectivity and objectivity, for this division constitutes that which we call "conditioned knowledge."

Playing on the etymological relationship between the German words "*bedingen*" and "*Ding*," Schelling calls the German word "*bedingen*":

> A superb word, of which one can say, that it almost contains all the treasure of philosophical truth. *Bedingen* (to condition) means that activity through which something becomes a thing, *bedingt* (conditioned) that which is made into a thing, from which it follows that it could not be posited through itself as a thing, which is to say, that an *unbedingtes Ding* (unconditioned thing) is a contradiction in terms. For *unbedingt* is precisely that which is not be made into a thing at all, which cannot become a thing.
>
> Hence, the problem whose solution we seek to present is changed into the more definite one of finding something that cannot originally be thought of as a thing (l. c., 166).

Schelling finds this nonobjective entity in the I, but you should not make the mistake of thinking of Fichte's I which is opposed to the Non-I and as such (in Schelling's conceptualization) forfeits the claim of being something unconditioned. For this reason, Schelling adds to the I the predicate of the Absolute (167; that therewith a self-contradiction is formulated is something which Schelling saw first around 1800 when he began to free himself of his dependence on Fichte. Indeed, after seeing this, he spoke only of the Absolute rather than of the I). In the notion 'I,' there should be no self-consciousness smuggled in. Because, just as was the case for Hölderlin, Schelling views self-consciousness as a consciousness of one's self, and so a consciousness conditioned by an object, an objective consciousness; and because it is articulated through a dual-linking (*Zweigliederkeit*), the temporal before and after cannot be excluded from it. According to Schelling:

> Self-consciousness presupposes the danger of losing the I. It is not a free act of the unchangeable, but rather a striving forced on the changeable I which

is conditioned through the Non-I, which strives to save its identity and to re-grasp itself in the on-going flow of change; (or do you feel yourselves to be really free in self-consciousness?) (180 f.).

Schelling says in fact that the I "as pure I [. . .] in consciousness (of which self-consciousness is only a special case) does not come into the picture at all" (206). If the absolute I should be subordinated to some modes of consciousness, it can be neither the I with an object nor the I encumbered with itself, hence it cannot be self-consciousness. We know that the early Schelling (just like Hölderlin) spoke of intellectual intuition (181). What he contributes to its structure is meager, but right now we are not concerned with this point anyway. What we want to investigate more closely is Schelling's consistent association of unconditioned knowledge with the unconditioned (in this context, the term 'knowledge' (*Wissen*) is questionable, but Schelling really doesn't need it anyway). Intellectual intuition may be called "unconditioned" for two reasons: it is, *qua* intuition, un-mediated consciousness of its object as an individual (this is how 'intuition' was defined by the Kantian School; and un-mediated knowledge is one which is not opposed to its object; for this reason we cannot speak here of an unmediated grasping of its object) and it is *qua* intellectual grasping not something given but rather a deed (*Tun*). (In the terminology of the Kantian School, something spontaneous—"Intellectual is that whose concept is a deed" [Reflection Nr. 4182, AA XVIII: 447]). So Schelling's "intellectual intuition" connects seamlessly with Jacobi's "feeling"—only Schelling does not settle beyond consciousnessss with a "salto mortale" (the concept of an unconscious feeling is self-contradictory anyway). Where Schelling remains tied to Jacobi is in his claim that the knowledge in which the unconditioned is made evident is cut off from all conceptual knowledge:

> The I cannot be given by any concept. For concepts are only possible within the sphere of the conditioned, only of objects. If the I were a concept, then there would have to be something higher in which its unity could be held and something lower that could contain its plurality; in short, the I would be completely conditioned. Hence, the I can only be determined by an intuition (181).

I think that this account of Schelling's early writings clearly demonstrates his reception of Jacobi's thought. Up until now, we have been concerned in particular with the way in which Schelling adopted the impulse of a first principle for philosophy generated by Jacobi's discussion of the regress problem involved in our knowledge claims. Even more interesting for contemporary philosophers, however, are the ontological commitments that

Schelling took over from Jacobi and which bring his work into surprising proximity to Hölderlin's *Urtheil und Seyn*. In both texts, an account of the copulative 'is' is provided, one which refers back to Kant through Jacobi. We are already familiar with this but must show how it works its way into these two texts.

The only two principles that Jacobi claims as fundamental ones of the understanding are the 'principle of identity' and the 'principle of reason.' The first functions as the principle of all logical-mathematical propositions; the second as the principle of all metaphysical and natural-science explanations of the world. "To understand" (literally, to grasp with the understanding) and "To establish" (*Begründen*) are reciprocal concepts (*Wechselbegriffe*), there is no logical certainty beyond the form of a proof; and the form of a proof has, in turn, the structure of judgments deduced from one another. Now, in Jacobi's time, it was a widely held view in logic that the 'is' in a judgment was a copula (Kant calls the 'is' a "connective"(*CPR* B141 f.), and Schelling spoke regularly in his philosophy of identity phase of a "connection" (*Band*) between subject and object). The copula—or the binding power of judgment—is read, in turn, as a sign of identity, whereby here "identity" can only have the weak sense of a connection (*Verknüpfung*) (for in a trivial way, in an informative or synthetic proposition, the meaning of a subject is something other than the meaning of the predicate). Two different representations are identified (in this weak sense) by the copula, usually a subject and a predicate, whereby one stands for the intuition-complex (*Anschauungskomplexion*), the other for a concept (cf. *SW* I/3: 363 f., 508; cf. I/1, 393 f.). When Jacobi says that the "principle of identity" underlies all logical operations of the understanding (and these are, according to Kant, judgments)— then he must mean this weak sense of identity—for in a synthetic proposition (in Kant's sense), the subject and the object are not identical.

Now, from the sheer distinction between the subject expression and the predicate expression, the achievement of the connection is not made comprehensible—for that Kant had already chosen the self-conscious identity of 'I think' for the instance from which the judicative connection makes its departure.

Hence, we have the following constellation. The synthesis of a judgment takes place in the name of a higher identity, which imparts a binding power to the synthesis Kant had already given to his followers. Insofar as Kant had placed both existential and predicative Being under the higher concept of 'positing,' he gave his followers two important pieces of information: (1) Being, in all of its applications, has one unique meaning. Jacobi took this in such a way that he attributed uniqueness to Being and held it to be one in all *Dasein*. Schelling goes even further in this direction when he combines the notion of Being with the Kantian synthesis of apperception in that he places the concepts of 'Being' and 'absolute identity' in the closest proximity; (2) Kant had pushed existential and predicative Being together so that it seemed that he held the latter as a derivative or minor form of the first. The "relative positing" would then be something like the predicative exposition (*Auseinanderlegung*) of that which in the unity of "absolute positing" can be thought as compact. "Absolutely posited" meant, in Kant, a concept if its object existed (as in the proposition, 'I am'—period; the 'am' does not express any new content for the concept 'I' which is synthesized with the first; rather, it only says that something like an I exists and is no mere figment of imagination). On the other hand, something is posited "relatively," if the positing—as in a predicative judgment—follows from the "connective 'is.'" In this case, nothing is posited absolutely, but rather a subject-expression is posited in relation to a predicate-expression. Such relations are what Kant called "judgments." They have the structure of "something-as-something." The first "something" stands for the object and the second for the concept under which the object is to be interpreted. Already Kant, and no less than Schelling, had thought that the copulative 'is' was (somehow) a modus descending from existential 'is.' The fact that this notion was perceived by the Kantians to be manifest is shown by a look at Reinhold's treatment of the modal-expression. There, "logical [. . .] Being, which is expressed in judgments through the word 'is,' as the sign of the connection between predicate and subject" in an unmediated relationship is exchanged with the Being of Absolute positing and differentiated from Being as mere representation (*Versuch*, pp. 478 f.). Jacobi, who in his turn would be followed by Schelling, Hölderlin, and Novalis, added—as we have already observed—the notion of the unity of Being: Existence and identity are somehow the same and the synthetic power of the connective 'is' in predicative judgments flows, in a mysterious way, from the seamless identity of Being.

Jacobi calls this higher identity "Being," Schelling calls this, in addition, and following in Fichte's footsteps—"Absolute I." In the "Absolute I," there is a seamless identity (a "sameness" [*Einerleiheit*] as Schelling would later say) between the intuition which refers to the subject-term and the concept which refers to the predicate-term. But the two terms of the synthesis are not exactly identical (otherwise they would not need to be "identified"). How, then, asks Schelling, can these two terms be understood as implied by the absolute I? In other words: How do the subject and object separate from each other? This, he tells us, is not possible "without a special activity through which both are opposed to each other in consciousness." Such an activity is that which is indicated expressively by the word 'judgment,' insofar as judgment is that activity through which what had been inseparably unified is first separated, namely, concept and intuition (*SW* I/3: 507 bottom). Hegel still emphasizes in section 166 of the Berlin *Encyclopedia* that: "The etymological meaning of judgment in our language is deeper and expresses the unity of the concept and its differentiation (*Unterscheidung*) as the original division, which is what judgment in reality is [. . .]." In another place he writes:

> The contemplation of judgment can now proceed from the original unity of the concept or from the independence of the extremes. Judgment is the diremption of the concept through itself, this unity is thus the ground (*Grund*), from which it is contemplated according to its true objectivity. It is in this respect the original division of the original one; the word: "*Ur-theil*" (judgment) refers thus to that which is in and for itself (GW 12:55, 4–10).

There are parallels with this mistaken etymology of the word "judgment" (as the effect of some original division)[4] in the work of C. G. Bardili who was a teacher at the seminary in Tübingen and whose courses had been attended by both Hegel and Hölderlin.[5] Violetta Waibel has shown that the direct model for this mistaken etymology is to be found in Fichte's Platner-Lectures from the winter semester of 1794–95.[6] These lectures were given in the evening. And because Hölderlin wrote that he went in the evenings to Fichte's lectures, we can surmise that he attended these lectures. Within the context of his theory of judgment, Fichte said the following:

> Judging (*Ur-theilen*—literally, to originally divide)—it is true that an original division underlies all judging.
>   There has to be a common sphere (a third term) to which both of the terms have to be related.
>   For example, The table is *red*: where do we here have the third term?
>   The table *isn't red*: what does this mean? How is 'it not red'? (GA II.4: 182).

Fichte too—like all Kantians—attempts to make the meaning of the copulative connection comprehensible from the originally unified and single sense of Being as existence. The absolute self-positing (or thetical) judgment forms a sphere, the essence of all reality. This sphere is the "third thing" by which, as Fichte expressed the matter, the terms of the judgment must be held. But in judgment, this sphere is cut up (*zerlegt*) into two expressions; that is, it is dis-integrated. One could also say: the "entire sphere of the concept" is "limited" to a partial sphere (183), in which I either can or (in the case of a negative judgment) cannot place an object. Fichte claims the following:

> In negative judgments I position (*setze*) something into a sphere disinct from the other ones, I draw a border. In positive judgments I put it into a sphere.—There I *exclude*, here I include. (183, top).

> Every positioning (Setzen) is at the same time an *exclusion,* and a
> positive judgment can also be considered to be negative one (184).

Hence, Fichte applies, in an ingenious way, his principle of determination through negation, or limitation, to the theory of judgment: A thing is what it is, insofar as it excludes everything that it is not from its sphere. The sphere is then the concept through which I indicate the thing. To judge simply means then: to draw a classificatory border and therewith to make clear to our conversation partner on which side of the border he/she should search for the object about which we are predicating something. Fichte's theory of judgment reappears in a contemporary light in Peter Strawson's work. Consider the following observation:

> One of the main purposes for which we use language is to report events and to describe things and persons. Such reports and descriptions are like answers to questions of the form: what was it like? What is it (he, she) like? We describe something, say what it is like, by applying to it words that we are also prepared to apply to other things. But not to all other things. A word that we are prepared to apply to everything without exception (such as certain words in current use in popular, especially military speech) would be useless for the purposes of description. For when we say what a thing is like, we not only compare it with other things, we also distinguish it from other things. (These are not two activities, but two aspects of the same activity.)[7]

The words of which Strawson here speaks are, of course, predicates. And in applying these predicates to objects, we classify these objects. We do this through a construction like the following: 'The table is monochrome red,' that is: it is not, for example, blue. Through the contrast between the propositions 'it is so' and 'it is not so,' we draw a boundary and thereby indicate on which side the object in question is to be found. Strawson speaks of spheres in which the objects are placed through predication, and also of these as "realms of incompatibility."[8] A realm of incompatibility is defined in the following way: Two predicates 'F' and 'G' are incompatible with each other and hence fall into the realm of incompatibility if the expression 'A is G' implies the claim 'A is not F' (hence, to remain with Fichte's example, 'The table is red' implies the claim 'The table is hence not blue') and vice versa. Because the proposition, 'The table is red' is only *one* way of its not being blue (if 'blue' and 'red' belong to the same realm of incompatibility), the proposition 'The table is red' stands equally in contradiction to the proposition 'The table is blue' and 'The table is not red.' One way for the table to be 'not red' (a way which Fichte mentions as well), would be for it to be square or marble. But 'square' and 'marble' do not lie within the same sphere of incompatibility as 'red' and can therefore be included under the same color-property, while properties from the same sphere, as Fichte said, exclude each other reciprocally, and they do this through a limitation of this sphere, that is, through the drawing of a boundary, indeed, through a judgment, which, if we return to the German word 'Ur-teilen,' takes us to an original dividing (*ursprünglich Teilen*). The judgment-structure, 'something-as-something' is the fundamental structure of all individuation: I determine something as precisely-this-and-not-that (*gerade-so-und-nicht-anders*), in that I keep at bay all that belongs to the sphere of predicates which do not correspond to this thing. According to Fichte,

> To determine in the *Wissenschaftslehre* means so much as to *limit* and this means to a specific *region* or *sphere* of our *knowledge*. (The absolute principle, in contrast, as the essence of all that is conscious, i.e., all reality), contains the entire *sphere* of our knowledge, for where we only speak of consciousness, the principle holds (GA IV. 2: 32 f., 43).

Fichte also spoke of "the law of reflection of all of our knowledge, namely: Nothing is known regarding what something is, without the thought of what it is not" (l.c., 41).

What does this anticipation of the understanding of logic and identity in *Urtheil und Seyn* have to do with our present set of questions? Now, Jacobi holds the logical operations of judgment to be applications of the principle of identity and understands 'identity' in the weak sense of connection. However, that which is connected is different, and each member of the relation stands in a conditioned relation to the other. The relation of conditions must be understood quite literally: a subject-term is determined more precisely through a predicate (and this is the operation that Jacobi calls "to condition"). A judgment is the classic case of a mediation (*Vermittelung*) of two into one. Precisely because of this, that which is comprehended in a judgment cannot be something unmediated (*das Un-mittelbare*) or unconditioned. Schelling adapts this insight in such a way that he attributes the division involved in a judgment to the work of conditioned consciousness— from which it follows that the unconditioned must be presupposed as prejudicative Being beyond (conditioned) consciousness. And, in fact, Schelling presupposes this. In the following he emphasizes this:

> The object and its concept are one and the same beyond our consciousness, and the dividing line first comes up with the awakening of consciousness. So, a philosophy that departs from consciousness will never be able to give an account of this correspondence [in which Schelling quite traditionally sees the criterion of truth], nor is it to be explained without recurring to an

original identity, the principle of which is necessarily located beyond our consciousness (*SW* I/3: 506).[9]

In this passage, it is clear that Schelling attempts to place his theory of judgment into combat with Jacobi's condemnation of mediated thought. Mediated thought is thought which is led by (or indeed conveys [*ver-mitteln*]) judgments. Judging presupposes counter-propositions, hence, relations of conditionedness. If the sphere of that which is grasped by judgment—in the broad sense—is the sphere of that grasped by objective thought of the same extension with consciousness, then it holds that the unconditioned cannot be represented in consciousness. And Hölderlin saw things the same way as did Jacobi, who, indeed, on the basis of this conviction, supports the bold venture of his "salto mortale" into the abyss of divine mercy (*Spin.* 2: 27).

Those acquainted with Hölderlin's work could object that in *Urtheil und Seyn* there is an additional complication that we do not find in Schelling's work. And with this complication, perhaps, Jacobi's influence comes more clearly into view. It appears that Hölderlin—like Jacobi—interprets the copulative 'is' in judgment as a sign of identity. And because the essence of judgment (or, according to Hölderlin, of the original division [*Ur-teilung*]) is generally characterized by this sign of identity, the sign of identity cannot be the highest (*das Höchste*). Above identity—making identity itself possible— stands "Being." "But this Being," says Hölderlin,

> must not to be confused with identity. When I say "I am I," the subject (I) and the object (I) are not unified in such a manner that no division could be carried out at all without injuring the essence of that which is to be divided; quite to the contrary, the I is possible only through this separation of the I from the I. How can I say I! without self-consciousness? But how is self-consciousness possible? It is possible in that I oppose myself to myself, in that I separate myself from myself, but despite this separation I recognize myself as the same self in that self which is opposed to me. But to what extent as the same self? I can, I must pose these questions, for in another respect the I is opposed to itself. Therefore, identity is not a unification of object and subject that takes place originally, hence, identity is not = to absolute Being (*FHA* 17: 156,$_2$).

Schelling would agree with Hölderlin's claim that self-consciousness is not an instantiation of the Absolute (for according to Schelling, self-consciousness has the structure of a judgment 'I = I,' that is, of a judgment of identity; but we will soon see that he interprets all judgment as a kind of identification). As a judgment, self-consciousness breaks up the highest (*das Höchste*) into two relata which are externally bound through the copula, it "relativizes" what is absolute about it, what, according to Schelling, must be thought of as "*omnibus relationibus absolutum.*" Therefore, the way in which knowledge of the Absolute is acquired must correspond to a mode of comprehension (*Auffassungsmodus*) other than that of consciousness (or self-consciousness). And for both Schelling and Hölderlin, this alternative mode is "intellectual intuition" (Schelling, Hölderlin, and Novalis always speak of "intellectual intuition" (*intellektualer*) while Kant and Fichte use the adjective '*intellektuell*'—leading us to ask whether this is a type of agreement on the part of the young Jena thinkers to separate themselves from Kant and Fichte). Hölderlin claims, exactly as Schelling had, that the Absolute (or Being) does not make self-consciousness evident, but rather makes "intellectual intuition" evident, in which, other than in the dividing and dispersing (*zerlegende*) judgment—the subject and object are "intimately unified" (l.c., p. 20). Accordingly, he distinguishes the judicative identification as a minor mode of Being in which unity finds its most intimate expression, that is, the strongest expression conceivable. In contrast, Schelling appears to identify the Absolute with identity (in fact, his philosophy came to be known, with his approval, as a philosophy of identity).

From this, certain interpreters have concluded that there is a notable difference between Schelling and Hölderlin—especially because we find in their written exchange direct communication regarding these differences (we have yet to discuss these). This difference, it seems to me, is of a purely terminological nature. For Schelling speaks occasionally of the Absolute (on this side of the division of consciousness or better, of "reflection") as of Being, as he generally determines the object of intellectual intuition through the "I am" and not through the self-reflection of the I. Hence, in this famous passage from the *Ich Schrift*:

> I am! My I contains a Being that precedes all thinking and representing. It is insofar as it is thought, and it is thought because it is. And this precisely because it is only insofar as it is and is only thought insofar as it is. This, in turn, is precisely because it is and is thought only insofar as it thinks itself (*SW* I/1: 167).

A bit earlier on the same page, Schelling had said, almost as decisively (though of the Absolute rather than of Being) that: "The Absolute can only be given through the Absolute, indeed, if it is to be Absolute, it must precede all thinking and representing."

How can we make sense of Hölderlin's and Schelling's use of language? Clearly, only if we take a closer look at the fundamental convictions which each of these thinkers articulated in slightly (but not fundamentally) different ways. They developed these convictions on the basis of conceptual points that are to be understood not only in terms of Jacobi's work. Now I shall give a sketch of the underlying theory that was never explicitly expressed by either Schelling or Hölderlin. I shall do this in my own words and then add some examples from their work.

Both Hölderlin and Schelling understood the "is" of assertive propositions (or, as they say in the Kantian tradition, of judgments) as an indication of identity. So they supported, in contrast to contemporary semanticists, an identity theory of predication. One can read more of this in Wolfram Hogrebe's book on Schelling entitled, *Prädikation als Genesis*.[10] Now, one can easily see that, in simple predicative propositions, that which is signaled by the subject-term does not mean the same thing as (hence, is not identical to) that for which the predicate stands. How does the identity theory of predication explain this? In such a way that, for this kind of case, a new term is introduced, that of synthesis (or connection). Accordingly, that which is synthesized is in part unified, and in part, not unified. The true sense of judgment would then be: "A is B," means: A is, in part B, and in part not B. That with respect to which both are strongly identical (that is, with respect to which both agree) is the Absolute (or X, as Fichte says in section 3 of the WL: WWI: 111). Or, as Schelling puts this (albeit much later):

> The true meaning of every judgment—for example, A is B—can only be this: *that which is* A *is that which is* B, or *that which is* A *and that which is* B are the same. Thus, a double-ness lies at the basis even of the simple concept: A in this judgment is not A, but something (=x) which is A; thus B is not B, but something (=x) which is B, and not the latter (not A and B in themselves) but the x which is A and the x which is B are the same, namely, the same x.[11]

Now, what does this x (which does not stand merely for the subject and object, respectively, or for the mere synthesis, but rather for the Absolute identity of A and B) have to do with Hölderlin's Being before all judgment? Here, one must keep in mind that Kant had characterized Being (in the sense of Scholastic *Quodditas* of "that-ness" or existence) as "positing" or "thesis." This explains Fichte's often puzzling use of language; he describes the Absolute I as a "positing of itself." Why? Because, also for him, in a certain sense, the highest state of affairs was not the reflexive (and in predicative "judgment," articulatable, cf. WWI: 95–94) self-relation of a subject I to an I itself-as-object but was rather the fact of the 'I am' (cf., l.c., 94 ff, esp., 98: "*To posit one's self* and *Being* are, as used by the I, exactly the same"). In the highest of all judgments, which Fichte calls "thetical judgments" (l.c., 115 ff.), there is no predicate assigned to the I (that it is this or that, this kind or that kind); it is without any predicate at all, "posited as being (*als seined*)" (l.c., 97). The pure identity-sense of the I comes into the picture only in this pre-predicative positing, and only this kind of positing can bring a radical "un-conditioned" into play: in the predicate's further determination (I is as a so-and-so) it falls under a "condition" (95).

Moreover, it holds that all further determination (predicative or judgment-like) of the I presupposes the Being of the I (that is, its being posited) (95). Hence, one must say that also in Fichte's theory, Being has precedence over judgment. Indeed, Fichte already has the synthesis of a judgment (in which something is related to something else in such a way that it is only partially of the same kind as the other—namely, with respect to being absolutely posited—and partially not, namely, with respect to its difference or the fact of its not-absolute positedness). That is to say, Fichte had already brought the synthesis of judgment into logical dependence with that which he calls the Absolute thesis (cf. esp. p. 151).

According to Fichte, a "thetical judgment" would be one in which,

> something is neither equated nor opposed to anything else, but only equated (*gleichgesetzt*) to itself; therefore it couldn't presuppose any principle of relation nor of differentiation: the common third which it has to presuppose due to its logical form, would only be a *task* to arrive at such a principle (*Grund*). The original and highest judgment of this kind is the assertion 'I am,' through which nothing [concrete] is asserted but the position of the predicate is indefinitely (*ins Unendliche*) left open for possible determination. All judgments which are contained under this one, that is, under the Absolute position, are of this kind (l. c., 116).

In the time we have remaining, I want to quickly substantiate the dependence which Schelling, Hölderlin, and Sinclair had on Fichte's work by looking at some comments by these authors. The following passage from Schelling's *System of Transcendental Idealism* indicates the influence of two of Fichte's views: (1) that he held judgment to be a way of identifying two representations, and (2) that he distinguished between Absolute "being posited" and mere (synthetic) "being posited."[12] Here is the relevant passage:

> The predicate [in judgment] is actually not different from the subject, since, precisely in the judgment, an identity of both is posited. So a division of subject and predicate is possible at all only by the fact, that one term stands for an intuition, the other for a concept. So in a judgment, concept and object should first be opposed to each other, then related to each other and posited as equal to one another.[13]

The "selfness-in-itself" (*an-sich-Selbigkeit*) between an intuition (or object) and concept takes place only in an absolute thesis. In judicative synthesis, the original, absolutely identified terms are subordinated to the sense criterion of that which is taken apart (*Auseinanderlegung*). And then the same holds for these terms as that which Hölderlin had claimed in *Urtheil und Seyn*: "The reciprocal relation of subject and object is already found in the concept of division, and the necessary presupposition of a whole (this is the Fichtean *x*) of which object and subject are the parts" (*FHA* 17: 156, lines 22–25). Earlier, this meant that in the judgment-like (*urteilsmäßige*) unification, "subject and object are [no longer] absolutely, [. . . but rather] merely [still] in part unified" (l.c., p. 2), that is: one is no longer completely but rather merely just a part of what the other is and in part not what the other is. Only in Being— therefore, in absolute or thetical judgment—are both *indistincte* one in such a way as presented by intellectual intuition. This can be made clear with the following description: In thetical judgment, the existence of the referent of the subject term is "posited," in this fact that I *am* (and to be sure, as the essence of all reality in general). If I say *what* I am, that is, that *as* which I determine myself, then I go beyond the pure identity of Being. When I say, for example: "I am sad." But the determination of sadness does not exhaust the content of thetical judgment; I am not *merely* sad. And insofar as this is the case, it holds that the predicate is "inadequate" (*unangemessen*) for the subject (for more on this use of expressions, see Schelling SW I/6: 183 ff., 192 bottom, 220–22). It is, as Hölderlin puts it, only "partly" what the Absolute contains, but for the most part, it is not what the Absolute contains. For this reason, that which is expressed in a predicative judgment is "inadequate" with respect to the con- tent of Absolute Being.)

So, too, again Schelling: In the thetical principle ("I am") a strong identity prevails (Schelling says: "an identical knowledge" [*SW* I/3: 363 bottom]), namely, the absolute sameness (*Gleichheit*) of one with itself. In a synthetic proposition, on the other hand, the subject of the proposition experiences a semantic furthering through something other than itself, namely, the predicate. And so Schelling claims, just like Hölderlin, that:

> Now, if an identical proposition is one in which the concept is compared exclusively with the concept, and a synthetical proposition is one in which the concept is compared with an object different from it, we have to put the task in the following terms: a point has to be found, *in which the object and its concept, the thing and its representation are absolutely and without any mediation one and the same* (l. c., 364).

This unmediated (*vermittlungslose*) identity of subject and object (as an un- mediated identity only graspable by intellectual intuition) (l.c., 369)) is indeed nothing other than that for which the completely synonymous expressions 'Being,' 'positing,' and 'thetical judgment' stand. This is clear already in section 16 of the early *Ich-Schrift*, in which Schelling explicitly adopts Fichte's theory of "thetical propositions." "An individual type [of class] of thetical propositions," he says there, "are identical propositions," like 'A=A,' hence, such propositions like ones in which the subject has only itself as a predicate (*SW* I/1: 218 bottom). "Synthetic propositions" (220–22) are then such propositions in which the subject meets in the predicate something (albeit partly, and not completely) different and thus articulates itself through a plurality of aspects. Now, the Absolute I is an *omnitudo realitatis* (from where, if not from itself, should an alternative-less single being [*Wesen*] attain its reality?). Hence, the synthetic relation of the subject to something other than itself can only be made known as negation, as a partial loss of reality (220 ff.). In Schelling's own words:

> Pure Being is conceivable only in the I. The I is posited as such. However, the Non-I is opposed to the I, so according to its original form is pure impossibility, that is not positable (setzbar) *in* the I. But now it has nevertheless to be posited in the I, and this positing of the Non-I in the I now mediates the synthesis in such a way that it strives to identify the form of the Non-I itself with the form of the I, that is to determine the Non-Being of the Non-I through the Being of the I (223).

Here we have the original form of Schelling's later notion of *identity*: Insofar as something *is* in an emphatic sense, it is absolute identity, entirely and undivided. In contrast, insofar as it stands under a (Jacobian) condition, that is, insofar as it is only conditionally that which it is (its Being is in something else which in turn has no Being without its being part of another, etc.) (*SW* I/6: 195 f.). Put another way: insofar as something is not absolute Being, but rather is relative Being, it just *is* not (μὴ ὄν); it is something which has been robbed from absolute Being. A reaction to this presentation is found in *Programmzettel b* where Isaac von Sinclair attempts to present a sketch of Hölderlin's argument: "Different beings are not different insofar as they are (I posit different beings as non-different insofar as I posit them)" (*Raisonnements*, 281).

The diverse modes of positibility in the I are articulated by the various modes of Being: possibility, actuality, and necessity—each of which are also discussed in *Urtheil und Seyn* in connection with the difference between absolute and merely relative or synthetic unification (*FHA* 17, lines 28–37). Of course, Schelling—unlike Hölderlin—associates the original act of the self-positing of the I (the original thesis or the notion of 'Being without further determination'), not with the mode of actuality, but rather with the mode of possibility. The "original forms of Being and non-Being," he claims, "underlie [. . .] all other (category) forms"—even the triad of the Kantian categories of modality (*SW* I/1: 221). And Being ("Thesis") is "objective-logical possibility," that is, "positedness in the synthesis generally" (225). Actuality, in contrast, presupposes antithesis, and therewith an oppositional effect of the Non-I, and therefore actuality cannot count as original. Accordingly, "Absolute Being" merges with "absolute positability" (226)—and that is certainly not Hölderlin's view. He follows the Kant-Jacobi use of language, according to which Being in its "existential" sense (as Schelling also says (cf. 224)) is not logical (and this means "objective-logical" [224, remark]), but rather something actual (*ein Wirkliches*). Actuality, however, is not grasped by logic or thought but by the senses, by intuition. The transcendence of Being with respect to thinking is founded precisely on the basis of this claim. And it is precisely for this reason that Hölderlin does not associate Being with judgment or a logical operation, but rather with an "intellectual *intuition.*" For only *intuitions* (and within these, only those which contain *sensation)* reach existential Being, such that it "reveals" itself in the original thesis. In contrast, Schelling believes that he can establish the three (concrete) modal-categories (possibility, actuality, and necessity) in the absolute I, only if as he traces them back to their pure *forms* (Being, non-Being, and Being determined through non-Being). He also calls these forms, following the terminology of the Kantian School (due to their strict universality and necessity), logical. Now Schelling, like Fichte but unlike Kant and Jacobi, does not adopt any so-called affection (*Affektion*) produced through independently given sense data ("sensation"). Hence, he must explain those modifications which Kant called the "meaning-acquisition of the categories" (*Bedeutung-Erlangen der Kategorien*) (through the schematism), by the collaboration of the original form, hence, as the effect of a "synthesis," so for Schelling, "*Dasein*"—which, for Kant, was the same as "absolute positing" and as such, independent of all concepts—is merely the "result of the first synthesis" (229, note). In short: the *objective* or *material* which the modal categories distinguish is something derived and minor and must be distinguished from the pure *forms* of the I which exist *before* all possibility or actuality. In this way, it becomes quite clear why Schelling, in sharp contrast to Hölderlin during the same period, recommends that,

> the term "pure, logical possibility" be given up: it necessarily gives rise to misunderstanding. Actually, there is nothing but real, objective possibility; the so-called logical possibility is nothing but pure Being such as it is expressed in the form of the thetical proposition (224, note).

Even the proposition that Kant draws upon for the characterization of the ontological status of pure apperception (*CPR* B422 f.), namely, the proposition "I am," already expresses an impure, empirical Being. For there is modal *Dasein* only within the realm of empirical (or objective) consciousness.[14] So, one can, of course, only speak if one subsumes actuality under possibility and (as in the ontological argument) would like to deduce the former from the latter. Only in his later work did Schelling follow Hölderlin's reversal of the ontological hierarchy of actuality and possibility, and of Being and Essence (Thought).[15]

We need not enter further into this now. It is enough to say that we can prove that in Schelling's work, as in Hölderlin's, the old Kantian distinction between absolute Being (and the positing of existence) and relative Being (as the joining of two nonidentical things through the concepts) is found in the realm of the speculative, in a more developed or expanded way—whereby the most speculative feature is, without a doubt, that which the synthesis of judgment brings into dependence with the absolute thesis (which is at the same time understood as identity). When Hölderlin (and, by the way, Novalis as well) wants to go beyond identity, there is no contradiction with Schelling's thought, but rather just another use of the words (perhaps modeled on Jacobi), according to which identity = synthesis. Even at the climax of his identity system (in Würzburg 1804), Schelling still insisted on the strict underivability of the Absolute from the synthesis of terms which in part exist independently of one another.[16] And he had connected this thesis to the opposed one according to which the synthesis depends unilaterally on the thesis (a view which dates from Fichte). This is a point that Schelling was already concerned about in the preface to the first edition of the *Ich-Schrift*. I quote the decisive passage, which discusses the hierarchy of forms of judgment or categories under one of the basic categories in Kant's table of categories:

> If you consider the matter more closely, you'll find that the synthesis entailed in judgment as well as the one contained in categories is only a derivated one, both expressing a more primitive synthesis which forms their basis (i. e. the synthesis of the manifold in the unity of the consciousness). And this higher synthesis is in its turn comprised by a still higher unity. Thus, the unity of consciousness is not determined by the forms of judgment, but the other way around: the forms of judgment are, together with the categories, determined uniquely by the principle of this unity (*SW* I/1: 154).

This higher (or rather highest) unity, Schelling continues, has only to be presupposed, but not established by the author of the *Critique of Pure Reason*—a diagnosis which fits perfectly with the one that we already know, that Kant had given the results but that the premises were still missing (letter to Hegel, January 6, 1795). The thought of an identical Being (graspable through intellectual intuition) prior to any synthesis of judgment and *Ur-teilung* was one of the first such premise candidates.

I have still to add one thing. There is a passage in the *Ich-Schrift* where Schelling ranks Being even above identity (as did Hölderlin). Whoever considers identity, he explains, as a "proposition" (as being a judgment of the form "A=A"), thereby conceives of it by the means of a *form* of judgment. True, the pure identity of A=A is the "original form" of the Absolute I, but this identity is itself a *consequens* of absolute Being, which is to say, that Being which is not conditioned through any *relata*, a Being-through-itself. In short: the judgment form, 'I=I' does adequately express absolute Being, but it is not this Being itself. Indeed, identity presupposes Being-itself. In closing, I cite the passage that offers support of this:

> The form of identity in general (A=A) is first established by the absolute I. If this form (A=A) *preceeded* the I itself, A couldn't express what is posited *in* the I, but only what is posited *exterior to* the I [. . .]. The I would then not be the Absolute, but rather conditioned (l. c., 178).

According to Schelling, the I would be conditioned by A and its self-relation. However, the I is absolute just by being *omnibus relationibus absolutum*, independent of any relations. And it could not be what it is when conditioned by a relation to an A. For either A is *in* it (given that the absolute I is *omnitudo realitatis*) and then it would be subsumed under the I; or it is *external to* it, and then the I would not be the Absolute-itself.

On Hölderlin's Disagreement with Schelling's *Ich-Schrift*

Our look at Schelling's *Vom Ich* (finished at the end of March or the beginning of April 1795—see *FHA* 17: 149) has brought us to a point in our account of the presuppositions of early romantic thought at which a basic stocktaking is in order. A tendency toward the re-Kantianization of philosophy—even before it withdrew, as Absolute or speculative idealism, "into the realm of nonsense"—is visible in the letters exchanged by von Herbert, Erhard and Niethammer concerning Reinhold's systematic turn in the summer of 1792, as well as in the works of Feuerbach, and even of Schmid and Forberg. Talk of absolute principles is not simply discredited; their Cartesian self-evidence is denied. They require justification. And thus they become, as Novalis says, "principles of approximation," ideas in the Kantian sense, which prove their correctness through their success.

Now, this was by no means the opinion of Hegel and Hölderlin's ingenious friend Schelling. Indeed, quite early on he sought the first principle of philosophy higher than Fichte had, in an Absolute that could be posited equiprimordially as subject and object, and at the same time as neither. He still called it the "I," not least because he attributed to it a knowing relation to itself (at least in the first paragraphs of *Vom Ich*; the conclusion, as we saw, veers mysteriously toward the paradigm of justification through postulates). But even then, "I" signified more for Schelling than for Fichte. It signified a structure that could be detached from the introspection of the human subject and set up as the fundamental process of the entire order of Being. There is spirit not only in self-consciousness, but also in nature. For "spirit, it seems to me, is that which is *for itself*, not for something else—and thus *originally* not an *object* at all, and much less an object *in itself*" (*SW* I/1: 367

note). In this sense, each natural being is not simply a "non-I," but rather a "subject-object," a thoroughly spiritualized being; likewise, human self-consciousness cannot be realized without a natural remainder. In 1796, Schelling writes in Niethammer's *Philosophisches Journal,* in a phrase that, later, will often be quoted: "the external world has been opened up before us, that we might find within it the history of our spirit" (383). "Hence there is something *symbolic* in every organization, and every plant is, so to speak, *the entangled prefiguration of the soul*" (386, 5). Since the publication of the *Timaeus* commentary,[1] we know that as early as 1794 Schelling had conceived the idea of a sequence of stages of nature leading to the development of self-consciousness. But we also know that Hölderlin didn't entirely agree with his friend. The point of disagreement was, of course, Schelling's continuing attachment to the Fichtean philosophy of the "I"—which he sought merely to extend into the domain of nature—and, more generally, to the method of derivation from a highest principle. It is very likely that as he began to write *Urtheil und Seyn* (not before April 1795), Hölderlin already had a copy of Schelling's *Vom Ich.* Schelling's *Vom Ich* is dated March 29 (Hölderlin's birthday, according to the seminary's printed list of students) but in fact appeared only at the Easter fair (on April 5). Two copies of this work were found in Hölderlin's estate. One of them bears Schelling's dedication and seems to be the one that Schelling gave to his friend during his visit to Tübingen in the summer. Hölderlin seems to have procured the other himself. Several passages in *Urtheil und Seyn* are comprehensible only if they are read as reactions to Schelling's *Vom Ich,* as the editor of the text of the *FHA* emphasizes (vol. 17, 149)—for instance, the claim that Being should not be confused with identity, and the claim that the absolute positing of the I should not be understood as the source of the category of possibility, but must rather be understood as the ground of actuality.

Schelling grounds the notion of his absolute I in an "intellectual intuition" (although he later considers a practical justification, like Fichte in the *Wissenschaftslehre,* whose practical part Schelling could not yet have read), and Hölderlin also speaks of such a faculty, as the organ through which *"Being pure and simple"* becomes evident (*FHA* 17: 156, lines 9 f.). Still, his argument leads in a direction quite different from Schelling's. Being—the Absolute—is no longer a content of consciousness, but rather a presupposition that we must necessarily make in order to render the unity of our self-consciousness—which is split into subject and object—comprehensible.

It was, essentially, the discussion among Reinhold's students that suggested this idea both to Hölderlin and to the friends who would soon follow him along this theoretical path.[2] Niethammer was doubtless the decisive mediating figure in Hölderlin's development. (For Novalis there were many other sources. He himself had been a student of Reinhold immediately prior to the decisive phase, and he remained in contact not only with Niethammer, but also with Herbert and Erhard.) Hölderlin, like Reinhold's students and like Novalis, also speaks of an infinite approximation of ("an infinite progress" toward) an idea that can never be realized (for instance in the letter to Schiller September 3, 1795 [FHA 18: 212 f.]). But he has an argument that (although prefigured in a few places, for example by Weißhuhn) is basically new—the same argument that we will soon hear again from Novalis: The objection to the self-evidence of the first principle does not take place only by means of a method which any philosophizing from first principles, that is, the justification of the first principle demands. The "I" is denied the status of a first principle because it stands in a relation of dependence upon a being that is neither the "I" itself nor something merely sensibly given. The unattainability of this presupposition motivates an infinite striving toward its appropriation, and through this striving the Being that was originally lacking takes on the status of an equally unattainable final idea. Granted, Fichte faced a similar problem. To the freedom which he thought of as the real ground of all consciousness, no consciousness could be attributed, precisely because of its status as the real ground of consciousness (see, for instance, the *Vorlesungen über die Bestimmung des Gelehrten* [Lectures on the Vocation of the Scholar] (GA I.3: 36). Since, however, freedom seemed to lie precisely in diametrical opposition to inert Being, it did not occur to him to baptize this real ground with that name. This, however, is exactly what Hölderlin and his friends do, following Jacobi's idea that Being is not a predicate, that it must be intuited and therefore must be thought of as preceding all possibilities of thought. Being is not a possible content of consciousness, as it is a "real substance." To this extent, it can even be called unconscious.

In earlier works, I saw only this second dimension (the priority of Being over self-consciousness) in the arguments of the early Romantics, and believed that in Hölderlin's main philosophical text of this period, *Urtheil und Seyn*, the point was as follows: The unity of our self-consciousness, and the notion of its simple and prepredicative positedness, cannot be explained on the basis of dual form of judgment. If self-consciousness *is*, it must have as its presupposition a "Being" that cannot be characterized by means of consciousness in the propositional form. It cannot even be characterized as "transcendental," for it is, precisely, transcendent.

Now this reconstruction is not exactly false. But is is nevertheless only half of the story. The presupposition Hölderlin invoked with the notion of "Being" cannot really be called a "principle." For "principle" means, after all, a beginning, and from this "principle" nothing can begin. An analysis of the notion of "pure positedness" cannot bring to light any further content, for "Being is not a genuine predicate." This is already demonstrated by the fact that Being's transcendence of judgment can be formulated as follows: Being—

the genuinely monistic principle, the quintessence of all actuality—cannot be adequately grasped in thought. (This is the cognitive gap that aesthetic intuition will soon be asked to fill, a solution Hölderlin shares with the early Romantics and with Schelling, but precisely not with Fichte and Hegel.) *Because* Being cannot be grasped in thought, the adequate scholarly treatment of Being becomes an idea in the Kantian sense. This means that "that which grounds the coherence of the world": "Being, in the true sense of the term" (in the words of the preface to the penultimate draft of *Hyperion*, a formulation that brings to mind Jacobi) will not at any point in time be graspable in thought. And so we can guess what Hölderlin was able to learn from the contributors to the *Philosophisches Journal*, who were skeptical about foundational principles; and we can also see which ideas he himself contributed.

In *Grund im Bewußtsein* (Ground in Consciousness), Henrich demonstrated the significance to our investigation of two theoretical fragments Hölderlin wrote at about the same time as *Urtheil und Seyn*. In the first, the sketch *Hermokrates an Cephalus* (Hermokrates to Cephalus), the unattainability of the highest is construed as something that can be captured only by the notion "of an infinite progress, a limitless time [which is necessary] to approach a limitless ideal" (*FHA* 17: 163, lines 12 f.). Exaggerated enthusiasm (*Schwärmerei*)—or as Hölerlin says, "scientific quietism"—would then be "the opinion that science could be brought to completion, or would be complete, within some determinate period of time" (l. c., lines 14–16). His skepticism about this is the exact counterpart of Schlegel's, as is the characterization of philosophy not as possession, but rather as "longing for the infinite." ("[. . .] *immer / Ins Ungebundene gehet eine Sehnsucht*" [*Mnemosyne*, third version]). Furthermore, the editors of the *FHA* suspect that this is actually a first draft of the *Fragments philosophischer Briefe* (Fragments of Philosophical Letters), which Hölderlin prepared for Niethammer's journal at the latter's invitation (see the letter to Niethammer of December 22, 1795). The choice of the correspondent's name also suggests Niethammer, who was known in the Schiller circle as "the brain"—the Greek κέφαλος means "head" and it was the chosen name for the correspondent of the letters. To be sure, this name, like that of "Hermokrates," also appears in Plato's dialogs (*FHA* 17: 157).

However, in the second fragment, *Über den Begriff des Straffe* (On the Concept of Punishment), we find—this time in a moral-philosophical context—an exact reproduction of Niethammer's or Feuerbach's critique of any form of transcendental argument, and their support of a foundationalist deductive program:

> It is the necessary fate of all enemies of principles that the sum of their assertions winds up being circular [. . .] If they want to avoid this, they have to begin from a principle (l. c., 147, lines 2 f., lines 7 f.).

In what follows, Hölderlin tries to explain how exactly the fact of "moral consciousness" can be related to a principle that can be understood merely negatively—that is, in a purely Kantian manner, as an "infinite" ideal, something never attainable in time. He tries to break the circle by separating the "ground of knowledge [of the principle]" from its "real ground" (148, lines 10 f.). I can, he says accordingly, recognize the principle by means of the fact (in the text: by means of its resistance); or I can, conversely, recognize the principle for the sake of the fact (in the text: for the sake of its resistance). Hölderlin's intuition (not entirely clear from this conclusion) was obviously that the (Kantian) "fact" of moral consciousness serves as the ground of knowledge for a principle (freedom, of course) that must itself be the real ground of the fact (the consciousness of the moral law). Here he follows Kant—who also spoke of a circle in this context—very closely. At any rate, the analogy between the relationship of Being and judgment on the one hand and that of freedom and the moral law on the other is immediately clear, even if 'freedom' cannot function as a semantic equivalent of 'Being.' This also gives us further evidence that the re-Kantianization of philosophy was continued by Hölderlin and the early Romantics along the path indicated by Reinhold's students.

Of course, we have to be clear about the fact that Hölderlin's reflections are only partially original. He relied to a large extent upon ideas that had been, or were in the course of being, developed among Reinhold's students. Novalis, who had studied with Reinhold and who knew Niethammer, Erhard, and von Herbert personally, probably became acquainted with these ideas more directly. Hölderlin, on the other hand, learned of Niethammer's version of the rejection of philosophy of first principles, which appeared in the latter's programmatic introductory essay for his *Philosophisches Journal* only first in May 1795. (Of course Hölderlin may well have seen the text before that time, since he was close to Niethammer, and since the essay had been completed long before its publication. He was surely also familiar with the various other critiques of the project of a philosophy of first principles that were leveled by Fichte's friend Weißhuhn and by Feuerbach. Many of the formulations found in *Urtheil und Seyn*, and in letters from this time period with philosophical content, are clearly direct borrowings from or allusions to these discussions, for which the *Philosophisches Journal* was intended to be a forum (at least until Fichte took it over).) Recall, for instance, his reproach (in a letter to Hegel dated the end of January 1795) to Fichte for wanting "to get beyond the fact of consciousness and into the great beyond of theory."

Niethammer seems to have been the first to formulate the basics of an alternative to Fichte's program for a philosophy of first principles, a program which the more intelligent among the students at Jena recognized as a mere regression to the long-discredited Reinholdian idea of a foundational philosophy. This recognition explains the unaninimity and promptness of the critique of Fichte's *Wissenschaftslehre* that all of them—Sinclair, Zwilling, Hölderlin, Herbart, Feuerbach, Novalis, and Friedrich Schlegel—were able to formulate between spring 1795 and fall 1796.

Let us not forget that these indispensable preliminaries and context reconstructions, however interesting they might be in themselves, are merely a means of clarifying, in the most complete way possible, the context into which *Urtheil und Seyn* fits like a piece of clay dug up by the archaeologist that is the very piece needed to make an ancient artifact whole. We have, in this process, already reconstructed and interpreted every single aspect, and indeed practically every sentence, of this little piece. Nonetheless, we do not yet have a clear picture of the whole to which Hölderlin is adding these parts.

Urtheil und Seyn was first published in 1961 (by Beißner in the large Stuttgart edition of Hölderlin's works: StA IV: 216 f.; we owe this title to Beißner as well; the editors of the Frankfurt edition chose the title *Seyn Urtheil Möglichkeit* [Being, Judgment, Possibility]: FHA 17: 149 ff.) The small but thematically weighty manuscript was deemed inconsequential by Christoph Theodor Schwab (Hölderlin's first biographer), and was given to a manuscript collector. It was auctioned through Liepmanssohn's and ended up in the Schokken Library in Jerusalem.[3] In 1970, it appeared once again in the catalog of an auction house, and this time it was acquired by the State Library of Württemberg, out of hastily raised funds and with the help of diplomatic pressure on competing bidders.

Urtheil und Seyn (as Beißner, the first editor, called the text) was originally written on the flyleaf of a book, out if which it was then torn. Comparison with the first editions has shown that the book could have been neither Fichte's *Wissenschaftslehre* nor Schelling's *Vom Ich*. The logic of the text suggests that what comes last in Beißner's edition—the part about Being—actually belongs at the beginning. Upon running out of space, Hölderlin would have continued writing upon the preceding page, because the text of the book itself would have begun on the succeeding page. If this is correct, then the fact that the remarks on judgment come first in the critical edition, which reproduces the original, is entirely accidental. The little excursus on the modes of Being that illogically functions as a joint between the passage on judgment and the one on Being in Beißner's edition would actually be the end, and the third part of the sketch.[4] The editors of the Frankfurt edition have restored the work to what is now presumed to be the original order.

The argumentation of this short metaphilosophical sketch can be quickly summarized. Being, the traditional and unique theme of philosophy (qua ontology), stands in a relation of tension with judgment, which conditions, epistemically and linguistically, how we express ourselves about something like Being. For while Being is absolute unity (Hölderlin says, somewhat misleadingly, "bond"), "judgment" expresses an original division. We should not, ultimately, allow Hölderlin's formulation to stand as it is. For, according to the traditional theory, a judgment expresses *precisely* a bond, that bond formed by the *copula* between subject and predicate. "Copula" means, after all, "connection." But Hölderlin seems to mean that the *form* of the judgment, which divides the expressions into subject and predicate, contradicts its *content*—for with respect to content, it is supposed to accomplish not a separation, but rather a unification. This is why Hölderlin says that the indefinite verbal expression "to be" (*sein*) expresses the connection of the terms that are then separated by the form of the judgment (he says "expresses," which shows that he's talking about an expression). But of course, the copulative "is" is only an inflected form of the binding Being. Judging means, therefore, what it meant in the Kant school: relativizing—in the relation of subject and predicate—the original Absolute position that we express by the term 'Being.'

Hölderlin could also have picked up the false, though expressive, etymology of the word 'judgment' as "original separation" from Fichte's popular lectures on *Logic and Metaphysics* (modeled after Platner's *Philosophische Aphorismen* [Philosophical Aphorisms]). Fichte gave these lectures—at the request of students overtaxed by the difficulty of the *Wissenschaftslehre*—for the first time in the winter semester of 1794–95, when Hölderlin, Zwilling, and Sinclair were his students. There Fichte, in addition to discussing the binding character of judgment, also emphasized the dividing character of judgment: "To judge means to posit a relation between different concepts [. . .] this becomes clear in the case of contrasts" (*Unpublished Writings*, edited by Hans Jacob, Berlin 1937, vol. II, sec. 469, p. 126). L. c., sec. 508, p. 129: "In the act of judging, concepts are held together; in the original act to which this [act of judging] refers, they can have been either held together or separated." Fichte also calls the ordering (*Einteilung*) of particular things under generic concepts "the *fundamentum divisionis*" (sec. 462, p. 124). Violetta Waibel has discovered a direct precursor of Hölderlin's etymology in Fichte's unpublished writings. Fichte claims that: "Judging (*Urtheilen*), to originally divide (*ursprünglich teilen*); [. . .] is based on an original dividing" (Fichte, *Unpublished Writings on "Platner's Aphorisms" 1794–1812*, edited by Reinhard Lauth und Hans Gliwitzky, in: GA II: 4, 182).[5] Reinhold's *Versuch* (435 ff.) might have been another source of Hölderlin's conception of the dividing character of judgment. There Reinhold speaks of judgment—in an apparently Kantian fashion—as an "act of the understanding by means of which two representations are linked, one of which is called the 'subject,' the other, however, which is linked with the first, the 'predicate' " (436). Subjects of propositions, Reinhold explains, generally stand for complexes of intuitions, predicates for the concepts according to which these are classified. So far, so good. But now, in order to characterize the relation of the judgment to the relata it binds together, Reinhold uses the metaphor of whole and part. In the subject there is a sort of "total representation," in the predicate a "partial representation" (437). In the subject, the unity of the intuitions as such is thought, in the predicate, (at least) one distinct aspect of the subject is "detached from it" (438).[6] After this, however, subject and predicate are "parts" of the judgment: judgment is "understood as the division of a whole into partial representations and a rejoining of these partial representations into a total representation."[7] This corresponds exactly not only to Hölderlin's conception of the structure of judgment, but also to his way of expressing this conception: "The idea of this division involves from the start the notion of the reciprocal relation of subject and object to one another, as well as the necessary presupposition of a whole of which subject and object are the parts" (FHA 17: 156, lines 22–25).

The distinction between unified Being and the originally divided act of apprehension forces us to distinguish between the object of an act of consciousness (in which a subject opposes something to itself) and the non-objective intuition in which Being is evident. Hölderlin, like Schelling, calls this latter "intellectual intuition" (l. c., line 6). As intuition it is an immediate consciousness (according to the terminology of the Kant school), and therefore not one that puts any distance between itself and what it is conscious of. Awareness of this originally united Being is thus not conceptual, for what is known through concepts is grasped mediately (again, according to Kantian terminology). That is, it is grasped "by means of" a concept that it shares with many other objects. Thus, intellectual intuition fulfills Jacobi's condition of the immediacy of the feeling in which Being is revealed. (Were the feeling not immediate, it would be conditioned through other knowledge, and thus no longer knowledge of the un-conditioned.) Kant had said that Being (in the sense of existence) is grasped only through perception, not through concepts (CPR, A 225/B 272 f.: "For that the concept precedes the perception means only that it is possible; perception (*i.e.*, feeling), which gives material to the concept, is the only mark of actuality.") This wording finds an echo in Hölderlin's reflection upon the modal categories. Existence, *Dasein* and actuality are synonyms, according to Kant. They simply express the act of positing. Now if Being, in the sense that Jacobi specified, is supposed to be accorded priority over all conceptualizations, then Hölderlin should give the category "actuality" priority over the category "possibility." And this is exactly what he does, distinguishing actuality and possibility in terms of immediate (perceptual) and mediated (conceptual) consciousness, and saying that the latter is dependent upon the former. (Hölderlin says the opposite, actually, but the context shows that this chiastic structure must have been due to inattention.) Actuality precedes possibility. This distinguishes Hölderlin from Schelling (as we have already seen), who in paragraph sixteen of *Vom Ich* deduces first the category of possibility from the thetical judgment ("I am") and then deduces actuality only out of the antithesis, true to the Kantian ordering and definition of the categories. ("1. That which accords with the formal conditions of experience (of intuitions and concepts) is *possible*. / 2. That which accords with the material conditions of experience (sensation) is *actual*. / 3. That whose connection with the actual is conditioned according to universal conditions of experience is (exists) *necessarily*" [*CPR* A 218/B 265 f.].) According to this, then, necessity is the synthesis of the characteristics of the possible and the actual, or: the actual itself taken up again into the category of possibility, or: as Schelling says, "*Existence* in *all* synthesis" (*Daseyn in aller Synthesis*) [*SW* I/1: 225, 227]. Further, the assignment of the understanding to possibility, of "perception and intuition" to actuality and of reason to necessity corresponds with the Kantian terminology. Hölderlin, however, takes the revolutionary step of extending the [modal] priority of actuality over possibility into the realm of consciousness, giving intuition priority over concept. For this reason, absolute Being can be grasped only by a limit concept of knowledge, namely, intellectual intuition; for only immediate intuition has access to being, an access which judgment, as knowledge mediated by concepts, lacks.

Such an intellectual intuition, Hölderlin continues, must not be confused with the awareness which we call self-consciousness (here again entirely "in accord" [*StA* VI: 1, 203] with Schelling's *Vom Ich*). Self-consciousness is an objectivizing consciousness, like every other—in other words, for the sake of determinacy (*omnis determinatio est negatio*), it distinguishes that which is conscious from that *of* which it is conscious, even though in this particular instance the object is the I itself. However, I-ness and self-consciousness are the same thing. And so it is more than a little odd to identify the I with absolute Being, as Schelling did. Whatever calls itself "I" always does this out of the distance of a relation. And we have to abandon this [distance] when Being in the strict sense of the word, as original union, is at issue. It is also entirely wrong to characterize the original union of Being as "identity." For identity is a relation—even if it is the very closest one—but absolute Being is not relationally structured at all. (One can see this already through a simple analysis of its meaning. For absolute is, as the late Schelling never tires of saying, *quod omnibus relationibus absolutum est*. Being is that which lies beyond all relations and which grounds their identity to begin with— even the identity relation of self-consciousness with itself expressed in the proposition 'I=I'.)

This is particularly clear in the example of self-consciousness (as Hölderlin suggests in the concluding passage). In the object in which I recognize myself *as* myself, the object is not an other at all, but rather me myself. Hölderlin's formulation recalls a familiar formulation of Reinhold, from the *Versuch* of 1789. There he said that it was not enough to define self-consciousness as a representation of the representing subject. Rather, in self-consciousness I must be related to the "*consciousness* of the representing [subject] as [a representing subject]" (*Versuch*, 326).[8] We can use a story told by Ernst Mach to illustrate why this complication of the formulation is necessary. Once, as he was entering a bus in Vienna, he saw a man entering the bus at the same time on the other side, of whom he thought: "What a pitiful pedagogue that is"[9]—not knowing, because he had not seen the mirror, that he was referring to himself.[10] (If Lacan were right about the mirror stage,[11] we would all spend our lives in the same unenviable situation.) For I could perfectly consciously relate myself to myself, without knowing that it was to *me* that I was relating myself. That this was perfectly clear to Hölderlin is shown by the formulation that he uses to characterize the particular problem that we have to deal with in self-consciousness: "But how is self-consciousness possible? In the following way: I oppose myself to myself, separate myself from myself, but despite this separation I still recognize myself as myself in the opposed term" (FHA 17: 156, lines 12–15). Jürgen Stolzenberg[12] has shown that Hölderlin's reconstruction of the self-consciousness problem is essentially identical to Reinhold's (although his solution, of course, is not the same). On the one hand, the "difference between subject and object [is . . .] essential to consciousness"; on the other hand, "in self-consciousness, the object of consciousness is represented *as identical* with the subject." This leads to precisely that aporia which Hölderlin's brief argument lays out before us, and in a strikingly similar formulation: "How is this *identity* in difference of subject and object, which is essential to consciousness, possible in one and the same consciousness?"(*Versuch*, 335).[13] In his *Einzigmöglichen Standpunkt* (Only Possible Standpoint), Jacob Sigismund Beck—taking off from Hölderlin—captured this point well:

> [Reinhold's] theory says that self-consciousness contains the representation not merely of the *representer*, but of the representer *as* representing. This is supposed to mean that in self-consciousness the object of consciousness is represented as being the same as the subject. And one has to ask how this *identity* in the difference of subject and object, which is essential to consciousness, is possible in one and the same consciousness.[14]

Hölderlin uses this problem, formulated preliminarily by Reinhold, in the following way: One cannot possibly see, in the mere intuition of the represented [object], that the representing [subject] in consciousness is identical with this represented [object]. Without some additional information, the objectivized intuition of himself must appear to the subject to be [the intuition] of an other, and precisely not of himself—as Fichte's critique of the reflective model of self-consciousness will demonstrate. An other is precisely an other and never oneself. It is useless to expect to learn anything about what is in principle no object at all from [such a represented object]. If I *know* the other *as* myself, a preobjective knowledge must underlie and authenticate this object-knowledge—a preobjective knowledge of the sort in which Being reveals itself (an intellectual intuition). So the linguistic form in which self-consciousness articulates itself (the judgment as original splitting of subject and object) is in principle unsuitable for expressing the unity of the knowledge we have of ourselves in self-consciousness. The material unity of that as which we experience ourselves in self-consciousness is thus contradicted by the duality of the form of the judgment we use to express this unity. But there *is* such an experience of unity (and not only the duality of judgment). And so we *must* presuppose a unified Being, and we can render the epistemic self-*relation* as *self*-relation comprehensible (and it is indeed self-evident, with Cartesian certainty) only if we think of it as the reflex of this unified Being. (Hölderlin repeated and clarified this thought in a rather long footnote to his literary-theoretical paper *Über die Verfahrungsweise des poetischen Geistes* (On the Method of the Poetic Spirit of 1800)—the Frankfurt *Hölderlin-Ausgabe* cites it according to the opening sentence [FHA 14, 312, lines 19–314, line 36].)

Here, even before idealism spread its wings, the self-sufficiency of self-consciousness is contested, in solidarity with Jacobi. Self-consciousness stands in a relation of dependency to Being, understood as preidentical existence. More explicitly stated (in a play on the famous line by Marx): Henceforth we must acknowledge: it is not consciousness that determines Being, but Being that determines consciousness.

In this sketch of the argument that, according to Henrich's reconstruction, could have been written no later than the beginning of May 1795, we have the first consummate expression of what I call "early Philosophical Romanticism"—not the dismissal of the theme of self-consciousness, but rather its relegation to a status secondary to that of Being. That is, self-consciousness is still an eminent theme of philosophy (indeed something like the touchstone of its ability to perform (*Leistungsfähigkeit*), but is no longer, as it was for Reinhold II and for Fichte, a principle of philosophy. This makes it clear how Hölderlin could connect the elevation of the ground of our consciousness with the renunciation of the philosophy of first principles. For Being is indeed higher than (self-)consciousness (and to this extent it is correct that the ground of our consciousness cannot itself be resolved into consciousness). But self-consciousness can no longer be claimed as the principle of deduction for philosophy. Rather, the transcendence of Being with respect to consciousness forces philosophy along the path of infinite progression, on which Being can never be given an adequate account through consciousness and so a path which can never offer a final interpretation of Being. Here one might recall something Gadamer said (not about self-consciousness, but rather about historically effective consciousness (*wirkungsgeschichtliches Bewußtsein*): "Historically effective consciousness is in an irreducible way more Being than consciousness."[15] This means that Being (or rather, actuality) always surpasses the understanding that we can gain of it. Thus, understanding becomes an infinite task.

In the context of his own and his contemporaries' efforts to get beyond Fichte, Hölderlin's reflection is not nearly as isolated as most have thought. It seems to me, quite apart from the affinity with Niethammer's anti-foundationalist tendency, that its proximity to Schelling's *Vom Ich* is much closer than Henrich, for instance, thinks. Granted, Schelling still calls the Absolute an I and he characterizes it as identity. And in the end he assigns not the category of actuality, but rather that of possibility, to thetical judgment. But these differences aside, both are *en route* to rather similar destinations.

We have, nonetheless, some evidence that Hölderlin did not always see it that way; but we also have evidence that Schelling, at the time of Easter 1795, still ungrudgingly credited his friend with a sort of philosophical superiority. In a later letter, Hölderlin reminds him discreetly of the "confidence that you seemed to have, back then, in my philosophical and poetic abilities" (Homburg in July 1799; StA VI:1, 347). Further proof of this are the words of encouragment Hölderlin bestowed upon his disheartened friend shortly after Easter 1795 on the way home to Nürtingen. Schelling, who at that point had already had his *Vom Ich* published, "complained about how far behind he still was in philosophy"—and could be genuinely comforted by Hölderlin, who had the good fortune of being a guest in the residence of the *Weltgeist*: "Don't worry, you've come just as far as Fichte. I've heard him, after all" (Schelling's son's account, in: *Plitt* I: 71). The consolation is, of course, double-edged. For as we know, Hölderlin believed himself to be already in possession of an argument that took him a good bit beyond Fichte's own starting point with the I, which Schelling, with a new Spinozistic interpretation strongly influenced by Jacobi, was just approaching. We cannot, by the way, take the statement of Hölderlin's philosophical superiority to be a judgment of modesty (see *Plitt*, I: 52 ff.). Schelling was not modest in the least. We known that he began to read the third part of the *Wissenschaftslehre* only in the spring of 1796 (letter to Niethammer, Stuttgart, January 22, 1796), and furthermore that he definitively shifted his predominantly theological studies to philosophical ones only in the second half of 1794. We also know that around the same time Hölderlin claimed to be in possession of an argument that had brought him (in aesthetic questions) "one more step beyond the Kantian border" than even Schiller had been able to go (letter to Neuffer October 10, 1794). The sketch *Urtheil und Seyn* seems to have been written in May at the latest. Only this work, however, justifies such a claim, even though it lacks any apparent aesthetic intention. Of course the same is true of Schelling's *Vom Ich*, just as the aesthetic-philosophical accord of Schelling with Hölderlin also found expression in the so-called *Earliest Program for a System of German Idealism* (although this appeared later), regardless of whom we take its author to be. On December 22, 1795, however, Hölderlin wrote from Frankfurt to Niethammer (who, he could assume, was well informed because of his proximity to Schelling in Jena): "Schelling has, as you must know, become a bit unfaithful to his first convictions"(*FHA* 18, 225; *StA* VI: 1, 191). The letter of February 24, 1796 (again to Niethammer) also attests to a lessening of their intellectual affinities. The decisive passage is the following:

> Schelling, whom I saw before my departure, is glad to be a collaborator in your journal, and to be introduced by you into the scholarly world. We did not agree with one another on everything, but we agreed that new ideas could most clearly be introduced in an epistolary format. He has, with his new convictions, embarked upon a better path before having reached his destination on the worse path, as you probably know. Tell me what you think of his latest things (*StA* VI: 1, 203).

Schelling carried out the idea of introducing new ideas in an epistolary form in his *Philosophical Letters on Dogmatism and Criticism*. And one can muse over the nature of this disaccord. Did Hölderlin mean, in an ironic and self-effacing way, that Schelling had not been satisfied with the "bad" path toward which Hölderlin had led him, and had taken the more comfortable path of Fichtean philosophy of first principles? This would correspond to the facts, and signify the period of particularly intensive association between Schelling and Fichte that found its end only in 1801.[16] Dieter Henrich has, however, proposed an entirely different hypothesis, according to which Hölderlin and Niethammer read Schelling's first work, *On the Possibility of a Form of Philosophy* (from the summer 1794) as a document of Fichtean philosophy based on first principles, and praised *Vom Ich* (in which he claimed that philosophy is based not upon propositions but rather upon practical demands [*SW* I/1: 243]) as, compared with the former, a better way. The note (cited above) that Schelling attached to *Vom Ich* in late fall 1796—as a response to Erhard's hostile review—would support this interpretation. There Schelling explains his work in retrospect as an attempt "to free philosophy from the debilitation to which it would inevitably have fallen victim through the infelicitous investigations into *a first grounding principle,*" and even claims "that abstract foundational propositions at the summit of this science mean the death of all philosophizing" (l. c., 242).

This, however, is a curious retrospective self-(re)interpretation, of which Hölderlin and Niethammer could have had no idea at the time of their correspondence in late 1795 and early 1796. For who could deny that *Vom Ich* indeed takes the absolute I as a "highest principle" (see especially the preface and the introductory paragraphs), and proceeds to deduce from it space, time, and the categories? Neither is it the case that Schelling takes the absolute I to be a mere postulate of reason. It has this status only from the perspective of finite self-consciousness, which, in acting, strives to recover absolute unity (l. c., 196 ff., 232 ff.). Schelling, however, does not postulate this unity (just as little as does Hölderlin), but rather grasps it immediately in intellectual intuition (l. c., 181). I also fail to see which of Schelling's changes of mind Hölderlin would have been willing to recognize (non-ironically) as a "better way" (given that it was not the epistolary form of the *Letters on Dogmatism and Criticism*). And so I still hold (against Henrich)[17] that Hölderlin applauded Schelling for having gone, in his questioning, beyond the relations of self-consciousness and having found there an unconditioned to which not even consciousness, and the unity typical of it, could be attributed.[18] The disagreement could have arisen from the fact that Schelling was willing to portray this transcendence of Being over consciousness less drastically than Hölderlin—and indeed, the more energetically he tried to bring his view closer to Fichte's on the one hand, and to work out the pantheistically conceived philosophy of nature on the other, the farther away he moved from Hölderlin's suggestion. (But I have already shown that Schelling's late work must be understood as a re-adoption of this once-abandoned idea that Hölderlin had.)[19]

One can still ponder whether Hölderlin had even read Schelling's *Vom Ich* by the time of the writing of *Urtheil und Seyn*. But evidence of this is provided, for example, by the fact that Hölderlin explicitly counters an argument that, so far as I know, had been advanced so explicitly *only* by Schelling: that the Absolute, Hölderlin's "Being," must be thought as identity. Schelling himself dated the work March 29 (Hölderlin's birthday, according to the records of the seminary), and it was available at the Easter fair (April 5). For the editors of the seventeenth volume of the *FHA* (140), this actually constitutes, alongside the fairly unambiguous orthographical peculiarity of the sketch, an indication of the date of *Urtheil und Seyn*. For they assume—rightly, in my opinion—that Schelling's piece was "acquired immediately by Hölderlin." Because, "[i]n Hölderlin's estate two *volumes* (copies) of this second publication of Schelling's are listed (see *book list (41)*) (one of them presumably the presentation copy given by Schelling to Hölderlin during the latter's visit to Tübingen, in the summer of 1795)" [l. c.]. So everything speaks for the fact that Hölderlin acquired the second copy himself right after the publication, and that it was with the line of thought in this work that he felt himself if not entirely, then at least partially "in accord."

On Hölderlin's Critique of Fichte

W hen Hölderlin's theory-fragment, which his first editor called *Urtheil und Seyn* (Judgment and Being), appeared, researchers found it difficult to place the piece, not only within the context of Hölderlin's work as a whole, but also within the contemporary theoretical context. However, Hölderlin's theoretical insight in this writing is not as isolated from the context of efforts, made both by him and his contemporaries, to get beyond Fichte, as it has hitherto been held to be. It seems to me that even if we leave aside the opposition to a philosophy based on a first principle, which Hölderlin shared with Niethammer, that Hölderlin's proximity to Schelling's *Vom Ich* is closer than Henrich makes it out to be. This we were able to conclude toward the end of the last lecture.

A different question has to do with how the sketch *Urtheil und Seyn* actually fits in with Hölderlin's own work, and whether we can point to any precursors of it there. After all, there is that letter to Hegel from January 26, 1795. It articulates for the first time an argument against Fichte (and another against Schelling) and appears to have been copied from another manuscript (now lost) consisting of notes Hölderlin wrote while reading the *Wissenschaftslehre*. This note taking habit served to aid his understanding of the texts he read. (We have a similar example of this practice in the notes he took on Jacobi's *Spinoza-Büchlein.*) Meanwhile, Hölderlin had read more than the three introductory paragraphs of the *Wissenschaftslehre*, and relates the following news to Hegel:[1]

> Fichte's speculative pages—the basis of the whole *Wissenschaftslehre*—and also his published lectures on the scholarly vocation will interest you very much. In the beginning I strongly suspected him of dogmatism; he seems,

I dare say, to have been on the fence [between critical philosophy and dogmatism], or still to be—he would like to get beyond the fact of consciousness within *theory* itself, as many of his statements show. This is just as transcendent, and more obviously so, as when the old metaphysicians wanted to get beyond the existing world. His absolute I (= Spinoza's substance) contains all reality; it is everything, and outside of it is nothing. There is, therefore, no object for this absolute I, for otherwise it would not contain all reality. A consciousness with no object is, however, unthinkable, and when I myself am this object, then I am, as such, necessarily limited, even if only in time, and thus not absolutely. And so no consciousness in the absolute I is thinkable. As absolute, I have no consciousness. And to the extent that I have no consciousness, to that extent I am nothing (for myself)—and so the Absolute is nothing (for me). I wrote these thoughts down already in Waltershausen, as I read his first pages, immediately after reading Spinoza; Fichte assures me [the remainder of the manuscript is torn off] (*FHA* 18, 198 f.; *StA* VI: 155 f.).

We first have to remind ourselves of the context—including the biographical context—in which this letter arose: Hölderlin had come to Jena in November from Waltershausen (where he had been a tutor in the von Kalb family, a position acquired with Schiller's help), and he gives the first account of his study with Fichte in a letter to Christian Ludwig Neuffer from the beginning or middle of November 1794:

Fichte is now the soul of Jena. And thank God he is! I know no other man with such depth and energy of mind. To seek out and determine the principles of knowledge, and with them those of right, in the most remote regions of human knowledge, and with the same strength of mind to think the most remote, clever conclusions from these principles, and despite the overwhelming force of obscurity to write and lecture about them, with a fire and an exactitude whose union would have seemed, without this example, a perhaps insoluble problem to wretched me—this, dear Neuffer, is certainly quite a lot, and yet is certainly not too much to say of this man. I attend his lectures every day, and I speak to him now and then (*FHA* 18, 187; *StA* VI: 139 f.).

Hölderlin speaks, in this letter, of Fichte's "lecturing ability" and of the courage "to write down" his "conclusions." Already in the von Kalb house, he may have *read* Fichte's writings on the Revolution, whose publication indeed demanded courage. And he might have *heard* Fichte's first lecture, *Über die Pflichten des Gelehrten* (On the Duties of the Scholar), given on November 9 (*GA* II. 3: 357–367), in which Fichte struck a blow to enlightenment, the establishment of universal rights, and the freedom of speech and action—with just the passion Hölderlin describes. Hölderlin writes to his mother that every day he attends only Fichte's lectures, no others (*FHA* 18, 191). Beyond the lectures *Über die Pflichten des Gelehrten* just mentioned (which he had to break off, because they conflicted with the Sunday church service), Fichte also lectured on the practical portion of the *Wissenschaftslehre* and—at the request of the students—on something with more popular appeal, namely, *Logic and Metaphysics*, based on Platner's *Philosophical Aphorisms* (*GA* III.2: 212; II.4: 38). These lectures took place in the evenings. And since Hölderlin writes about going to Fichte's class in the evenings, we can conclude that he heard these lectures. (There is also a textual basis for this supposition: Hölderlin came upon the idea of conceptualizing judgment as "original division" through Fichte [*GA* II.4: 182].)

Beginning in the middle of January 1795, after he had given up his tutoring job in Waltershausen bei Meiningen for good, Hölderlin lived "next door to Fichte's house" (letter to his mother of the 16th of January 1795 [*FHA* 18, 194; *StA* VI: 149]). This proximity may well have given rise to some opportunities for conversation, and Fichte also offered a philosophical *Konservatorium* (a class devoted to discussion of various philosophical themes) that winter semester (Saturday evenings from 5:00–7:00), which would have provided other such opportunities. In the important letter to Hegel cited above (January 26, 1795 [*FHA* 18, 199; *StA* VI: 156]), he recounts a conversation with Fichte in which he presented a decisive critique of the *Wissenschaftslehre*: "Fichte assures me"—here the remainder of the letter is torn off, apparently by a manuscript collector, so that we can only conjecture what Fichte might have responded to Hölderlin's criticism. But first let us look at this critique itself.

One observes a certain indecisiveness, even a retreat, in the course of the argument. Hölderlin begins with the observation—in solidarity with the spirit of Kantian criticism—that the search for a prerelational I upon which our knowledge rests would be an excessive undertaking, and forgetful of the limits of possible experience. A little later he remarks that an I could in any case not be called absolute if it were seen as an object of knowledge, for all objectification requires limitation. His conclusion is still aporetic: an absolute I beyond the limits of my understanding would be unthinkable for me and therefore nothing. In this he remains true to Reinhold's terminology, according to which consciousness must always be regarded as characterizing the representation of something different from itself. It could not take place within an absolute, if it is part of the definition of an absolute that no subject-object opposition can take place within it.

But Hölderlin's reasoning is faithful not only to Reinhold's, but also to Fichte's basic epistemological conviction. As we know, Fichte also connected consciousness with the condition of a limitation upon infinitely proceeding activity (or with the condition of an object opposed to the one who is conscious). From this it also follows that consciousness must be suspended in anything posited as the Absolute—from which the problem addressed by Hölderlin follows directly.

The preliminary sketches for *Hyperion*—some of which predate Hölderlin's attendance of Fichte's classes, some of which are contemporaneous with it—are also marked by the (thoroughly Fichtean) conviction that consciousness presupposes opposition and that the Absolute must therefore be unconscious. The preface of the *Fragment of Hyperion*, written already in mid-1794, distinguishes "a state of highest simplicity" based on "*the mere organization of nature*" from a "state of highest cultivation [. . .] *through the organization that we are able to give ourselves*" (KTA 10, 33). Between these two points runs the famous "eccentric path." I do not intend to interpret this much-interpreted report (*Prädikator*) once again. Parallel contexts clearly show that the natural unity as well as that achieved through culture—irrespective of its transreflexivity—are not unarticulated: In them there are "in general and in particular" '*essential tendencies.*' The *Preface to the Penultimate Draft of Hyperion* (KTA 10, 162 u.; StA III: 235 f.) also speaks of the "eccentric path": "and there is no other way possible from childhood to maturity." Here also the essential tendencies are present, in this case as "that eternal tension between our self and the world," which will ultimately restore "the peace of all peace that is higher than all reason." The talk of 'restoration' points to an original loss, and this is in fact how it is:

> The blessed unity, Being in the only sense of the word, is lost to us [,] and we had to lose it, if we were to strive for it, to gain it back. We tear ourselves loose from the peaceful *en kai pan* of the world, in order to produce it through our self. We, with nature, are fallen, and what once, one can believe, was one, now struggles against itself, and mastery and servitude alternate on both sides. Often it seems to us as if the world were all and we ourselves nothing, but often too as if we were all and the world nothing. Even Hyperion was split between these two extremes.

Other texts portray these extremes as antagonistic essential tendencies within the unconditioned or love, above all the prose and the verse drafts of winter 1794–95. It is an exciting thought, which remains hidden in *Urtheil und Seyn*, with which Hölderlin takes his leave of the Jacobian idea that the unconditioned, according to the very meaning of the term, must be thought of as entirely free of any opposite to which it would stand in relation—or in other words, relative to which it would be conditioned. We are already familiar with the beautiful iambs in which Hyperion (in the verse draft of winter 1794–95) lets "a wise man" (line 27) free him from his devotion to the modern subject-object schema, and distinguishes a state of unconscious purity, sincerity, and freedom (corresponding exactly to the natural state of 'highest simplicity' of the preface to the *Fragment of Hyperion*) from a state of consciousness ("On the day the beautiful world began for us, the poverty of life also began, and we exchanged our purity and freedom for consciousness" [lines 127–130]). And now the wise man develops a conception of the essence of unity as a structure articulated through opposition that is not only incompatible with Descartes' and Kant's—but also Fichte's—dualistic intuitions, and that, despite its inconspicuous appearance, marks a turning point in modern thought:

> The pure untroubled spirit does not concern itself with material, but is conscious neither of itself nor of any thing. For it there is no world, for outside of it is nothing.—Of course, what I'm saying is just a thought.— The unchecked power struggles impatiently against its fetters, and the spirit longs to return to the unclouded aether. But there is indeed something in us that prefers to keep the chains; for were the divine within us not constrained by any resistance, we would feel neither ourselves nor others. But not to feel oneself is death. To know nothing and to cease to be are, for us, the same.—How could we disavow the drive for endless progress, the drive to purify, refine and free ourselves? This would be bestial. But neither should we presume to deny the drive for constraint, for receptivity. This would not be human, but would be suicide. The opposition of these drives, both indispensable, is united by love. (lines 131–154)

The first verses essentially reproduce the position of the "preface" to the *Hyperion* fragment, reflected in the above-cited letter to Hegel—the report of his experiences in Fichte's class—from January 26, 1795. The unity (oneness, Hume's simplicity) that remains only a presupposition in the self-relation of consciousness cannot itself be consciously thought—this is why it is 'nothing for us.' But this means that it is no longer something that merely precedes reflection (as synonymous with 'consciousness'), but rather a properly transcendent ground of the latter. Friedrich Daniel Ernst Schleiermacher, characteristically, will replace the expression "transcendental ground" with the expression "transcendent ground" in his *Lectures on Dialectic*.[2] Already in 1795, Friedrich Hölderlin and Friedrich von Hardenberg had reached this conclusion, via distinct but closely allied paths. In fact it follows directly from Fichte's critique of the tradition, although its implications are not, in the end, reconcilable with a consciousness-immanent idealism.

Although, as we have said, the breaking off of the text prevents us from knowing what Fichte's reaction to Hölderlin's critique might have been, we do know very well which of Fichte's ideas particularly bothered Hölderlin. The letter to Hegel from January 26, 1795, continues at the top of the other side of the page as follows: "[Fichte's interpretation] of the reciprocal relation

(*Wechselbeziehung*) of I and Non-I (to use his terminology) is certainly note-worthy" (*FHA* 18, 199; *StA* VI: 156). Hölderlin was unfortunately in too much of a hurry to elaborate further. But the importance of this theorem to him—a theorem which also, incidentally, influenced Schiller's *Aesthetic Letters* (Letters 10–17),[3]—and above all of how he planned to use it, is demonstrated by two important pieces of evidence: the above-cited *Draft in Verse of Hyperion*, and the letter to his brother of April 3, 1795.

With his talk of "reciprocal determination," Fichte had transformed the old dualistic conception of a reciprocal play of material and formal drives (with which Schiller also worked) into a monistic concept: In the sphere of the all-encompassing I, which must be seen as the quintessence of all reality, nothing would come to determinacy in the absence of some negation that would allow for individuation: *omnis determinatio est negatio*. The basic idea is simple (and is taken up again in Fichte's conception of judgment): each being is what it is insofar as it excludes everything that it is not. Once I have distinguished from a particular everything which lies outside of it, I have thoroughly individuated that particular—that is, fully determined it—in accordance with the old scholastic definition of the individual as an *ens omnimodo determinatum*. Fichte goes on to specify this determination within the absolute I as follows: the I creates a sphere in which precisely those parts which the I cannot ascribe to itself are occupied by the Non-I—and conversely. The sum of both parts, in which it is always the absolute I that is at work, comes to 100 percent. Fichte also likes to illustrate this reciprocal determination with the image of an infinitely progressing activity [or: an activity proceeding to infinity], which activity, for the sake of its own determinacy, needs a counteractive or limiting activity. This latter exercises a "check" (*Anstoß*) upon the infinite activity, turns it back upon itself and so allows the I to acquire a consciousness of itself (for consciousness, according to Fichte, is always consciousness of something finite, particular). This consciousness is, of course, no longer the consciousness of the absolute I, for the absolute I, as the sphere itself, always underlies the determination and knows no negation/limitation.

Hölderlin explains this basic idea of Fichte's to his thoroughly unphilosophical brother, in the following words:

> I see that I still have a lot to say, but I will stop here because I would like to tell you, to the extent that this is possible in few words, about one of the main characteristics of Fichte's philosophy. There is in man a striving towards the infinite, an activity for which absolutely no barrier is insurmountable, which makes absolutely no rest possible, but aspires to become ever more expansive, ever freer, ever more independent. This drive toward infinite activity is limited. In the nature of a being that has consciousness (an "I,"

as Fichte calls it), this drive it has toward unlimited activity is necessary, but the limitation of this activity is also necessary in a being that has consciousness. For were this activity not limited, not deficient, then this activity would be all, and outside of it nothing. If our activity suffered no resistance from the outside, there would be nothing outside of us—we would know nothing, we would have no consciousness. Were there nothing opposed to us, there would be no object for us. But just as necessary as the limitation, the resistance and the suffering caused by the resistance is for consciousness, equally necessary is the striving toward the infinite, an instinctively limitless activity in the being that has consciousness. For if we did not strive to be infinite, free from all limitations, then we would not feel that something opposes this striving; we would again feel nothing different from ourselves, we would know of nothing, and we would have no consciousness. I have tried to be as clear as possible given the brevity with which I had to express myself. At the beginning of the winter, until I had worked my way into this, the thing sometimes gave me a bit of a headache—the more so as I had become accustomed, through the study of Kant, to examine before accepting what was said (StA VI: 164).

The restraint of the infinitely striving activity—which Fichte also calls a "drive" in paragraphs 6–11, and in particular paragraph 7, of the *Wissenschaftslehre*—is therefore the condition of becoming conscious.

Whatever Fichte might ultimately have answered to Hölderlin's objection, on what basis could he claim that the Absolute could have no consciousness? Hölderlin's argument went as follows: Precisely because the Absolute is not determined by the reciprocal action of the infinite and of the limitative activity, it is, at least for us, nothing—and therefore not a possible theme for any defensible philosophical theory. This last point is particularly important. Hölderlin specifies his critique in a formulation that we have thus far let pass unremarked: Fichte "would like to get beyond the fact of consciousness within the realm of *theory* itself, as many of his statements show. This is just as certainly transcendent, and even more obviously so, as when the previous metaphysicians wanted to get beyond the existing world."

We know, from Erhard's and Niethammer's critiques of Fichte, what Hölderlin is alluding to here. In the announcement and again in the preliminary report of his *Philosophisches Journal*, Niethammer had spoken of philosophers who placed their principles beyond the limit of possible knowledge as "transcendentists," thereby infuriating Fichte. The expression "transcendentism" was at the time common coin in the critique of first principles; Carl Christian Erhard Schmid and Friedrich Schlegel also use it often. On the other hand, since 1792 Erhard had pointed out repeatedly, first against Reinhold and then against Fichte, that a theoretical principle is unfit to be a grounding principle and cannot provide an adequate defense against attack from the skeptic—whereas no conceivable doubt is possible of the apodictic command of the moral law. Once we introduce this background information into the sketch of Hölderlin's critique of Fichte of January 26, 1795, we can see that this critique makes use of the resources provided by the critics of foundationalism among Reinhold's students—resources that were known to him, at least through his exchange with Niethammer.

Of course, Fichte was aware of them as well—possibly through remarks of his listeners and colleagues, of whom a few had been Reinhold's students (e.g., Forberg and Niethammer), and certainly from reading the announcement of the *Philosophisches Journal*. When Hölderlin compares Fichte's I with Spinoza's substance and, consistently, describes it as the quintessence of all reality, he can appeal in so doing to several of Fichte's own formulations, in particular to that of sec. 3 of the *Wissenschaftslehre*, where consciousness is announced as "encompassing *all* reality" and hence as a Spinozistic *omnitudo realitatis* (WW I: 109). This quintessence of all reality would describe a sphere that the (relative) I and the Non-I would have to share, according to the laws of reciprocal determination.

In the first paragraphs of the *Wissenschaftslehre*, Fichte does indeed admonish his readers against the comparison with Spinoza (WW I: 100 f.)—not thoroughly, however, but rather only with the aim of showing the superiority of beginning from the I. This does not satisfy Hölderlin: Fichte's absolute I, he says, is even more obviously transcendent than the substance of the dogmatic metaphysicians. For precisely when the I, a term with the connotation of consciousness, is placed in the position of a first principle, it becomes clear that it, as absolute, is as much beyond the limits of consciousness as Spinozistic substance. And to the extent that there can be no consciousness of the absolute I, to that very extent its employment as a principle of all knowledge rests upon a transcendent speculation.

When Fichte was confronted with this accusation he was already on the way toward a correction in his system. Fichte no longer wanted to get beyond the "fact of consciousness" within the frame of *theory* itself—as one had to conclude if one was familiar only with the first three (or even four) paragraphs of the *Grundlage*—rather, he now wanted to get beyond the "fact of consciousness" and into *praxis* (secs. 5–11). The Absolute is now no immediate possession of some epistemic capacity (some sort of intellectual intuition); rather, it appears as a Kantian idea, something we can only approach, through an infinite striving directed by the moral law. With this correction—which he never made explicit—the author of the practical part of the *Wissenschaftslehre* comes around, in large part, to the course set by Erhard.

Violetta Waibel has attempted to demonstrate traces of a possible dialogue with Hölderlin precisely in sec. 5, in which Fichte develops his theory of striving. There, Fichte says that the absolute I must go out of itself and posit itself for itself, because otherwise it "would be for nothing" (*WW* I: 271 f.)—a turn or phrase that sounds like an appropriation of a similar idea of Hölderlin's. This is true also of the following more well-known passage:

> The I should not only posit itself [as was required in the opening paragraph] for some intelligence outside of it; it should also posit itself *for itself*; it should posit itself *as* posited through itself. It should therefore, just as certainly as it is an I, have the principle of life and consciousness exclusively within itself. This means that the I, just as certainly as it is an I, must have within itself, absolutely and without any [further] basis, the principle of reflection upon itself. And so we have from the beginning the I in two respects: one, insofar as it is reflecting, and in this respect the orientation of its activity is centripetal; another, insofar as *it* is that which is reflected upon, and in this respect the orientation of its activity is centrifugal, and indeed centrifugally [striving] out into infinity (l. c., 274).

According to this idea, the I fills the entire sphere of the reality posited within it (l. c.). But this is a transcendental idea, to the extent that it cannot be transferred into a consciousness "for itself." For this reason, the I must oppose one part of its sphere to itself. This it does through reflection. As reflecting and reflected it is, however, no longer *omnitudo realitatis*, but rather a finite for-itself, able to make that part of the sphere that is outside of it epistemically accessible only through the schema of an infinite approximation. And this schema is the I as the idea of a "practical need." Thus, Fichte seems to follow Hölderlin's critique, in giving not the theoretical I, but rather the *practical* I, the task of answering the question of whether it actually "contains all reality within it" (l. c., 277). Fichte had indeed shown signs of being convinced, in earlier publications and also in his *Eigene Meditationen*, that the practical I should take precedence over the theoretical. But this thought was not well-developed, and it was obscured by the strategy of using the I as a principle of a philosophical deduction, and in particular as the ground of explanation of all *knowledge*. Knowledge, however, if there is such, must rest upon one *theoretical* principle. And Fichte, with his talk of a "self-positing I," had indeed given no indication that this was intended not as a first principle but rather as a final principle that could be appropriated only by an infinite striving (that is, that could *never* be reached here below).

With this newly acquired information in hand, let us now take another look at the verse draft of *Hyperion*. Its second half does not rest with the claim of a unity above reflection. The highest—unconscious—unity is not opaque, but is articulated. It displays, in fact, two antagonistic drives, in which we recognize the precursor of Schelling's "reciprocal play of hindrance and striving,"[4] also articulated as the opposition of an infinitely expansive real activity and an ideal activity that turns the first back in upon itself. If the Absolute (or unconditioned) presented itself as an infinite striving, this would remain unconscious. If it presented itself as limited, it would contradict its own concept (determinacy requires negation, therefore limitation, therefore conditionedness; but the infinite is *completudo realitatis*). So it must present itself—for Novalis, Friedrich Schlegel, and for Schelling—as an inhibited striving, one that places transitory limits upon itself in order that it may present itself, and then, for the sake of its infinitude, surpasses these limits. In brief, it presents itself as ex-centricity or as ecstatic, as the temporality of consciousness, where "temporal," according to a famous definition, describes a being "that is what it is not, and that is not what it is."

The disharmony between the "drive to progress endlessly" (Hölderlin and Schelling call this "real activity") and the "drive to be limited" ("ideal activity") is not such as to destroy the structure of the Absolute. It is, rather, its very articulation: "The opposition of these drives, both indispensable, is united by love." By "love" we generally understand a cosubstantial relation between beings that are equal in rank and autonomy, a relation that excludes servitude and domination. In Schelling's beautiful formulation:

> This is the secret of love, that those it binds could be each for itself, and yet they are not, and cannot be without the other (SW I: 7, 408; also 174).

In loving, an individual oversteps the "sphere" of its individuality, whose center of gravity seems to lie outside of it. The one who is, as they said back then, "inflamed" by love of the other seeks his or her self-worth outside of him- or herself, seeks to win back his or her own Being, in a heightened form, from the beloved. The one in love, says Schiller, does not desire the other like an object (possessively); he or she values the beloved, as one respects a person.[5] Love appeals—contrary to all dualistic intuition à la Kant and Fichte—to a principle superior to the dichotomy of self and other, one that embraces both equiprimordially, without sacrificing one or the other to the "God ruling within us."[6] Rather, the lovers experience the bond encompassing both as "God in us."[7]

With this speculative conception of love, an entirely new notion of the essence of identity also comes into play, again with no apparent counterpart in *Urtheil und Seyn*. Since it was first developed in connection with the structure of self-regulating beings (i.e., of organisms), the high degree of distinction allotted to the concept of nature as a thoroughly organized being (*Wesen*) in this regard is also essentially comprehensible. Hölderlin and Schelling go farther, however: not only nature as a whole, but also the mind, is organically structured. It consists of the absolute identity of the real and the ideal. And this identity articulates itself as the complete equiprimordiality of identity and difference. This formula, (normally, if also unjustly) associated with Hegel, is an attempt to express above all the following: in contrast with a tautology (where one and the same thing is simply reiterated, A=A), identity is a genuine relation, and thus nontrivial. It is represented by: A=B. "How (to use a very convenient example) one man who has two names is nonetheless one and the same man" (*SW* I: 6, 501, sec. 270)—an example that reminds us of Frege's Venus, specified differently by the terms morning star and evening star, but neither deprived of its identity nor, as evening star, trivially identical with the morning star. (In fact it took thousands of years for humanity to become aware of this identity. Schelling would say: it took tens of thousands of years for humanity to grasp its identity with nature in a nonreductive way—that is, neither realistically nor idealistically.) The same is true of absolute identity—it identifies two semantically distinct things: the real and the ideal, the infinitely progressing activity [or: activity progressing to infinity] and the limiting activity. This difference nevertheless remains virtual in the womb of the Absolute, becoming actual only when one disregards the bond that unites the two. This means: two terms only virtually opposed to one another can subsist together, since that which is able only to be real, but is not, cannot displace that which is able only to be ideal, but is not. Only when the moments are realized must one displace the other and determine it as its predecessor or its follower. Considered apart from the bond of "substantial identity," the real sets itself in opposition to the ideal and only as a result of this activated relativity can the world actualize itself as finite and temporal reality that is opposed to the Absolute.[8]

Nevertheless, Hölderlin's philosophy of love could not typify a philosophy of *absolute* identity, if its Absolute did not contain within itself that which it is not: relativity, the difference of separate essential tendencies. Relativity proves to be, on the one hand, a moment within the structure of the Absolute—for whatever *Being* relativity has is nothing but the presence of the whole in the part, and the whole is precisely the complete indifference of difference and identity. The structure of the Absolute is thus connected with that of the organism, which, in an analogous way, includes within itself that which is opposed to it: mechanism. (This organic structure of the Absolute is explained especially beautifully in Hölderlin's letter to Sinclair from Bad Homburg, December 24, 1798.)

One thing, of course, remains ambiguous and indistinct in the poetic sketches of this philosophy of love. The identity whose seamlessness guarantees that the relation between the endlessly striving and the limiting activity is a genuine self-relation, cannot be understood on the basis of the sheer duality of the reflecting and the reflected: it remains a presupposition, not a claim, of reflection (a demand that reflection makes upon *praxis*, Sinclair would say). Still, we can, and indeed must, ask whether this conception of love is compatible with the thought of the absolute unarticulated unity of

Being. In *Urtheil und Seyn* there is no such suggestion. Of course Hölderlin does claim that Being expresses the highest "bond"—a bond could not very well be called unarticulated. Sinclair, however, distinguishes in Manuscript A (of *Philosophische Raisonnements*) between union (*Einigkeit*) and the mere unity of the I (*Ich-Einheit*): unity is an oppositional term opposed to multiplicity. For this reason Being cannot be unity, but only union: non-distinctness of the I and the Non-I (which are divided only conceptually, not in reality). This is quite a different thought from that of the suppression of manifoldness through unity. In union there is no "despotism," no "one-sidedness," no "subjugation" (*Raisonnements*, manuscript B: 267, and 274[4]). For this reason alone Sinclair is (with *Hyperion*) able to call Being "peace."

Hölderlin himself became concerned with finding a solution to this difficulty, apparently in May 1795, a few months after the draft in verse. I shall try to sketch the essence of that argument called, in the Frankfurt edition of Hölderlin's Works, *Seyn, Urtheil, Möglichkeit* (Being, Judgment, Possibility).

Kant had identified judgment with the activity of thought, following Rousseau's *Savoyard Vicar*. Each judgment is in the service of a synthetic unity, for to judge is to connect a subject term and a predicate term to one another, so that if the proposition formed thereby is true, one knows what the fact of the matter is about, the object that it indicates. (Analytical judgments either presuppose previous syntheses or are tautologous, like the judgments of logic, which rest solely upon the principle of noncontradiction.) Now Hölderlin, still following in Kant's footsteps, interprets the expression 'judgment' to indicate an original division (the German term for judgment, 'urteilen,' can be broken up into 'ur,' which means 'original,' or 'primitive' and 'teilen,' which means 'to divide'), according to a widespread, if incorrect, etymology. Something that was considered as one is analyzed into two members or *relata*, whose relation at once conceals and reveals the original unity. This relation *reveals*, because in a judgment two distinct representations are bound together, and so connected with a unity that makes possible this [binding together]; but it also *conceals*, for the unity appears not as such, but only as the distinctness of two classes of representation (articulated in subject terms and in concepts) that refer to one another. Hölderlin then applies this basic observation to the particular case of the judgment 'I am I.' Here also there is a differentiation; an original division separates the *relata* (for otherwise the determinacy of that which is judged would be submerged). This happens, of course, in such a way that the *content* of the judgment contradicts its *form*. What is expressed in and by the judgment is precisely the non-distinctness of the *relata*; the *form* of the judgment consists, however, in distinguishing these non-distinct terms. Hölderlin draws the following conclusion from this observation: if, on the one hand, I can gain no knowledge about a state of affairs unless I make a judgment about it (which means depriving it of its absolute identity); and if, on the other hand, a judgment must refer to an underlying, no longer relative, identity in order to be a relation (of something to something else, e.g., of the I to itself); then the synthesis that takes place in judgment must be distinguished in the sharpest possible way from a prejudgment-like and nonrelative unity. Hölderlin, like Spinoza and Jacobi, calls this unity "Being." Being lies beyond the relative identity of which Fichte spoke. It cannot be thought (for to think is to judge, and to judge is to differentiate), and yet I cannot dispense with it, for without postulating a grounding unity of the terms of the relation, the factual and evident experience of 'I am I'—as the identity of the I—would have to remain unexplained.

Strictly speaking, it is not only the preidentical unity that is underivable from relations of judgment. Hölderlin assumes that self-consciousness is possible only through the fact that "I oppose myself to myself, separate myself from myself, but despite this separation recognize myself as the same in the opposition" (FHA 17: 156, lines 13–15). In other words: not only the *fact* of the sameness of subject and object remains unclear according to the reflexive model of self-consciousness, but also and in particular the *consciousness* that in the other (of myself) I am dealing *not*, in fact, with another, but *with myself* ("as one and the same"). (For it is, after all, possible that the subject and object in self-consciousness be the same, without this sameness being present to consciousness—just as a person properly identified as X can know regarding X that he is thus-and-so without thereby knowing that he stands in a knowledge relation *to himself*.)[9]

This is the initial idea that, in my opinion, expresses the basic conviction common to the early German Romantics. It consists in the supposition that Being—as the simple seamless sameness (*Einerleiheit*), in contrast to the identity of the Kantian-Fichtean *cogito*—cannot be understood on the basis of the relations of judgment and reflection, all of which are occupied with reuniting original divisions and can always merely presuppose an original simple unity. Hölderlin's critique of Fichte consists, therefore, in the fact that he opposes, in the sharpest terms, "intellectual intuition" (as he calls it) to the act of judging and thus to the determinate consciousness of something.

The formula for intellectual intuition (in Fichte's sense) does indeed fall short of the radicality of this reflection, for it actually articulates a supposedly immediate unity in a mediated way: through a duality of concepts (intuition/intellection). Now, a duality could perhaps bear witness to a unity, but only under the circular presupposition that an immediate awareness of this unity is already present before the original division. If awareness is connected with consciousness, however, then one must go further still: there can in principle be no consciousness of the absolute unity that is at work only mediately in the play of reflection.

Hölderlin presents this objection more distinctly and in greater detail in a long footnote to his paper, *Über die Verfahrungsweise des poetischen Geistes* (On the Method of the Poetic Spirit) (which was, however, not destined for publication [1800, = FHA 14: 312–314]). Of this, as well, I shall give only a summary.[10] Hölderlin argues roughly as follows: The two basic characteristics of the representation 'I'—its simultaneous absoluteness and self-relationality—mutually exclude one another. For were I-ness bound by the condition of relating itself to itself *realiter*—in the form of a synthetic judgment—then its unconditionality would thereby be denied (it would depend upon a condition; but conditionedness is the semantic opposite of absoluteness). Conversely, one cannot simply renounce the unconditionedness of the I with respect to its presentation (*Darstellung*), for otherwise the moment of having *oneself*, the self-evident feeling of identity and non-distinctness in the consciousness of oneself, would have to remain unexplained, in favor of the distinctness of two nonidentical elements. Therefore neither of the two aspects can be suspended. It must be emphasized, however, that the active self-relation of the I does not *create* the awareness of the absolute identity of those elements bound together in it (but not through it). Yet I nevertheless have this awareness, and indeed infallibly—on which basis Hölderlin concludes that "in the infinite unity of the self . . . a *united* and uniting something *of the highest order*, which [is] not in itself an I reveals itself" (Letter to his brother from mid-1801 [StA V: 419]). Hölderlin soon calls this the "One" and "Being"—as opposed to identity, which can ground only relative (synthetic) relations between *relata*, and therefore relies upon a criterion that cannot be gained from the self-relation itself, but must always be presupposed by it. This can be seen as the foundation of consciousness, but not as conscious (so long as consciousness is regarded as synonymous with reflection, as it is in the entire post-Leibnizian tradition). In this sense, one could speak of the primacy of Being over thinking: the light in which consciousness subsists does not arise from itself, but from a (non-causally conceptualized) ground, which consciousness itself can never entirely illuminate. It can be portrayed as such—as reflexively *unrepresentable*—by the darkness (semantical inexhaustability) of aesthetic representation; therein consists the superiority of the artistic over the speculative mode of expression. This is the consequence Hölderlin draws from the aporia at the end of the aforementioned footnote.

On Isaac von Sinclair

E ven if the footnotes from the *Verfahrungsweise des poetischen Geistes* (Mode of Procedure of the Poetic Spirit), with whose interpretation we ended the last lecture, were not written before 1800, we do know something more precise concerning the content of Hölderlin's thought around 1795 from the so-called *Philosophische Raisonnements* written by Hölderlin's friend Isaac von Sinclair. Furthermore, we also know something more about the aesthetic consequences that he drew from the failure of reflection to epistemically secure the Absolute. Unlike Hölderlin, Sinclair was already in Jena during the Spring of 1794 and belonged to the group of listeners of the first (theoretical) part of Fichte's *Wissenschaftslehre*. Sinclair also listened to C. C. E. Schmid's lectures. Schmid was, at least in Fichte's eyes, Fichte's archenemy. Schmid was Friedrich von Hardenberg's tutor and would have been acquainted with the fate of the *Wissenschaftslehre,* and the discussions going on in Jena about it. Sinclair praised both Fichte and Schmid, above all due to political considerations:

> Their cold proofs, their *Raisonnement* which springs forth from the depths
> of reason and spreads itself out to all the branches of human actions, will
> vindicate the rights of humanity and overthrow all thrones (Letter to
> Prinzenerzieher in Homburg, Heinrich Brühl, from June 6, 1794).[1]

Isaac von Sinclair was from a German-Scottish family that had been in Hessen for two generations.[2] He was born on October 3, 1775 in Bad Homburg von der Höhe, so he was the same age as Schelling and five years younger than Hölderlin. Sinclair's father was a teacher at the estate of Count Friedrich V. Ludwig von Hessen in Homburg, but he died quite young. Sinclair's much beloved mother remarried the Count's chamberlain (*landgräflichen Kammerjunker*) von Proeck, whom the poor woman lost very soon (through an accident on March 26, 1796). Isaac was raised with the two sons (Philipp and Gustav) of the Count.

Next, Sinclair registered for law at Tübingen (in October 1792), but excepting the company of Jakob Friedrich Abel, Schiller's teacher and friend from Carlsschule, Tübingen was much despised by Sinclair. So great was his hatred that he "cursed the place and its people." I take the following passage from a letter that he wrote to his father-figure, friend, and mentor, Franz Wilhelm Jung. The letter was written from Tübingen on December 1, 1793. Sinclair wrote the following:[3]

> The miserable place where I live becomes day by day more unbearable and unpleasant. Lifeless and living objects alike disgust me. Everywhere one sees the reigning ignorance and short-sightedness and the coarse egoism, that is not once removed through even a trace of finesse. Tübingen is so despicable to me that I curse the place and its people.

This harsh judgment is surprising, for in Tübingen Sinclair came to know Hegel somewhat well and to know Hölderlin at least superficially. We don't know whether he also attended lectures on philosophy. At the end of January 1794, Sinclair transferred to Jena, compared it to Athens ("Thank God that I am within these walls"), and soon was excited about Fichte's lectures, and (as we just saw) about Schmid's lectures.

Nevertheless, the desire to attend Fichte's lectures was certainly not Sinclair's motive for moving to Jena from Tübingen. He went to Jena, as did everyone else, in order to attend Reinhold's lectures, yet when Sinclair arrived in Jena, Reinhold's chair in philosophy had already been given to Fichte. During the winter semester of 1794–95 Sinclair (together with Hölderlin, Zwilling, and Herbart) became an enthusiastic member of Fichte's audience. The fact that Sinclair knew Herbart is documented in Sinclair's letter to Johann Smidt from October 26, 1802.[4] In addition to his engagement with Fichte and Schmid, Sinclair became involved with a fraternity, becoming a member of the order of the "Black Brothers," created in the spirit of Freemasonry within an already established fraternity. From statements of the young Feuerbach, we know that the members of this order did not always behave in conformity with the strong moral demands of the order: besides wild drinking, there were duels, brawls, and proper beatings with a knobbed stick (*Knotenstock*). This was surely not the motive behind Sinclair's decision to join the fraternity. The members of the fraternity shared with him an enthusiasm for the ideals of the French Revolution. There were other sorts of groups dedicated to some of the ideals of the French Revolution. One of these was the well-known "literary society" or "Society of Free Men," to which Hölderlin, Herbart, Johann Georg Rist, Friedrich Horn, Friedrich

Muhrbeck, Casimir Ulrich Böhlendorff, and others belonged. Sinclair never officially joined this group, but he was a sympathizer. The group admired Fichte, had revolutionary ambitions, and Sinclair was early on, not only enthusiastic about the group, but he was also an active member of it. The fact that Sinclair was not immediately a member may hang together with the fact that the group had more "literary" ambitions, while Sinclair tended to prefer the company of true activists. He enjoyed, for example, the company of figures like the Alcase revolutionary, Jakob Brechtel and Johann Joachim Orthmann, who had signed himself into a registry with the following sentence: "Who would not prefer to honor the death of bloodthirsty tyrants on the altar, rather than living ones on the throne?"[5] For his part, Brechtel, with whom Sinclair had lived during the winter semester of 1793–94, left Reinhold, upon the occasion of the latter's departure from Jena, the following passage in his registry (*Stammbuch*): "*La République française est invincible comme la raison; elle est immortelle comme la vérité*" (The French Republic is invincible like reason; it is immortal like truth") and he signed it: "in memory of a true Sansculotte *qui se nomme Brechtel du départment du Bas-Rhin, l'an second de la République française ou 1794 vieux stile.*"[6]

In May and July 1795 there was student unrest in Jena. By no means would it be accurate to claim that the students' unrest can be attributed to revolutionary motives; their unrest was a reaction against the very reasonable attempts by Minister Voit and by Fichte to dissolve some of the boisterous activity of the student groups, their unpolitical riots, the duels, and their dangerous *Säbelrasselns*. The members of the order took revenge upon Fichte by breaking the windows of his home and threatening his wife by throwing stones. Sinclair (with others) signed a written petition to the Emperor Carl August in Weimar. The petition was yet another measure taken against the attempts to curb the activities of the student groups. On July 19, there were public disturbances in which the hot-blooded Sinclair was said to have played a role. These disturbances, as I said, did not have any revolutionary background at all; they were rather matters between members of the Jena community. Sinclair was entrusted by the order with a sort of spokesman's role in negotiations with the Jena academic senate and the Weimar government. He was accused of participating in the unrest, but this was never conclusively proven. Then, the *consilium abeundi* was given to him, the expulsion from the university (there were even harsher punishments, the *Relegium cum infamii*, which would have forbade studies at other universities too). Sinclair had already left Jena at the beginning of August. He did make sure the dean and senate of the Jena University received a very detailed and passionate letter of justification from Bad Homburg (dated November 25, 1795).

Naturally, more important than all of this activity in Jena is the fact that Sinclair had met with Hölderlin during Fichte's lectures of 1794.

Immediately, Sinclair suggested that the two plan to live together in one of the garden houses in front of the towers of Jena. Sinclair also, in his unique and somewhat violently protective way, suggested Hölderlin as a prospective *Prinzenerzieher* (tutor to the prince) in Homburg (cf. Sinclair's letter to Jung from March 26, 1795). Through Sinclair's arrangements, Hölderlin actually is said to have come once to the Homburg Court estate, but under what sad auspices!

On January 1, Sinclair (much to his mother's liking) began his service for the *Landgraf* and began a steep ascension in his career as a civil servant (from assistant to the privy councillor to the justice councillor and finally to general councillor, like Goethe). The prince must have been very fond of him and had great faith in him. But none of this altered the so-called Württemberg high-treason trial, that is, the process in which Sinclair became enmeshed in 1805 and during which he was accused of making an attempt on the life of the elector of Württemberg. The whole thing was nothing more than an intrigue with revenge as its motive. The accusations stood on thin ground; this was shown when the committee of investigation, which must have had a great interest in the case, did not find any solid justification for the suspicions at all. Just how revolutionary Sinclair's attitude really was can only be supposed; it seems that he had flirted with the rhetoric of subversion rather than with its politics. In any case, the Prince of Homburg allowed him to be the diplomatic representative at the famous (revolutionary) Rastatt Congress, and then in 1802 at the Regensburg Congress.

When in 1796 Hölderlin went to Frankfurt to work as a tutor, and Hegel followed one year later, a circle of friends formed. This circle became the third most important one for the development of German idealism— after Tübingen and Jena. To this *Bund der Geister* (Fraternity of Spirits) belonged F. W. Jung, Siegfried Schmid, Johann Gottfried Ebel, Joseph Franz Molitor, Jakob Zwilling, the priest, Ph. J. Leutwein, Friedrich Muhrbeck, Friedrich Horn, Casimir Böhlendorff and, of course, from 1797 onwards, also Georg W. F. Hegel. Later, Sinclair was to do a great deal to help the sick and disheartened Hölderlin. After the *eclat* in the Gontard house (the love story between Hölderlin and Susette Gontard, the wife of a banker), Sinclair generously gave Hölderlin shelter in Homburg and from there Hölderlin often met with Hegel and (more interestingly) secretly with his Diotima. Hölderlin also accompanied Sinclair to Rastatt (a trip that was joined to the hope of a proclamation of a republic after the model of the French Republic or the recently established Helvetic Republic). Hölderlin was also allowed to follow his friend to Regensburg in 1800. The trip allowed him a closer contract with the *Landgraf* (who is honored in the *Patmos Hymm*). Shortly before and probably in conjunction with the news of Susette's death, Hölderlin's schizophrenia broke out, if it was schizophrenia. Sinclair obtained a position for Hölderlin as chief librarian in Homburg. When, in the winter of 1804–05, Sinclair returned from a diplomatic mission in Paris, he was arrested for treason. Because of his bad state of health, Hölderlin was spared, but he appeared to be terribly frightened by the course of events. When his new "caregiver," the psychiatrist Anstalt took him in, Hölderlin went into a frenzy and cried: "I don't want to be a Jacobinian, away with all Jacobinians. I can walk before the eyes of my merciful *Kurfürsten* with a clear conscience!" When Friedrich Schlegel arrived in Homburg, Hölderlin was no longer presentable. On August 3, 1801, Sinclair had asked Hölderlin's mother to have her son picked up—with a gruffness and coolness, the meaning of which remains a puzzle for researchers. Hölderlin arrived at the Autenrieth Clinic (the Old Burse, where the department of philosophy is currently located in Tübingen) and then stayed in what has become known as the Hölderlin Tower on the banks of the Neckar River in Tübingen, in the custody of a carpenter by the name of Zimmer. Neither Sinclair, Hegel, nor Schelling ever visited Hölderlin there, but Bettine Brentano did. In her enthusiastic empathy for Hölderlin she said that he was "at one with language":

> She [language] gave him her most secret inner charm, not like what she gave to Goethe, through the untouched intimacy of feeling, but through her personal acquaintance. So true! He must have kissed language.—Yes, that's how it goes with those who come too close to the god, she turns them to misery" (cited in Christopher Jamme, *Isaac von Sinclair*, 35).

Sinclair was one of the very few connecting links between the Schlegel and Hölderlin circles. Sinclair went hiking with Schlegel on August 10, 1806, after Hölderlin had already been sent for "treatment" in the Autenrieth Clinic. In mid-September he met with the Brentano's, again with Friedrich Schlegel and Ludwig Tieck (who, for his part, was inspired by Sinclair's dramatized *Cevennen* Trilogy to write his novel/fragment, *Der Aufruhr in den Cevennen* (The Riot in the Cevennen). "All of these men," wrote Sinclair on September 26, to Princess Marianne, "have been the greatest admirers of Hölderlin and place him first among all of the poets of Germany." (Bettine reported most comprehensively on this in her exchange with Günderode, who had, as the neighbor of the Gontard's, the family for whom Hölderlin worked as a tutor, an especially intensive access to the famed poet.)

After great diplomatic achievements for Hessen-Homburg, Sinclair died of a stroke on April 15, 1815 during the Napoleanic occupation. In the meantime, he had become quite a reactionary—raving about old Germany, praising Machiavelli, championing the cause of an old-established constitution with the Kaiser as its leader. (What things can become of those who were revolutionaries in their youth! But one must keep in mind the double disappointment regarding France: first the deterioration of the Jacobinian leadership into a reign of terror [Sinclair, Hölderlin, and also Friedrich Schlegel and Wackenroder had yet to deal with this], and then its transformation into the murderous Napleonic imperialism.) Death overtook Sinclair unexpectedly as he was traveling to Vienna, where he was to be named major of the Austrian General Staff (more precisely, the stroke befell the zealously converted reactionary in a clothing store, where he apparently wanted to find an appropriate suit for his appointment ceremony that evening at eight o'clock).[7] He was buried in Vienna, in a ceremony of reformed confession in the Catholic Matzleinsdorf Cemetery.

Sinclair's main philosophical work appeared in 1811 in three volumes under the title, *Wahrheit und Gewissheit* (Truth and Certainty). Like the *Phenomenology of Spirit* written by his friend, Hegel, and also typical of the generation influenced by Reinhold's turn, Sinclair does not begin with a first principle possessing certainty but rather from skeptical doubt, in order to approximate the position of certainty. Sinclair, with Jacobi, calls this position of certainty, "faith" (*Glauben*). The magic dialectical formula "the uniting of differentiation and non-differentiation" (*das Vereinigen des Unterscheidens und Nicht-Unterscheidens*) reminds one not only of Hegel, but also of Hölderlin's antagonistic tendencies of beings (*Wesentendenzen*) that are united in love. Sinclair extended one chapter (*Physik*) of his main work to create a text entitled, *Versuch einer durch Metaphysik begründeten Physik* (Attempt at a Physics based upon Metaphysics) (Frankfurt/M. 1813). The numerous surviving notes for an *Allgemeine Sprachlehre* (General Theory of Language) were never published.

In the winter semester, Hölderlin came to Jena, along with Jakob Zwilling, another friend whom Hölderlin would meet again in Bad Homburg.[8] Of the three, Sinclair, who had arrived first, was, without a doubt, the one most informed of the entire discussion which was taking place amongst the circle formed by the students of Reinhold and the friends of Niethammer. He also had the advantage of having heard Fichte's lectures on the *Wissenschaftslehre* from the beginning. We have clear evidence of the period during which his notes were taken, for they were written on the backside of a program announcing a concert on December 6, 1795. In a letter dated April 26, 1796, Zwilling reports to a Jena professor (whose identity is, unfortunately, unknown) that Sinclair "who is very strong in the Greek language" had told him "that Prometheus means as much as reflection" that he himself, however, sets our faculty of imagination against "this Prometheus who tore us away from Olympus," "who had brought us back up again" (in Christoph Jamme and Dieter Henrich, editors, *Jakob Zwillings Nachlaß. Eine Rekonstruktion*, l.c., 43)—and these remarks have a place only within the context of the *Raisonnements*. Later, Sinclair revised his hasty and rhaspodic *Raisonnements*, and created a second version, which simply extended the main ideas of his earlier version. Dieter Henrich and Hannelore Hegel, in whose doctoral thesis the *Raisonnements* were first published, have speculated that Sinclair's *Theorie-Skizze* (Theory-Sketch) presupposes knowledge of Hölderlin's *Urtheil und Seyn*. In spite of this connection with Hölderlin's work, Sinclair's *Raisonnements* are more instructive, more conceptually nuanced, and established with greater care and argumentation by Sinclair than by Hölderlin.

The *Raisonnements* present four theses: reflection (whose linguistic expression is judgment [247, 271]) is a separation (*Trennung*), in which a demand for unity survives and is posited therewith as a demand; Fichte's I is not a substance, but rather something in which and through which reflection forms itself; *praxis* cannot be grasped from theory; and the *unpresentability* of Being through reflection makes the aesthetic the unsurpassable expression of that upon which philosophy founders.

Of these theses, the first and the last are of interest to us. In the way that I have formulated these theses, the first thesis corresponds to Hölderlin's conviction that the reference of one thing to another is always (for us or from the he/she perspective) a self-reference, in which, however, the self *itself* can only grasp *its* act in another, if beyond the separation it also possesses knowledge of the ongoing unity *as its own*. Sinclair identified reflection with "consciousness," "theory" ("Consciousness is theory" [270]; "Theory, I, consciousness is one" [247]) or "Form of knowledge" (271), and he must then consistently say that God "[has] no consciousness" (272). If consciousness is always and in principle burdened with an object and if, moreover, it is true that the notion of Being leaves no room for any separation, then it is clear that there can be no consciousness corresponding to Being. In a letter to Hegel dated January 24, 1795, Hölderlin treated this consequence (exhibited in Fichte's talk of absolute I) as an aporia. And in *Urtheil und Seyn* he himself allows Being on the side of consciousness to correspond to an intellectual intuition (which he later, in a letter to Schiller from September 4, 1795, characterized as an aesthetic intuition and distinguished from the theory which reaches Being "only through an infinite approximation"). Sinclair boldly surpasses these final (and completely unclear) theoretical limits and allows reflection to be grounded in that which—precisely because of its uninterrupted unity—cannot correspond to any consciousness at all and of which nothing more can even be known.

> The word "judgment" (*Urtheilung*) contains that beyond which one cannot go higher than this division (*Theilung*): that this division occurs is independent from the I and from that in which the division (*Theilung*) as a part (*Theil*) is thought (271).

In other words: the I is only one part (next to the Non-I) within the structure of reflection, which must be thought as overlapping both parts. Whoever thinks of I and Non-I as 'parts' (*Theile*), thinks of them necessarily as coming forth from one whole:

> For the separation ([. . .] of Reflection) is not opposed to anything and so is not appropriate for the positing of the whole (282).

The notion 'I' corresponds to unity, the notion of the Non-I corresponds to the notion of the manifold. Already for that reason it is clear that the 'unity' represented by the I, as it is opposed to the manifold of the Non-I, is no expression for that higher unity in which the opposition (*Gegensatz*) is dissolved (259, penultimate section).

Whoever says 'I' grasps a certain thought, that is, a thought whose comprehensibility consists in the limitation of at (least) one term of opposition (Non-I). Already for that reason, it is completely misguided to hold the I as a principle of philosophy or to give it priority over the notion of the Non-I. (Later we will see that this consideration was the one which led Jakob Zwilling to the view that the structure of reflection is autonomous, above both the I and the Non-I.) When Sinclair claims that I and Non-I are both "not beyond reflection" (273 bottom; cf. 247: "Positing and separating through the freedom of reflection is no positing, no separating of an I, it [the I] becomes such only through these"), he therewith declassifies their interaction as an appropriate expression of Being: "It consists in [:] the unity is not thinkable for reflection" (216). The expression "intellectual intuition" can now fall by the side. It only throws sand in the eyes of the reader in that, on the one hand it simulates an epistemic character and on the other (also in Hölderlin and Schelling) should be strictly unconscious or over-conscious (*überbewußt*). Here Sinclair creates clear relationships: the ground of consciousness is a Being which is not resolvable in consciousness, because there is nothing other than thetical consciousness (that is, there is nothing other than a consciousness opposed to its own objects).

You will ask: In this radical framing of the problem isn't Fichte's genial insight upset or even more, made obsolete? Fichte had shown that self-consciousness, whose Cartesian certainty is compelling to all as a fact, cannot be clarified through the structure of reflection, that is, through the subject-object schema. And he introduces the expression 'intellectual intuition' only to indicate that unmediated consciousness in which we are factically entrusted with ourselves. Unmediated consciousness in Kant's tradition is called "intuition"; and because it consists in the spontaneity of apperception itself, it is further called "intellectual." Now, Hölderlin and Sinclair remain true to this insight. But they hold the role of 'intellectual intuition' as something completely unclarified. First because in the duality of terms ('intuition' and 'intellectual') the desired unity is only a pretense, it is never realized (for this reason Sinclair claims that "the unity" is posited as "a should" or as a "demand" [272]). Second, because Fichte's whole construction is unillumi-nating. Fichte strictly follows the rule of language according to which con-sciousness equals objective consciousness (throughout the lectures on the *Wissenschaftslehre nova methodo*). On the other hand, Sinclair holds that there is one consciousness that is nonobjective (*ungegenständlich*) (given in intellectual intuition). So we have a fundamental unclarity in the use of the word "consciousness." This unclarity compels Fichte to explain (as Hölderlin had shown very early in his letter to Hegel from the end of January 1795) the absolute I first as self-conscious, then as unconscious, and to distinguish between the 'I as intellectual intuition' and the 'I as ideal,' which can only be communicated (*vermittelt*) to consciousness in an infinite approximation. However, as Fichte correctly saw, the ground of self-consciousness indicates no connection (*Gliederung*) in subject and object and if this distinction is characteristic for consciousness, then it follows that the ground of conscious-ness must be assigned to some ground even higher than consciousness. In this moment the ground is transformed from a transcendental one into a transcendent one. A transcendental ground is the condition of possibility of all that follows from it. In contrast, nothing can be deduced from a transcen-dent ground. A transcendent ground brings the program of a deductive philosophy of first principles to a standstill.

Sinclair is (with Novalis) the first to treat the achievement of con-sciousness as a positing ("Thesis") (268). According to Sinclair, that which is posited by one is the other of one's self (the object or itself as object). Because judgment—as the original expression of the self-division of Being (*Selbstentzweiung des Seins*) or of (271)—consists of such a thesis, Being itself must, in contrast, be thought as nonobjective (*ungegenständlich*) (not as thetical or a-thetical): to that there corresponds a mode of consciousness of the non-positing cogito, "the Athesis" (268). The Aisthesis—which Sinclair indi-cates with an adventurous etymology as "Aeisthesis" or "A Εις (εαυτον) Θεσις" [sic! 254] (ongoing positing, ongoing its-self-positing), is what makes the content of the unposited and unpositable first comprehensible to the positing consciousness. In this sense, "aesthetic reality is [. . .] a self-denial of the I, a rejection of the pure thesis": a return of its raggedness in athetical oneness (269)—which incidentally (once again) should not be confused with unity (*Einheit*). Unity (*Einheit*) (the Ἕν) still stands in opposition to manifoldness (the Παν); athetical oneness (*Einigkeit*) is, however, completely beyond oppositions (*über-gegensätzlich*) (259, cf. 275). This (positive) sense of 'aesthetic' stands in opposition to another: the (Kantian) sense of the sensible world; and then 'Aeisthesis' means the perpetuation of the separations of finite understanding and the dissolution of what is intuited in intellectual intuition into a non-completable (*unabschliessbaren*) progress of knowledge: "Knowledge is always incomplete (*unvollkommen*) for the aesthetic, for insofar as it is a product of reflection, it always presupposes judgment and this makes it impossible for oneness (*Einigkeit*) as enduring to be thought, for the aesthetic ideal to be thought" (269). One observes in this citation the alteration of the second (negative) meaning of 'aesthetic' into the first (positive) meaning, in which the aesthetic becomes an ideal of understanding: it becomes a utopia of sensible, presented oneness (*dargestellte Einigkeit*). In context:

> As soon as one posits the Θεος knowledge (the athetical unity, essence), one makes it into an I (into the absolute I of Fichte). In reflecting upon his highest essence, in positing it, one separates it and gives back to it, after this separation, the character of non-separation through unification (*Vereinigung*), whereby, hence, separation is at the same time presupposed by Being: it is the incomplete concept Εν και παν (268/9).

If separation were not presupposed for Being—which is absolute "oneness" (*Einigkeit*) (Sinclair distingushes absolute unity from mere relative unity of synthesis [e.g. 271, 9], then this could not be read as "the proposition: I am I" (282). In order to find myself and not merely others in other *Relata*, that oneness (*Einigkeit*) which was denied for the sake of the judgment form, must survive in the postulate form ("reflection of limits is only possible under the presuppositions of unity as a should (*ein Sollen*) (269, cf. 272). In other words, insofar as the (material) unity (*Einheit*) of Being in the *form* of (judicative) separation cannot as such be claimed, it becomes something that can only be postulated (it becomes a demand to be met). For this demand there must, however, be a rational motive in the structure of self-consciousness; and this motive is the factical knowledge of myself as a unified (not a divided) being (*Wesen*).

Sinclair, like Weißhuhn, Niethammer, and Feuerbach, rejects Jacobi's recourse to "feeling," which would be given to absolute oneness (*Einigkeit*) as such (270, 10). That would mean: to go beyond consciousness to transcendent explanation (l.c. and 273). Philosophy cannot go beyond reflection and that which is presented in it "as reaction" (the impressions which seem to stem from the Non-I and which are probably processed by the I). That does not prevent philosophy, as a result of the relative unity (*Einheit*) of self-consciousness, from possessing a motive for its "demand" for absolute oneness (*Einigkeit*); and so the justificatory ground of the oneness (*Einigkeit*)-postulate lies in the fact that, "reflection [. . .] reflects upon itself" (273). So it recognizes the laws of form, which prevent philosophy from grasping the notion of the Absolute at once with the insight of the undeniability of the Absolute as an established presupposition: "The demand of unity (*Einheit*): so it appears in reflection and so it takes on trascendent theory independently of reflection" (259).

> [T]ranscendental reflection [. . .] does not demand consciousness in order to establish consciousness: it does indeed feel the necessity of this demand, but because this demand once led reflection away from consciousness, reflection also abandons the form of consciousness and no longer separates or posits consciousness against it (273).

Of the demanded unity (*Einheit*) it holds, therefore, that it must be left to stand symbolically by the aesthetic; but by philosophizing reflection it must be left to stand as something transcendent or, what amounts to the same, this demanded unity can only be reached through an infinite approximation, which is to say, it can never by reached at all. This unreachability of pure Being, of "peace higher than all reason," which accordingly—precisely as in Hölderlin—is a necessary presupposition of that whole whose part is subject and object, and is exactly that which makes the thought of Being into a mere "demand" (and one that will never be met).

> [The proposition: I am I] contains, Should is higher than *Dasein*: oneness (*Einigkeit*) is, but reflection destroys it immediately, and nothing is left but an infinite task (261).
>
> What is the result of the investigations of certainty? That its demand presents an infinite task whose satisfaction, if one were to seek it, would contradict itself: one would, namely, want to posit something for an I, that was not posited for an I (275).

On the basis of the demand and on the strength of it alone, the necessary connection survives for reflection itself (actualized in separations and contrapositings). This connection really survives in the subject and object of self-consciousness, which judgment misrepresents ("in that in each separation I am made aware of the demand posed by the infinite" [282]). Therewith it is also clear that Sinclair must depart from a philosophy based on first principles: "The highest ideal (so that at which the demand is aimed) is not the highest principle" (267), but rather a final idea.

Sinclair was passionately interested in theories of truth and certainty. The title of his main philosophical work of 1811 indicates this. If I am right, he was also inclined (as were Niethammer and Schlegel) toward a sort of probabilistic coherence theory of truth. Truth is not discernable from a highest principle, but rather from "agreement with all propositions." Because I cannot proceed from a first principle, I don't know in advance "whether a proposition is true," for to know that "I must compare it to all of infinity" (l.c.). This compels philosophy to a hypothetical-deductive method. With this method, a proposition is taken and then one seeks to clarify it from a first hyposthesis. The method goes on, driven by the *Fakten*, getting eventually to "a second hypothesis" (277 f.) and so on. Only through a continually increasing establishment of context (*Zusammenhang-Stiftung*) can it make its assumptions probable.

Hölderlin referred the semantics of the term 'judgment' to the faculty of judgment, which Kant had understood not as an absolute positing but rather as a relative positing (as the relation of a subject to a predicate). But in Hölderlin's work too, in addition to the judicative meaning, another conceptual component manifests itself. Judgment 'divides,' that is, it breaks the original subject-object unity into parts. This (non-judicative) sense of 'judgment' is even clearer in Sinclair's work. It leads to that which, "in the division is thought as a part" (271), to the unwhole (*Unganze*). Because, however, that which *is*, is everywhere only one, a part *is* in the demand for a reinstated completion (*Wiederergänzug*) and independent of this demand, this Being is merely appearance, a thought-thing (*Gedankending*), an image of reflection, indeed a μὴ ὄv (cf. 281). Sinclair claims that "reflection and its separations are something that appear, but not something that are (*etwas seiendes*) and are something which should not be" (276). He also claims: "Those things which are different are not different insofar as they are. (I posit those things which are different as not different insofar as I posit them)" (281).

Sinclair, however, also adopts Hölderlin's meaning of copulative Being (in judgment) as an imperfect product of absolute Being and therewith indirectly adopts Kant's distinction between absolute and relative Being. Insofar as he allows the copulative word in a predicate judgment to be a sign of truth, he can mean, like Kant, that it stands for the actuality of the expressed and distance it is therewith from illusion (*Schein*). Illusion (*Schein*) would be separation, "actuality [. . .] is oneness (*Einigkeit*)." "Even when I say this is really the table, there are not two (different) things, they are through the relationship one (the same)" (l.c.). Truth itself should, therefore, be made clear from the notion (not of unity (*Einheit*) opposed to manifoldness, but certainly) from oneness (*Einigkeit*). And this goes together with the apprehension of truth as coherence and knowledge as an infinite progression. In order to convince one's self of this, one need only substitute '*Einigkeit*' with 'should' ("What happens when reflection occurs? *Einigkeit* is posited as a should" [272]). And then I come easily to the demand "that truth should be" (279). Underlying reflection, which is interweaved with separations, is the task of overcoming the separations, negating illusion (*Schein*) and so making free a view of the truth which should stand alone. (In the *Fichte-Studien*, Novalis develops an amazingly similar theory of truth and illusion [*Schein*].)

We will turn to Novalis during our next meeting—not without first taking a look at the theory-sketch (*Theorieskizze*), *Über das Alles* (On the All), by Jakob Zwilling, a friend of both Sinclair and Hölderlin.

Lecture 8

On Jakob Zwilling's *Über das Alles*

We have prepared a "constellation portrait" of Hölderlin's sketch *Seyn und Urtheil* and also discussed the *Raisonnements* by Hölderlin's friend Isaac von Sinclair (to do him justice, we must acknowledge that they are argumentatively less crude and in the details more pointed than Hölderlin's all too brief sketches). Now, we must turn our attention to the third of the group (who later showed up in the 'Brotherhood [*Bund*] of spirits' in Homburg and fruitfully continued the discussion begun in Jena).

I am talking about Jakob Zwilling. He was born on September 12, 1776 in Bad Homburg—so he was one year younger than Sinclair and Schelling; six years younger than Hölderlin and Hegel.[1] Zwilling was the oldest son of Christian Zwilling, a *landgrafliche Hofprediger* who later became *Oberhofprediger* and *Konsistorialrat* and his wife Marie Sara, née Weiker. Zwilling's father shared a close relationship with the *Landgraf*, and he was appreciated not only in his capacity as *Hofprediger*, but also as his constant advisor, mentor, and dialogue partner. This constellation explains Zwilling's early contact with Sinclair, who was raised and educated with the children of the *Landgraf*. On September 29, 1794, Zwilling traveled to Jena where he matriculated one week later. (Zwilling, like Hölderlin, did not attend Fichte's lectures on the first, theoretical part of the *Wissenschaftslehre*.) We don't know what or where (other than with Fichte) Zwilling studied. We do know that he first left Jena in the fall of 1795 (after Hölderlin and Sinclair had left). The next winter he wrote to the crown prince and asked for a place in his regime (the *Chevauxlegerregiment* Modena, which then, as was so nicely expressed, "stood" in Poland). The *Landgraf* himself supported the request and a few months later the prince did indeed appoint the young Zwilling for a position that had been made available. On May 18, 1796, Zwilling traveled from the area of

Lublin in order to enter as a cadette in the brigade. On October 12 he notified his father of his promotion to second lieutenant. This time he returned at year's end and was back in Bad Homburg by early 1797. "This must be the time at which the *Bund der Geister* formed between him, Sinclair, Hölderlin, and Hegel, who since January (as *Hofmeister* for the wine merchant Gogel) had been in Frankfurt" (L. Strauß. 371). Zwilling, who was always moving from place to place in order to serve his brigade, accompanied (together with Hölderlin) Sinclair on his trip to the Rastatter Congress from December 1799 to January 1799. Friedrich Muhrbeck (also a member of Fichte's audience in Jena and later a professor of philosophy in Greifswald) was introduced to Zwilling. Sinclair wrote to Hölderlin that Muhrbeck was "completely enchanted by him [Sinclair]"(372). In the time during which these letters were written, there is talk of a summer spent together in Homburg, which "would mark an epoch in our life" (Sinclair to Muhrbeck, Rastatt, January 19, 1799, cited in Strauß, 373, the "our" refers to: Zwilling, Sinclair, Hölderlin, Fritz Horn [also a Rastatter acquaintance] and Friedrich Muhrbeck). Yet because of the constant draft calls and a dangerous illness suffered by Zwilling, nothing came of this plan to pass a summer together; only letters testify to the ongoing, intense friendship, especially with Sinclair. In wars there are deaths: Zwilling was killed on July 6, 1809 in the Battle of Wagram, he had reached the level of first riding master (*Premierrittmeister*) and squadron commander (*Eskadrons-Kommandant*). In the end, he was a Napoleon enthusiast, as Hölderlin had been (to be more accurate we should say that he was an enthusiast of General Bonaparte of the French Revolution). Napoleon had been the arch enemy of the *Landgraf*. For this reason, Zwilling's evening raid on Napoleon's camp before the battle must have seemed even more ambivalent. The brigade "belonged" to the brother of the crown prince, whom Zwilling, in a premonition of his death, had appointed as his universal heir. The crown prince wrote this of Zwilling's death:

> The regiment of my brother has been almost eliminated on the 6th, among others the poor Zwilling was killed; it is in every respect a pity: he was a brave and insightful officer. The manner of his death was quick but terrible for the ones around him; an entire *Kartätschen-Büchse* hit his body and only there the bullets separated, so that they exited his body again (cited in Strauß, p. 381).

And one year later, on August 16, 1810, Sinclair wrote to Hegel (on the occasion of the announcement of his main philosophical work, *Wahrheit und Gewißheit*):

> [I hope] to agree with you in most of the results. Thus, it would make me glad if this bond of truth would further strengthen that of our old friend-

ship, for the others are no longer with us [the poor mentally disabled Hölderlin in the tower of Tübingen thus no longer counted as alive for Sinclair] and from those who shared our vision of the truth, you alone have remained to me. For I must tell you that Zwilling has been killed in the battle of Wagram on the second day. He was head squadron of the hussars of the division Hessen-Homburg, was to become major and had the greatest expectations [for the future]. In the army, he was known as one of the most able and brave officers and had led several *coups* for himself. In the battle he remained in the most dangerous place on the left wing where his regiment lost two thirds of their officers and men. A *Kartätschen-Büchse* burst in his side and even injured those around him. Yet he still lived a few minutes and when he had fallen off his horse and the hussars had picked him up and carried him away from the front line, he still conversed with them to the end and said that they should only put him under the earth, alive or dead, so that the enemy when advancing would not find one additional Austrian officer. He had had an intimation of his death, had made his will only two days earlier, so that I would be returned a debt that he had with me, and on the evening of the first battle he said that he would not survive the next day. That same night he attacked the Saxons with his division, which alarmed the whole camp and almost provoked an entire derouting and made Napoleon himself take to his horse. All these circumstances I have from the best sources (cited in Strauß, p. 382).

From Jakob Zwilling's literary remains, it seems (according to the information at that time) that all we have is the thirty page outline, *Über das Alles* (in Ludwig Strauß, *Jakob Zwilling und sein Nachlaß*, l.c., 390–2; reprinted in: Henrich/Jamme, editors, *Jakob Zwillings Nachlaß in Rekonstruktion*, l.c., 63–65). From the notes of a letter to a professor in Jena (whose name, unfortunately, we don't know; was it Schmid, Niethammer, or perhaps even Fichte?), Ludwig Strauß prepared a few excerpts and a sort of table of contents for the short piece:

These outlines (from the 26th of April 1796, writes Strauß) polemize against Fichte's *Wissenschaftslehre*, above all against the concept of the absolute I. The primacy of relation, the rejection of the isolation of a concept from the relation to its counter-concept, the tendency toward symmetry, are already well-defined here. With the positing of the relation between I and Non-I as impenetrable, Zwilling accomplishes–before Schelling's philosophy of nature—a new expression of Fichte's subjective thought, not an objective one, but rather a synthetic expression, as Hölderlin had attempted to do since his departure from Jena, but had only first formulated later in a letter to Sinclair from the 24th of December 1798. In this letter he writes: "Each result and product is the result of the subjective and objective, of the individual and whole." And in the essay, *Über die Verfahrungsweise des poetischen Geistes*, especially in the sentence: "It is in vain that humans seek to attain their determination in an overly subjective condition as well as in an overly objective condition, and this accounts for the fact that humans recognize themselves as unity in the divine, and containing that which is opposed to harmony, and they also recognize, inversely, the divine, the one (*Einige*), opposition to harmony in themselves as contained in unity." Here as everywhere in Hölderlin's philosophy it is also clear how much the principle of "equilibrium" suited him. But Zwilling's outlines from the 26th of April also touch upon the notions that were of decisive interest to both Hölderlin and Schelling: for example, the conclusive place of the aesthetic within philosophy. In Hölderlin's case, this was expressed, after long preparation, in letters written to his brother in March and June 2, 1796 and in the preface to *Hyperion* of 1796. In systematic context, we find the notion outlined in the text that Franz Rosenzweig (who discovered the text) has rightfully attributed to Schelling, the so-called, *Earliest Program for a System of German Idealism*. As there, in Zwilling's work imagination is granted a key role, as there, the "aesthetic perspective" is the highest one. The "one," which is only given to feeling (*Empfindung*), and "separation" which is accomplished by "reflection," meet in it. At the same time, however, a very notable critical demarcation of the aesthetic is given. Namely, only from that meeting can the aesthetic be determined according to its form, but in no way according to its content and is "therewith closed within its principle"; "for the attempt [,] to penetrate its content would result in an oscillation, which would consist in an infinite over-leaning towards either feeling or reflection and so would be now a theory of feeling (*Gefühl*), now a logical analysis, from which the rules of art are general proofs." At the end of the letter he writes: "Whenever I look at the *Wissenschaftslehre,* I am pleased by the sumblime thoughts concerning the imagination. Sinclaire [*sic*], who is very strong in the Greek language [in the original version of the letter, Zwilling writes "*Griechischen*" as "*Grigischen*"[2]], tells me that Prometheus means reflection; in contrast to this Prometheus which tore us away from Mount Olympus, I place imagination as that which has reinstated us there." Hence [adds Strauß], Zwilling had philosophical conversations with Sinclair, and in all likelihood with Hölderlin as well. Hölderlin surely discussed the notion of the primacy of the beautiful with Schelling, and probably with Sinclair and Zwilling as well. At the same time, Zwilling could very well have taken over Hölderlin's fundamental conception, while bringing to it his own critique of the aesthetic as science. And as Schelling crowned Hölderlin's conclusive concept of the beautiful with a systematic wholeness, which is profoundly different from Hölderlin's complete insight (*Gesamtanschauung*), so Zwilling places above it the familiar concepts of unity and separtation, which turn up again in the essay, *Über das Alles* and perhaps in other places as well (Strauß, l.c., 387 f.).

You have probably noticed that Ludwig Strauß is overtaxed by the philosophical aspects of the letter and its context. But it makes no sense to complain about the fact that he paraphrases so much of the letter with little understanding of its philosophical content, instead of citing the letter directly and completely, because this paraphrasing of the letter and the few direct excerpts from it are all that we have. And Strauß knew nothing at all about Sinclair's *Raisonnements*, which confirm conjectures, but also indicate the independence of each of the three thinkers (Zwilling, Sinclair, and Hölderlin). Regarding Schelling, during the trip from Stuttgart to Leipzig (to the commencement of his service as *Hofmeister* in the house of the Baron von Riedesel), he visited Hölderlin in April 1796 and perhaps also had met Sinclair and Zwilling and been engaged in discussions with them. The dialogue concerning the role of beauty in giving a conclusion to the system, could, therefore, really have taken place, and the foundations of the *Earliest Program for a System of German Idealism* could have been worked out then as well. It has even been conjectured that Schelling, who is surely the author of the *Earliest Program for a System of German Idealism*, brought the text to Hölderlin on the journey from Stuttgart to Leipzig and that Hegel transcribed it during the winter (the only surviving copy of the fragment is in Hegel's handwriting).

Disregarding this, Strauß's citations offer us some reference points: it seems that Zwilling, precisely like Sinclair, placed reflection beyond the *relata* I and Non-I. The fact that the notion of the highest unity beyond all separation was important only seems to contradict the place of reflection as beyond the *relata* I and Non-I. In the end, Sinclair also distinguished between the notion of Being and the union (*Einigkeit*) expressed therein from that which is merely an expression of relation, namely, the unity (of the I) in opposition to the manifoldness (of the Non-I). If the I and Non-I (as *relata*) are formed first through reflection, this attests to the fact that reflection is vis-à-vis the I and Non-I, marked as a higher unity; even if reflection, as the draft of the letter indicates, is responsible for the "separation." In any case, that unity which is grasped through "sensation" (not through reflection) cannot be the oneness (*Einigkeit*) of which Sinclair speaks (otherwise, reflection would not be that which is the highest [*das Höchste*]). This union (*Einigkeit*) can only be an undifferentiated unity (*Einheit*) (in contrast to manifoldness). And then we find ourselves once again in a Kantian language game, according to which 'sensation' alone is that through which 'Being' is grasped, because sensation alone is unmediated, nonconceptual consciousness. But I do concede that Strauß's report is not precise enough to support my interpretation. Nonetheless, the conviction concerning the importance of the imagination and the beautiful is interesting. This notion is not surprising for a period inspired by Plato, especially after the appearance of Schiller's *Letters on Aesthetics*. But the "aesthetic viewpoint" becomes, in Zwilling, the "highest" overall because only this aesthetic viewpoint can overcome the oscillation between reflection/separation and sensation (*Empfindung*)/unity (*Einheit*) in such a way that the highest union (*Einigkeit*) of both becomes an event (in Schiller as in Kant, the aesthetic condition remains merely a sort of trace (*Vorschein*)—a "Symbol"—of the impossible unity of nature and freedom: a unity-as-if, but no actually occurring unity.

We find more clues in the theory sketch, *Über das Alles*. Unlike Sinclair and Hölderlin, Zwilling seems, by this time, to trust reflection and reflection alone to heal the maladies of the separation, "because together with a relation [according to the law of cognition-through-counterpositing (*Erkennens-durch-Entgegensetzung*)] a non-relation is conceived. So the related must be posited against the related as non-related, or the relation must, by all means, be posited as the relation of proposition and counter-proposition (*Satz und Gegensatz*) (Strauß 391; Jamme/Henrich, *Jakob Zwillings Nachlaß*, 64 f.): a notion, which, as always, flows, albeit in an unexecuted and only suggested way, from Hegel's absolute positing of the self-referential negation (or reflection). The autonomously posited "category of relation in general," concludes Zwilling, is the true infinite, indeed, it is "infinity itself" (Strauß 392; Jamme/Henrich 65). It should also be noted that Hölderlin and Sinclair's characteristic opposition between union (*Einigkeit*) "according to content" and separation "according to form" is found throughout Zwilling's fragment (L.c.).

But we must go into more detail. Dieter Henrich reads Zwilling's short draft of a system against the background of a basic ambiguity which flows through all of the drafts of the Homburg Circle: the indecision, namely, between the development of a conceptual form of metaphysical monism (so the theory of the unity of the all) and philosophically real interests (*realphilosophischen Interessen*) (Being, the Subject, the Non-I are not merely logical, but real quantities).[3] One does not know, after reading *Urtheil und Seyn* or the *Raisonnements* exactly whether the original unified Being survives judgment-through-reflection (so that reflection, in its conceptual spheres, merely does not come into contact with Being), or whether after the original division or judgment (as Being in Hegelian logic) it is completely dissolved in reflection as in its richer further determination. For Hölderlin and Sinclair one would have to deny the first part of the alternative, for how should an infinite striving of reflection for a reappropriation of the lost One (*verlorenen Einen*) be made comprehensible if reflection could completely dissolve Being within it (that is to say: to clarify Being through its own conceptual means)? We cannot forget that the presupposition of an 'absolute Being' which cannot be characterized through difference is also and above all, 'necessary' because otherwise the unity of that principle cannot be established from which Fichte departs as though it were established: namely, the I which Hölderlin and Sinclair, without further ado, identified with self-consciousness (and that means: with a consciousness distinguished by a division). If the notion of Being is dissolved in reflection (which is distinguished by a self-

reference), then a problem would surface which would make the presupposition of a no-longer-self-conscious unity absolutely necessary: namely, the explanation of a self-*reference* as *self*-reference. If this doesn't exist, then Hölderlin's notion of a unity that cannot be traced to relation and the reflexive relation of the Subject-I to the Object-I, could no longer be intelligible as a *self*-reference.

Zwilling's proposed solution is much different. If, according to the motto, ἓν καὶ πᾶν, unified Being and different manifoldness are one and the same (if, therefore, between them, the continuity of further development should rule), then the notion of Being must be able to be translated without loss into the notion of judgment. Then, of course, there can be no insurmountable abyss gaping between Being and judgment. In the short treatise, *Über das Alles*, the aesthetic escape path is largely omitted (it survives in the mention of imagination, which forms the synthetic idea of the All (Strauß 390; Jamme/Henrich, 63). So reflection alone must come up with the unbroken mediation of the One with the All.

One can imagine, even without looking at Zwilling's text, under which conditions such a text could have been possible at all. Reflection must be able, on its own, to make the notion of relationlessness (*Beziehungslosigkeit*), as it is presented in Being, comprehensible. And from Hegel's 'Logic of Being,' we know how that can take place: somewhat slyly, one interprets the non-refereniality (*Unbezuglichkeit*) of Being itself as a relation, namely, as a "relation only to itself" (in opposition to a relation-to-something-else). From this, as it were, one-place relation, it is to be shown that it—if more fundamentally developed—is identical with the relation of one *relata* to another (hence, a two-place relation); for also in a self-reference (*Selbst-bezug*) of a *relata* only to itself there is still *per definitionem*, a relation. Now, in a third step, we have only to show that the relation-only-to-itself (*Beziehung-nur-auf-sich*) is identical with the explicit relation of a *relata* with its correlate because in a monistic system the correlate can only be itself (or a modification of itself). And so it would be shown that the undeveloped relation, which is called 'Being' at the beginning, collides in its conceptual development with that which we called 'reflection'—and in such a way that no moment of that which was thought in the initial thoughts is missing from the further determined concepts (*fortbestimmten Begriffen*). These further determinations would be rather like operative concepts, hence such concepts, which throw a retroactively richer light upon the initial concepts, but which at the beginning cannot yet be fully determined and so appeal to a conceptual differentiation. Here, Diez's critique of Reinhold's philosophy based on first principles is taken into account. This critique had shown that Reinhold's supposed self-sufficient principle really assumed premises, which Reinhold could only justify from more robustly determined conceptual relations.

These presuppositions underlie Zwilling's small system, however not in the explicit Hegelian way that I have just sketched. Yet Hegel's principle, one he formulated while still in Frankfurt, namely, that all relations contain within them something relationless (indicated as a relation-*only*-to-itself) can be read as a direct echo of Zwilling's thesis that, "together with a relation a non-relation is conceived" (Strauß 391, Jamme/Henrich 64) and "that the contemplation of relation at its highest level is the relation with the non-relation" (392/65; cf. *Konstellationen*, 98 ff.; the parallel formulation can be found in Hegel's early theological writings (*Hegels theologische Jugendschriften*, ed. H. Nohl [Tübingen, 1907; reprint; Frankfurt/M.: Suhrkamp 1966], 348). Only in this way can Zwilling suppose that he can accommodate the notion of in-itself non-differentiated Being (which he describes as a non-relation) in the structure of reflection itself.

Of course, Zwilling decisively distinguishes his concept of absolute knowledge from Hegel's concept of the same in that he explains the reflexive re-appropriation of the notion of Being as point of departure (*die reflexive Wiederaneignung des Ausgangsgedankens 'Sein'*) (so the notion of the 'All') as "an idea of the imagination, as something presented as a perfect whole" (Strauß 390, Jamme/Henrich 63)—hence as a mere idea,

> Whose concept, in order to be mastered, must be contemplated as a progressive alteration of reflections, which are all merely different modifications of the first reflections and whose resolution lies in infinity (l.c.).

This means that, even in Zwilling, unity maintains precedence over separation. And this precedence makes itself valid insofar as (like in Sinclair) it operates within reflection as a demand to reestablish unity under the conditions of reflection (but this time unity-enriched-with-manifoldness (*Einheit-um-Mannigfaltigkeit-bereichert*), ἕν καὶ πᾶν. Zwilling characteristically speaks of a "reunification" of the separated [391/64; edited by M. Frank]. To actualize the All is an infinite task, an idea in the Kantian sense. But we have in the "Idea of the All," an indispensable standard measure, against which we can measure the dividedness (*Zerteiltheit*) of the reflexive world, through which we can relate this raggedness (*Zerrissenheit*) even to the maintained unity:

> We possess the idea of the All in each moment of the separation from the unification. As certain as every moment is a portion or interval (*Zeitraum*), which always, in order to appear as time to me, must be so related to infinity [which is, in other words, the lack of any relation to determination (*Bestimmungsunbezogenheit*), cf. 64: "infinite is, that which sustains no determination more"] that they reciporcally dissolve and conditon each other. And therein lies the connection between consciousness and the unity of

memory, that each reflection has a negative association with the other, insofar as they all, in a similar way, abolish (*aufheben*) infinity (Strauß 390; Jamme/Henrich, 63).

Now, of course, one does not easily see how the incipient "infinity" which becomes at once "finite" and the "correlate" of "reflection" is supposed to be able to preserve its own power in the stream of "infinite serially arranged and self-potentializing reflections" (*unendlich aneinandergereihten und sich potenzierenden Reflexionen*) (L.c.). One sees that even less, when Zwilling explicitly says that there occurs with the "first mutual relation" (*Auf-einander-Beziehung*), the dissolution of all that is Absolute (l.c.), indeed, there is, "according to form, positively no Absolute other than the fact that we can absolutely assume that there is nothing absolute" (392/65). From this self-destruction of the infinite (or absoluteness) Zwilling infers that "the relation of proposition and counter-proposition [hence, the *relata* of the relation] must be absolutely posited" (391/65). Therewith, however, we find ourselves again in the theoretical situation that Hölderlin, through the demand of an "absolute Being" beyond all relation (including the self-relation of consciousness) wanted to avoid. For a relation is no self-sufficient structure. If it is able to stand out from the merely indifferent differences (or, in other words, should the members be recognizable not as related to another externally, but rather internally), then a unity must hold sway over them, which cannot be made clear from the play of the relation itself. Indeed, this notion is found in Zwilling too. But precisely as is the case later with Hegel, Zwilling cannot claim to be against the other notion of the restless dissolution (*Auflösung*) of Being in reflection. Unity goes under in the relationships of reflection, which can only preserve the property of *self*-relation through a trick.[4] Of course, Zwilling distinguishes between matter and form and then claims that the incipient "infinity is only overcome with respect to form, with respect to matter it remains" (392/650). But if that is the case, then we find ourselves once more in Hölderlin's theoretical framework, no longer in Hegel's context: "with respect to content" only the unified Being endures; "with respect to form," we are dealing with a correlation of two things which cannot be distinguished as roughly "something" and "nothing." The something (*Etwas*) originates from making original Being finite under the gaze of reflection. It can, however, present itself as something valid only in distinction (*Abhebung*) from Nothingness. Thus, one can (admittedly in a somewhat Sartrean way) say that reflection "negates" the formerly opaque original Being and makes it into an object of a consciousness that is focussed upon it. Because consciousness cannot objectify all of Being, in other words: because Being surpasses every possible consciousness-of-Being, there arises the regulative idea of the 'All' as the goal of an impossible but demanded perfect presentation of Being in consciousness.

But this is precisely the path Zwilling doesn't take. He positions him-self resolutely at the point of view of reflection as a kind of medium that is the only way we can make unified Being comprehensible. To speak of Being is an "impossibility" "an idea which goes beyond reflection [. . .] or [. . .] an abstraction" (391/64). And even if this abstraction were feasible, it would have no content for us and no determination. For that which is recognizable (according to the "highest principle of a relation to each other" [*Auf-einander-Beziehung*]) withdraws from a counter-proposition (*Gegensatz*), in other words: only that which is determined within a relation is recognizable. And the pure 'negative idea' of infinity as the non-referential determination (*Bestim-mungsunbezogenheit*) proves, if I define it in this sense, to be related to deter-mination. Hence, the dimension of relation cannot be skipped over, it must be acknowledged as the true infinity (and admittedly, with this and only with this, comes the notion of relationlessness).

On the other hand, Hölderlin and Sinclair claimed (and I will con-clude with their arguments) that reflection is certainly insurmountable in the sense that beyond reflection we lose our consciousness, and it is with con-sciousness that we must prove all of our theses if we don't want to fall into the transcendent speculation of precritical philosophy. But it does not follow from this that reflection could clarify its unity to self-consciousness on its own. And that was precisely the reason for going beyond the identity I=I (and therewith for going "beyond the Kantian boundary lines") to postulate a Being, that, itself unconscious, could mete its unity out to consciousness. In Zwilling reflection is overtaxed: it must be both the ground of knowledge and the real ground of unity at the same time. For the fact that we recognize unity (and not constant cleaving [*Gespaltenheit*]), can be attributed not to reflection but rather to the intervention of Being. But we owe to reflection the fact that we really *recognize* (*erkennen*) this intervention. Reflection is what allows Being to appear, but reflection does not create Being.

Zwilling's systematic approach leads to absolute idealism, just as the sketch of Hölderlin's argument, in its first steps, immediately distances itself from absolute idealism. Later, Schelling will distinguish between the two models as between negative and positive philosophy and identify the first with Hegel's, the second with his own (late) philosophy. The first or negative philosophy says only (for that reason it is called 'negative'), what Being is not, namely, appearance for a consciousness. The second kind of philosophy speaks of a reality beyond consciousness, hence it is called 'positive' (still in the framework of the Kantian terminology concerning Being qua Being posited) 'positive.'

We shall see that Novalis shares this conviction.

Lecture 9

On Novalis' Pivotal Role in
Early German Romanticism

Although the most important contribution of early German Romanticism to the philosophical discussion of these years is put forward with the fragmentary work of Novalis, no other area of research has been so bitterly neglected as this one. Dieter Henrich also works on the early German Romantics, yet within his Jena Project, he does not look beyond Diez, Niethammer, Hölderlin, and their circles. I once wrote to Henrich telling him that it is difficult to deny that Novalis, in his philosophical writings, shows himself to be more explicit and analytically and argumentatively agile than Hölderlin. Henrich did not deny this. He does, however, insist that Novalis' work came much later than Hölderlin's, and insofar as Hölderlin's work was done earlier than that of Novalis, we must—he thinks—consider Hölderlin the pioneer in overcoming of a philosophy of reflection. Indeed, according to Henrich, Novalis simply wrote down thoughts similar to Hölderlin's, and he did so *after* Hölderlin. Henrich's Jena Project concerns exclusively the investigation of the actual priorities in and relations of dependence between the works of this period. According to Henrich's criterion, Friedrich Schlegel and Novalis emerge as secondary figures.

Aside from the obvious fact that one can justifiably question this conclusion, we should also question the feasibility of Henrich's thesis concerning Novalis as a mere follower of Hölderlin. Is there evidence in the work of Novalis to justify such a claim? In this lecture, I would like to explore this issue in more detail, and to this end, we must turn to some philological and biographical information on Novalis.

In an important passage from his work, *Konstellationen*, Henrich compares the quick rise of authentic speculative philosophy to the ascent of a supernova. Moreover, he claims that this process, "in principle came to an

151

end already in 1796 with the beginning of romantic theory, with the establishment of the Homburg Circle and with Schelling's early work"—within this context, Novalis' name comes to us, but only as a contrast to the "early" Hölderlin (in a similar way, Friedrich Schlegel's name is included on p. 228). In another work, *Grund im Bewußtsein* (127), Henrich elaborates:

> Syntheses of Fichte and Spinoza, which were first made available through Jacobi, were then worked out in detail by many others just a short time later. The most important of these were Novalis and Friedrich Schlegel. But *only* Hölderlin with his conception of "judgment and being," in which such a synthesis is really produced, was able to work this out in detail, both with more precise knowledge of and in unmediated proximity to the metaphysical debates of the Jena Period.

One can contest this claim, especially if one keeps in mind the technical-argumentative superiority of Hardenberg (Novalis) as compared with Hölderlin's rather rudimentary notes. Henrich, however, continues in the following way:

> Already in the seventies, I had undertaken a first yet quite unsatisfactorily oriented attempt at gaining some clarity about the common presuppositions of Hölderlin, Novalis, and Schlegel in the Jena situation. In fact, Novalis, too, had been a Jena student, even one of Reinhold's auditors in 1790. During this period, four Ph.D. theses were written: one by Manfred Frank entitled, *Das Problem Zeit in der deutschen Romantik*, München, 1972, 1990, the other by Stefan Summerer, *Wirkliche Sittlichkeit und ästhetische Illusion*, Bonn, 1974, the third by Hermann Timm, *Gott und die Freiheit*, Frankfurt, 1974, and the fourth one by Panajotis Kondylis, *Die Entstehung der Dialektik*, Stuttgart, 1979, all of them dedicated to this topic. But none of them, despite all their merits, succeeded in actually penetrating the interior part of this explosive transformation of thought.[1]

So, we all had to do our homework again, and do it better. One of my attempts to do this, still, I think, inadequate, is my book, *Einführung in die frühromantische Ästhetik* (Introduction to Early-Romantic Aesthetics) (Frankfurt/M.: Suhrkamp, 1989). In this work, the philosophical thought of Novalis and Friedrich Schlegel is freed of the sort of limited presentation found in my doctoral dissertation and is presented in view of its practical and poetic consequences. In the course of this work, I had much opportunity to consider the parallels between the work of Novalis and Schlegel, on the one hand, with that of Hölderlin and Sinclair on the other (and once again, with even more detail, in the epilogue to my book, *Selbstbewußtseinstheorien von Fichte bis Sartre* (Theories of Self-consciousness from Fichte to Sartre) (Frankfurt/

M.: Suhrkamp, 1991). But still I was missing—and this given the lack of knowledge of the results of Henrich's Jena Project—the full picture regarding Novalis' engagement in this period, that is, the material which would clarify his involvement not only with respect to the parallels to be found between his work and Hölderlin's, but also to the background of his education and his reception of various works of the period. We have such material for Hölderlin and his friends. In the period between 1991 and today, we have gained much in the way of knowledge regarding many aspects of Novalis' work and his life. We know, for example, that Novalis knew Niethammer well, and von Herbert and Erhard, too. Indeed, they all studied for a while under Reinhold in Jena (Hardenberg's matriculation was canceled at the beginning of October 1791; but according to Tieck, he "remained until 1792" [NS IV: 552, line 24]; in fact, at Christmas, Novalis visited Schiller, who was sick [cf. l.c., 98, lines 12, f.], further, Schiller's correspondence to Göschen from January 15, likewise on January 20, 1792 [571, lines 19 ff.]). The mediating role of Novalis' private tutor, Carl Christian Erhard Schmid, whose classes he attended too, must have been of extreme importance during the conception of the *Fichte-Studien*—this is shown in the written exchange between Novalis and Friedrich Schlegel and is also indicated in other documents from the period. Schmid's role is also clear in Novalis' *Allgemeiner Brouillon* of 1798, for Novalis cites Schmid's Kant Dictionary. (Unfortunately, we have no record of correspondence between Schmid and Novalis. Schmid's literary remains have not been sorted through and a part of Novalis' have been lost. We don't even have the correspondence between Novalis and Niethammer, a certain Mr. Döderlein—a descendant of the Niethammer familiy—had information on this correspondence. It is supposed that this correspondence is in some unknown place held by an heir or someone who purchased the documents, and like the dragon Fafner in *Siegfried*, "lies and holds them in possession." We are also missing the entries from Niethammer's diary from the period during which Novalis was in Tennstedt, and there we would have found information regarding Novalis' collaboration with Niethammer's new journal, the *Philosophisches Journal*.) We know that through Schlegel (not first and not only through his review of the journal), Novalis regularly received the *Philosophisches Journal* and so was acquainted with the debates concerning the feasibility of a philosophy based on first principles and some of the skeptical attacks against any attempt to secure first principles for philosophy. We must remember, too, that the *Philosophisches Journal* had a relation to Schmid; it was his orphaned journal that was taken over by Niethammer and renamed the *Philosophisches Journal*. Moreover, in the first group of the *Fichte-Studien*, Novalis makes detailed reference to Fichte's essay, "Von der Sprachfähigkeit und dem Ursprunge der Sprache" (On linguistic ability and the origin of language) (NS II: 155 ff., = Nr. 9–11 [central passages in the

Fichte-Studien, cf. l.c., 43], 130–1, 183, 185, 219, 249 f.); and this essay appeared in Niethammer's *Philosophisches Journal* (Vol. I, No. 3 (1795): 255–273, and No. 4: 287–326). Hence, Novalis read and was acquainted with the *Journal* even earlier, that is, before 1797 (cf. *NS* II: 44). Incidentally, the skepticism regarding the feasibility of Reinhold's philosophy of first principles began with Reinhold's students during the time that Novalis formed part of this group (1790–91, perhaps until January 1792). Hence, the seed of his skepticism regarding a philosophy based on first principles may have been planted in him then. In a long, biographically rich outline for a letter to the finance chancellor, Julius Wilhelm von Oppel (*NS* IV: 304–314)[2] from the end of January 1800, Novalis appraises his period in Jena thus:

> In Jena I came to know excellent scholars and acquired a love for the muses, the more the fashion of the democracy of the time made me disloyal to the old credence of the aristocracy. Philosophy was of interest to me, but I was far too fickle to bring this interest to anything more than some fluency in the language of philosophy (l.c., 310, lines 1–6).

So, the presumption that in this period Novalis already had caught references to the feasibility of a philosophy based on first principles can only be called possible or likely, but not certain. The long and enthusiastic farewell letter to Reinhold dated October 5, 1791 (l.c., 91–98) goes on more about generalities and about Schiller in particular, than about anything philosophical (nonetheless, it confirms the intensity of his contact with Reinhold and his fellow students). So in contrast to the case of Hölderlin, where we have precise evidence of his philosophical development, we have, in the case of Novalis, only conjectures regarding the same. Nonetheless, in Novalis' *Fichte-Studien*, we find good evidence to support our conjectures regarding the development of his thought. In particular, we find a decisive argument for the move to go beyond the limits of reflection, and we find this presented in full in the first pages of the *Fichte-Studien*. Thus, Novalis' thoughts regarding the move to go beyond the limits of reflection are not the result of a laborious process of learning to which Novalis would have had access first in 1796. For the first notes of the *Fichte-Studien*, the same holds as that which Henrich claims for Hölderlin's work: namely, that such revolutionary thoughts could not be the result of just a few weeks of deep thought, but rather the result of a long process of thinking and rethinking a given issue. In the particular case of Novalis, his work in the *Fichte-Studien* could not have been the result of Fichte's influence. For Fichte had only just begun to present his *Wissenschaftslehre*, which was almost unanimously rejected by the young intellectuals of Jena. (When Fichte began to teach in Jena, Novalis was no longer living there and was not present on a regular basis. Sinclair, Herbart,

Zwilling, and Hölderlin, in contrast, attended Fichte's lectures regularly.) The rejection of Fichte's philosophy was the result of the general skepticism regarding the possibility of a philosophy based on first principles. This skepticism was substantiated by arguments which were sophisticated and were, after a short period of respectful listening, learning, and waiting, used against Fichte's thought. Fichte's debut in Jena with this concept of a philosophy based on first principles must have seemed to his craftier listeners like a return to times already overcome, indeed, like an anachronism. Fichte would *mutatis mutandis*, be attacked with the same weapons that had been used successfully against Reinhold, and they would work just as well against Fichte. The supposition that the same tools used to attack Reinhold's philosophy would work against Fichte's helps account for the fact that when Novalis had a few peaceful days, he began immediately to work on what would become his *Fichte-Studien*. The writing was the result of what was, without a doubt, the fruit of previous and intense meditations. In a letter to me, Henrich expressed doubt regarding the early date of the writing of these notes (in September 1795).³ But, as I have said, I find in Henrich's *Der Grund im Bewußtsein* an argument in favor of Hölderlin, which can also be applied to Novalis: "Such dense texts, which are in accordance with a robust argumentation, can only be the result of the sum of a process of reflection, with some distance to a single reading [. . .]" (389).

For Novalis, the conditions surrounding him as he wrote the first sentences of the *Fichte-Studien* were the following (this is what he wrote to his brother Erasmus between November 11–13):

> I have around three hours a day free, that is, when I can work for myself. Urgent introductory studies for my complete future life, essential gaps in my knowledge and necessary exercises of my mental powers in general take the larger part of these hours away (*NS* IV: 159, lines 7–11).

If we take these comments together with the more detailed glimpse of his life provided in the letter to the finance counselor von Oppel, then we see that already during his time in Tennstedt, Novalis devoted his "extra hours to the old favorite ideas and to a labored investigation of Fichtean philosophy" (311, lines 3 f.). An assignation of a later date is not only obstructed by the comparison of handwriting types,⁴ but also by the fact that Novalis writes to von Oppel that his Fichte "investigations" took place in Tennstedt, where Novalis lived since October 25, 1794 (on December 30, he was appointed to the saltworks directory (*Salinendirektion*) of Weißenfels, and he left at the beginning of January; for one month in the early part of 1797 he was again in Tennstedt, but that was during the time of Sophie's death: his writings from that time are limited to entries in a diary, which clearly show other characteristics than those of the early *Fichte-Studien*). I don't think that there is any reason to contest the assignation of date given by the publisher.

Novalis' *Fichte-Studien* share the fate of their reception with Hölderlin's *Urtheil und Seyn*, and the literary remains of Zwilling and Sinclair: they first became accessible to the public in the twentieth century. Novalis' "Fragmente vermischten Inhalts" (Fragments of Mixed Content) (reprinted in *NS* V: 201/3–361), which were made accessible in the second part of *Schriften* (Writings) (Berlin, 1802) by Ludwig Tieck and Friedrich von Schlegel, are often not fragments by birth at all. Rather, they are pieces taken arbitrarily and artificially from treatises, essays, and notes, far from any chronological order or any order according to subject, and so artificially made into fragments. Hence, the reader of that time had no idea that the fragments belonged to different collections that were themselves coherent; and lacking the unifying power of this context, the reader could hardly come to an understanding of the single sentences ripped from their larger context. This, admittedly, added to the impression that Romanticism was something akin to anarchy and magic. Ernst Heilborn, asked by the publisher Reimer, on the occasion of the hundredth birthday of Novalis, to prepare an edition of Novalis' work, was the first to gain access to the Hardenberg family archive. Novalis' literary remains had been organized by one of his nieces, Sophie von Hardenberg (1821–98), with help of her sister Karoline (1823–1900). "They provided large manuscripts from groups of manuscripts with Latin letters from A to V or pages with Arabic digits (everything in red ink) and divided these— partially bound—into folders or envelopes" (*NS* II: VII). Heilborn went to work on the manuscripts much more conscientiously than Tieck and Schlegel had, but he published the so-called *Fragments* in the same contingent order in which he had found them. In contrast, Eduard von Bülow had already arranged the fragments according to subject, and in this he was followed by, for example, Kamnitzer in the twentieth century. It is clear, that even from the actual order, the connection by subject or the chronology of the frag- ments, one does not get any clear impression of their meaning. Not until the 1920s did Paul Kluckhohn reorganize, in part, based upon the criteria of handwriting, all of the manuscripts available at the time, in order to create the first halfway critical edition of Novalis' works. But some manuscripts were lost and others were not examined thoroughly enough in the Hardenberg house. In short, one had to wait until the end of the World War II, to breathe new life into the critical edition of Novalis' work.

This happened in the following way: Novalis' literary remains were auctioned in 1930.[5] A part of the philosophical papers came into the posses- sion of Salman Schocken who had taken the papers with him into exile in 1933; he died in 1959. Only first in 1960, just after Schocken's death, could his collection be acquired by the Frankfurter *Freies Deutsches Hochstift*. And only since then has there been an edition of Novalis' "Philosophical Works" worthy of being called a critical edition (volumes II and III, 1965 and 1968). It is more complete than any earlier edition, and it is the first one to present the groups of manuscripts in a chronological order rather than in a piecemeal fashion, and to present the works according to strict criteria. This was, for the most part, the work of a Germanist from Kiel, Hans-Joachim Mähl. "He was in a position to completely re-organize the works from 1795–96 which had been left quite incoherent in the first edition and to do this according to inner criteria and handwriting observations, thus, creating a logically connected order which brought a new continuity to Friedrich von Hardenberg's work and resulted in what is known as the *Fichte-Studien* (section II)" (l.c., X). Therefore, only since Mähl's work was done, that is, only since 1965, do we know something of the character of these notes, with many of them first edited then. Mähl shows, in two synoptic comparisons on page 39 and on pages 88 f., how much the new reconstruction differs from Kluckhohn's first edition and how much more is added; and his reconstruction offers, in addition, the most reliably justified ordering of the seven different text groups, which again, are brought together from many different individual manuscripts.

Once the very important sequence of the notes can be more or less secured, we want to know with more precision, how degrees of probability can be assigned to the dates of the *Fichte-Studien*. Now, we have one clear *terminus post quem*, which is that Novalis used—and this can be clearly deduced from his notes—besides the manifesto (*Programmschrift*) *Über den Begriff der Wissenschaftslehre* (On the concept of the Wissenschaftslehre), the *Vorlegungen über die Bestimmung des Gelehrten* (Lectures on the Vocation of the Scholar) (both from 1794), the three parts of Fichte's *Wissenschaftslehre*, the last part of which, just like the *Grundriß des Eigentümlichen der Wissenschaftslehre* (Outline of the Particulars of the *Wissenschaftslehre*), appeared in 1795 (1795 was also the year, as we have already mentioned, in which Fichte's essay on the origin of language appeared in volume three of the *Philosophisches Journal*, and Novalis made strong use of this as well). One can assume that Novalis had already received the pages of the *Wissenschaftslehre* and received as well the books of Fichte (cf. Mähl, *NS* II: 30 f.). This can be assumed because Fichte was not an unknown name in the Hardenberg house; the Baron Ernst Haubold von Miltitz (1739–74) was a relative of the Hardenberg's and the father of Novalis' cousin and friend, Dietrich Freiherr von Miltitz (1769–1853). The relationship became still closer, when, after the death of Ernst Haubold, Novalis' father became the guardian of the twenty-five-year-old Dietrich.[6] The elder Miltitz was a man of property and had, one day, taken on the task of inspecting his estates. In Rammenau, a priest had been recommended to him, whose sermon he wished to hear. His carriage broke down however, and he arrived too late to hear the sermon. Yet, the people of the village told him of a young boy, Johann Gottlieb, who watched over the geese, and who could recite the sermon, which he had missed. The good humored and curious man heard the sermon from the young boy and was so impressed by the talent of the boy, that he spoke with the boy's father and arranged to take responsibility for the education of the young Fichte. And so Fichte came first to Father Krebel in Meißen, then to the elementary (Latin) school there, and finally to the advanced school (*Fürstenschule*) in Pforta. It is hard to imagine what would have become of Fichte without this fateful stroke of luck!

For us, however, it is more important that the relation between Fichte and the Hardenberg's was anything but superficial. It was not only the case that the elder Miltitz took the most active share in Fichte's development. With the close relation he had with the Hardenberg family, it is easy to imagine, "that Fichte's works were accessible to the young Hardenberg from the beginning, and that already in 1794 he could have occupied himself with them" (*NS* II: 30 ff.)—but, of course, it is just as possible that Novalis was also familiar with Fichte's early publications, which were discussed actively in the Reinhold circle, and which had been reviewed by friends and colleagues of Novalis (for example, by Johann Benjamin Erhard and Leonhard Creuzer). In any case, one may assume that Fichte's works could be found in the Hardenberg house earlier than in any other place. After all, they had taken over the guardianship of Miltitzen's only son and therefore had become the sole recipients of Fichte's gratitude. Hence, Novalis had priviledged access to Fichte's works, although he met Fichte first in May 1795 (together with Hölderlin) at Niethammer's house.[7] This priviledged access to Fichte's work may have put Novalis in an intensive "inside position" comparable to that of Hölderlin's. The fact that Fichte later sent the elder Hardenberg books on occasion is not, by the way, mere conjecture: it has been verified by a letter which Novalis sent to Dietrich von Miltitz on February 6, 1799, in which he enclosed Fichte's *Appellation* (*NS* IV: 277).[8]

We know of Novalis' earliest philosophical interest during his study with Reinhold from his letter to von Oppel. Although in this letter he describes his studies as "far too cursory" (because of his well-known affairs with women, his teachers Schmid and Schiller had to personally remind him to work with more diligence); we know from a Jena note, that, in 1791, he had taken on a study of Kant as his main philosophical task and hence probably visited the introductory lectures on Kant which Schmid gave. In any case, in 1791, Novalis writes, cryptically and proudly, under the keyword "Philosophy," the names "Schiller, Herder, Lessing, I myself, Kant" (*NS* IV: 4, line, 18): an indication, if not of achievements, at least of ambition. In

Leipzig, Novalis also occupied himself constantly with philosophy, in spite of his continued and rather frivolous student life-style. And from his correspondence with Schlegel we learn that in the early part of 1793 he grappled seriously with Kant's moral philosophy. Friedrich Schlegel found this impressive enough to write the following lines to Novalis on July 3, 1793:

> Your letter has heightened my expectation of the next one—let me remind you of your promise to share your thoughts on ethics and their relation to Kant's theory and more open information about your new love (NS IV: 355).

Novalis could have occupied himself with Fichte's works early on—precisely because of the close relationship with Miltitz—why then claim that he did so first "beginning in 1794," that is, upon the appearance of the *Begriff der Wissenschaftslehre* (Concept of the *Wissenschaftslehre*) and the first pages of the *Grundlage der Wissenschaftslehre* (Foundation of the *Wissenschaftslehre*) (NS II: 31)? It may be that the meeting with Fichte at Niethammer's home (in May 1795) stimulated him to intensify his studies of Fichte. In any case, the letter to von Oppel confirms a "more arduous investigation of Fichtean philosophy." Still during the time he was in Tennstedt (Novalis worked there as an actuary at the district office (interruptedly) between October 25, 1794 and February 5, 1796; on February 5, he shifted to a position as *Akzessist* for the saltworks directory in Weißenfels—where, until the autumn of 1796, his philosophical notes were finished.) Since we have no evidence to the contrary, we must assume that the *Fichte-Studien* were the result of this first, more foundational and, according to Novalis, "more systematic" occupation with Fichte. From a letter that Novalis wrote to his brother, Erasmus (previously cited), we know that the completion of the *Fichte-Studien* was accomplished with difficulty because of the office work in which Novalis was entrenched. Novalis—whose diligence and industriousness astonished all of his acquaintances[9]—apologizes to his brother for not having been able to reply to him sooner.

> First consider that I am rarely fully free to allow myself to come to ideas without pressure and in a connected way; second, consider how many priorities make their claims upon me during these free periods. One cannot always give the first mortgage to the favorite creditor (NS IV: 159 top).

There follows the report on the three hours of free time per day that are devoted to his studies of philosophy. "I know, you do not demand its [studies of philosophy] neglect. But you know me too well anyway and know how intimately my friendship for you is interwoven with my whole self, than that you should assume from such an ambiguous proof anything proved" (l. c.).

In the saltworks directory of Weißenfels Novalis had to wrest his study time from his obligations at work, and this was no easy task. So he writes to Friedrich Schlegel on July 8, 1796, that he lives "in a bearable freedom—with adequate leisure to carry out my inner calling" (*NS* IV: 187, lines 14 ff.). Meanwhile, he reports, that he already has a "system of philosophy," which he would like to dedicate to his spiritual brother. "Then my reflection would become quite dear to me. It would contain an inexhaustible source of comfort and peace. Of course, it is still in need of its finishing touches" (l.c., p. 172, lines 9/10–13).[10] In a letter to Caroline Just dated April 10, 1796, Novalis complains again about job-related distractions so hostile to his work in philosophy:

> Now under a heavy workload, I gratuitously study the philosophy of compulsion (*Philosophie des Zwangs*) and make for myself a small, useful capital, of which I would not have otherwise thought. Incidentally, I am still the same old person—maybe a little merrier. Sciences and love fill my entire soul (l.c., p. 181, lines 21–25).

That this letter really alludes to the *Fichte-Studien*, can be determined from a characteristic alteration of Novalis' manuscripts, which also shows up in the philosophical notes from the end of March/beginning of April (*NS* II: 33 top). Concerning this issue, Mähl writes:

> It is noteworthy that in the preceding manuscript group (from No. 249 and following) traces of a subsequent revision and correction show up for the first time, which run throughout the entire collection of papers. So the supposition is to be not dismissed, that, during this time, Novalis intended to publish a philosophical work and at the same time wanted to make recourse to his *Fichte-Studien*. An explanation of this will surely first be given in the correspondence with Niethammer (l.c.).

In this context, one should introduce L. Döderleins letter to Mähl as one, even if indirect, document that attests to Novalis' deepened occupation with philosophical topics. In Niethammer's literary remains, there were two (unpublished) letters from the time that Novalis spent in Tennstedt. And Niethammer mentions Novalis' name many times in his (not yet edited) diary, "whereby it has almost always to do with an intended collaboration of Hardenberg's on the *Philosophisches Journal*. If these statements were to be confirmed, another piece of evidence would be won for the philosophical writings from this time period, which Novalis would have made use of for the proposed collaboration" (*NS* II: 32 f). In any case, Niethammer must have expected that Novalis be capable of providing the *Philosophisches Journal* with a worthy philosophical contribution containing a solid argument, perhaps even one expressing skepticism regarding the possibility of basing philosophy on first principles; he would not have been disappointed.

A famous passage from a letter dated July 8, 1796, in which Novalis tells Friedrich Schlegel of his engagement with Sophie von Kühn, also reveals a longer, prolonged period of philosophical activity:

> My favorite study is, in essence, called the same as my bride. Her name is Sofie—philosophy is the soul of my life and the key to my deepest self. Since that acquaintance, I am also bound to this study completely. You will test me. To write something and to marry is a goal of almost all of my wishes. I am indebted to Fichte for the encouragement—He is the one who awakened me and indirectly incited me (*NS* IV: 188, lines 8–14).

As a mild criticism in the same letter, we find talk of the fact that Fichte, unlike Spinoza or Zinzendorf, does not explore "the infinite idea of love" and has not "divined" its method and its "breath of creation" (*Schöpfungsathem*), and that this is "a shame" (l.c., p.188), a thought which Novalis shared with Hölderlin's philosophy of love, even when Novalis' source was, above all, Hemsterhuis. Soon an intensive correspondence with Friedrich Schlegel began again, after having been interrupted for almost two years (subsequent to a serious argument about one of Novalis' love relations), the friends see each other frequently, discuss philosophy and call it "fichtesizing" (*fichtisieren*). Thus, Friedrich Schlegel writes on January 2, 1797, that in Jena there is no one with whom he can speak of the "I," as we did "on the last evening of our merry time together" (l.c., p. 467, 1. Brief-Abschn.); and still on June 8, 1797, he wishes: "Oh, if we could only fichtesize, so sincerely, so warmly, so comfortably, as happened sometimes during this winter" (l.c., p. 487, lines 32–34). Novalis had a longer conversation with Fichte in August 1797, concerning which he writes to his friend on September 5, that:

> At Fichte's I spoke of my favorite topic—he did not agree with me—but with what tender consideration did he speak, for he held my opinion to be eccentric (*Abgedrungne*). This will remain unforgettable.
>
> He praised Schelling's ideas, as well as Schmidt [*sic*], very highly—especially the introduction (l.c., p. 236).

But we must not enter any further into the meaning of the remark in this letter—both cryptic and enthusiastic, since it lies beyond the time period that we must take into account now.

With this clear view of the constellation and the precarious circumstances under which Novalis began to write the *Fichte-Studien*, one can hardly assume that he achieved his breakthrough first in late-autumn 1795 (therefore on the occasion of the studies, about which he informs his brother), with the decisive thoughts coming at lightening speed. In other words: Nothing speaks against the fact that Novalis had his decisive insight just as early as Hölderlin did (with whom he had conversed in May). In 1805, Novalis' superior official, the *Kreisamt* (district official) Just (1750–1822) in Tennstedt, confirms in an affectionate obituary for his friend who died too early, the significance of Fichte for Novalis during his Tennstedt period.[11] He characterizes the spiritual physiognomy of Novalis so well, that I will read you the entire passage:

> There were three things for which—then and, as far as I know, until his death—he showed resolute preference: Consistency (*Consequenz*) in thought and action, *aesthetic beauty*, and *science*.
>   . . .
>
> The preference, which he gave to the first, misled him, occasionally, so that he could, for example, for the sake of consistency (*Consequenz*) give a talk praising Robespierre's reign of terror even while he must have hated it on account of its repulsiveness. So, at the end of his life, he also gave a devout catholic friend, who was staying with me, a feast for the soul (*Seelenschmaus*), in which he described the consequences of the hierarchy, and in this long, long account interwove the entire history of the papacy, and with a wealth of reasons and images, which reason and fantasy offered him, became the panegyrist of the papal autocracy.
>   . . .
>
> He showed a similar preference for aesthetic beauty. In spite of the fact that his inner self was not yet inclined to the rational-religiosity of the Christian religion, the Bible was, nonetheless, due to its aesthetic beauty, dear and valuable to him; of course, however, he could fall in love with just such a religion, which offered for worship a mother of God, a madonna.
>   . . .
>
> *Fichte gave the word "science" (Wissenschaft) a new meaning; and this had much value for my friend.* For his wish and aspiration was, not only to attribute everything, which up until then had been called art and science, to one principle and so to achieve a true science, but also to unify into one all sciences and arts. For, he was convinced that the one offered its hand to the other as a sister, and a splendid unity bound all. For this reason, he did not exclude any subject from his investigations and studies; (so in Wittenberg, completely on his own, he obtained information on the history of the church) and he couldn't study all of them: So this certainly is already an indication of his extraordinary genius, that he *wanted* to study all subjects and from these to create *one* science (*NS* IV: 540/1; emphasis in the fourth section added).
>   . . .
>
> His lively imagination was accompanied by a tranquil reason. How else could he have had the desire and the strength to explore the depths of speculative philosophy? But his study was not an end, but only a means.

He set limits upon speculation, and Jakobi's [sic] letter to Fichte spoke loudly to his heart.

"Philosophy now lies next to me"—he wrote in February 1800—"only in the bookcase" (l. c., pp. 548 f.).

If everything speaks in favor of the claim that Novalis began his *Fichte-Studien* in the autumn of 1795, then one thinks of the earliest possible date as sometime in November—that is the time he wrote the letter to his brother Erasmus (Novalis wrote many letters during this period for from September 21 onwards, he traveled frequently). But Mähl also considers "an inception in September" as possible, indeed, on the basis of writing samples as "more likely" (*NS* II: 43). For—we should recall—the significant change in writing begins first at the end of November, and up until then there were already 114 manuscript pages available! In fact, there are, in every manuscript group, temporal interruptions, subsequent deletions or improvements, so that the early writing style or ink types mix with the later ones. But the only writing style which can be demonstrated to have been abandoned in the late-autumn of 1795 and which is available in the supplement to the *Fichte-Studien*, counts to place Novalis, as far as the period of his revolutionary contributions is concerned, in the closest company of Hölderlin, Sinclair, and Zwilling.

Now the question is: how do the *Fichte-Studien* (from 1795–96) relate to the metaphilosophical reflections entertained in Hölderlin's circle? In order to attempt an answer to this question, I shall first give a preliminary articulation of the main theses of Novalis' manuscript. Novalis (1) raises the problem of how an entity which is supposed to be unconscious (the original Being) can nonetheless be mediated with consciousness; (2) tries to show how the thought of transreflexive unity (or simplicity) of Being can be attuned to the other (thought) according to which the Absolute is not devoid of an inner articulation (into synthetic and analytic I, opposition (*Gegensatz*) and object (*Gegenstand*), state (*Zustand*) and object, essence and property and however else Novalis construes this opposition); and (3) establishes a well-substantiated connection between the two thoughts, namely, that Being is beyond consciousness and that philosophy consists in an infinite approximation. This latter idea, on the one hand, takes up the skepticism manifested towards the project of a foundational philosophy (Erhard's and Niethammer's critique of Reinhold and Fichte), and on the other hand, prepares an aesthetic solution: what philosophy attains to only in the long run (so never actually), aesthetic intuition can grasp immediately even though taking it *as* a content inexhaustible by any concept.

When the character of a given problem is unsolvability, then we solve it if we present its unsolvability (as such).

We know enough of *a*, when we realize that its predicate is a (*NS* III: 376, Nr. 612).

Art is able to achieve this as "presentation of that which is unpresentable" (*Darstellung des Undarstellbaren*) (*NS* III: 685, Nr. 671).

My three theses about the basic arguments of the *Fichte-Studien* stand in need of a sort of overture. In fact, the question of how Being, which is *unpresentable* (*undarstellbar*), can nevertheless be grasped by consciousness is preceded by a reflection on the relationship between Being and consciousness. And you will soon see that Novalis is inspired—as was Hölderlin—first by Kant's theory of judgment and second by Spinoza's (or rather Jacobi's) idea that all phenomena are sustained (or permeated) by a single Being. In short, Novalis, too, assumes that the copulative 'is' of predicative judgment derives from Being, understood as 'existence' or 'identity,' and so presupposes this meaning as its condition.

So Novalis' earliest independent attempts at philosophy, like those of Hölderlin (whom he had met briefly at Niethammer's house), start with a consideration of the form of judgment. Like Hölderlin, he assumes that the original sense of Being is identity and that the function of the copulative 'is' is to connect something to something, even though only partly or relatively (namely, in relation to a third: A and B are not the same *as* A or *as* B, but they both express the same Absolute, which is in the strictest imaginable sense identical with itself). However, in order to present the identity in judgment, we have to step outside of it: "We leave the *identical*, in order to present it" (*NS* II: 104, Nr. 1). Novalis also claims that; "[w]e speak of the [Absolute] as of one, but there are in fact two, essentially distinguished from each other—even though absolutely correlated" (249, Nr. 462, lines 3–5). Insofar each "judgment is de-composition" (562, Nr. 181), namely, decomposition of a prior unity into two interrelated terms. On the other hand: without this original division the unity would not be presented to our mind. So presentation produces a "*Scheinsatz*"—a pseudo-proposition. In other words: the Being of original identity transforms or disfigures itself into a synthesis which, precisely in disclosing identity to our consciousness, hides it from our consciousness. So if the act of judging reveals to us a kind of identity, it does so only "seemingly." The forms of our judgments attribute to objects only relative or partial identities;[12] and the very Being of absolute identity finds itself expressed in forms which are alien to Being and therefore opposed to itself: "non-Being, non-identity, signs"—substitute forms of what was actually meant but systematically missed.

Like Hölderlin and Sinclair, Novalis identifies consciousness, on the one hand, with thetical consciousness ("all that is known is *posited*" [241, line 33]) and, on the other hand, holds the object of consciousness to be that which is known in judgment. He means that knowledge derives from a 'what' (*Was*) (105, line 23), hence the reference to an object is essential to his view of knowledge.[13] Now, if you add to this the other claims put forward by Novalis, namely, that the presentation of the content of a judgment produces a pseudo-proposition (*Scheinsatz*), that, therefore the conditions of the appearance-in-consciousness disguise Being, then you will more or less understand Novalis' definition of 'consciousness': "Consciousness is a Being outside of Being within Being" (106, line 4), a formulation which, by the way, will turn up in Fichte's later versions of the *Wissenschaftslehre*.[14] What does 'outside of Being' mean? Novalis responds, that it is "no real, no genuine Being" (line 6). It has, so to speak, less being (*seiend*) than its object, true Being. The ancient Greeks spoke of μὴ ὄν, of something that does not entirely lack existence (this would then be a οὐκ ὄν) but exists only in some respect, namely, in and by its relation to Being, and does *not* exist in another respect, namely, independently of Being. Being itself—as unconditioned existence or as Jacobi's "original Being" (142, line 13)—is *not* subject to this condition. That is why it is not conscious, not known to us (it is "without consciousness" [lines 6–7]; "in the realm of the unknown" [144, line 29]). There would be Being even if there were no consciousness, knowledge, or judgment of it:

> No modification or concept clings to mere Being—one cannot oppose anything to it except verbally—Non-Being. This is however a copulative hook that is placed there merely *pro forma*—it only seems to be. It grasps only a handful of darkness (lines 20–23).

Consciousness, on the other hand, exists only as intentionality, as the essential reference to Being. All reference distinguishes, and it is in the differentiation that the determinancy of the differentiated is grounded: "Everything is knowable only through its opposite" (171, line 14). So Being itself is in a way determined too: with regard to what is accessible to consciousness; but as "mere Being—or chaos [absolute indetermination]" (line 26), and offers a reflex space, which can only be apprehended by 'feeling.' Novalis transcribes this withdrawal with the words that the genuine spirit of the Absolute is "there beyond" the contemplation of reflection (114, line 9); and he sometimes says that the "original action" (*Urhandlung*) which is given to feeling, disappears under the gaze of reflection.

One can also characterize the effect of intentional relation of consciousness to Being in the following way: the reference produces "an image of Being" (lines 8–10) or a "sign" (line 10). The sign is then the "presentation" or the image of "Non-Being in Being, so that Being for itself, in a certain way, allows for its existence" (lines 11f.; on the theory of signs cf. 108 ff., Nr. 11). In other words, transcendent Being lets itself appear before consciousness through a representative related to consciousness, which is not consciousness itself.

In developing these ideas, Novalis applied Fichte's law of reciprocal determination (*Wechselbestimmung*) of the I and Non-I to the differential nature of a linguistic system: "Each schema or linguistic sign," he writes, "is only what it is in its place, through the others" (*NS* II: 109, lines 34 ff.).[15] This anticipates (for Novalis could not have known of this) Wilhelm von Humboldt's insights concerning the differentiality of signs, whose meaning is generated through the functioning in an (open) system of differences in the material of expression. But more interesting is what Novalis observes about the process of mutual communication. He first raises a question: Given that a sign is first presented as an organized physical matter and second that a linguistic system does not automatically entail comprehension and meaningfulness, how then can the addressee of a communicative act understand what a speaker means? Novalis' response is that the addressee has to depict her image like a painter "before the mirror of reflection in such a way [. . .], that even this feature is not forgotten, namely, that the image is depicted in the position of depicting itself" (110, lines 20–24). The parable betrays dazzling insight into the treacherous character of the circles entailed by the reflection model, but does not really resolve them. In fact, we may ask Novalis in virtue of which necessity (if it cannot be the one imposed by the differentiality of signs) is it that the addressee of a message interprets the physical uttering (*Verlautbarung*) as a *sign* and as *this* sign? At best what Novalis manages to explain is that and how an addressee comes to realize that the physical sound is a signifier, a material token loaded with an intention, a meaning.

I leave out some remarks concerning another source for Novalis' linguistic-semantical reflections: his reading of a manual of logic the author of which was a certain Johann Christoph Hoffbauer (191, 21).[16] In fact, Hoffbauer had distinguished between the content of a judgment and the linguistic form in and through which this content is represented. According to his symbolism, '*a*' is the linguistic representation (or a sign) of A, and the judgment '*a* = *a*' presents explicitly and in logical 'form' to our consciousness what was implied (but not known) in the content of A. This somewhat subtle distinction not only left some mark on Novalis' own symbolism but may have given rise to his thoroughgoing talk of a distinction between the matter and form of judgments. From Hoffbauer, Novalis learned that matter is what the judgment is about (its object), and form is "the representation of the relation itself in which objects in the same [relation] are thought" (sec. 145, p. 82). Of course, what is entirely lacking in Hoffbauer's description (as well as in Fichte's text on the origin of language) is the emphasis Novalis puts on the idea that the linguistic and judgment-like (*urteilsmäßige*) presentation is at the same time a conversion of Being into illusion (*Schein*).

Perfectly consistent with this conceptual switch is Novalis' claim that "thinking [is] an art of illusion (*Schein*)" (181, lines 1 f.): "All matter of thought is illusionary matter" (line 14). "Thinking is an expression of Non-Being" (146, lines 25 f.). In fact, objectifying thought makes us lose our intuition of Being as nonobjective (194, Nrs. 278 ff.). Novalis calls this un-objective essence of Being, first 'object' (*Gegenstand*) and then 'state' (*Zustand*) (pp. 210 ff.). When the thinking subject's gaze believes itself to have met with something, the subject "actually" or "really" thematizes nothing (115, lines 28 and 6; 118, lines 16 ff.). So the following note fits nicely with this line of thinking:

> When the subject reflects on the pure I, it has nothing—insofar as it has something for itself—but if, on the other hand, it does not reflect upon this—then it has nothing for itself just in having something (137 f., Nr. 49).[17]

In this context, it is relevant to consider note Nr. 41 in which Novalis claims that the subject—beyond its intentional relation to the Absolute—is denied all Being (for the subject is precisely a μὴ ὄv in that it only *is* insofar as Being makes of it an object and so is contained/supported by Being but is *not* apart from this relation). Without presupposing Being, consciousness could not at all subsist as a reference to Being (*Seins-Bezug*).[18] "From which we see, by the way, that the I is basically nothing—everything has to be *given* to it" (273, lines 31 ff.).

But not only consciousness of Being (*Seins-Bewußtseins*) must convert Being into illusion. A corresponding inversion occurs to *reflection* (as a special instance of objectifying consciousness). Reflection—as consciousness' turning back onto itself—produces a result, that we may call self-consciousness. Self-consciousness is consciousness of a particular object, namely, of the subject itself. But should the relation of inversion proper to reflection here be suspended? Not at all: reflection produces an illusion with regard to the self as well as with regard to Being. But what does the illusion consist in? It consists in making the subject believe that what appears first to itself (to consciousness), is also first in the order of Being. But, says Novalis, "what reflection *finds*, seems already to have *been there*" (l.c., 112, Nr. 14). What already seems to have been there is what grounds reflection as an epistemic self-relation, and this ground, Novalis calls "feeling." Feeling is a way in which consciousness is not objectifyingly opposed *to* but is immediately familiar *with* itself. This feeling, to which the seamless identity of Being is revealed, can ground the relation of the self to itself as a knowing relation to itself *as itself*. The mere relation of a subject to itself could not do this.

Novalis' talk of feeling was stimulated by several readings. He was acquainted with sections 7–10 of Fichte's *Grundlage der gesammten Wissenschaftslehre*

(1795), so when he speaks of a "*Selbstgefühl*" (self feeling) (113, 25), it is clear that he has Ficthe's rather developed *Gefühlstheorie* (theory of feeling) in mind.[19] Yet, Fichte was concerned with something somewhat different than Novalis was. Fichte's reference to *Selbstgefühl* was used to clarify how the I (which in his theory cannot exercise two intentions at the same time) can become conscious of its own unconscious striving or, as it was to be called later, "longing" (*Sehnen*). Because here we are concerned not with the consciousness of a counter effect of the Non-I but rather with the effect of the activity of the I itself, the required conscious apprehension (*Bewußtnahme*) must fall in the realm of the Being-for-itself (*für-sich-Seins*). And for the designation of such a conscious apprehension, the term "feeling" recommends itself. For in feeling, I am "passive and not active" (*WW* I: 289). This also holds for the term, 'feeling of longing' (304, 302 ff.), which was so important for the early Romantics.

The general rule, that Fichte put forth for any conscious apprehension (including feeling), namely, that this conscious apprehension is tied to a limitation and an opposition expresses itself as a "compulsion (*Zwang*) an inability (*Nicht-könnens*)" (289). Consequently, the thought that there is something external to me results as an almost natural "illusion" (*Täuschung*) that there is something existent external to me (*ein außer mir Befindliches*) that restrictively affects my activity and drives it back—a structure of my conscious life for which the designation "feeling" is most fitting (290).

Fichte tries to explain our belief that opposed objects act on us, as a necessary illusion. This illusion is due to the fact that, using the category of causality (which is a priori and hence subjective), we are inclined to take the view that those parts of our psychological life which we are unable to attribute to ourselves (to our own activity) as intended acts, are the effect of the things on us. Whatever is determined in our psychological life must be the effect of some opposite action. Now, for example, the mood of longing for something is determined in that it is plainly distinguished from some (or any) other mood. And since we cannot self-attribute the cause of this limitation/determination, we feel somehow passive: we cannot help but long. This is the origin of our talk of feeling, according to Fichte. On the one hand, feeling is something quite internal (manifesting itself *in me*); on the other hand, it is the work of an opposing action, the authorship of which I cannot ascribe to myself, unless I consider (but how could I?) that I myself produce it. "What is felt," says Fichte, "is the inhibition (*Hemmung*) of the spontaneity of our faculty of reprensntation" (*WW* I: 339). (Fichte, by the way, as do Novalis and Schelling, tries to explain the German word "*empfinden*" as "to find inwardly in oneself"—where "finding" is the expression of an inactivity, which, however, takes places in the inner world of consciousness.)

Yet, while Fichte thinks that what makes the empirical I feel passive is, in the end, the absolute I itself, Novalis is convinced that the I is, from the outset, struck by a passivity that it can never overcome. This is the decisive motive for his ontological realism: Being is prior to our consciousness; we feel it but don't produce nor even constitute it. Fichte, aiming at an absolute idealism, has, of course, no use for an original passivity by which our mind is struck; since, if one accepts such a sensory passivity to be uncircumventable, one cannot at the same time hold that *all* activity comes from the mind. In more detail, Fichte distinguishes between two forms of sensory passivity: sensation (*Empfindung*) and feeling *sensu stricto* (*Gefühl*). Sensation turns up when the spontaneity of our *faculty of representation* feels inhibited and attributes the cause of this inhibition to the action of the thing-in-itself. According to Fichte, there is no such thing-in-itself; but using the category of causality and being misguided by a natural self-deception, we automatically attribute what we cannot immediately self-attribute to the world instead of to the absolute I—only the philosopher pretends to know that this is, of course, the work of the absolute I which causes the empirical I's sensations, and not, as Kant held, the world of objects. So goes this story of the German term 'Empfindung' (sensation). The German term, 'Gefühl' (feeling), on the contrary, is not the apprehension of an inhibition of the spontaneity of our *representation*, but of our *action*, given that the determinacy that shapes our actions and makes them distinguishable from each other, cannot be self-attributed by and to these actions themselves. So just in acting we (finite human beings in the world) feel the compulsion to admit that this action is not all encompassing and does not exhaust the totality of activity which is the privilege of the absolute I and of it alone.

Now, what happens when Novalis transposes Fichte's theory of feeling from a practical to a theoretical context? Nothing less than a break with the highest premise of an absolute idealism (and ipso facto with any philosophy believing in principles from which the totality of facts—objects of justified true beliefs—can be deduced). Prior to representation and to action is *Being*, and Being is originally apprehended by feeling. Feeling is, as it were, the way our consciousness testifies to the insurmountable superiority of Being in each and every initiative of its own.

Now remember what we know about Kant's thesis about Being: Being (in the sense of actuality) is apprehended by sensation alone (*CPR* A: 225/ B: 272 f.). And Novalis' former tutor Carl Christian Erhard Schmid (whose *Empirische Psychologie* Novalis used while writing his *Fichte-Studien*) had distinguished between sensations and feelings in a narrower sense. Something is given to feeling, something with regard to which the feelings are passive or receptive. Unlike Fichte, Schmid was convinced that feelings belong (or fit) not into a theory of will but into theoretical philosophy (*Empirische Psychologie,* Jena 1791, 199). That is why Novalis at times replaces the term 'feeling' with the term 'sensation,' that is to say that he does not delimit the former consistently from the latter (as Fichte does). And in occasionally describing that which is given to sensation "as *intuition, image*" (l. c., 187, sec. 16), he is falling back on Schmid rather than on Fichte.

Let us now try to make the connection between a feeling (defined along the lines sketched above) and Kant's thesis about Being. Rousseau's *savoyard vicar* states the following about feeling in view of a theory of self-consciousness, namely: "Exister, pour nous, c'est sentir" (*Œuvres complètes,* éd. de la Pléiade, volume IV [Paris: 1969], 600). Now sensations (through which actuality is apprehended) form a subclass of intuitions. This is also true for Novalis: "The concept 'actual' rests on intuition," he notes and then refers to Kant's categories of modality (160, Nr. 161). Like Hölderlin, he then applies the mode of actuality to the highest or original Being emphasizing that it is apprehended by feeling, not grasped by reflection (or thought). What corresponds to Being on the side of consciousness (or in other words: the epistemological mode of feeling), is a "not positing" (125, 1), a "not knowing" (105, 11–13; sensations are non-intentional [cf. Schmid's *Empirical Psychologie,* 1. part, sec. 2, 154 ff.; II. part, sec. I, 179 ff.; esp. III, part, secs. 258 ff.]), while reflexive consciousness *posits* (and *knows)* that of which it is conscious. (Hölderlin's friend Sinclair spoke of an "original athesis," and Jean-Paul Sartre will speak of the original mode of consciousness as being "non-positional" or "non-thetic.") If every knowledge is positing, then it is obvious that feeling—or rather the "spirit" which reveals itself to feeling—cannot be knowledge at all. To know means: to be liable to be mistaken; knowledge claims are fallible. But there is no sense in which we could speak of a feeling's being mistaken: it just occurs and, while occurring, is familiar with itself (or, as Novalis puts it, feels itself). Since what is felt (or is prereflexively intimate), is not known, we may say that it is "believed." This was Jacobi's terminological suggestion, and Novalis knew it very well. That which is believed is that which cannot be known, but has to be presupposed implicitly in every instance of knowing. "What I do not know but do feel," says Novalis, "(and the I feels itself as content)—that I believe" (105, lines 11–13).[20] So, it is not the case that belief lacks epistemological justification (Nr. 3). It is only by and through belief that a necessary presupposition is epistemologically acknowledged:

> The only aim of philosophy is toward *Being.* The human feels the limit which emcompasses everything for him, including himself; call it the *first action.* He has to believe it, as certain as he knows everything else. Consequently, we are not yet, in this respect, transcendent [enough], we are only in the I and for the I (107, lines 1–4).

We now have reached the point where I can substantiate my first thesis about the *Fichte-Studien*. For if it is the case that the highest Being exceeds the possibilities of our cognitive faculties, then the question immediately arises of how there can be any consciousness regarding it. That is the question to which Novalis, who always remained faithful to the basic critical inspiration of Kant (and, in a way, of Fichte), has dedicated a series of reflections that one has to call ingenious both because they are without precedent and because of their effect on subsequent intellectual history. These reflections open up nothing less than an independent course of idealist speculation. At its end there does not stand an "absolute idealism" (or an "absolute knowledge") in the manner of Hegel. Rather, ontological idealism is overcome in favor of an epistemologically enlightened realism. One should speak of a return to Kant even before absolute idealism had time to spread its wings. Here I can sketch only the most basic of Novalis' arguments.

At the beginning of Novalis' thought experiment stands a consideration of the etymology of the word *reflection*.[21] Apparently, Novalis was moved to such a consideration because, as we just saw, he thinks of consciousness as, in principle, related to an object (or "positing"). From this he does not exempt reflection, that is, the consciousness through which we are acquainted with ourselves. With this he distinguishes himself radically from Fichte and his followers who are adherents of an "intellectual intuition." Even the alleged intellectual intuition that (as in Hölderlin) directly grasps Being in its undivided entirety is, upon closer inspection, characterized by an opposition: that of intuition and intellect (Novalis uses the terms 'feeling' and 'reflection'). What would it mean, asks Novalis, if the knowledge that we do indeed possess of ourselves could not be made intelligible *from* the thought of reflection? And what if this were the case for the same reasons that prevent us from representing Being in a simple predicative proposition (a "judgment")? We can only grasp something objective *as ourselves* if we are already acquainted with ourselves prior to all objectification. For that a special consciousness would be needed, one which Novalis calls "feeling." It would be distinguished by the fact that it would posit itself opposite to that which is felt, as is the case with reflection. And yet Novalis does not really resort to this nonobjective mode of consciousness for his argumentation. "Feeling" is rather the name for an ideal limiting case of consciousness on which we cannot count in an epistemic respect. That is, feeling is originally not a case of "knowledge." Following Jacobi's language, Novalis ascribes to it the epistemic mode of "faith" (*Glaube*). Thus, we have acknowledged a presupposition that cannot be questioned, that cannot be resolved into knowledge, and without which philosophy cannot advance a single step.

We are thus referred back to reflection. Out of it we are not able to explicate our actual *self*-consciousness. But *without* it, we have no *consciousness* of our self. Now, a consideration of the meaning of "reflection" reveals, according to Novalis, a connection with mirroring, indeed, for him "reflection" means mirroring, and all that appears in a mirror is inverted. If I hold an object in front of the mirror, the right is reflected as the left and the left as the right. Novalis claims, "Image and Being change. The image is always inverted Being. What is right in the person is left in the image" (142, lines 15–17; cf. 153, Nr. 107, lines 1–2); "It is the right in the consideration of the image/—the image is to the left—the original is to the right—." Furthermore, the ray of light, which approaches the glass, appears to come out of the glass and move towards the opposite direction. Novalis calls this order, which is characteristic for the finite world of consciousness, the "ordo inversus" (127, line 20; 128, lines 30 ff.; 131, line 3; 133, line 26; 136, line 6). In this order, consciousness is "not what it represents, and does not represent what it is" (226, Nr. 330, lines 13 ff.).

Now Novalis asks whether things should be different with the reflection due to which we cognize our self. Could it be the case that it is the fault of reflection that we disfigure Being into judgment (thus into the oppositional play of two synthesized statements)? And that we similarly misrecognize our identity as the interplay of two reflections, an I-subject and an I-object? In that case, the advice of Parsifal would be the only remedy: "The wound can be healed only by the very spear that opened it."[22] In reflecting upon itself, reflection discovers in its own structure the means for mirroring the reversed relations back again into the right order. This is done through self-application or doubling: a reflection that is again reflected upon turns the reversal of relations back around and thus reestablishes the order that obtained prior to the first mirroring. That which first had the appearance of tending "from the limited to the unlimited" thus reveals itself in the light of doubled reflection as an "apparent passing from the unlimited to the limited."[23]

Novalis takes himself to have established two things: first, the origin of the idealist illusion according to which consciousness comprehends all objects and their sum total, "Being," only in the perspective of consciousness, since it starts from itself as that which is first (for itself); and second, the truth of realism according to which Being "fundamentally," that is, in the ontological order, precedes all consciousness and exists independently of it.

The object of the first reflection is by no means the Absolute itself (that would be nonsensical, transcendent speculation) but rather its lack. That is why Novalis calls that which occupies the place of the failed object of this first reflection a "what"[24] and later also "matter."[25] Now, reflection does indeed have an object, but not that which it originally intended: the Absolute. The position of nonobjective Being has been taken over by that of the objective appearance. As soon as feeling—the organ of this experience of deprivation—is in turn "observed" (thus reflectively objectified), its "spirit" necessarily disappears: "It [the feeling] can be observed only in reflection. The spirit of the feeling [that which reveals itself in it properly] is then gone. From the product [the intellectual intuition] one can infer the producer, according to the schema of reflection."[26]

Novalis' attempt at a solution is unusual even in the context of the reflection on self-consciousness at the time. Like Kant and Fichte, he does concede to self-consciousness an eminent position and thus, distinguishes himself from, for example, "post modern" detractors of subjectivity. But he no longer takes self-consciousness to be a principle. It is rather something "dependent" on Being.[27] "I am," Novalis notes, "*not* insofar as I posit myself but insofar as I suspend myself."[28] Thus, a negation of reflection opens the path to Being—the dream of the sovereign self-origination of the subject is ended. However, Being, which has now adopted the fundamental position, does not exercise the abandoned function of grounding, which the tradition from Descartes to Fichte had assigned to the subject. Being is an ontic, not a logical matter. Nothing follows from it in the logical sense of the word, except that the self is no longer the master in its own house. By the way: Could there be a more striking difference to Hegel? Being is not created, but posited as subsisting prior to its negation through any work of any concept.

I will touch briefly upon the other two theses. The second thesis states that Novalis—who differs here from the author of *Urtheil und Seyn*—does not simply juxtapose the thought of "original Being" and that of the internal articulation of consciousness. For Novalis, the internal differentiation of consciousness follows from its unavoidable reflexivity. Therefore, we have to distinguish that which is reflected from the activity of reflecting. In order not to betray the position of philosophical monism, the differentiation of Being in reflection has to be made intelligible by recourse to the very structure of the Absolute. Otherwise the difference would fall outside the sphere of the Absolute. That, however, would mean that the Absolute was not the sum total of all reality but existed along with something else (independent of it). And that would be an internal contradiction for the Being that carries in its very name the specification "*quod est omnibus relationibus absolutum.*"

The determination of this internal differentiation is spelled out by recourse to the opposition of feeling and reflection. Terminological successors to this pair are (in that order) "matter and form," "synthetic and analytic I," "opposition and object" (alternatively, "state and object"), and "essence and property." It is thus always the case that the statement that stands in the position of the subject in the model loses its identity with the application of the predicate and becomes the correlate of a relation. Thus, at a higher level, Novalis regains his initial definition of consciousness as "Being in Being outside of Being," namely, through a consideration of the "significant etymology" of "existence."[29] We "ex-ist" by standing outside of our own Being, thus, transforming it into an appearance and relating to it as something lost. Recall that for Novalis, consciousness "is not what it represents, and does not represent what it is."[30] From here, we are not far from Hegel's determination of time as Being which is, insofar as it is not, and is not, insofar as it is.[31] Lost Being is thus represented under the schema of the past; Being which is not yet under that of the future. Split between the two, the self loses its strict identity and is transformed into the continuity of a life history.

But, you will say: If I capture pure Being always in only one of its predicates and thus fail to reach it properly, then how can I be sure Being is at all a meaningful concept? To this Novalis responds with impressive clarity that there is no such thing as the pure (as such):[32] "[Pure would be] what is neither related nor relatable. . . . The *concept* pure is thus an empty, *necessary* fiction."[33] This fiction is "necessary" because without it we could not understand the connection among the members of the judgment, expressed through the short relational word 'is' of predication. Thus, it remains the unknown "sum total of the properties known by us,"[34] an ideal, a thought-entity that our knowledge can only approximate infinitely but the content of which it can never exhaust.[35]

And with this thought we enter into the realm of my third thesis. It states that Novalis, unlike Hölderlin, establishes an explicit connection between the thought that Being is beyond knowledge and the characterization of philosophy as an infinite task.[36] To be sure, Hardenberg's reasoning is inspired by the doctrines of drive and striving with which he had familiarized himself through his reading of the third part of the *Wissenschaftslehre* (1795).[37] Novalis' thoughts on drive and striving, which are more radical in their point of departure than those of Fichte, fall completely outside the frame of the philosophy that had trusted self-consciousness with the function of the ultimate foundation of the *Wissenschaftslehre*. For Novalis, the formula of philosophy as a "longing for the infinite" is thus an indication of philosophy's intrinisic openness (or the non-final nature of its claims).

This happens in the context of a characterization of philosophy as the search for an absolute foundation. This search for a foundation, so the argument goes, is necessarily infinite since an absolute foundation cannot be given to consciousness. Now, if "this . . . were not given, if this concept contained an impossibility—then the drive to philosophize would be an infinite one—and therefore without end, since there would be an eternal need for an absolute foundation which could be satisfied only relatively—and therefore would never cease."[38]

Once one has convinced oneself of the impossibility of completing the search (or rather of the impossibility of realizing what is sought), Novalis claims, one will "freely renounce the Absolute."[39] "That way, there originates in us an infinite free activity—the only possible Absolute which can be given to us and which we find only through our inability to reach the Absolute and know it. This Absolute given to us can be known only negatively by acting and finding that what we are looking for cannot be reached through any action at all."[40]

> The I signifies that Absolute which is to be known [only] negatively—which remains left over after all abstraction. That which can be known only through acting and which realizes itself through its eternal lack. / Thus, eternity is realized through time, although time contradicts eternity. /[41]

Novalis also calls this futile "searching for one principle" an "absolute postulate"—like a "squaring of the circle," the "*perpetuum mobile*," or the "philosopher's stone."[42] And from the impossibility of ultimately justifying the truth of our conviction he draws the conclusion that truth is to be replaced with probability. Probable is what "is maximally well connected," that is, what has been made as coherent as possible without there being an ultimate justification to support the harmony of our fallible assumptions regarding the world. The coherence of our convictions must replace the lack of an evident Archimedean point of departure. If someone wanted more than that, wanted to bring before consciousness the unknowable foundation as such, which can only be postulated, then that person would land "in the realm of the nonsensical."[43] The fact that the fiction of an absolute justification is called "necessary"[44] does not by itself make it something actual: "we are thus searching for a non-thing (*Unding*), an absurdity."[45]

It has been my intention to document, while staying quite close to his texts, the conclusions drawn by Hardenberg, that philosophy does *not* reach its ideal. Why bother with this point? Because the predominant tendency of researchers is to count Hardenberg among the idealist absolutists—and a proper understanding of his claims concerning the nature of philosophy as a kind of infinite task clearly shows that he was not an absolutist. He did indeed follow his former tutor, Carl Christian Schmid, on the path toward a re-Kantianization of philosophy and away from the arrogation of claims to absolute knowledge put forth by Fichte and Schelling. The position of these latter thinkers was sometimes called "transcendentalism" by Schmid and Niethammer, because it boldly oversteps the limits of knowability. Of course, the fact that the ideal is unreachable by any intellectual effort implies that the propositions obtained by philosophy may never be ultimately justified. After all, something that is justified by Kantian ideas is justified only hypothetically. And thus the early work of Novalis fits organically into the constellation surrounding the *Philosophisches Journal*, with its skepticism regarding the possibility of a philosophy based on first principles.

Early German Romanticism was much more skeptical and modern than its reputation would have it seem. Yet, as its reputation is based on stereotypes and ignorance of some of the most fundamental texts of this movement, the reputation is easily redeemed when one examines these texts with depth and care. What we have learned from our tour through the "constellation" of early German Romantic philosophy that follows Jacobi and the second stage of Reinhold's work are two insights that the materialist and positivist philosophy of the nineteenth century have repressed rather than forgotten and that could be regained only with difficulty toward the end of the twentieth century. The first of these is that self-consciousness has to be described in terms totally unlike those for consciousness of objects and that it therefore cannot be reduced to objective consciousness (not even an objective consciousness that is developed and practiced in intersubjective encounters). The second insight is one of modesty: if self-consciousness is indeed a position that cannot be given up in the economy of philosophy, because otherwise the talk of a distinctive dignity of human beings could not be justified at all—it is still not a principle, especially not one from which eternal truths could be derived. Rather, our *self* has the double experience that it cannot be made intelligible through a reflective turning upon itself and that it depends on some "Being prior to all thinking," which it is not itself. At one point, Kant had considered whether the intelligible substrate of "thinking nature" could be thought of as "matter" or at least as founded in a principle that would equally be the cause of "matter"[46] and of the "subject of thoughts."[47] According to Novalis, our mind is not self-sufficient but rather has its root in some Being (outside of consciousness) that resists its might. The fact that he did not draw any reductionist conclusions from this treatment of self-consciousness is what makes his position so incredibly contemporary.

Lecture 10

On Friedrich Schlegel's Place
in the Jena Constellation

Friedrich Schlegel has been mentioned throughout these lectures, but we have not yet dealt with him in a comprehensive way. He did not get involved with the working out and transformation of the critical philosophy as early or as productively as his peers Erhard, Hölderlin, and Novalis. On the other hand, it can be said of Schlegel (who presumably came to his own viewpoint first in conversation and written correspondence with Novalis) that he carried out the break with a philosophy of first principles most vigorously. Nowhere is philosophizing as an infinite activity so clearly defined as with him. He writes: "The nature of philosophy consists in a longing for the infinite [. . .]" (*KA* XVIII: 418, Nr. 1168; cf. 420, Nr. 1200). From the inaccessibility of a first principle he also drew what is perhaps the most decisive consequence of all for a coherence theory of truth (first around 1800–1801). It was, in any case, Schlegel who wanted to draw from the impossibility of any absolute knowledge and the agreement that exists between our various claims, a negative criteria for the "infinite probability" of our truth claims (*KA* XIX: 301 ff., Nr. 50). The thought of the infinite progression (consider the famous Athenäum-Fragment Nr. 116 which makes reference to a "progressive universal poetry"), and also the love of skepticism are nowhere as obvious as in the work of Schlegel. One need only look through the indexes of the critical edition of his work to see that these concepts and their variations are abundant in his work. Schlegel was, together with Hölderlin, one of the first to draw aesthetic consequences from the fact that the Absolute transcended reflection. This distinguishes him clearly from that constellation which one usually refers to as "idealist philosophy." For idealism holds some absolute principle, whether it be at the beginning or the end of the system, to be epistemically accessible.

I have, as you remember, repeatedly and in an emphasized opposition to the *communis opinio*, proposed that a sharp distinction be drawn between idealism and early Romanticism. Under idealism I understand the conviction—made especially compulsory by Hegel—that consciousness is a self-sufficient phenomenon, one which is still able to make the presuppositions of its existence comprehensible by its own means. In contrast, early Romanticism is convinced, that self-being owes its existence to a transcendent foundation, which does not leave itself to be dissolved into the immanence of consciousness. The same holds for Fichte's philosophy:

> In Fichte's philosophy something creeps in which is not I, nor comes from the I, and which is also not merely Non-I (*KA* XVIII: 25, Nr. 83).

So the foundation of self-being becomes an inexplicable puzzle. This puzzle can no longer be handled by reflection alone. Therefore, philosophy is completed in and as art. Schlegel remarks that: "[. . .] the beautiful insofar as it is, is an absolute" (*KA* XVIII: 26, Nr. 92). This is the case because in the beautiful, a structure is given to us whose meaning (sense-fullness [*Sinnfülle*]) cannot be exhausted by any possible thought. Hence, the inexhaustible wealth of thought with which we are confronted in the experience of the beauty of art (*Kunstschönen*), becomes a symbol of that which in reflection is the unrecoverable foundation of unity, which must, due to structural reasons, escape the mental capacity of dual self-consciousness. Early German Romanticism, in a polemic dismissal of the classical use of this term, names this type of symbolic representation allegory.

In order to understand the particular difference between the early German Romantic aesthetic and the classical view of so-called idealism, it is useful to take another look at Jacobi's notion of the transreflexivity of Being—this time, admittedly, with a concentration on Friedrich Schlegel's reception of this thought. Jacobi believed that he could achieve a perfect dualism between the unmediated certainty of Being and the infinite relativity of rational justification. Therewith he helped the philosophers of Tübingen and also Jena to reach the insight that guided the rest of their thinking, namely, that the unconditioned cannot be reached from any chain of conditions. Friedrich Schlegel's thinking takes a turn different from that of Jacobi's on the one hand, and from the absolute idealism of Schelling and Hegel on the other hand. The latter two believe that knowledge of the Absolute is one with the self-dissolution of relativity; conversely, Jacobi attempts to overcome relativity though a higher faculty of knowledge which he calls "feeling."

Friedrich Schlegel is convinced with Jacobi, that "[. . .] the unknowability of the absolute is an identical triviality" (*KA* XVIII: 511, Nr. 64).[1] With Hegel and Schelling, in contrast, he shares the insight that the concept of finitude is dialectically bound to that of infinity and cannot be isolated from it. He doesn't conclude from this however, that we can represent the Absolute positively in knowledge. It has the status of a regulative idea (as in Kant), without which finite thought would be comprehended as a series of fragments and patchworks, but through which finite thought cannot simply disregard its limitedness. Schlegel expressed this by claiming in 1804 that: "The actual contradiction in our I is that we feel at the same time finite and infinite" (*KA* XII: 334). The unity of these two conditions constitutes the life of I-ness itself. However, this unity is not for the I; it is impossible for the I to secure in one and the same consciousness both its finitude and its infinitude, for both modes of consciousness are opposed to each other both temporally and qualitatively (*KA* XVIII: 298, Nr. 1243). The Being of the I never becomes an object of reflection; and the I becomes an object of reflection only insofar as it dispenses with Being. Schlegel notes that, "A person as individual is not completely but only piecemeal there. A person can never be there" (*KA* XVIII: 506, Nr. 9 [note from autumn 1796]). The Being-in-itself (*An-sich-Sein*), which the reflexive I can never get a look at, is expressed *ex negativo* as freedom; insofar as it cannot establish itself in its finitude but rather must always strive to move beyond its limits, never able to remain absorbed in its identity with its respective condition. Removed from its foundational past, with whose memory the light of self-consciousness is filled, the self continually feels new possibilities sent against it, which do not grant it any definitive self-identity. To the three dimensions of time there correspond (in the Cologne lectures and the corresponding fragments from this period) the following modes of consciousness: memory, intuition, and premonition (*Ahnung*). Their triad is only the threefold nuanced expression of an essential 'inadequacy' (*Unangemessenheit*) of the essence of time to its actuality. "Time," Schlegel says, "is only eternity brought in from its disorder, from its disjointment" (*KA* X: 550). Time, therefore, reveals itself in the loss of Being (the eternal) in the finite I and perpetuates itself in a reflexive grip. Hence, Schlegel concurs with Schelling's diagnosis of Fichte's philosophy. According to Schelling's diagnosis, whoever doesn't seize the Absolute immediately and completely, must make reference to an infinite progress (*SW* I: 4, 358), which in time vainly, that is to say, infinitely, anticipates eternity. Because Schlegel explains the Absolute as unknowable, he must agree at first with Schelling's somewhat jesting presentation of the consequence of Fichte's position. This becomes the point of departure for Schlegel's theory of the fragment. The paradox defended by Fichte (on the one hand the I exists only under the presupposition of an Absolute, on the other hand the Absolute exists only in and for the I) becomes the motor for Schlegel's discovery of irony and indeed the general driving force of his entire thought. In the autumn of 1796 he notes laconically: "Knowing (*Erkennen*) already indicates some conditioned knowledge (*bedingtes Wissen*). The unknowability of the Absolute is therefore an identical triviality" (KA XVIII: 511, Nr. 64; cf. 512, Nr. 71: ["The Absolute is itself undemonstratable."]). In these claims, whose obvious reference to Jacobi is in no need of any further commentary, absolute idealism is radically refuted. Schlegel's own suggestion for the solution to the problem assumes a progressive postponement (*Hinausschiebbarkeit*) of the limits of knowledge: that is, we can attain no positive (demonstrative, intuitive) knowledge of the Absolute. To believe that we could, would be something akin to a sort of mysticism which Schlegel refers to as, "the striving (*Trachten*) for absolute unity" (7, Nr. 40), for "perfect identity of subject and object" (8, Nr. 42). An absolute unity of consciousness with that which is conscious is, however, incompatible with the conditions of conscious apprehension (511, Nr. 64). Therefore, "the mystic ends with dull journeys into itself" (4, Nr. 6). Fichte's *Wissenschaftslehre*, which Schlegel describes in each of the following ways, is a type of mysticism: it is "an arbitrary positing of an unknowable and 'absolutely contingent' something as its beginning point" (31, Nr. 127); "a denial of an intersubjective communicable-ness (*Mitteilbarkeit*)" (4, Nr. 7); "a contempt for the critical limits of knowledge." Schlegel continues with this classification of Fichte's *Wissenschaftslehre* by claiming that: "In the *Wissenschaftslehre*, the method must also be critical; but that is what Fichte is not" (8, Nr. 52). Schlegel continues this line of thought by adding in another fragment that: "That which Fichte presupposes as given and self-explanatory can almost always be boldly refuted" (31, Nr. 126).

According to Schlegel, "mysticism is in fact the abyss into which everything sinks" (3, Nr. 4), even, he adds, "the most sober and most solid of all furies" (5, Nr. 13); it is a form of dogmatism (5, Nr. 10). So the "newer mystic," Fichte, falls like "the pope in his own realm, and has the infallible power to open and close heavens and hell with his key"(3, Nr. 2). This accounts for Fichte's arrogant dismissal of all people who don't want to follow him through thick and thin and to whom, according to Schlegel, Fichte "throughout his work repeats that he really doesn't want to speak nor could he, even if he cared to" (37, Nr. 200).

Hence, mysticism is not a plausible alternative to critical philosophy. Skepticism remains in sympathetic relation to critical philosophy insofar as it assumes no principle secured through evidence by virtue of which our fallible convictions would be certain. The fallibility can also be interpreted as the non-conclusiveness (*Nichtendgültigkeit*) of our previous state of knowledge. And then a view of the growth of our knowledge is opened. Schlegel interprets this as 'progression' or as 'infinite approximation.' In other words: the inconclusiveness (*Unendgültigkeit*) of our knowledge doesn't keep us from making cognitive progress, quite the contrary; it in fact allows us to make advances in our acquisition of knowledge. So, on the other side of the limits of our actual knowledge, we do not find the realm of the unknowable or the nonsensical. We are always rather at the same time on this side of these limits and just beyond these same limits. Schlegel expresses this in the following way:

> The claim (against Schelling and Fichte), that all positing beyond the limits of the knowable is transcendent, contradicts itself and brings all philosophy to an end. Further, if the theoretically Absolute is posited, then the limits of the knowable are not even known.—One can determine no limits, if one is not at once, on this side of the Absolute and beyond it. Therefore it is impossible to determine the limits of knowledge if we cannot, in some way, (even if not recognizing ourselves to be) get beyond these same limits (*KA* XVIII: 521, Nr. 23; cf. *KA* XIX: 120, Nr. 348).

We are always in some condition of relative self-identity (as a relatively closed condition of knowledge), and we overstep this condition (as our past) always in the direction of a future. Irony is the response which consciousness of the relativity of each relationship and fixation receives—as, for example, occurs in the selective union of wit (*Witz*). Irony is that which refers "allegorically" to the infinite, exposing its provisionality and incompleteness.

That will be Schlegel's solution to the problem of the limits of our knowledge and the necessity of the Absolute. But we do not yet know how he reaches this solution. From the fact that we cannot immediately represent the union of unity and plenitude, it does not follow that we can adjust ourselves constantly to one of the two moments. The flow of life constantly drives us from a relative unity to a relative plenitude; no consciousness grasps both parts at once. Which philosophical method can do justice to this temporally disparate 'not only but also'?

"In my system," Schlegel explains (in fragments from August 1796, when Schlegel moved to Jena [Cf. Ernst Behler's commentary in *KA* XIX: 527 ff.]), "the frist principle is really a *Wechselerweis* (alternating proof). In Fichte's a postulate an unconditioned proposition" (*KA* XVIII: 520 ff., Nr. 22).[2] The reciprocally self-supporting propositions that Schlegel is thinking of here are, in some passages, identified in the following way: "The I posits itself"—that would be an unconditioned proposition—and "The I should posit itself"—that would be the postulate. Schlegel says in another place (e.g. l.c., 36, Nr. 193) that:

> "The I posits itself" and "The I should posit itself" are not two propositions deduced from a higher one; one is as high as the other; further they are two first principles, not one. *Wechselgrundsatz.*

The fragment is located in a collection of notes entitled, "On the spirit of Fichte's *Wissenschaftslehre*" (from 1797–1798, pp. 31 ff.). Interestingly, Schlegel no longer makes reference to a 'Wechselerweis' (alternating proof), but rather directly to a 'Wechselgrundsatz' (alternating principle). And the weakness of Fichte's *Wissenschaftslehre* (the one from 1794–95, not the 'nova methodo' which would come during the next winter semester) is seen to consist in the insistence that one could create a science of knowledge based on one proposition as the first principle. Schlegel was quick to point out that "[i]n Fichte's [system] there is a postulate *and* an unconditioned proposition" (521, Nr. 22, italics added). Hence, there are two candidates for the first principle, and not only one as a philosophy based on a single first principle would have it. If one of them were self-evident and moreover sufficient to ground all of philosophy, there would be no need for a *Wechselerweis*. This means that Schlegel cannot follow Fichte in his use of the general principle which states that, "The I posits itself absolutely" because this proposition is not self-sufficient. The proposition passes itself off as evidence (hence as of theoretical use), while it is really the case that, according to Schlegel "the Absolute is itself indemonstrable" (512, Nr., 71), that is, in Schlegel's words "not knowable" (511, Nr. 64).[3] A beginning point like "I am" is (as Fichte demonstrates himself in the *Grundlage der Wissenschaft des Praktischen* [Foundation for a Science of the Practical]) is to be referred to *praxis* and will only then be completely comprehensible. One can formulate this in the following way: The principle which the first section of the *Wissenschaftslehre* presents sustains itself as weakly as Schmid and Diez had proven to the followers of Rheinhold: it relies upon presuppositions which can only be clarified in the practical part of the *Wissenschaftslehre*. This turn was not forseeable before the third part of the *Wissenschaftslehre* had been presented (and this part had not yet been worked out by Fichte at the beginning of his lectures in Jena; indeed, he may not even had conceived of it yet). When Hölderlin (as we saw) writes to Hegel on January 26, 1795, that he has the impression, based upon what he has heard at Fichte's lectures, that Fichte would like to go "beyond the fact of consciousness into theory," an obviously transcendent beginning, he communicates an impression which many of the listeners of the lectures shared. Like other skeptics, Hölderlin (as we saw) argues that the absolute I is unknowable, that "at least for us" it can be nothing. Along similar lines, Schlegel claims that "the limits of knowability are still not known, even if the *theoretically* Absolute is posited" (521, Nr. 23 [italics added]). The theoretically Absolute is expressed in the proposition 'I am' (or 'The I posits itself absolutely'). If this proposition were a principle that was self-evident, it would be in no need of the support of the practical proposition: 'The I should be.' Insofar as this practical proposition is ascribed a task of justification, which the proposition 'I am' cannot achieve alone, the "claim (against Schelling and Fichte), that all positing beyond the limits of the knowable is transcendent" is refuted (l. c.). Because now this proposition is referred to an idea, from which one day it will become comprehensible (admittedly even then, to be precise, never in the way of knowing).

Schlegel not only argues that a theoretical proposition (which, afterall, is made fully meaningful only through *praxis*) cannot be the foundation of philosophy. He also affirms that the notion 'I' cannot express any Absolute because it is conditioned (*KA* XII: 147 f.). "It is conditioned" means: it includes something from outside of itself (one must assume "something besides the proposition"). In this respect it is not self-sufficient but strives always after an ever more perfect determination:

> And so that would lead to always another proposition, *ad infinitum*, without ever coming to an end, that is without ever resolving the task satisfactorily, since the mistake lies in the first sentence and it cannot, even with full refinement [. . .] be removed; in this way, there is always something, even if just the finest speck (*Atömchen*) which remains besides and above the I (l.c., 150,5).

Therefore the first proposition of Fichte's philosophy cannot be considered to be a self-sufficient principle. Fichte himself must assume another proposition beyond this so-called first principle: the principle of reaction (*Gegenwirkung*), of limitative activity, the "check (*Anstoß*)," which the conscious (and therefore already limited) I cannot, in any way, attribute to itself and must therefore posit outside itself: another argument for the preference of the operation with a double or alternating principle (*Wechselgrundsatz*).

Even in the muddled version of the lectures on transcendental philosophy which Schlegel delivered in Jena from October 27, 1800 through March 24, 1801 in his capacity as lecturer in philosophy at the university there, the baselines of the operation with the *Wechselgrundsatz* can be somewhat recognized. In these lectures, Schlegel distinguishes between that with which philosophy must begin and that through which philosophy can be sufficiently grounded. He calls the first a principle and the second an "idea." The beginning point in philosophy is just one part of an infinite chain, whose first part or origin, just as any part in general, is something individual. The original (*Ursprüngliche*) is also called the primitive, the opposite of which is totality (*KA* XII: 4). To begin with a first and primitive—yet individual—is not to begin with something certain. Only the baselines, the first principles, are given, to give more is not possible at the beginning, "because applicability is infinite"(49), that is, through a beginning principle applicability cannot be mastered or exhausted. (Schlegel confirms that this is the right interpretation, insofar as he translates "infinite" as "not perfectible.") The first principle, then, does not contain its consequences epistemically *in nuce*, so the motive to philosophize is not a successful intuition of an *omnitudo realitatis*, but rather (as had been the case with Novalis) the "feeling" of a lack, also referred to by Schlegel as an imperfection (*Unvollendung*): "a striving towards knowledge" (p. 3), a "tendency [. . .] *toward the Absolute*" (p. 4), "*a longing* [. . . .] *for the infinite*" (pp. 7 ff.). The departure point of all philosophizing is caught up in a tension with the whole. And it is this feeling of an initial incompleteness (*Unganzheit*) (or a feeling of the whole pulling one into its grip), which gives rise to the process of philosophizing—as longing for knowledge. Schlegel can say therefore on the one hand that philosophy results from two 'elements': the consciousness that we have of ourselves as incomplete (or, what amounts to the same, finite) beings and the infinite as that through which we strive to complete ourselves (make ourselves whole) (p. 5). This corresponds to his later announcement that the "constitution of philosophy" results from "two fundamental concepts" (p. 48). Let the consciousness from which one departs, which is the most primitive (Schlegel calls this "feeling" [7; cf. 355,1]), carry the name of 'intellectual intuition' (17): it does not stand for the full possession of reality but for the "minimum of reality," as opposed to "the infinite [. . .] the positive or maximum of reality." With this equal positioning of consciousness and the infinite, Schlegel can now portray the one and the all, ἓν καὶ πᾶν (clearly following Spinoza's lead, cf. p. 7, passim). Thirdly, however, he can bring to mind his earlier claim that philosophy cannot be grounded upon one principle but rather upon an alternating principle (*Wechselprinzip*). For, the relationship of the individual with the infinite from which it has been torn is, one could say, the alternating proof (*Wechselerweis*) between a principle and an idea. For we begin with this torn off individual and the infinite is experienced by consciousness as a constant pulling force or aspiration (*Sog*). Schlegel expresses this as follows:

> Knowledge of the origin or primitive gives us principles. And knowledge of the totality gives us ideas. *A principle is therefore knowledge of the origin.* An idea is knowledge of the whole (4).

One must probably read this in the following way: the first kind of knowledge (*Wissen*) only directs us to knowledge (*Erkenntnis*) of the departure points, which are indicated by their deficiency. This kind of knowledge does not put us any closer to knowledge of the all (*Totum*) towards which we strive and for which we long. That could only be done by a knowledge that would instruct us regarding the justification deficit of the departure point, and that is the anticipating knowledge of ideas. For philosophy, however, we need both. The self-contained, completely determined Absolute would be both: unity of the one *and* the infinite (cf. p. 20, note, p. 25). Or else: first in the infinite approximation toward the (unreachable) infinite do we find retroactive justification and enlightenment regarding the departure point of philosophy.

Confirmation for this interpretation of Schlegel's conception of philosophy's starting point is found later in a series of private lectures that Schlegel delivered in Cologne in 1804–05 (*Kölner Privatvorlesungen*). Here he claims that "the beginning point of philosophy [. . .] does not consist in a positive knowledge of the unconditioned, but rather in the uncertainty of natural knowledge of reason on the one hand, and in experience, on the other"(*KA* XII: 324). This double lack commits philosophical method to "a middle course between experience and higher sources," the upshot of the preconceptual self-intuition (for intuition is the relative minimum in the development of the notion of a complete and absolute I [l.c.]) is the exit of a preconceptual self-view. A bit later Schlegel claims that precisely because intuition, as a starting point, can offer "certainty but no knowledge" (331,3), "it has an effect on our hunger for knowledge (*Wißbegierde*); intuition convinces us of our great lack of knowledge (*Unwissenheit*), it makes us more perceptive [. . .] [through its effect on our hunger for knowledge] intuition receives from this increasing indication of our lack of knowledge the most powerful stimulants for investigation and material for future knowledge" (330, 1).

Already in Schlegel's notes from 1796–97 this enlightenment happens genetically, therefore progressively and, since the principle of the entire *Wissenschaftslehre* proves, in the end, to be an idea in the Kantian sense, this principle can never be final. The I is not really given (as Fichte's first principle would suggest) as the result of an activity (*Tathandlung*), but rather proves itself to be assigned as one task in the series of tasks which must be completed (7, Nr., 32).[4] Parallel formulations from the Cologne Private Lectures of 1804–05 speak of "the object of philosophy" as the "positive knowledge (*positive Erkenntnis*) of infinite reality." So certainly it is "easy to see, that this task can never be accomplished" (*KA* XII: 166). Schlegel writes that:

> If knowledge of the infinite is itself infinite, therefore always only incomplete, imperfect, then philosophy as a science can never be completed, closed and perfect, it can always only strive for these high goals, and try all possible ways to come closer and closer to them. Philosophy is in general more of a quest or a striving for a science than itself a science. (l.c.).

This has much to do with the fact that the philosophizing I is never presented in an original intellectual intuition. Rather it has knowledge of itself as an idea in the Kantian sense, hence, as an emptiness that looks for completion, or as a task, that through no time and no activity could ever be fully executed. The perfect "I always remains, not as a clear object of knowledge but perhaps as an insoluble puzzle, therefore it is also always only a likelihood" (330; cf. pp. 333 f.). So—as with Niethammer, Novalis, Sinclair, Feuerbach, or Forberg—the notion of an infinite progress comes into play, so that we part with philosophizing from the certainty of a an absolute, self-grounding, first principle. If "deducing" means, to produce a foundation for our validity claims, then it holds in philosophy that: "deducing never has an end, and should never have an end" (KA XVIII: 31, Nr., 129). In the end, a "demonstration of the I" is not only not possible, but it would be "also not at all necessary for the beginning of philosophy" (KA XII: 331), and this is because we have a "certainty" (l.c., 3) in our prereflexive self-consciousness which cannot be denied by anyone without generating contradictions (l.c., 2), which however "no knowledge" (l.c., 2) can present. This original self-intuition concerns what is close to Novalis' concept of "self-feeling." According to this, the I is certain but this certainty does not have the status of a complete or demonstrative knowing. Knowledge implies truth, while feeling does not. Hence, there is "an enormous gap between truth and feeling" (335, 3).

> In the future we will call self-consciousness feeling (*Empfindung*), as a finding in oneself (*in sich finden*), because the I cannot, ultimately be proved but only found. (334, 2).

"Self-feeling (*Selbst-Gefühl*)" (or "Self-consciousness"), adds Schlegel, delivers "[insofar as it is] related to knowledge and the possibility of knowledge, [. . . only] the certainty of something incomprehensible"(333, 5; cf. 334, 3). According to Schlegel:

> The puzzle of self-feeling which always accompanies us, is also indeed the reason why thoughtful people are put into doubt by philosophers who try to explain everything. They feel certain (even if perhaps they cannot express this) that there exists something incomprehensible; that they themselves are incomprehensible. (334, 1).

The infinite regress (*Begründungsregress*) involved in our search for knowledge or hunger for knowledge, which was referred to by both Jacobi and Niethammer, (and according to which philosophy is defined) is recognized by Schlegel to be a reality of all philosophizing, without exception. It is, however, reinterpreted as an endless progress. In the "I as idea" an "original image" is introduced to us, which, according to Schlegel, "we can approximate only 1/0 (infinitely)" (KA XVIII: 26, Nr. 85).[5] Because the approximation is itself infinite and the I is an inexplicable puzzle (and, as such only presentable through art), there will be no time at which an absolute knowledge of the searched for takes place. Talk of an "infinite approximation" refers us to the day when pigs will fly, not to some long awaited Hegelian absolute knowledge. Schlegel speaks of an "antinomy of intuition" (329, top; 335 f.). This antinomy arises as a result of the fact that we must understand ourselves as at once infinite and (for the sake of the condition of consciousness [cf. 325]) limited. The solution of the antinomy will consist, according to Schlegel, in that "we cannot explain the feeling of limitation which constantly accompanies us in life, in any other way than by assuming that we are only one piece of ourselves" (337). Therefore, we must distinguish between our conscious I and an absolute or original I (337 ff.). The feeling of ourselves as limited beings implies the notion of "the elevation of the I through the idea of *becoming* an original I" (339), as well as, inversely, the notion of a theory of 'memory' as the thinking-of the lost whole in the "torn off, dismembered, derived I" (pp. 348 ff., 380 ff.). In memory, the "incompleteness of our I" as such is presented to us (354), and therewith the "suffering (*leidenden*)," the inaccessible parts of our reason (just as in understanding we are presented with the active, free parts, those parts which overstep the deficiency they point to [op. cit.]). Schlegel defines the epistemic attitude of the striving I which goes in the opposite direction, that is, the future oriented I, as "premonition" (377 ff.). This orientation toward the strived for must be called "premonition" (in the restrictive sense), because there is no positive knowledge connected with it. Since the remembered, lost I is one and the I anticipated by premonition is multiple and in itself varied, Schlegel believes that he may "deduce" our familiarity with the notion of unity from memory and that of infinite plenitude from premonition (381).

To be sure, Schlegel is not completely content with shifting the philosophical task of justification from the posited (or "intellectually intuited") I to the "I as idea" (or to the "original I"). He claims that: "The Absolute is no idea" (513, Nr. 80). And he continues, "Postulates are only propositions derived from imperatives, therefore they are not suitable for the foundation of knowledge" (518, Nr. 14). Most importantly, a postulated proposition is unburdened by the difficulty to be ad hoc and as such proven:

> The Absolute itself is indemonstrable, but the philosophical assumption of the same must be justified analytically and proven (512, Nr. 71).

That is: I must justify the goal of the "infinite progression" as a movement towards the Absolute, namely, precisely then, when I cannot "prove" the Absolute through some initial knowledge belonging to a sort of intellectual intuition. Schlegel is quite clear regarding this point, when he characterizes the absolute I—the goal of infinite approximation—as something which cannot be intuited but can merely be thought. From this it follows that the notion of intellectual intuition is not operative in his philosophy. And again in this context the expression 'analytic' which we will pay close attention to comes into use:

> The "I should be" must also be able to be demonstrated analytically in and of itself, independently of I = I. (36, Nr. 187).[6]

This follows from the thesis directed against Fichte that, "the I does not posit itself because it posits itself but rather because it should posit itself; herein lies a very big difference" (35, Nr., 176). The difference is big because the validity of the self-positing is restricted here by an ought. The I *is* only insofar as it *should* be. This means, however, that I cannot derive one of the propositions from the other non-circularly, I must rather posit both as equally primitive. Fichte's "entire W[issenschafts]l[ehre]," which initially subordinates the first under the second and in the last part, the second under the first, can therefore be criticized as "a Hysteronproteron" (35, Nr. 170). The absolutely necessary prerequisite has then however only "lemmatic" validity (as Reinhold would say). It holds only under the proviso of later substantiation. And just this procedure of subsequent substantiation is what Schlegel calls "analytic." He also speaks occasionally of a "logical imperative" (e.g., 514, Nrs. 89, 91; 518, Nr. 11)—in contrast to a "logical fact" (*Datum*). A logical fact would be something like the proposition from which Schelling's *Ich-Schrift* departs, namely, "a system of knowledge exists" (*Wissenschaft ist*). In contrast, the logical imperative does not presuppose knowledge as given but rather departs from the proposition: "a system of knowledge should be" (*Wissenschaft soll sein*). To "prove analytically," Schlegel says, is left to the experts too, "who, perhaps philosophize without even knowing or willing to do so, that is, who indeed strive toward a totality (*Allheit*) of knowledge or even make claims to have possession of the same" (514, Nr. 90; cf. 506, Nr. 10). This demand, which is essentially inherent to the drive toward philosophy (and is contained in the etymology of the word itself), is "the given with which the philosopher begins" (5, Nr. 18).[7] In a note from 1798, Schlegel writes: "The whole must begin with a reflection on the infinitude of the drive towards knowledge" (283, Nr. 1048). That may well be the "middle" from which Schlegel says, philosophy, "like the epic poem" must start (518, Nr. 16). At times its vehicle is "feeling," at times "self-intuition."

Already a fragment, which Schlegel had written in July 1797 during a visit with Novalis in Weißenfels, we see a move in this direction: "According to its formation, philosophy must begin with infinitely many propositions (not with one)" (KA XVIII: 26, Nr. 93). Hence, we can conclude the following: genetically ("according to its formation") philosophy cannot begin with one proposition; any arbitrary proposition could be its beginning point;

therefore, philosophy can begin in *media res* (in the middle). And the impulse (*Antrieb*) to philosophizing from the middle is a reflection on "the infinitude of the drive towards knowledge." The beginning of philosophy is therefore not a positive principle grasped by knowledge, but rather the feeling of a lack of knowledge. We can also express this in the following way: Knowledge is not *given*, but rather the feeling of an emptiness. This appears to reflection as an aspiration toward fulfillment, as a striving for what is lacking, as what Novalis called "a drive toward completion" (*Ergänzungstrieb*). Schlegel writes: "A person as individual is not completely, but only piecemeal there. A person can never be there" (506, Nr. 9).[8] The person can only refer to his own lack by anticipating the totality (or completeness) of that which escapes him. In the Cologne private lectures Schlegel expresses this state of affairs with even clearer hermeneutical conceptualness as follows: the advance, which the path of philosophy opens to original-immediate self-perception (as a private being [*Seienden*]), consists therein, that first through this, "the true meaning of the departure proposition is gradually understood. The self-understanding of the beoming I grows as it were. The "essence" of A is well-understood as that which the I perceives directly, not A itself but rather its meaning" (*KA* XII: 350). So I am not (completely or in my full meaning—I am only piecemeal), I should however (completely and fully comprehensibly) be. And this "single [. . .] correct presupposition is discovered on the analytic path; all that is synthetic goes from there. The analysis must be led up as highly as possible, up to the: *The I should be*" (*KA* XVIII: 519, Nr. 17).[9]

Lecture 11

On the Origins of Schlegel's Talk of a *Wechselerweis* and His Move Away from a Philosophy of First Principles

S chlegel was not the first to use the terms 'analytic' and 'synthetic' in the context of an attack on a philosophy based on first principles.[1] Yet, his use of these terms adds important new nuances to their meaning. In Schlegel's work, 'analytic' doesn't mean (as in Kant's use of it to describe analytic judgments) that which is apprehended simply by knowledge of the meaning of words and the principle of noncontradiction. Rather it is here used in a second sense, one which can also be traced to Kantian models: as reflective ascending movement from one proposition (provisionally assumed to be true) to its ground. So Schlegel can say: "The single correct presupposition (of philosophy) is discovered on the analytic path" (519, Nr. 17). The ascent to the right presupposition is motivated by the will to know. If the presupposed reason for holding a certain proposition to be true is an idea, as is the case with merely postulated reasons, then the proposition is merely hypothetical, therefore it cannot be absolutely justified. The proposition with which we are concerned here is 'The I posits itself.' As such, it is not yet justified and must be referred to the other proposition ('The I should be'), which, in turn, thematizes the I not as something actual, but as an idea. Schlegel says: "All *thetical propositions* can, insofar as proof or verification should be *philosophical*, only be analytically proved <invented>" (511, Nr. 62; cf. 513 f., Nr. 88). He continues, asserting that: "The analysis must be taken as high as possible, up until: 'The I should be'" (519, Nr. 17). If the true principles are not deductive but rather principles that have been discovered, then they cannot be presupposed but rather they must be approached progressively. Indeed, precisely because of this, as the last citation shows, these principles are postulative rather than demonstrative. This conviction is reflected in Schlegel's frequent references to "infinite progression,"[2] or "infinite approximation"[3] and "striving for the infinite" (e.g., 9, Nr. 62) or "longing for the infinite" (418, Nr. 1168; 420, Nr. 1200). This conviction is also found in Schlegel's claim that: "Every proof is infinitely perfectible" (518, Nr. 9; cf. 506, Nr. 12). After all, that this ascent leads to the infinite, rather than into an aimless wandering or to a dead end, can and must be justified analytically. And this analytic justification, Schlegel seems to assume, is in need of both the proposition, 'I am' as well as the proposition, 'I should be,' with neither standing on its own but rather with each depending on the other in a reciprocal way.

Schlegel's "ultimate ground" (*letzter Grund*) is therefore avowedly not a single first (Fichtean) principle,[4] but rather a consortium of two, or indeed (as we shall see after looking at some other fragments) several propositions.[5] We can locate this move towards a plurality regarding first principles (usually a dualism) and the corresponding polemic against the desire to depart with a single first principle, in many of Schlegel's writings. In the second half of 1797, Schlegel notes: "αρχαι—principles are always in plural, they construct themselves together; there is never just one as the fanatics of first principles think"(105, Nr. 910). Already in the autumn of 1796 he had noted that: "The basic science (*Grundwissenschaft*) must be deduced from two ideas, principles, concepts, intuitions without any other matter" (518, Nr. 16). This is similar to the idea expressed in his claim (88, Nr. 708) that: "Principles are facts which construct themselves together" and (in 108, Nr. 942) that: "Two foundations and an alternating construction (*Wechselconstruktion*), these seem to suit [systematic philosophy] and absol[ute] [philosophy]."

As original as this idea is to Schlegel, one could nevertheless speculate that in the choice of his expression, he may have been inspired by Fichte.[6] In the first section of the *Grundlage des Naturrechts nach Principien der Wissenschaftslehre* (from 1796), a work which Schlegel knew well, indeed, one for which he had written a review, Fichte spoke of *Wechselsätze* [alternating propositions] and *Wechselbegriffe[n]* [alternating concepts] (*WW* III: 17)[7] and explained his use of these terms as follows: "one says, what the other says" that is, "one means what the other means." Accordingly, *Wechselbegriffe* are, for example, "finite rational entities" and the "limitation of the object of their reflection." Further *Wechselsätze* are: "The self-positing of the I" and "Reflection of one's self." The I, Fichte explains, can only meet with that which is limited in this realization of self-reflection. Otherwise, the act would not be a conscious act. This is because consciousness of a given object presupposes the determination of this object. And something is determined as that which it is, if it is distinguished unequivocally from all others that it is *not*. Such characterizations and distinctions are precisely that which one calls the function of concepts.

Of course, this is not the sense in which Schlegel uses the terms *Wechselbegriffe* or *Wechselerweis*. In Schlegel's use there is no move towards equating these terms with the meaning of concepts—these terms refer to propositions none of which could serve as a first principle because none is comprehensible in and of itself, but is rather in need of another principle, for which the same holds. Otherwise it would not be at all comprehensible how Schlegel could hope, with the expression '*Wechselbegriff*,' to formulate an alternative to (or, more precisely, *against*) a philosophy based on first principles (of Fichte's type).

One could think of another, much closer source of Schlegel's talk of *Wechselerweis*: Fichte's use of *Wechselbestimmung* (alternating or reciprocal-determination) at the beginning of the theoretical part of his *Wissenschaftslehre*.[8] Hölderlin, in his famous letter to Hegel from January 26, 1795, calls this, "certainly peculiar"(*StA* VI: 156); and Schiller refers in the first comment of the thirteenth *Brief über die ästhetische Erziehung* (Letter on aesthetic education) to the "concept of *Wechselwirkung* (reciprocal effect)," which one finds in Fichte's *Wissenschaftslehre*, "admirably analyzed" (*NA* 20, 347 f.). With "*Wechselbestimmung*" (reciprocal determination), Fichte understood the interaction of two activities, in which the absolute I, in order to become conscious, internally articulates. That part of activity that the I cannot attribute to itself, it posits as the Non-I and vice versa. Hence, it is clear that the two concepts determine each other reciprocally; for more activity on the part of the Non-I is immediately reflected as less activity on the part of the I. Or also: the activity which strives toward the infinite will have exactly that extension which is set down by the limitative activity that strives away from the Absolute (cf. *GA* I: 2, 289 f.; *WW* I: 130 f.).

Novalis was impressed by this idea, especially as Fichte had attempted to show the structure of the *Wechselbestimmung* (reciprocal determination) through the "hovering of the imagination" (*Schweben der Einbildungskraft*) between acting and nonacting. Further, *Wechselbestimmungen* play a powerful role in Novalis' *Fichte-Studien*: "The unconditioned I changes absolutely in itself" (*NS* II: 123, line 31) means that, under the gaze of reflection, the two poles of the unconditioned I transform always into each other, therefore, their "roles switch places."[9] It may be that Schlegel, who had extensively discussed Fichte's notion of the I with Novalis in the summer of 1796 (between July 29, and August 6), had his first contact with the concept '*Wechselbestimmung*' from Novalis.[10] But it is clear, that the recollection of the definite use of the concept in Novalis or Fichte's thought, does not fully explain Schlegel's fundamental use of the term '*Wechselerweis*.' It would make no sense, one wants to say, that the I and Non-I or infinite and limiting activity or feeling and reflection determine each other (where possible still *ordine inverso*). Furthermore Fichte and Novalis use the expression to indicate the inner-differentiation (*Binnendifferenziertheit*) within the Absolute and not as the name for an alternative to a philosophy based upon first principles, which departs from an evident Absolute. And it is precisely this alternative that concerns Schlegel.

Neither Novalis nor Schlegel allowed their philosophical differences with Fichte to cool their personal relationship with him. Quite the contrary; on January 30, 1797, Schlegel wrote the following to Christian Gottfried Körner:

> I have been led with overwhelming force into speculation this winter. I have also come to an understanding of the main issue of Fichte's system. However my philosophy can easily rest ten years on my desk. I myself speak with Fichte always only about the outer work. I find much more to like in his person since I separated myself definitively from the *Wissenschaftslehre* (*KA* XXIII: 343, cf. letters to Novalis: letters dated May 24 and 26, 1797 [l.c., 367, 4; 369, 5]).

Novalis—in fact a good three-fourths of a year earlier—had also announced his dismissal of a philosophy based upon first principles with the announcement of a *Wechselbestimmungssatz* (reciprocal proposition of determination) (*NS* II: 177, lines, 12–14. "A type of *Wechselbestimmungssatz* (reciprocal proposition of determination), a pure law of association, it seems to me, must be the highest principle, a hypothetical proposition.") There was, as mentioned, a philosophical conversation between the friends which took place in Weißenfels and Dürrenberg from July 29 through August 6, 1796, a discussion which was warm but seemed not entirely free of old and new sensitive reactions to the views of each (cf. *KA* XXIII: 319; 326 ff.; cf. Commentary 509, letter 165, comment 2); later it seems that Schlegel gave Novalis a look at some of his work (later referred to by Behler as the *Beilage I* and *Beilage II* [*KA* XVIII: 505–516, 517–521]).[11] Novalis sent the notebooks back to Schlegel on New Year's day 1797 with the following remark:

> Here with much thanks, I return your *Philosophica*. They were very valuable to me. I have them in my mind where they have built strong nests. My difficult (*cainitisches*) life hinders me; otherwise you would have received a thick heap of replies and *Additamenta* (*KA* XXIII: 340).

We don't know whether Novalis received more from Schlegel than the *Beilage I* and *II*. We do, however, know that five of Schlegel's philosophical notebooks from the years 1796–97 have been lost. They should have been found in the estate of the Viennese theologian Anton Günther, but were not (cf. *KA* XVIII, XLIII: Windischmann's letter to Dorothea). Still another notebook from 1797, with the title *Zur Grundlehre* (Concerning the Theory of First Principles), is missing: according to the title, it is presumably a notebook concerning the problem of first principles (cf. Behler's report in *KA XI*, XVII, and *KA XVIII*, XLIV f.). For these reasons, we are limited from the start, to a contingent selection of texts in our attempt to reconstruct the context surrounding Schlegel's use of the term 'Wechselerweis.' Incidentally, Novalis hesitated a while before supporting Schlegel's position over and against the position developed in Fichte's *Wissenschaftslehre*. But on June 14, 1797, he writes to Schlegel:

> Incidentally [. . .] I most warmly participate in your philosophical plans, which I first now begin to give my full support [. . .]. Your notebooks haunt my inside with an overwhelming force, and as little as I can finish with the single thoughts, so dearly I unite with the view of the whole and divine an abundance of the good, and the true [. . .]. Regarding Fichte, you are without a doubt right—I move evermore towards your view of his *Wissenschaftslehre*. [. . .] Fichte is the most dangerous of all thinkers whom I know. He casts a spell over all who enter his circle. [. . .] You are chosen to protect all aspiring independent thinkers from Fichte's magic (*NS IV*: 230).

The context plainly shows that Novalis' insight regarding Fichte's position increased as a result of his reading of Schlegel's notebooks and further that he read Schlegel's work on Fichte as part of the critique of any attempt to establish a single, absolute first principle for philosophy. This accounts for the reference to the danger of Fichte's thought. It seems to me, that also the famous diary entry from May 29 and 30, that "the actual concept of the Fichtean I" struck him like an illumination between the Tennstadt barrier and Grüningen (l.c., 42, lines 3 f.), is meant to be critical: as the ascent of the insight of its infeasibility (cf. also Mähls commentary *NS II*: 303 in the context).

Regarding the search for contexts in which Schlegel's key term 'Wechselerweis' could be made comprehensible, Dieter Henrich has reminded me of Schlegel's study of Schelling's work in the autumn of 1796.[12] Indeed, during this time, Schlegel had read not only Schelling's work *Über die Möglichkeit einer Form der Philosophie* (On the Possibility of a Form of Philosophy) but also his *Ich Schrift*. He had read both thoroughly and taken notes on them (cf. sporadically the *Beilage I* of the *Philosophische Lehrjahre*). Amongst these notes we find the following claim, which seems to be really significant: "*Wechselbegründung* (reciprocal establishment) of matter and form in the first principle of knowledge" (*KA XVIII*: 510, Nr. 54). This claim, however, stands alone and has no parallel to other claims in which the *Wechselbegründung* takes place between the thetical and postulatory character of the I. Morevoer, Schlegel's notes on Schelling are, although sprinkled with praise for him, in general more critical than laudatory. Hence, Schlegel claims that Schelling does not depart from the hunger for knowledge, that is, from the postulate that, "[t]here should be a system of knowledge (*Wissenschaft soll seyn*)" but rather from the arbitrary claim that, "[t]here is a system of knowledge (*Wissenschaft ist*)" (l.c., 514, Nr. 89)—and this goes along with Schlegel's critique of Fichte. Moreover, Schlegel finds that the first proposition of the *Form-Schrift*, namely, that philosophy is a system of knowledge and has a determinant content and form (*SW* I: 1, 89), is "conspicously false" (*KA* XVIII: 51, Nr. 79). With it, a meaningful postulate becomes replaced by a logical fact (l.c., Nr. 89); that science is, can only be a presupposition, never something taken as an unquestionable given. Later Schlegel writes that Schelling, "can develop the concept of the Non-I from the absolute I, but he cannot develop the concept of the actual, absolute positedness (*Gesetztseyns*) of the same. There he is lame" (513, Nr. 94). On the other hand, Schlegel finds Schelling's opinion "very important against Kant," that the form of the highest thetical principle cannot be synthetic, but its content in contrast the "anti-thetical proposition A=B can only be demonstrated analytically" (511, Nr., 62; cf. Nr. 60, and Nr. 86). I however, see no hint in the note to Nr. 54 of *Beilage I* that Schlegel was inspired by Schelling's notion of the *Wechselbegründung* between content and form.

This thought is found worked out in Schelling's *Form-Schrift* from the autumn of 1794 (still before the reading of Fichte's *Grundlage*). Schelling speaks there of a "*wechselseitige[n] Begründung* (reciprocal foundation) between the content and form of the highest principle of the philosophy (*SW* I: 1, 95; cf. 94). This source, with which Schlegel was in fact acquainted and of which had taken note, is according to Henrich, a more probable source of Schlegel's use of the term '*Wechselerweis*' than the one traced by me. With his suggestion, Schelling was trying to find some point of reconciliation for the dispute between Reinhold and Fichte, on the one hand, and Eberhard, Schwab, Rehberg, and Aenesidemus on the other hand, regarding the relation between the highest formal first principle of philosophy, the principle of noncontradiction, to which the determined (at least with respect to content) principle of consciousness (for example, Fichte's absolute I) had been led. But, in the first place, I can see in Schelling no gesture in the direction of a relativization of a philosophy based on first principles. And, furthermore, Schlegel ties his talk of a *Wechselbegründung* more to a Fichtean context: the tension between the self-positing evidence and the postulatory character of the I (the "concept of positing" and "the demand that it be justified" [*KA* XVIII: 510, Nr. 55]). Already in his earliest notes Schlegel laments that Fichte wants to get out of this problem with "only one concept" (510, Nr.

58), and this while, according to Schlegel, there is a need for at least two related concepts, indeed, of a *Wechselbegriff* (518, Nr. 16).[13]

A fourth source could prove to be more significant. For a while Schlegel lived with "Fichte's first student," Herbart, in Döderlein's house.[14] The devil must have had a hand in bringing the two together under one roof and together as regular guests in Fichte's house—meanwhile, they supposedly never spoke to each other about philosophy—admittedly, we are missing supporting evidence for this. (Nevertheless, the collection of letters in Herbart's collected works contains letters to and from Feuerbach). Herbart was from Oldenburg and had arrived in Jena during the winter semester of 1794 and through an acquaintance with the historian Woltmann had found access to the circle around Fichte, Weißhuhn, and Niethammer.[15] He was a member of the "Fraternity of Free Men." Other members of this group (with different dates of entrance) were: Friedrich Muhrbeck, Johann Smidt, Fritz Horn, and Casimir Ulrich Böhlensdorff. Some of them made the acquaintance of Hölderlin during the Homburg period or even during the Rastatter Congress. It seems that Herbart did not meet Hölderlin in Jena, but in his correspondence with Böhlensdorff and Muhrbeck in 1799, he expresses an interest in one day meeting Hölderlin (*StA* VII: 2, 130 ff.). In this circle, Herbart gave several lectures, for example, "On the Principles of Philosophy," "On the Fichtean Principles of the Natural Law," and on "Spinoza and Schelling."[16] Herbart, who would prove to be a merciless Fichte-critic,[17] already had misgivings regarding the feasibility of the *Wissenschaftslehre*,[18] yet he followed the new turn which Fichte introduced beginning October 18, 1796 with *Lectures on the Wissenschaftslehre nova methodo*.[19] (It is likely that Friedrich Schlegel heard these lectures as well as the Platner lectures.)[20] Herbart's two attempts to critically review Schelling's *Form* and *Ich-Schrift*[21] did not meet with Fichte's approval.[22] Herbart holds Schelling's own basic idea that "two absolutely unconditioned entities (*Unbedingtheiten*), which are *connected* but not *unified*, condition each other mutually" (volume 1, 21, 2) to be untenable. Herbart charges Schelling with having allowed the subjective (epistemic) unconditionedness (*Unbedingtheit*) to flow into the objective (real) unconditionedness, insofar as he *confuses* "the unconditionedness of becoming thought (*Unbedingtheit des Gedachtwerdens*) with unconditionedness that is thought (*gedachter Unbedingtheit*)" (20, 2). One could think that Herbart is blind to Schelling's parallel thoughts of the *Wechselbegründung* of the form and content of the highest principle. But on the one hand, this is not entirely the same problem; and on the other hand, Herbart, in his judgment of Schelling's *Form-Schrift* had paid special attention to the notion of the *Wechselbegründung*. Herbart presents an account of Schelling's view, that, if there were several first principles, which stood in reciprocal relation to one another, all that would be proved by this relation is that the relation itself would be superceded by a common third principle (L. C., 13,4; with reference on *SW* I: 1, 91). Herbart elaborates as follows:

> The following position will make this interpretation doubtful; and therefore it will be necessary to immediately urge that any proof for the singleness of a first principle is not fitting if it attempts to establish the *entire content* of philosophy. Several absolutely certain propositions can refer to each other without becoming lost in each other. If, for example, the Kantian School wants to be consistent, then, as it explains the manifold of experience through sensation and through sensation the thinking being, including its pure intuitions, categories, and ideas—it must first allow these to develop (see p. 1 of the *CPR*). Further, all single sensations must be assumed to be absolute (absolutely certain, which in *Wissenschaft* would not be conditioned by any proof), which join each other in an equally unconditioned rational being and first in this unification make all thinking possible and from which, within *Wissenschaft*, genetically explain thinking, as something from which one must start *absolutis*. The process may always have errors, but the errors do not lie in the mere concept of many absolutes which relate to one another; one cannot confuse the absolute, unconditioned with the infinite (l.c., pp. 13 f.).

Hence, Herbart defends a purely logical form of dualism: the Kantian form of dualism which admits, with the same evidence, the individual entities given through sense (*Sinnesgegebenheiten*) and the understanding's general rules of connection. Herbart defends this position against Schelling's position regarding a philosophical first principle, which holds that a plurality of integrating elementary facts would have to be brought under a common third principle, which would be the highest principle. Incidentally Herbart refers to Schelling's own formulation (*SW* I: 1, 91 f.) with the words: "[h]ere comes a very similar argument again."[23] Hence, Herbart saw through Schelling's own talk of the *Wechselbegründung* of a formal and material first principle as insufficient and defended, as Aenesidemus and Schmid, the possibility of evident, reciprocally self-supporting principles that would not be reducible to a third, higher principle. If we knew more of Herbart's thinking in Jena, we would not hesitate to establish a remarkable parallel, to the form, if not to the content, with Schlegel's notion of a *Wechselerweis*. It would be tempting to reconstruct the conversations which the housemates, Herbart and Schlegel, shared as they made their way to or from Fichte's lectures.

A fifth source comes into the picture when we come to give an explanation of the ancestry of the strange talk of a *Wechselgrundsatz*, and this is Johann Heinrich Abicht's essay "On the freedom of the will" (from 1789).[24] At the time it was the center of much attention. Abicht (1762–1816) was a philosophy professor in Erlangen and an important defender of the new

Kantian philosophy (incidentally, together with Johann Christoph Schwab, *ex aequo* winner of the competition of the Prussian Academy of the Sciences on the question regarding the "Progress of Philosophy since Leibniz and Wolff"). The short treatise stands within the context of deterministic doubt, which the traditional Leibnizians had expressed regarding Kant's theory of freedom (from the *Critique of Practical Reason*), above all the Jena professor of philosophy, Johann August Heinrich Ulrich (1746–1813), with whom Carl Christian Erhard Schmid and Friedrich Karl Forberg had studied.[25] Abicht rejects (according to the matter) Ulrich's weakly reasoned attempt to reduce freedom to contingent indetermination or "groundlessness," "namely choice without ground or what is really the same: nothing."[26] Freedom is rather "the faculty [. . .] *to be the sole self-ground (Selbstgrund) of its willing*" (l. c.). A 'self-ground' can only be called freedom however, when the subject and object of its acting is in a person, that is, when it places *itself* under the pressure of constraint (*Nötigung*) which it exerts upon itself *freely* (like the Kantian 'self-affection' of the I, which as spontaneous, determines itself as empirical; Abicht speaks of a "Self-constraint or better, self-determination" [231]). Only when we think of both objects, spontaneity and the passive person, which are unified in the notion of self-determination, as two distinct objects, does there arise the illusion (*Schein*) of an anonymous process of becoming constrained (*Genötigtwerdens*) (anonymous because "transcendental" freedom is epistemically "unreachable and hidden"). And it is within this context that talk of *Wechselgründen* shows up:

> If we want to be convinced by the existence (*Dasein*) of this ground of the self (*Selbstgrund*), then we must proceed approximately in the following way, as if we were to attempt to prove the existence of substances in space and their relationships to one another as *Wechselgründe* (reciprocal grounds). For precisely in this case we allow for appearances, to which we attribute necessary grounds, namely, substances; we allow for a *change* of appearances, to which we attribute *Wechselgründe*, namely, reciprocal substances which have an effect on each other. . . .
>
> In the same way, we must allow for inner-appearances in consciousness, to which we could attribute substantial grounds. At the same time, however, we must see precisely whether these given appearances of willing are of the kind and so created that we would be obliged to posit under them external substantial grounds as well. These substantial grounds are different from the principle of the I and from the substantial grounds that are contained within the I, e.g., from the substantial grounds of the appearances of the understanding (231 f.).

Abicht seems to mean the following: Because the ground of our free action is "transcendental," it does not make itself known to our consciousness directly.

We know only appearances, which, like all appearances, stand under causal laws. That which indeed appears in appearances is something of which we can never be aware, but we think of it as the ground of the changes within appearances. We also only know free will through its outer manifestations (in inner sense). But we presuppose a substantial will as the ground of the manifestations, which we, in the world of sense, recognize as nothing other than external cause (under a universal conformity to nature). Abicht's *Wechselgründe* are, therefore, grounds for the interaction between substances (which exist in themselves), from which, in the world of sense, they are the expressions of the sequences of appearing phenomena—a notion which lies rather far from Schlegel's operation with the *Wechselgrundsatz*. There is, however, something that the positions share in common: Abicht assumes that there must be two sorts of reciprocally supporting grounds in order to make the phenomenon of a free self-determination comprehensible. These are: "substantial, transcendental, first grounds" (232) through which the first become capable of being perceived. And Schlegel assumes that the first principle does not show itself as such and in singular, but rather is in need of completion through another, which compensates for its deficit. In any case, it may be that Schlegel was familiar with Abicht's use of the term *Wechselgrund* (Novalis had read Abicht, he made fun of the "absolute and infinite boringness" of his writings: NS II: 457/9, Nr., 103 as well as 462/4, Nr. 111).

On Schlegel's Role in the Genesis of Early German Romantic Theory of Art

I shall now attempt to give a summary of Schlegel's thought, as he himself presented it, that is, independently of other possible models and sources. In a second step, however, I want to come back to Schlegel's reference to Jacobi's *Spinoza-Büchlein*; Schlegel spoke for the first time openly of 'Wechselerweis' in his review of Jacobi's novel, *Woldemar* (found under the title, *Woldemar-Rezension*, in Behler's critical edition of Schlegel's work). The review was published at the latest in September (and at the earliest at the beginning of August) 1796. Novalis' insights regarding this were first published in the 1960's and 1970's, that is, first in *this* century (and unfortunately, given the hopeless state of the sources, only in a very incomplete form).

A highest principle—so Schlegel is convinced—has proven to be unattainable to finite consciousness.[1] A highest principle could not consist of the notion of an 'absolute I,' because absoluteness excludes the relationship to a necessarily finite I. In a claim against Schelling's *Ich-Schrift*, Schlegel notes: "It is thick empir[ical] egoism with regard to the absolute I, to say: *my* I" (*KA* XVIII: 512, Nr. 73). If we don't reach the highest (*das Höchste*) in direct intuition, then we must be content with indirect evidence for the existence of one of the whole chain's governing unity. This evidence can be found. It is not as if the moments of unity and infinity would fall apart in the river of life. Time does not only divide, it also joins, although only relatively. Meanwhile, this relativity decreases, if one reads the *Wechselbegriff* (l.c., 518, Nr. 16) between unity and infinity as indirect evidence for an "absolute approximating," provisional, spontaneous self-constitution of the series. In the same way, there would follow a finite (we can say: provisional or ad hoc) "proof" of the Absolute which never shows itself in the finite but which supports the whole series and guarantees its coherence (l.c., 329, Nr., 55; 298, Nr. 1241): one phase "proves" the other and so on forever. This leads Schlegel to claim that: "Philosophy must begin, like the epic poem, in the middle"[2] (l.c., 518, Nr. 16; cf. XII: 328)—that would be what Benjamin calls the "medium of reflection" in his doctoral dissertation, "The Concept of Critique of Art in German Romanticism."[3] Schlegel continues with his point, claiming that, "it is impossible to carry out philosophy in such a way, piece by piece, so that even the first step would be completely grounded and explained" (l.c.). In the medium of reflection the individual parts of the successful synthesis formation support and negate each other reciprocally. They are not derived from a principle, which had previously been established by "more demonstrative evidence" (*KA* XII: 331), but rather they make the existence of this principle only "ever more probable" (l.c., 327 ff.). For this reason, in place of a demonstrative or accomplished knowledge, we find a "belief in the [absolute] I" (331).[4] The likelihood (or credibility) of an established unity increases to the same extent as does the selective unity, where each phase of the process exists, and the coherence, which connects everything, and which cannot be explained solely by means of the mechanism of reflection that separates everything. Separation and connection, which are brought again under the clamp of a predominant unity by the continuity of time itself, that as such doesn't become an event, point to something amid finitude which is no longer finite, and which is therefore the absolute unity of both. So the line comes to an end in a circle, because the schema of the linear flow is corrected piece by piece through the validation of that higher unity, the infinite turned into totality (*Allheit*): "It is a whole, and the way to recognize it, is, therefore, no straight line but a circle" (*KA* XVIII: 518, Nr. 16). An excerpt from the Cologne private lectures of 1804–05 summarizes Schlegel's basic idea very nicely:

> Our philosophy does not begin like the others with a first principle—where the first proposition is like the center or first ring of a comet—with the rest a long tail of mist—we depart from a small but living seed—our center lies in the middle. From an unlikely and modest beginning—doubt regarding the "thing" which, to some degree shows itself in all thoughtful people and the always present, prevalent probability of the I—our philosophy will develop in a steady progression and become strengthened until it reaches the highest point of human knowledge and shows the breadth and limits of all knowledge (*KA* XII: 328, 3).

Now, the concept of the *Wechselerweis*—as has been said—was brought by Schlegel himself into connection with a passage from Jacobi's *Spinoza-Büchlein*, namely, in the description of Jacobi's *Woldemar* (*KA* II: 72; the quotation refers explicitly to p. 225 of the second edition of the *Spinoza Büchlein*).[5] It

would in fact be embarrassing if Behler's—admittedly not further substantiated—claim regarding the date of this were correct, because, according to
Behler, Schlegel's description of Jacobi's *Woldemar* was written during Schlegel's
visit with Novalis, that is between July 29, and August 6, 1796.[6] And, if this
were the case, then we would have to assume either some sort of wonderful
effects to have flowed from Schlegel's discussions with Novalis (this is in no
way corroborated by Schlegel's portrayal of these conversations to Caroline
from August 2, 1796 [KA XXIII: 326 f.]).[7] Or Schlegel must have had freed
himself from the prejudices of a philosophy based on first principles on his
own and independently of any influence from the Jena discussion groups,
which he did not enter into before August 7. For the reconstruction of such
a pre-Jena development, however, we are missing all evidence. And the
enthusiastic letters, written to Novalis regarding the speculative stimulation
which Schlegel received through his involvement with the Jena milieu, also
speak completely against any such attempt to establish Schlegel's break with
a philosophy of first principles independently of his involvement with the
Jena group.[8]

Meanwhile, concerning the function of the quotation from the
Woldemar-Charakteristik, we have acquired provisional clarity. That the highest principle of philosophy can only be a *Wechselerweis* should simply mean
here, that a concept or a proposition can never alone per se, that is to say
from Cartesian evidence, be established; rather, it is established first through
a further and second (provisional) concept or proposition (for which the
same holds, so that through a coherence formation of truth we come ever
closer to the truth without ever grasping it in one single thought).[9] This was
precisely that primary insight which Jacobi had formulated in the second
edition of his *Spinoza-Büchlein*: All of our thinking takes place within conditions. To justify something means: to lead it back to something else which
itself is not established or fully grounded and in turn refers to some other
reason or ground which is without a basis, and so on ad infinitum. In this
way, all of our knowledge gets lost in that which is unfounded and in infinitely
many conditions—unless there would arise at some point in this chain of
conditions an unconditioned, which as such would be in no need of a further
condition. Jacobi himself found this in that which he called "feeling" or
"belief" (*Glauben*) (which, by the way, caused Kant to rebuke him); Reinhold
thought he had found the solution to the problem of the infinite regress in
the "principle of consciousness," hence, he shared with Jacobi this attempt
to put an end to the regress involved in searching for the condition of any
given knowledge claim.

Friedrich Schlegel now joins—and this should draw our attention—
Jacobi's insight very closely to Reinhold's and criticizes in the name of
Reinhold II both Jacobi and Reinhold I. After dismissing Jacobi's *salto mortale*[10]

(which places belief as that intuition which will stop the infinite regress involved in our search for the unconditioned condition of all knowledge) as a general "absurdity" which any philosophy of elements (*Elementarphilosophie* was the title of Reinhold's theory) that departs from a fact will have to meet, Schlegel goes on to observe the following:

> That every proof presupposes something proved holds only for those thinkers who depart from one, single proof. What if, however, an externally unconditioned yet at the same time conditioned and conditioning *Wechselerweis* were the foundation of philosophy? (l.c., p. 72).

That which Schlegel introduces as the alternative, which he opposes to Jacobi's solution, remains shadowy in his review of *Woldemar*; however, we can shed light on this issue by looking ahead to Schlegel's notes from the autumn of 1796, for these reveal a clearly recognizable connection to the constellation of philosophers around Niethammer who were opposed to a philosophy based on first principles. My concern here is with proving Schlegel's dependence on Jacobi's thought. In the citation quoted above (*Spinoza-Büchlein*, 2d ed., 225), Jacobi himself refers in a footnote to a letter written to Mendelssohn (215–217) in which he defends himself from the charge to have broken off with rational argumentation in favor of a leap to a higher revelation (or, to have recommended such a break). He says (I quote the passage in its entirety):

> Dear Mendelssohn, we are all born in faith and must remain within this faith, just as we are all born in society and must remain within society. *Totum parte prius esse necesse est.* How can we strive for certainty when certainty is not known to us in advance; and how can it be known to us, other than through something that we already recognize with certainty? This leads to the concept of an unmediated certainty, which stands in no need of explanation (*Gründe*), but rather excludes all such explanation, and solely and alone is the corresponding representation itself of the represented thing. Conviction based on argument is secondhand conviction. Reasons are only properties of similarity to things of which we are certain. The conviction which these bring about arises from a comparison and can never be totally certain or complete. If faith is an act of holding something to be true without relying upon argument, then the very security we place in arguments of reason must be rooted in faith (*Glaube*) and so arguments of reason must take their strength from faith (215 f.).[11]

Jacobi's thesis would be misrepresented, if one were to characterize it as a recommendation to break from the discourse of rational argumentation (therefore from the language of justification). What Jacobi actually claims is that argumentation, which is led by the search for foundations, involves us in an infinite chain of relativity, because we cannot at all indicate at which point we should put an end to this search. Jacobi's thesis is: We have indeed certainty (or at least claim to have it). And if this is the case, then at least one single fact amongst the facts of our consciousness must be immediately certain—whereby 'immediate' means: without the mediation of further reasons or states of consciousness. To want to justify the assumption of such a fact once again, means that one has not understood what is involved in our having to make recourse to an infinite regress in the language of justification. Therefore immediate consciousness (Jacobi calls this "feeling"—Novalis and Schleiermacher will follow him in this terminology) must be understood literally to be a ground-less, unjustified assumption, that is, as a belief (*Glauben*). Schlegel's claim that, "[e]very proof already presupposes something proved" means then: without an immediate and original certainty, each further foundation would be lacking support and foundation.

Now Schlegel follows Jacobi regarding the consequences of the infinite relativity of our knowledge (under the condition of the unattainability of an ultimate foundation). Against Jacobi, he considers infinite relativity to be inevitable. Yet he does not break completely with the notion of first principles: Yet, the "first principle" cannot be one, but rather should consist of two "externally unconditioned," but "internally, mutually conditioning" principles (or—what is not the same—'proofs'). No one of them alone creates its own validity. Therefore, philosophy cannot be supported by *one* highest principle. Not one of the candidates alone is self-sufficient in itself; however, through reciprocal self-support, together they generate something like the idea of unconditioned validity. Therefore, it would be wrong to claim that Schlegel is an unrestrained relativist. Like Novalis, he holds fast to a negative concept of perfect knowledge—in any case with the condition, that this be considered as a transcendental ideal and not as an actually produced instance of Cartesian certainty. We shall see that Schlegel, without a view of the Absolute-*ex–negativo*, could not bring the dialectic of the reciprocal annihilation (*Wechselvernichtung*) into play, which he grasps as irony. The only positions which reciprocally cancel out their relativity are those that are related as contradictory determinations to one and the same thing. This thing is the positively *unpresentable* (*undarstellbare*) Absolute.

Now that the context in which Schlegel's reference to (and correction to) the main thesis of the *Spinoza-Buchlein* can be understood has been made somewhat clear, I will return to Schlegel's theory of the ubiquitous centrality of reflection. According to Schlegel's theory, the main problem of Fichte's philosophy, which consists of the dilemma (indicated also by Schelling, even if first in 1802) presented by the problem of the in-and-for-itself (*An-sich-für-sich*), should be solved by a progressive reflection-proof (*Reflexionserweis*). Each single phase establishes the prior one and is, in turn, established by it. The Absolute permeates the whole series by offering continuity; and in this respect the series proves (other than what Jacobi thought, just through its essential relation to the whole) the synthetic effect of the Absolute through its verifiable manifestation in relative (particular) syntheses. On the other hand, this principle is elusive, and the series is revived by a loan from something which is, within the series, unprovable, and about which the only thing that can be said is that it is ever more probable. From this paradox springs an "infinite agility," a reciprocal affirmation and negation, from which is finally freed a straight and linear striving for a "progressive," ironic "dialectic" as the true method (KA XVIII: 83, Nr. 646). "Whence it comes," Schlegel writes later, after 1803 (l.c., 564, Nr. 49), "that some philosophers come as close to the true as Fichte does, but nonetheless don't reach it, is from my construction, quite clear."

The strange transcendence of the Absolute vis-à-vis the series, which Schlegel conveys alternatively with the terms "infinite plenitude" or "chaos," can be explained by the two phenomena: *allegory* and *wit* (*Witz*). Allegory is—briefly put—the tendency toward the Absolute amidst the finite itself. As allegory, the individual exceeds itself in the direction of the infinite, while as wit the infinite allows the unity that breaks from the wholeness of the series to appear selectively. In Schelling's terminology we could also say: allegory is the synthesis of "infinite unity" and "infinite plenitude" under the exponent of the infinite (or better: with a tendency towards the infinite); while the selective igniting of wit presents this same synthesis under the preponderance of unity.

However, in which way should the infinite present itself in the finite? Not through thinking, not through concepts: "Pure thinking and cognition (*Erkennen*) of the highest can never be adequately presented"—this is the "principle of the relative unpresentability of the highest" (KA XII: 214). Yet how then? Through the fact that art steps onto the scene (KA XIII: 55 f. and 173 f.):

> Philosophy taught us that the divine can only be hinted at (*andeuten*), only presupposed with probability, and that we must therefore assume revelation to be the highest truth. Revelation is, however, for people of senses too sublime a knowledge (*Erkenntnis*), and so art steps onto the scene very nicely, in order to place, through sense presentation and clarity, the objects of revelation before the eyes (l.c., 174).

This is an observation from the years 1804–05. You may have noticed that Schlegel's claim (according to which we know about the Absolute through revelation) pulls us out a bit from the context of Schlegel's epistemological commitments and into something else. The formulation attests to Schlegel's developing conversion to the Catholic faith during this period. The conversion became official on April 16, 1808 in the Cathedral of Cologne (he converted with his wife Dorothea, who was, by the way, the daughter of philosopher Moses Mendelssohn). Even on this solemn occasion, Schlegel's wit was not wanting. To his perplexed friends he answered (regarding his conversion) that: "To become Catholic is not to change, but only first to acknowledge religion" (*KA* XIX: 230, Nr. 236; cf. l.c., 223, Nrs. 184, and 163, Nr. 81). In the (incidentally great, stimulating, and far too neglected) Cologne private lectures for the brothers Boisserée, we also find proclaimed "as the higher law," that "all poetry must be mythological and Catholic" (*KA* XIII: 55). That is why Tieck has one of his characters in his comedy *Prince Zerbino* exclaim in despair: "What's happening here is such as to make you become Catholic!" His emphasis on the Catholic religion, however, does not hinder Schlegel from noting during the same period that: "The dissolution of consciousness into poetry is as necessary for idealism as the divinity of the elements. <Idealism is itself poetry>" (*KA* XIX: 172, Nr. 150).

During the Jena period, art does not appear merely to make a certainty acquired elsewhere (that of revelation) perceptible in a popularizing way. Rather, it supplements the absolute unpresentability of the Absolute that can be overcome neither religiously (during this time Schlegel was a strong atheist) nor conceptually, nor sensibly, but only by "alluding to" (*andeuten*) it indirectly. This is only possible if art is able to go beyond what it presents (and that is always, in relation to the Absolute, too little), by alluding to that which it does not succeed in saying. Schlegel calls this saying-more (*Mehr-sagen*) in all poetic saying (*poetische Sagen*), *allegory*. It is a mode or specification of imagination. In Kant, as you remember, imagination is the faculty of the synthesis of the manifold under the command of the understanding. In Schlegel understanding and sensibility join and work together, therefore neither is "under command" of the other. Therefore, imagination is the ideal middle joint (*Mittelglied*) or *medius terminus*, inserted between the notion of the infinitude of the highest and that of the sensible finitude, imagination drafts an image of that which otherwise would remain unpresentable: the absolute unity between "infinite plenitude" and "infinite unity." (Because this image is also the image of truth, as it is expressed in the copula "is" of any judgment, we see here once again that like art, allegory is committed to truth.) Already in Fichte, imagination was that "faculty hovering in the middle between the infinite and the finite." Its boundary poles are the concrete individual on the one hand, and the purely determinable infinite on the other hand.

> *Why* (so asks Schlegel in the lectures on Transcendental Philosophy which he delivered in Jena during the winter semester of 1800–01) *has the infinite gone out of itself and made itself finite?*—that means, in other words: *Why are*

*there individuals? Or: Why doesn't the play of nature (Spiel der Natur) end
immediately, so that absolutely nothing exists?* The answer to this question is
only possible if we insert a concept. We have, namely, the concepts: one
infinite substance—and individuals. If we want to explain to ourselves
the transition from the one to the other, then we cannot do other than to
insert another concept between the two, namely, the concept of image or
presentation, allegory. The individual is therefore *an image of an infinite
substance* (KA XII: 39).

From *allegory* (explanation of the existence (*Daseyn*) of the world) it
follows that there is in each individual only so much actuality, as it *has
sense, as it has meaning, (allusive power), spirit* (l.c., 40).

This theorem comes to us only from a bad student version (obviously abbre-
viated)—the version is, unfortunately, not Hegel's, although he had attended
Schlegel's lectures. It corresponds, approximately, to Schelling's notion (from
1800), according to which art must symbolically represent that which slips
away from a conflicted reflection that is free and necessary (*zwieschlächtige,
notwendig-freie Reflexion*): the link between the universal and the individual,
the unconscious and the conscious, the real and the ideal, the infinite and
the finite—or, however, the idealistic original opposition (*idealistische
Urgegensatz*) is expressed. But Schlegel's view is more radical than anything
Schelling maintained, for according to Schlegel's view, we *don't* have any
view of the highest other than through allegory.

The allegorical is an artistic procedure that extinguishes the finitely
presented as that which is not meant (*das nicht Gemeinte*) and steers our view
towards that which was not grasped by this singular synthesis. Allegory (as
pars per toto for all artistic forms of expression) is, therefore, a necessary
manifestation of the unpresentability (*Undarstellbarkeit*) of the infinite. This
can happen only poetically. Poetry is, namely, the collective expression for
that which is inexpressible, the presentation of the unpresentable: that which,
as such, cannot be presented in any speculative concept. "All beauty," Schlegel
writes, "is allegory. The highest, precisely because it is inexpressible, can only
be said allegorically" (KA II: 324). But each single poem wants to present in
itself the whole, "the one everywhere and, that is, in its undivided unity."
And "that it can do only through allegory" (l.c., 414). It can do this, therefore, insofar as, in that which it presents, it includes the features of the
unpresentable. Schlegel also calls the presentation of the unpresentable
"meaning"—whereby he understands "meaning" (*Bedeutung*) in the sense of
"suggestion," (*Hindeutung*) "hinting at," (*Anspielung*) "indirect allusion."
"Every allegory," claims Schlegel, "means (*bedeutet*) God and one can only
speak of God allegorically" (KA XVIII: 347, Nr. 315). Elsewhere he expresses
the following:

> Every poem, every work should mean (*bedeuten*) the whole, really and in-
> deed mean, and through the meaning and the copy also be real and in fact
> be, because besides the higher (meaning) to which they make reference,
> only meaning has existence (*Dasein*) and reality (*KA* II: 414; on the appli-
> cation of this word cf. also *KA* XIII: 55 f., and 173 f.).

That constitutes the ecstatic trait of the finite, that it does not realize its
reality in itself, but only points beyond itself. With meaning, allegory alludes
to ("points to") the Absolute (*KA* XVIII: 416, Nr. 1140). Literally, allegory
is translated as ἀλληγορεῖν: to mean something other than what one says.
That which is said, the body of the word, becomes the expression for the
unpresentable which can be meant only insofar as it points beyond what lies
within its reach: the infinite. Allegorical *Be-deuten* is not itself that which is
only "alluded to" (*KA* XII: 208–09, 126, 166). Elsewhere: "Allegory is an
allusion to the infinite [. . .], an indirect glimpse caught of it" (l.c., 211; cf.
XI: 119). Its negativity consists in the positive, extinguishing release of the
gaze at what is absolutely meant by all thought and images: "It gets as far as
to the door of the highest (*das Höchste*), and satisfies itself in merely suggest-
ing indefinitely the infinite, the divine, which cannot be described or explained philosophically" (l.c., 210). So the principle, which as such, remains
in the realm of the *unpresentable*, makes itself noticeable only through self-
negation of the finite. "The tendency of principles is to destroy the illusion
(*Schein*) of the finite" (*KA* XVIII: 416, Nr. 1139); for the finite only has a
semblance of life (*Scheinleben*) insofar as, in the finite, the principle lives
negatively" (cf. l.c., 412, Nr. 1095; 413; Nrs. 1107, and 1108). So the device
of allegorical expression frees the finite from its material fixedness and refers
it to the infinite. One could say: in and as allegory, the tendency of finite
actuality toward the inactual and infinite makes itself felt.

Wit is the counterpart to allegory in the realm of the actual itself:
selective flashing (*Aufblitzen*) of the unity within unity and of the infinite in
the finite. The metaphor of flashing which is favored by Schlegel, indicates
that the synthesis makes itself noticeable only in the flaring up and a dwin-
dling of light and does not present itself as positively enduring. Wit is an
embodiment, "the external appearance, the external flash of fantasy" (*KA* II:
334, l.c., 258, Nr. 26), which is, in turn—clearly a Kantian reminiscence—
the synthesizing faculty of the spirit. "Wit is applied fantasy" (l.c., 356), "an
indirect form of expression of the same (fantasy)." Fantasy is the organ of the
bonding power of the Absolute itself—in the world of finite production its
expression can only appear occasionally. "Wit," Schlegel explains, "does not
itself lie in the realm of the Absolute, but, admittedly, the more absolute it
is, the more developed it is" (*KA* XVIII: 113, Nr. 1002). Wit is a chaotic
synthesis which Schlegel also characterizes as a "sudden startling and setting,"

as "a petrifying" of that "fiery liquid of representation" (*KA* XIX: 171, Nr. 148). As if shortened to an instantaneous insight, in the synthesis of wit, the shifing, surging chaos of the imagination is solidified. If allegory is devoted to the "annihilation of the individual qua individual," then "wit (in contrast) is directed to the unification of plenitude" (*KA* XVIII: 18). In wit, the undemonstrable principle reveals itself through effects condensed into singularities. Wit is "fragmentary geniality" (l.c., 102, Nr. 881).

Wit is, therefore, *not* the power which makes a system from fragments, for that it would need the *unpresentable*, absolute unity (unity of chaos and plenitude). Instead of constructing a system of chaos, wit constructs, as a "chemical faculty" (*KA* XVIII: 129, Nr. 90), as an "ars combinatoria" (l.c., 124, Nr. 20), only a "chaos of systems," that is, a variety of partial unions without a systematic center. Therefore, witty syntheses can also contradict themselves everywhere. Many of the definitions provided by Schlegel tell us that the "content" of wit must be "always paradoxical" (l.c., 94, Nr. 781), for it unifies the infinite and the finite in *Aperçu*. This union, on the other hand, is accomplished in finite form, namely, as a fragment. So the units contradict themselves in their details and so exclude themselves from that highest dialectical unity, which the infinite would encompass and to which allegory merely alludes negatively.

Allegory and wit are, therefore, the view—and turning point of reflection, which can, however, never be taken up at the same time: in wit the tendency toward unity without plenitude is presented; in allegory the tendency toward the infinite, removed from unity, is presented. There is an agent missing, which would gather both points of view at once or in the unity of one consciousness.

The elusiveness of this central perspective of the infinite series leaves upon this series, what Schlegel calls "chaotic universality." And exactly here we find the philosophical place of the *fragment*. Its relationship with wit is evident. For, just as wit deflects the synthetic power of absolute unity, as it were, into a single appearance, so only—in/as fragment—"can a single notion receive a type of wholeness, through the sharpest direction to a point [. . .]" (*KA* II: 169, Nr. 109; *KA* XII: 393; XVIII: 305, Nr. 1333; l.c., 69, Nr. 499; II: 197, Nr. 206). The witty faculty of selective synthesis, which manifests its indivisible unity precisely through intensive concentration on "singularity" (*Einzelheit*), is what Schlegel calls "fragmentary genius" (*KA* II: 149, Nr. 9). Fragmentary genius is the "form of derived, fragmentary consciousness" (*KA* XII: 393), of the real, the disseminal I, whose ontological status Schlegel explains as the "dismembered" (*zerstückelte*) or "incomplete" I (*KA* XII: 374, 348, 352; cf. *KA* XVIII: 506, Nr. 9; 512, Nr. 73), and which is the consequence of an unavailable going-out-of-itself, a fragmentation of the bond between unity and infinity in a mythically projected "original I" (*KA*

XII: 348). As dowry (*Mitgift*) for this dismemberment, "the particular, [. . .] *specific* [. . .] form of human consciousness" guards "the fragmentary" nature as the nature of "derived, rational consciousness" (l.c., 392).

> It is exactly through this singleness (*Einzelnheit*) and disjointedness [adds Schlegel] that derived consciousness distinguishes itself. The one activity, however, through which consciousness announces itself most as a fragment (*Bruchstück*) is through wit. The essence of wit is to be found precisely in disjointedness and originates in turn from the disjointedness and derivation of consciousness itself. This ability, which is not usually given enough attention, is the *particular, individual form* in which *the highest* appears to human consciousness, insofar as it is derived and subordinated at all. (l.c., cf. 440 ff.).

As the expression of a consciousness torn asunder, the fragment therefore bears the following contradiction: it grants unity to chaos, because it inherits the synthesis-effecting power of absolute unity; however, it steers the bonding power of the Absolute from the infinite to the particular, that is, it creates not totality but rather an ensemble ("chaos") of individual positions, each one of which goes against the other. This spirit of a contradictoriness woven into the fragment is a necessary effect of the detotalization or decomposition of the highest unity, which is no longer a unity of a whole (or a system), but rather only a unity of a single thing and without systematic relationship to other single things: From the fragmentary universe there results no system but (as Schelling puts it in 1820) "asystasy," "instability" (*Unbestand*), "disharmony" (*Uneinigkeit*) (SW I: 9, 209 [ff.]), incoherence, lack of connection (*Zusammenhanglosigkeit*): characteristics which, above all in the fragments of Novalis, not only appear compositionally but are constantly the theme of his considerations.

Romanticism is often presented as a movement of thinkers drunk with harmony and in love with the Absolute, so much so that one can no longer see in this vulgar *Wirkungsgeschichte*, why the romantics drew the scorn of the classicists Goethe, Schiller, and Hegel and the devout Christian, Kierkegaard, or the bourgeois realist Rudolf Haym, or what makes Romanticism radically modern. Indeed, it is in the discovery of the multiple layers of human character—its insecurity inconsistency, contradictoriy nature—that Romanticism distinguishes itself from an optimistic tradition, be it based on the joy of God or of an absolutely grounded metaphyics. "So humans are" declares Theodore in one of Ludwig Tieck's *Phantasus-conversations*, "nothing but inconsistency and contradiction!"[12] Theodore's exclamation summarizes one of the deepest convictions of Tieck's poetry, which always presses thematically and stylistically for new modes of representation. I quote—*partem pro toto*—the seventeenth chapter of the *Sieben Weiber des Blaubart* (The Seven Wives of

Bluebeard) (written in 1797), in which the hero, Peter Berner, is conversing with his patron, Bernard:

> If you would reflect upon the fact that in the whole of human life there is no purpose and no connection to be found, you would give up gladly the attempt to bring these things into my life.
>
> Truly, you are right, said Bernard, and you are really much more intelligent, than I thought.
>
> I am, perhaps, more clever than you, said Peter, I only rarely let myself notice anything.
>
> Therefore, said Bernard deep in thought, should it be the case that the entire, grand human existence is not something solid and well-founded? It leads, perhaps, to nothing and would mean nothing, it would be foolish to search here for a historical connection and a grand poetic composition, a Bambocchiade or a Wouvermann would have expressed it, perhaps, most correctly (*TS* 9: 193).

In Rudolf Köpke's collection of conversations with Tieck during the last years of his life, we find the following remark:

> One of the most resistant (*widerstrebende*) notions is, for me, that of connection (*Zusammenhang*). Are we really in a position to recognize this at all? Is it not more devout, more noble and upstanding, to simply acknowledge that we cannot perceive this, that our knowledge can only relate to the individual, and that we must resign [to any further claim]?[13]

Ludoviko says in *Sternbald* (1798):

> One cannot forget his purpose [. . .], because the most sensible person is already so arranged that he doesn't have any purpose at all. I must only laugh when I see people making such preparations to lead a life. Life has passed even before they are ready with these preliminaries (*TS* 16, 338).

Friedrich Schlegel also counts "confusion," "inconsistency, lack of character" under the "flaws of progressive people" (*KA* XVIII: 24, Nr. 66). In infinite becoming there is no middle around which constant qualities could crystallize. Therefore, the irregular form of art represents the truth that "all life is like a bent line (*krummlinicht*)" (*KA* XVIII: 171, Nr. 551). From this follows the romantic inclination to "undetermined feelings" (*unbestimmte Gefühle*) and contingent arrangements—the preference for language (whose allegorical functions Schlegel emphasized early on [*KA* II: 348]) and for the language of all languages, music. Concerning sound (referring to both media as a common basis for this), Schlegel claims that: "It has an infinite advantage, insofar as it is something completely mobile; for through this, one distances oneself one step further from the rigidity and immobility of the thing and [one step closer] to freedom" (*KA* XII: 345). According to Schlegel, hearing is "the noblest sense." "It is, as the sense for the mobile, much more closely connected to freedom and insofar much more suitable than any other sense, to free us from the tyranny of the thing" (l.c., 346; cf. *KA* XVIII: 57 f, 217 f.). Music, a completely temporal art form, corresponds best to the fluidity of the substance-less I. The definiteness of three-dimensional space as the medium of art becomes polemicized. It conjures up an untruthful self-identity in the presentation of human beings. However, as we heard, the essence of transitory art types is infinite progressivity. So music wins against all others, because it allegorizes the temporality/instability of this essence most easily.

"[Everything] contradicts itself," notes Schlegel succinctly (*KA* XVIII: 86, Nr. 673). And what holds for reality, holds just as well for consciousness: "The form of consciousness is altogether chaotic" (l.c., 290, Nr. 1136; 123, Nr. 2). In order to handle this, consciousness needs a "polemic against consistency" (*KA* XVIII: 309, Nr. 1383). So the fragment, which carries the contradiction of the infinite and the finite in itself—but only selectively— does not avoid stepping into new contradictions with other fragments, which in fact all share the tendency towards the infinite, but on the basis of their individuality provoke new reciprocal contradictions. This fact explains the special import which Schlegel bestows to the concept "tendency": Each fragment relates to totality, as determinateness relates to the infinitely determinable: a relationship, which explains "the multitude of poetic sketches, studies, fragments, tendencies, ruins, and materials" (*KA* II: 147, Nr. 4). All rash totalizing originates from "spiritual gout" (*KA* XVIII: 221, Nr. 318), from "spiritual petrifaction."[14] "All classical forms of poetry in their strict purity are now ridiculous" (*KA* II: 154, Nr. 60). The fragment is "no work but only a piece (*Bruchstück*) [. . .], a mass, a sketch, a [pre]disposition, an incentive" (l.c., 159, Nr. 103; cf. 209, Nr. 259).

"The authentic contradicting-ness in our I," says Schlegel, "is that we feel at one and the same time both finite and infinite" (*KA* XII: 334). This contradiction frustrates the I, which "looks for itself," without finding itself (*KA* XIX: 22, Nr. 197), for it is missing the possibility to grasp itself with "one single [encompassing] look" (*KA* XII: 381). This impossible total impression, which denies the pieces (*Bruchstücke*) of consciousness "connection and foundation" (*KA* XII: 393, 402), makes itself observable *ex negativo* as "a gap (*Lücke*) in existence" (*KA* XII: 192). It splits and dismembers the self, but does so in such a way that the fragments, in which its *Weltanschauung* dissolves, also become groundless and changeable: they dissolve themselves reciprocally and correct, as it were, the totalitarianism of the analytic spirit, in that they defend—ironically—the synthesis which *is* not but *ought* to be, against the existing dissolution. In this respect, the fragment stands in the service of a new totality; the enthusiasm which Schlegel raises for the notions of "Confusion [. . .], inconsistency, lack of character, etc" (KA XVIII: 24, Nr. 66), would otherwise hardly be clear: he feels himself justified by his "love for the Absolute" (KA II: 164, Nr. 26). In such and similar terms, the structure of Friedrich Schlegel's completely realistic foundation of art and philosophy is represented in exemplary fashion throughout. He says, for example: "Because nature and humankind contradict so often and so sharply, philosophy may perhaps not avoid doing the same" (KA II: 240, Nr. 397). Another illustration: "Life too is fragmentarily rhapsodic" (KA XVIII: 109, Nr. 955), and "the confusion" of perfect poetry "is actually a faithful image of life itself" (l.c., 198, Nr. 21). Indeed, "if one has a sense for the infinite, [. . .], he expresses himself decisively, through pure contradictions" (KA II: 243, Nr. 412; cf. 164, Nr. 26 [inserted in *Blüthenstaub*, the collection of fragments by Novalis]).

Inconsistency and asystasy form only one aspect of the fragment. If, in the fragment, the synthetic dowry would be lifted completely from the Absolute, then an unlimited multiplicity of forms would result from the instability of the single positions, but these would never step into any real contradiction with each other. Contradiction can only appear insofar as logically incompatible determinations are attributed to the same thing; and that is a crucial point for the negative dialectic of early Romanticism. In other words: the fragment would not be comprehensible as that which it is, had it not, *ex negativo*, its place within the framework of a system (KA XVIII: 80, Nr. 614; 287, Nr. 1091; 100, Nr. 857).

One could also formulate this consequence as follows: until now we have only viewed the oppositions which the fragments enter into amongst each other on the basis of the finitude or individuality of their position, which in each case fall into contradiction with the individuality of every other position. There is a contradiction meanwhile, without which the latter cannot even take place, namely, that which appears between the fragmentary-particular positions, on the one hand, and the idea of the Absolute, on the other hand. The fragment not only breaks into other fragments like it, but the sum total of the particular positings also stands in contradiction to the idea of the Absolute, which is found outside of and beyond all opposition. It is precisely this perspective that leaves all fragments—and the unity embodied in them—to appear as the failed expression of the Absolute, which as such, remains incomprehensible.

It is from these considerations that the basic idea of the so-called romantic *irony* originates. The idea of the Absolute, which remains inadequate to all single positions, moves these into an ironic light. On the other hand, we can get our bearings in our finitude only by such single positions, while the Absolute remains ungraspable. For this reason, irony plays into both directions. Irony is a derisive gesture toward the finite, because it is denied by another finite and by the notion of the Absolute is altogether shamed; but irony can also laugh at the Absolute because, as Novalis said, pure identity does not even exist (*NS* II: 177, lines 10/11). *Pure* would be, "something neither related nor relatable [. . .] The concept *pure* is, therefore, an empty concept—[. . .] everything pure is therefore a deception of the imagination, a necessary fiction" (II: 179, lines, 17 ff.).

> All philosophizing must [. . .] terminate in an absolute foundation. Now, if this were not given, if this concept contained an impossibility—then the drive to philosophize would be an infinite activity—and therefore without end, because there would always exist the eternal requirement of an absolute foundation, that could, however, only be fulfilled in a relative way—and so never completely. Through the voluntary renunciation of the Absolute, there arises within us infinitely free activity—the only possible Absolute which can be given to us and which we find only through our incapacity to reach or to recognize any Absolute. This Absolute which is given to us, can only be recognized negatively, insofar as we act and find that it cannot be reached through any act. This can be called an absolute postulate. All searching for such a principle would therefore be like trying to square a circle.
> [. . .]
> [. . .] This Absolute which we can only recognize negatively, realizes itself through an eternal absence [. . .]. So eternity becomes realized through time, even though time contradicts eternity (l.c., 269 f., Nr. 566).

This sort of back and forth looking from eternal unity to the temporal manifold is something that irony shares with what Fichte had said about imagination in the earliest *Wissenschaftslehre* (*WW* I: 212 ff., esp., 215–17). Imagination was introduced there as a hovering between irreconcilables, as a middle faculty at once unifying and dividing. The irreconcilable entities are, for Fichte, the two conflicting activities of the I: its expanding (determinable) activity, the I moving towards the infinite and its limitative (dermining) activity.

> The imagination is a faculty, which hovers in the middle between determination and non-determination, between the finite and the infinite; and accordingly is indeed determined as A+B *simultaneously* through the determinant A and the indeterminant B, which is that synthesis of the imagination of which we just spoke.—Precisely this hovering marks the imagination through its product; the imagination brings forth its product during and through this hovering (l.c., 216 f.).

In order to become comprehensible, that which is pure must limit itself; any border contradicts the essential infinity of that which is pure, however; therefore it must always overstep the limits which it sets to itself, and then limit itself again, and then overstep these limits, and so on and on. This is Schlegel's model of irony. He speaks of "a divided spirit," which emerges from "self-limitation, therefore as a result of self-creation and self-destruction" (*KA* II: 149, Nr. 28). This happens in the following way: the limits conflict with the infinite activity, which itself dismisses any limit imposed upon it. Precisely this surpassing of all self-imposed limits is what Schlegel calls irony. You can now see clearly, that irony is the searched for structure of the whole whose abstract parts are wit and allegory. In wit, the spirit takes "the sharpest direction to a point" (*KA* II: 160, Nr. 10; cf. XII: 393; XVIII: 305, Nr. 1333; 69, Nr. 499; II: 197, Nr. 206), and so acquires "a type of wholeness." The bonding power of the Absolute is deflected, as it were, into the single syntheses of the individuated world; the world is grasped as fettered within limits. Precisely the reverse tendency, the striving beyond all limits to the limitless, becomes in allegory the event which corrects, through the opening into the infinite, the "derived" and "fragmentary character of human consciousness" (*KA* XII: 392 ff., cf., l.c., 348, 352, 374; XVIII: 506, Nr. 9; 512, Nr. 73). Irony is the synthesis of wit and allegory; due to its activity of going beyond limits it corrects the onesidedness of the unity that was meant to include the Absolute, but only embodied the particular unity of the witty synthesis.

> It contains and excites a feeling of the insoluble opposition between the unconditioned and the conditioned, between the impossibility and the necessity of an exhaustive communication. It is the freest of all licenses, because through it [irony], one clears oneself away from [or transcends] oneself; and indeed even the most lawful because it is absolutely necessary. It is a very good sign, if the harmonious philistines do not at all know how they have to take this constant self-parody, always and again believe and mistrust, until they are swindled into taking the joke for something serious and something serious as a joke (*KA* II: 160, Nr. 108).

Something of this swindle can be felt through listening to a song from Tieck which is at the same time cryptic and charming:

> Mit Leiden
> *Und Freuden*
> Gleich lieblich zu spielen
> Und Schmerzen
> Im Scherzen
> So leise zu fühlen,
> Ist wen'gen beschieden.
> Sie wählen zum Frieden
> Das eine von beiden,

Sind nicht zu beneiden:
Ach gar zu bescheiden
Sind doch ihre Freuden
Und kaum von Leiden
Zu unterscheiden.
(TS 10, 96).

With pain
And joy
To play equally dearly,
And pains
In joking
To feel so quietly,
Is granted to few.
They choose for the peace
That one of the two,
Is not to be envied:
Oh, even to summon,
Are their joys
And hardly from their pains
To distinguish.

Joys, when observed closely, lose their distinctive characteristics and become similar to their opposite, pains, for which the same holds. There are, therefore, determinacy (*Bestimmtheit*) and difference (*Unterschiedenheit*) throughout; they are, however, treated poetically in such a way that their positing is mysteriously overdetermined through the dissolution of what is posited: its being transcended toward that which it is not. This stepping over, which always anew passes beyond that self-contraction, which is carried out by the infinite activity as wit, is made into an allegory of the unlimited; it opens outlooks, "échappées de vue into the infinite" (*KA* II: 200, Nr. 220). So irony becomes an επιδειξις (idendification, indication) of the infinite" (*KA* XVIII: 128, Nr. 76). Through irony, "one clears oneself away from oneself" (*KA* II: 160; Nr. 108)—away from oneself, namely, insofar as this self has become torn off and fragmentary, a self lost from the infinite. Irony consists in a "constant alternation (*Wechsel*) between self-creation and self-destruction" (*KA* II: 172, Nr. 151), in a "wonderful, eternal alternation between enthusiasm and irony" (l.c., 319), between "creation and destruction" (*KA* XVIII: 198, Nr. 11), an "eternal oscillation between self-expansion and self-limitation of thought" (l.c., 305, Nr. 1333), a "reciprocal play (*Wechselspiel*) between the infinite and the finite" (l.c., 361, Nr. 495), it is "the pulse and alternation between universality and individuality" (l.c., 259, Nr. 782)—no matter how the contrasting pairs may be articulated. In any case, irony is the place in which human beings express and present that which Schlegel calls "the authentic contradiction of our I," namely, "that we feel at the same time finite and infinite" (*KA* XII: 334). This contradiction frustrates the I, which, Schlegel writes: "doesn't really posit, but rather searches"; it is essentially "longing," not possessing (*KA* XIX: 22, Nr. 197). The finite I "finds itself as inwardly split and divided, full of contradictions and incomprehensibilities, in short, as a patchwork, rather opposed to unity" (*KA* XII: 381 bottom). An "all-encompassing look" at its states is missing; that is why it can only grasp fragments of itself without cohesion and foundation (l.c., 393, 402)—it appears to itself as "a gap in existence" (l.c., 192). This splits and dismembers the self, in fact so thoroughly, that the fragments and witty aperçus, in which this dismemberment is manifested, don't dissolve in favor of a single world view. Quite the contrary, these fragments neutralize themselves reciprocally. In this way they correct the onesidedness and the false semblance of their finite existence, so that what is meant to be presented though their annihilation—not intuitively, but via premonition—, is not the fragments themselves but that which should have presented in their place: the infinite. It is in this sense that Schlegel can say that "irony [is] merely the surrogate of that which should go into the infinite" (*KA* XVIII: 112, Nr. 995). Seen so, irony already gives evidence in this world for the truth of that which should be, which must, in the meantime, appear as nothingness. Whenever someone expresses something finite, he/she will have committed a contradiction; which is only lifted if the Absolute—that which was really intended—shines through all finite natures (*KA* II: 243, 412; cf. 164, Nr. 26)—and that it can only do negatively, as a vector, which pushes the shattered space into the direction of what is not itself finite. So irony, with a laugh, corrects the false esteem of an atomized world, in that it—for the time being only within the realm of the imaginary—mocks as null, that which spreads itself out as substantial reality. On the other hand, through the fact that irony uncovers the "discord" and "incongruity" within the whole context of "life," it is also a "negative [. . .] proof against providence and for immortality": as cipher of the "Labyrinth of the infinite" (*KA* XVIII: 218, Nr. 293) it entails, at the same time, the hidden chance for the advent of a restored totality. This, according to Schlegel, is because "the faintest discord is, for the religious, evidence for eternity" (l.c., 213, Nr. 207). This is so because each contradiction alludes to its own self-dissolution; and through the inconsistency and the fragility of a fragmented world, the infinite announces itself. The means it employs in order to make this contradictory experience perceptible is a serenity (*Heiterkeit*), which is left to hover above the self-affirmation of all finite positions. Admittedly, philosophy can explain this but cannot set it in motion. To say something determined in such a way that while expressing it this determinacy dissolves into some indeterminacy; to say something as if one were not saying anything at all, is something that only the poet can do. Here, too, philosophy finds its supplement, indeed, its completion, in and as poetry. Nowhere did Schlegel determine the function of art more clearly than in a private lecture from 1807: "It should be brought to mind, that the necessity of poetry is based on the requirement to present the infinite, which emerges from the imperfection of philosophy."[15] But already in Fragment 48 of *Ideas* (from 1800), Schlegel noted that: "Where philosophy ends, poetry must begin" (*KA* II: 261).

Notes

Acknowledgments

1. Karl Ameriks and Dieter Sturma, eds., *The Modern Subject. Conceptions of the Self in Classical German Philosophy* (Albany, NY: State University of New York Press, 1995), 65–86.

Introduction

1. For the philosophers of this period, that is, immediately following the publication of Kant's *Critique of Pure Reason*, the foundations of knowledge *are* the foundations of philosophy as well.

2. See for example, Peter Viereck, *Metapolitics: The Roots of the Nazi Mind* (New York: Capricorn Books, 1965); and Georg Lukács, *The Destruction of Reason*, trans. Peter Palmer (Atlantic Highlands, NJ: Humanities Press, 1981).

3. The most recent example of this schizophrenic characterization of German Romanticism is to be found in Isaiah Berlin's, *The Roots of Romanticism* (Princeton, NJ: Princeton University Press, 1999).

4. Theodor Ziolkowski, *Das Wunderjahr in Jena: Geist und Gesellschaft 1794–95* (Stuttgart: Klett-Cotta, 1998).

5. *Loci classici* of works dealing with the literary strengths of early German Romanticism are: Rudolf Haym, *Die Romantische Schule* (Berlin: Gaertner, 1882); Richarda Huch, *Die Blütezeit der Romantik—Ausbreitung, Blütezeit und Verfall der Romantik* (Tübingen: Rainer Wunderlich, 1951); Georg Lukács, *Soul and Form*, trans. Anna Bostock (Cambridge, MA: MIT Press, 1974); Oskar Walzel, *German Romanticism*, trans. Alma Elsie Lussky (New York: Capricorn Books, 1966); Paul Kluckhohn, *Das Ideengut der deutschen Romantik*, 3rd ed. (Tübingen: Niemeyer, 1953).

6. I refer here to *Das Athenäum*, a journal published between 1798 and 1800, edited by Friedrich and August Wilhelm Schlegel. This journal became the most

important literary vehicle of early German Romanticism. For a good taste of the tone of the journal, see Schlegel's essay, *On Incomprehensibility, KA* II: 363–72. Translated in *Theory as Practice: A Critical Anthology of Early German Romantic Writings*, ed. and trans. Jochen Schulte-Sasse, Haynes Horne, Andreas Michel, Elizabeth Mittman, Assenka Oksiloff, Lisa C. Roetzel, and Mary R. Strand (Minneapolis, MN: University of Minnesota Press, 1997), 118–128. All references to Schlegel's work in German are to *Friedrich Schlegel Kritische Ausgabe* (*KA*), in thirty-five volumes, edited by Ernst Behler, Ernst Behler, editor (in collaboration with Jean-Jacques Anstett, Jakob Baka, Ursula Behler, Liselotte Dieckmann, Hans Eichner, Raymond Immerwahr, Robert L. Kahn, Eugene Susini, Bertold Sutter, A. Leslie Wilson and others) (Paderborn: Ferdinand Schönigh, 1958 ff.). The *Athenäum Fragments* as well as selections of the *Critical Fragments* and *Ideas* have been translated by Peter Firchow in *Friedrich Schlegel: Philosophical Fragments* (Minneapolis: University of Minnesota Press, 1991).

7. This trend is finally beginning to turn around. Stanley Cavell and Frederick Beiser have paid serious attention to the philosophical dimensions of early German Romanticism, and their work will be discussed below. Other promising signs of a change in this trend are Robert J. Richards, *The Romantic Conception of Life: Science and Philosophy in the Age of Goethe* (Chicago: University of Chicago Press, 2002), Frederick Beiser, *German Idealism: The Struggle against Subjectivism, 1781–1801* (Cambridge, MA: Harvard University Press, 2002), and Terry Pinkard, *German Philosophy 1760–1860: The Legacy of Idealism* (Cambridge: Cambridge University Press, 2002). The approaches of each of these philosophers differ in substantial ways from Frank's, and this kind of disagreement is most welcome, for philosophers are finally beginning to dispute the nature and relevance of the *philosophical* dimensions of the early German Romanticism. A recent *Cambridge Companion to German Idealism*, ed. Karl Ameriks (Cambridge: Cambridge University Press, 2000), includes several excellent articles on Romanticism, though the sharp boundary that Frank wants to maintain between early German Romanticism and German idealism is not always upheld.

8. See Wilhelm Dilthey, *Das Leben Schleiermachers*, vol. I, book 2 (Berlin: Walter de Gruyter, 1970); and *Die Entstehung der Hermeneutik* (Göttingen: Vandenhoeck & Ruprecht, 1961). Both Dilthey and Hans-Georg Gadamer acknowledge that Schlegel's thought was an important turning point in the history of hermeneutics, the point at which the act of understanding became its own subject.

9. Walter Benjamin, *Der Begriff der Kunstkritik in der deutschen Romantik: Band I Gesammelte Schriften* (Frankfurt a.Main: Suhrkamp, 1974). Translated into English as, *The Concept of Criticism in German Romanticism*, in *Walter Benjamin: Selected Writings; Volume 1—1913–1926*, eds. Marcus Bullock and Michael W. Jennings (Cambridge, MA: Harvard University Press, 1996), 116–200.

10. Ernst Behler, "Friedrich Schlegels Theorie des Verstehens: Hermeneutik oder Dekonstuktion?" in *Die Aktualität der Frühromantik* (Paderborn: Ferdinand Schöningh, 1987), 141–160. Also, Klaus Peter, "Friedrich Schlegel und Adorno: Die Dialektik der Aufklärung in der Romantik und heute," in *Die Aktualität der Frühromantik* (Paderborn: Ferdinand Schöningh, 1987), 219–235.

11. Works which clearly mark Beiser as a leading authority of early German Romanticism include: *The Fate of Reason: German Philosophy from Kant to Fichte*

(Cambridge, MA: Harvard University Press, 1987); *Enlightenment, Revolution, and Romanticism: The Genesis of Modern German Political Thought* (Cambridge, MA: Harvard University Press, 1992), and *German Idealism: The Struggle against Subjectivism, 1781–1801* (Cambridge, MA: Harvard University Press, 2002). Beiser has also edited and translated a collection of texts by the early German Romantics, *The Early Political Writings of the German Romantics* (Cambridge, England: Cambridge University Press, 1996), and is the author of many articles on the movement.

12. See for example his article, Andrew Bowie, "John McDowell's *Mind and World*, and Early Romantic Epistemology," *Revue Internationale de Philosohie* 3 (1996): 515–554.

13. Richard Eldridge, "Some Remarks on Logical Truth: Human Nature and Romanticism," *Midwest Studies in Philosophy* 19 (1994): 220–242. Although Eldridge does not discuss early German Romanticism, his claim that: "Romanticism is one reasonably accurate name for the sense that human beings are thus perenially between the aspiration to establish the ultimate terms of human responsibility and that aspiration's disappointment" (Ibid., p. 238), nicely captures a major theme in Schlegel's thought, that of the tension between the infinite and the finite and the feeling of longing which arises from this state of eternal longing after that which can never be attained. Frank discusses these issues in lecture twelve.

14. See, Robert Richards, *The Romantic Conception of Life: Science and Philosophy in the Age of Goethe* (Chicago: University of Chicago Press, 2002).

15. See, Dieter Heinrich, *Konstellationen. Probleme und Debatten am Ursprung der idealistischen Philosophie (1789–1795)* (Stuttgart: Klett-Cotta, 1991); and *Der Grund im Bewusstsein. Hölderlin's Denken in Jena 1794–95* (Stuttgart: Klett-Cotta, 1995). Neither of these works have been translated in English, while Henrich's work on Kant's philosophy has. See, for example, Dieter Heinrich, "The Proof-Structure of Kant's Transcendental Dialectic," *The Review of Metaphysics* 22 (1969): 640–59; *Aesthetic Judgment and the Moral Image of the World: Studies in Kant* (Stanford, CA: Stanford University Press, 1994); *The Unity of Reason: Essays on Kant's Philosophy*, ed. Richard Velkley (Cambridge, MA: Harvard University Press, 1994).

16. Especially: Manfred Frank, *Unendliche Annaehuerung: Die Anfaenge der philosophischen Fruehromantik* (Frankfurt/M: Suhrkamp, 1997); "*Philosophische Grundlagen der Frühromantik,*" *Athenäum Jahrbuch fur Romantik* (1994); *Eine Einführung in die frühromantische Ästhetik,* (Frankfurt/M: Suhrkamp, 1989); *Das Problem "Zeit" in der deutschen Romantik: Zeitbewußtsein und Bewußtsein von Zeitlichkeit in der frühromantischen Philosophie und in Tiecks Dichtung* (München: Winkler, 1972). While Frank's book, *What is Neo-Structuralism?* has been translated (Minneapolis: University of Minnesota Press,), most of his work on early German Romanticism is available only in German. One exception is his article, "The Philosophical Foundations of Early Romanticism," *The Modern Subject: Conceptions of the Self in Classical German Philosophy*, K. Ameriks and D. Sturma, eds. (Albany: State University of New York Press, 1995), 65–85.

17. Manfred Frank, "*Les fondements philosophiques du premier romantisme allemande,* vol. 50, no. 197 (1996).

18. A good example of this is *Die Aktualität der Fruhromantik*, Ernst Behler, ed. (Paderborn: Schöningh, 1987). This is a series of articles by the leading scholars in

this field (e.g., R. Brinkmann, J. Hörisch, R. Bubner, M. Frank, E. Behler, K. Peter, H. Schanze). Most of these articles deal with specific philosophical issues of early German Romanticism.

19. Stanley Cavell, *This New Yet Unapproachable America* (Albuquerque: Living Batch Press, 1989).

20. Phillipa Lacoue-Labarthe and Jean-Luc Nancy, *The Literary Absolute*, trans. Phillip Barnard and Cheryl Lester (Albany: State University of New York Press, 1988).

21. Ibid., pp. 4–6.

22. Richard Eldridge, "A Continuing Task: Cavell and the Truth of Skepticism," in *The Sense of Stanley Cavell*, Richard Fleming and Michael Payne, eds. (Lewisburg: Bucknell University Press, 1989), 76.

23. *KA* XII, p. 328.

24. *KA* XII, pp. 109–115.

25. *KA* XII, p. 307.

26. Michael Krausz, "Relativism and Foundationalism," *The Monist* 67, no. 3 (July 1984): 395–404. For another account of this kind of "middle position," see J. Margolis, *Pragamatism without Foundations: Reconciling Realism and Relativism* (Oxford: Blackwell, 1986).

27. *KA* XII, p. 110.

28. *KA* XII, p. 111.

29. "weil ein philosophisches System sich aus das andere stützt, zur Verständigung des einen immer wieder Kenntnis des anderen vorhergehenden erforderlich ist, und die Philosophien eine zusammenhängende Kette bilden, wovon die Kenntnis eines Glieder immer wieder zur Kenntnis des anderen nötigt" (*KA* XII, p. 111).

30. "es kommt auf die Ideen, Meinungen, und Gedanken der verschiedenen Philosophen an, welche zu untersuchen, zu erklären und zu beurteilen nicht Sache der Geschichte, sondern der Kritik ist" (*KA* XII, p. 112).

31. This is a far cry from Berlin's claims in *The Roots of Romanticism* (Princeton, NJ: Princeton University Press, 1999). Berlin characterizes Romanticism (not distinguishing between early, middle, or late Romanticism) as an anti-Enlightenment movement that was rooted in irrationalism and the blind forces of the will that led to a kind of poetic mythology culminating in a glorified nationalism. He argues that the two most prominent consequences of Romanticism were existentialism and fascism.

32. This critique is concentrated in two series of fragments entitled: *Zur Wissenschaftslehre 1796* (*KA* XVIII, pp. 3–14, Nrs. 1–125); and *Geist der Wissenschaftslehre 1797–1798* (*KA* XVIII, pp. 31–39, Nrs. 126–227).

33. *KA* XVIII, p. 7, Nr. 36.

34. This early usage of the term might explain, though not justify, the endemic mistake of considering early German Romanticism as merely a literary movement.

35. A. O. Lovejoy, "The Meaning of 'Romantic' in Early-German Romanticism," and "Schiller and the Genesis of German Romanticism," in *Essays in the History of Ideas* (Baltimore: The Johns Hopkins Press, 1948), 183–206, and 207–227. Lovejoy's purpose in both of these articles is to present his view of the source and original meaning of the term "romantic" (in its use by the early German Romantics) and of the sources and content of the aesthetic and philosophical ideas for which the

word stood (p. 185). He contrasts his view to that of Rudolf Haym's (*Die Romantische Schule*, 5th ed. 1870; reprint, Berlin: Weidmann). Haym claimed that "romantic" poetry simply meant "Romanpoesie" or writings possessed of the qualities of Goethe's *Wilhelm Meister*. Haym equates "romantic" with the German word for "novel" which is *Roman*. This, according to Lovejoy, is problematic for several reasons: (a) it does not explain then what the term could have meant as we find it in Schlegel's pre-Meister writings; (b) every modern novel may be romantic, but not everything romantic is a novel (Shakespeare's work is romantic, as are the medieval tales of romance, and some songs and poems); (c) to reduce the origin of the term "romantic" to its relation with the novel is to limit its philosophical relevance. Lovejoy claims that

> The genesis of Romanticism, then, is very seriously misconceived, when it is supposed (as by Haym and many others after him) that the conception of "Romantic poetry" was formed by Schlegel only about 1796 or later, that he "abstracted it" from *Wilhelm Meister*; that it implied a sort of apoetheosis of the novel among the literary genres; and that Schlegel's first elucidation of it was in the *Athenäum* in 1798. The theory of Romanticism was, so to say, a by-product of the prevalent classicism of the early 1790s (p. 203).

According to Lovejoy, the most important text in Schlegel's conversion from classicism to Romanticism was not Goethe's *Meister*, but Schiller's essay "Über naive und sentimentalische Dichtung" (published in *Horen* in 1795). Schiller's essay offers a vindication of the moderns.

36. For more on the genesis and use of this term see René Welleck, "The Concept of Romanticism in Literary History," *Concepts of Criticism* (New Haven: Yale University Press, 1963), 128–198; and Hans Eichner "Romantisch—Romantik— Romantiker," *'Romantic' and Its Cognates—The European History of a Word*, Hans Eichner, ed. (Toronto: University of Toronto Press, 1972), 98–156.

37. Ernst Behler, *German Romantic Literary Theory* (Cambridge, England: Cambridge University Press, 1993), 25.

38. *KA* II, p. 335.

39. Behler, *German Romantic Literary Theory*, p. 26.

40. *KA* II, p. 333.

41. *KA* II, p. 182, Nr. 116

42. For a thorough dissection of this fragment, see Eichner's introduction to *KA* II, LIX–LXIV.

43. Behler, *German Romantic Literary Theory*, p. 30. The term "romantic" took on a polemical, caricaturing designation later, with the advent of the Heidelberg Romantics. The Homer translator, Johann F. Voss, applied the term disparagingly to the proponents of this style, and thus, the term took on a negative connotation. In the 1830s and 1840s there arose a group of ardent opponents of Romanticism, these were the representatives of the New Germany (*das Junge Deutschland*) and included Heinrich Heine, Arnold Ruge, Theodor Echtermeyer. (Behler 1993, 32). Hegel was also highly critical of Romanticism, deeming it a type of subjectivity without any continents, the "apex of subjectivity separating itself from the unifying substance"

(Behler 1993, 32). In the late 1800s and early 1900s several efforts were undertaken to investigate the contributions of the early Romantics. Important contributors to this endeavor include: Richarda Huch, Carl Schmitt, Georg Lukács, Oskar Walzel, Josef Körner, Paul Kluckhohn. It was within this context that the term "Romantic School" became broken down into early Romanticism or Jena Romantics, middle Romanticism or Heidelberg Romantics, and late Romanticism.

44. Kant characterizes his age in this way in a note at Axi of the *Critique of Pure Reason*.

45. KA XII, p. 286.

46. For more on the important distinction between classification and comparison, especially within the context of early German Romanticism, see Rodolphe Gasché, "Comparatively Theoretical," *Germanistik und Komparastik*, H. Birus, ed. (Stuttgart: Metzler Verlag, 1995), 417–32. Gasché explores the relation between early German Romanticism and the rise of comparative literature, arguing that early German Romanticism forms the prehistory of the discipline known today as comparative literature.

47. For translations of texts by K. L. Reinhold, G. E. Schulze, S. Maimon, and J. S. Beck, see *Between Kant and Hegel: Texts in the Development of Post-Kantian Idealism*, trans. with intro. George di Giovanni and H. S. Harris, 2d ed. (Indianapolis, IN: Hackett Publishing, 2000). Also, see *Kant's Early Critics: The Empiricist Critique of the Theoretical Philosophy*, trans. and ed. Brigitte Sassen (Cambridge: Cambridge University Press, 2000).

48. Recently, Manfred Frank edited a volume of Gottlob E. Schulze's work, *Aenesidemus oder über die Fundamente der von Herrn Professor Reinhold in Jena gelieferten Elementar-Philosophie* (Frankfurt: Meiner Verlag, 1996).

49. Schlegel became a contributor to Niethammer's (later Fichte's) *Philosophisches Journal* (cf. KA XVII, p. 22 ff. und 49 ff.). We know that Schlegel was occupied with Fichte's work in 1795 and stimulated by Fichte's *Vorlesungen über die Bestimmung des Gelehrten* of 1794 (cf. Behler's commentary KA XIX, 370 ff.).

50. See Frederick Beiser, *The Fate of Reason: German Philosophy from Kant to Fichte* (Cambridge, MA: Harvard University Press, 1987).

51. *Philosophische Lehrjahre* (1796–1806): *Beilage II Aus der ersten Epoche. Zur Logik und Philosophie 1796 (Jena)*, KA XVIII: 517–21.

52. KA XVIII: 506–507, esp. Nrs. 12, 15.

Lecture 1: On Early German Romanticism As an Essentially Skeptical Movement

1. Karl Leonhard Reinhold, *Versuch einer neuen Theorie des menschlichen Vorstellungsvermögens* (Prague and Jena: Widtmann and Mauke, 1789).

2. Georg Lukács, *The Destruction of Reason*, trans. Peter Palmer (Atlantic Highlands, NJ: Humanities Press, 1981).

3. For evidence of this, see Manfred Frank, "Wie reaktionär war eigentlich die Frühromantik? (Elemente zur Aufstörung der Meinungsbildung)," in *Athenäum. Jahrbuch für Romantik* (Paderborn: Ferdinand Schöningh, 1997), 141–166.

4. Translator's note: The German term is *Grundsatzphilosophie*, which I have translated as "philosophy of first principles."

5. Emil Petzhold, *Hölderlins Brot und Wein: Ein theoretisches Versuch* (Sambor: Schwarz und Trojan, 1896, New ed., Darmstadt: Wissenschaftliche Buchgesellschaft, 1967), 41.

6. More than rudimentary comprehension of Kant's basic positions is presupposed. An understanding of Kant's *Critique of Pure Reason* is indispensable for a full appreciation of the philosophical foundations of the early German Romantics.

7. Friedrich Heinrich Jacobi, *Über die Lehre des Spinoza in Briefen an den Herrn Moses Mendelssohn, Neue vermehrte Ausgabe* (Breslau: Löwe, 1789). In English translation by George di Giovanni as, "Concerning the Doctrine of Spinoza in Letters to Moses Mendelssohn, excerpts," in Friedrich Heinrich Jacobi, *The Main Philosophical Writings and the Novel Allwill*, translated with an introductory study, notes and bibliography by George di Giovanni (Montreal: McGill-Queen's University Press, 1994), 339–378.

8. Another critical text for an understanding of Reinhold's work during this period is, *Über das Fundament des philosophischen Wissens* (Concerning the Foundation of Philosophical Knowledge), Jena: Widtmann and Mauke, 1794. A significant excerpt from this work has been translated by George di Giovanni in *Between Kant and Hegel: Texts in the Development of Post-Kantian Idealism* (Indianapolis, IN: Hackett Publishing Company, 2000), 53–103.

9. There were around thirty-one pieces of mail from eighteen senders, six of them anonymous. (General administrative archives: Polizeihofstelle, Geheimakten 102/1794, folio 172). The letters first made their way out of the Viennese police possession in 1923 at the urging of the then Vice-Chancellor of the Seipel Regiment, Dr. Felix Frank. They are now in the Viennese National Library, under catalogue number 130/1. For a comprehensive account of this, see, Walter Goldinger, "Kant und die österreichischen Jakobiner," in: *Beiträge zur neueren Geschichte Österreichs*, eds., Heinrich Fichtenau and Erich Zöllner (Vienna-Cologne-Graz: Hermann Böhlaus Nachf., 1974), 299–308; also see, Wilhelm Baum, "Staatspolize und Kärntner Geistesleben," in *Forum* 36, no. 432 (1989): 20–23. Goldinger names Max Pirker (*Die Zukunft der deutschösterreichischen Alpenländer*, 1919) as the discoverer of a part of Herbert's correspondence. Also see the thorough and most up-to-date evaluation by Wilhelm Baum, "Die Aufklärung und die Jakobiner in Österreich: Der Klagenfurter Herbert-Kreis," in *Verdrängter Humanismus—verzögerte Aufklärung: Österreichische Philosophie zur Zeit der Revolution und Restauration (1750–1829)*, eds., Wilhelm Baum, Michael Benedikt, and Reinhard Knoll (Vienna: Turia and Kant, 1992), 803–827. Goldinger's research (which includes abundant literature on the affair and on Herbert's circle of friends, including Johann Benjamin Erhard and Jens Baggesen) is also Dieter Henrich's source.

10. Letter to Niethammer from February 24, 1796. *FHA* 14, cf. also 11; e.g., *StA* VI: 202 ff.; cf. 190 ff.

11. Dieter Henrich, *Der Grund im Bewußtsein*, 832 (cf., the highly relevant passage from the letter, l.c., 828–834). Henrich did not publish the second, equally comprehensive, half of the letter; it was first published by Wilhelm Baum in, *Korrespondenz mit dem Klagenfurter Herbert-Kreis/Friedrich* Immanuel Niethemmer

(Vienna: Turia and Kant, 1995), 81–96, here, p. 88 to the conclusion. Niethammer's thought was, by that time, no longer original: his formulation only summarized the much more radically formulated issue concerning skepticism, which Herbert und Erhard had established in their letters May 6, 1794 (cf. l.c., 75–77; also *Denkwürdigkeiten*, 393–5) and from May 19, 1794 (l.c., 79 ff.; cf. *Denkwürdigkeiten*, 395 ff.). Niethammer's letter is nothing more than a reply to this.

12. Accessible in Weimar's Goethe-Schiller-Archive under number 76/II: 3, 2. The decisive passage reads as follows in the original (my transcription): "He [Diez] has studied my writings as well as those of Kant. He has, on the occasion of my lectures, which he attends, presented doubts, which are for me and my Philosophy of Elements, of the upmost importance, and along with *some* (I say *some*, because most are not really useful) passages in Schmid's review of my essay on the foundation of knowledge, have provided the material for the second part of the essay." The talk is of Schmid's review of the *Fundament* from April 9 and 10 in Jena's *Allgmeinen Literatur-Zeitung* (49–60). I have provided a precise account of the objections in my contribution to the *Revue internationale de philosophie* (op. cit.), and also in my essay, "Hölderlins philosophische Grundlagen," in *Hölderlin und die Moderne: Eine Bestandsaufnahme*, eds., Gerhard Kurz, Valérie Lawitschka, and Jürgen Wertheimer (Tübingen: Attempto/ Studium Generale, 1995), 174–194.

13. Reinhold's account of Schmid and Diez's objection goes as follows: "Now I clearly see that in the first part of the fundamental theory of the Philosophy of Elements, theorems come forth which I myself should have explicitly shown not to follow immediately from the principle of consciousness, but rather *through* other principles, which I, in this theory of Elements, present without proof, as the claims of common sense, and which can only become proved claims of philosophizing reason if the other principles of consciousness are presented and developed. For example, the theorem that content is given, form is brought forth, representation is produced, whereby self-consciousness and consciousness of self-activity, which does not lie within consciousness at all, is presupposed. Only the claims of common sense *must* in any case be taken up lemmatically in the Philosophy of Elements, for it is only through common understanding that the passage to philosophizing reason can be made; but the claims must be justified by the latter.

The foundation of the Philosophy of Elements are pure facts of consciousness, amongst which one?, which the principle of consciousness expresses, is the most general and insofar, in the system, the *first*. The Philosophy of Elements first exhibits the principles of philosophy, and so cannot depart from these principles, but rather from the mere *facts*, which are explained through their difference and connection, and from which the principles come forth" (in, *Briefwechsel und Kantische Schriften: Wissensbegründung in der Glaubenskrise Tübingen-Jena (1790–1792)*, ed., Dieter Henrich (Stuttgart: Klett-Cotta, 1997), 912 ff.

14. *NS* III: 296, Nr. 314, lines 15 ff.

15. Metaphors which Hölderlin also uses in the same context in his letter to Schiller from September 5, 1795. It seems that Novalis picked these up in Friedrich Karl Forberg's *Fragmenten aus meinen Papieren* (Jena: bey. J. G. Voigt, 1796), 74 ff.; moreover, a citation of Erhard), with which he demonstrated familiarity: cf. the

adoption of 'Anecdotes' on Platner's Self-bias (*Selbsteingenommenheit*) in *NS* II: 567, Nr. 205 from *Fragmenten* 10.

16. Henrich was able to prove this to be the case for Hölderlin in *Der Grund im Bewußtsein* (Stuttgart: Klett-Cotta, 1992).

17. Friedrich Immanuel Niethammer, "Concerning the Demands of Common Sense on Philosophy," *Philosophisches Journal* 1 (May 1795): 1–45.

18. Paul Johann Anselm Feuerbach, "Über die Unmöglichkeit eines ersten absoluten Grundsatzes der Philosophie," *Philosophisches Journal* 2, no. 4 (1795): 306–322.

19. Leibniz had already understood self-consciousness to be an immediatedly clarifying truth which was, nonetheless, an a posteriori (that is, factual) truth.

20. The decisive passages in support of this are to be found in *Philosophische Lehrjahre* (*KA* XVIII: 7, Nr. 36; 36, Nr. 193; 505, Nr. 2; 510, Nr. 54 (with a reference to Schelling's "Reciprocal grounding of content and form in the first principle of knowledge" (*SW* I: 1, 94 f.); 518, Nr. 16; 520 f., Nr. 22). In his Jacobi-Review, Schlegel traces a direct reference to this expression in a passage from the *Spinozabüchlein* where Jacobi claims: "that each proof already presupposes something proven" (*Spin*[2], 225, *KA* II: 72). I have undertaken a rather thorough investigation of the meaning of the function of this talk of a reciprocal or alternating first principle in the afore-mentioned essays, "*Alle Wahrheit ist relativ*" (*Revue internationele di Philosophie* (1996), and "*Wechselgrundsatz*"(*Zeitschrift f. p. Forschung* 50 (1996).

21. Carl Christian Erhard Schmid, *Empirische Psychologie* (Empirical Psychology), 1st ed. (Jena, 1791).

Lecture 2: On the Historical Origins of Novalis' Critique of Fichte

1. Novalis, *Schriften: Die Werke Friedrich von Hardenbergs*, eds., Paul Kluckhohn and Richard Samuel (Stuttgart: Kohlhammer, 1960 ff), (abbr.: *NS*), Vol. IV: 159, pp. 7–11.

2. Novalis, *op. cit*, vol. IV, 269, Nr. 566.

3. And during the beginning of the year he returned once again (according to some accounts he returned to Jena in February again). For more on Novalis' intimate contact to the Reinhold and Schmid circles, see Hermann F. Weiss, "Eine Reise nach Thüringen im Jahre 1791: Zu einer unbeachteten Begegnung Karl Wilhelm Justis und Joseph Friedrich Engelschalls mit Schiller und Novalis," *Zeitschrift für hessische Geschichte und Landeskunde* 101 (1991): 43–56.

4. Cf. Friedrich Heinrich Jacobi, *Über die Lehre des Spinoza in Briefen an Herrn Moses Mendelssohn*, new, expanded ed. (Leipzig: Löwe, 1789), 389–434, esp., 424 ff., 430 ff.

5. Reinhold's *Elementarphilosophie* and the arguments of its most important critics are presented with great detail in lecture 10 of Manfred Frank, "Unendliche Annäherung," *Die Anfänge der philosophischen Frühromantik* (Frankfurt/M: Suhrkamp, 1997), 252–285.

6. *NS* II: 16 ff.

7. *NS* III: 356, Nr. 524. Cf. Komm. 943.

8. Cf., l. c., 1009, Nr. 81.

9. *NS* IV: 203, pp. 19 ff.; cf. pp. 85 ff.

10. On Novalis' relation to Erhard see lecture 14 of Manfred Frank, "Unendliche Annäherung," *Die Anfänge der philosophischen Frühromantik* (Frankfurt/M: Suhrkamp, 1997), 363–395.

11. Schmid attributes the corresponding faculties, for example, powers, to these acts, but as an irreducible plurality: "The manifold of appearances of the mind leads us to the notion of a manifold of faculties and powers as the conditions of their determinant possibility and existence (*Daseyn*)" (*Empirische Psychologie*, Jena (1791): part one, 158, sec. VII).

12. *Empirische Psychologie*, 18 ff. (sec. VI of the introduction); cf.—under reference to Crusius—also the twelfth section of the first part (164): "[. . .] that hereafter, everything that should be explained, will, on the contrary, be presumed." Here we find the historical source of Nietzsche's taunt (*Spott*) that Kant answered the question concerning the possibility of a priori synthetic judgments with the claim: "faculty of a faculty" (*Vermöge eines Vermögens*) (Part 11 of, *Jenseits von Gut und Böse* (Beyond Good and Evil), Kritische Studienausgabe 5, eds., by Giorgio Colli and Mazzino Montinari (Munich: Deutscher Taschenbuch Verlag, 1988), 23–25). For more on the entire context, cf. Frank,*"Unendliche Anäherung,"* pp. 275 ff.

13. K. L. Reinhold, *Beyträge zur Berichtigung bisheriger Mißverständnisse der Philosophen*, vol. 1 (Jena: Widtmann and Mauke, 1790), 424 ff.; for more on the consequences that he drew from Heydenreich's critique, see, l. c., 115 ff.

14. Cf. Schmid, *Empirische Psychologie*, 163 ff. (sec. 12), 167 ff. (sec. 14).

15. Cf. Kant's famous comment in sec. 61 of the *Critique of Judgment*, "[. . .] For when we point, for example, to the structure of birds regarding how their bones are hollow, how their wings are positioned to produce motion and their tails to permit steering, and so on, we are saying that all of this is utterly contingent if we go by the mere *nexus effectivus* in nature and do not yet resort to a special kind of causality, namley, the causality of purposes (the *nexus finalis*); in other words, we are saying that nature, considered as mere mechanism, could have structured itself differently in a thousand ways without hitting on precisely the unity in terms of a principle of purposes, and so we cannot hope to find a priori the slightest basis for that unity unless we seek it beyond the concept of nature rather than in it" (*Critique of Judgment*, trans., Werner S. Pluhar (Indianapolis, IN: Hackett Publishing Company, 1987), 236.

16. Cf. lecture 12 in Frank's *"Unendliche Annäherung,"* esp., pp. 314 ff., and 341 ff.

17. So we see in his letter to Reinhold from July 30, 1792. Impressed with how Fichte had outbid Reinhold, Erhard once again takes up the line of argument from this letter in his correspondence with Niethammer from May 19, 1794: "Kant's philosophy is still not at all prevalent amongst the young scholars, for they want reason to be completely constitutive. Ideas would be recognized by us as a priori in us, but they would not be recognized by us a priori but rather analytically, and as they have, as ideas, features of the genus, we believe that in these features, that we have abstracted from the ideas, we have actually discovered the ideas. I have already written to Reinhold about this [. . .]" *Niethammer: Korrespondenz*, 79.

18. Reinhold, *Beyträge* I: 117.

19. Reinhold, *Beyträge* I: 16 (in context, pp. 15 ff.).

20. Reinhold, *Beyträge* I: 358 (in context, pp. 357 ff.).

21. Cf. Lecture 20 in Frank, *"Unendliche[n] Annäherung,"* 532–568, esp., pp. 538 ff.

22. *WW* I (edition of I. H. Fichte, reprint Berlin 1971), 244. Fichte's theory of abstraction was to be reproduced by Schelling in his, *System of transcendental Idealism.* Cf. the transition from the second to the third epoch. Schelling adopts the expression 'absolute abstraction' in *SW* I: 3, 336 (third epoch); usually, however, he speaks of a 'transcendental' abstraction. See especially, pp. 516 ff., 523 ff.

23. Reinhold, *Beyträge* I: 427 ff.

24. Novalis had an even more fundamental objection to this concept, which was aimed more against Fichte and even challenged his idealism: "A self-determining activity is a non-thing—all determined activity absolutely presupposes something posited, something given" (242, Nr. 444, pp. 7–10).

25. Cf. the entire section which collectively, in the name of "theory," proves the concept 'definition' to "contain the objective concept of the thing" (262, Nr. 526).

26. Cf. l. c., pp. 2 ff.: "If we speak of genera, what do we understand therewith: a common basic character—but don't we always find the genera contained in that which surrounds them[?]"

27. Cf., p. 256, Nr. 478, line 3: " 'I' is an expression of the individual, who 'has representations' and judges."

28. Cf. Frank,*"Unendliche Annäherung,"* lecture 11, pp. 286 ff.; lecture 15, second half, pp. 418 ff.; lecture 18, pp. 485 ff.

29. Cf. Forberg, *Fragmente aus meinen Papieren*, pp. 23 ff. Philosophical explanations are, he claims, mostly only expositions and not definitions at all. "An exposition is an incomplete explanation, a definition a complete explanation" (l. c., pp. 23 f.). In order to be able to give definitions, we must be able to produce compelling proofs. And to do that we need indubitable propositions. Kant's wisdom consisted partly in seldom giving more than expositions. "If his students [. . .] needed definitions, that is not his fault" (l. c., 24). Kant's explanations never make claim to an ultimate justification. Only a few definitions follow from the concepts of understanding. A foundation of ideas—infinite presentations, which our finite understanding cannot grasp through concepts (l. c., 14; cf. 40 ff.)—can only lead to flawed explanations.

30. The presupposition of self-activity was, already brought up in Heydenreich's critique, and, in many ways, Schmid adopts this. Cf. Reinhold, *Beyträge* I, 428.

31. This accusation is, however, unjustified.

32. Translator's note: The term 'Wechselerweis' can be broken down into two parts, 'Wechsel' which means change, or reciprocal and which in Schlegel's term suggests a process of mutual alteration between the elements, and 'Erweis' which means proof. The term 'Wechselerweis' then, means some sort of alternating proof structure. In most cases, I leave it untranslated as there is not English term that can capture this in an accurate, elegant way.

33. *SW* I/1, p. 242.

34. This appeared in Jena's *Allgemeine Literatur-Zeitung* Nr. 319, Tuesday, October 1796, pp. 89–91.

35. Letter to Niethammer from May 19, 1794 (in, *Niethammer Korrespondenz,* 79).

36. Cf. esp. Manfred Frank, *Unendlichen Annäherung,* lectures 15 and 17.

37. In the Peirceian sense.

38. Dieter Henrich, ed., *Immanuel Carl Diez, Briefwechsel und Kantische Schriften: Wissensbegründung in der Glaubenskrise Tübingen-Jena (1790–1792)* (Stuttgart: Klett-Cotta, 1997): 911–914; esp. the introduction by Marcelo Stamm, pp. 898 ff. Also, for more on the beginnings of philosophical early Romanticism, see Manfred Frank, *Unendliche Annäherung,* lecture 15.

39. *NS* II: 252, line 6; p. 254, lines 11 ff.; p. 255, lines 12 ff.

40. Ludwig Wittgenstein, *Werkausgabe* (Frankfurt/M: Suhrkamp, 1984), 8: 342, Nr. 301; cf., pp. 346 ff., Nr. 314: "The difficulty here is: to come to a stop."

41. *NS* II: 179, lines 17 ff.

42. L. c., p. 273, lines 22–24. Cf. the later comment (from 1798–99): "Analysis is (*Divination,* or) the art of invention brought to rules" (*NS* III: 434, Nr. 858). The danger with this experience is to lose oneself in "immense spaces and in, quite simply, the infinite," indeed, "even in the senseless," in the "ill-reputed, false mysticism—the belief in the penetration of the thing in itself" (cf. p. 442, Nr. 906).

43. Cf. Johann Christoph Hoffbauer's determination of analytic method in his revised prize essay, *Über die Analyse in der Philosophie* (Berlin, 1810), 6–8. Hoffbauer there refers to section 416 as well as sections 503–505 from Alexander Gottlieb Baumgarten's *Acroasis logica in Christian: Wolff* (Halle, 1761).

44. C. Wolff, *Philosophia rationalis, sive logica methodo scientifica pertractata et ad usum scientiarum atque vitae aptata* (Frankfurt and Leipzig, 1728, ²1732); reproduced reprint (Hildesheim/Zürich/NewYork: Olms, 1983), sec. 885: "Appellatur [. . .] methodus analytica, qua veritates ita proponuntur, prout, vel inventae fuerunt vel minimum inveneri potuerunt."

45. In his *Vernunftlehre,* sec. 259.

46. Johann Christoph Hoffbauer, *Über die Analyse in der Philosophie,* 23 ff., 25 ff. Hoffbauer's own considerations concerning this point are of great interest, and not only because we find traces of his views concerning analytic method in Novalis' *Fichte-Studien.*

47. *SSD* 7: 239.

48. Translator's note: Spitzberg is Europe's northernmost town, which is almost on the Arctic Circle. Novalis may be referring to this town.

49. *NS* IV: 321; Letter to *Kreisamtmann* just dated February 1800.

50. Hoffbauer defends this view, expressly against Kant, in his, *Über das Genie und die Fähigkeit des Kopfs,* l. c., 101–113, here: pp. 102 [ff.]. To be sure, in the *Logic* Kant had already called "[t]he analytic method [. . .] the method of discovery" (AA IX, comment to sec.117, 149).

51. *NS* III: 685, Nr. 671.

52. *NS* III: 413, Nr. 745; Nr. Nr. 748.

53. *NS* III: 376, Nr. 612.

54. Ludwig Tieck's *Schriften* (Berlin, 1828–1854), 11: 89–90; *NS* III: 664, Nr. 603.

55. Friedrich von Schlegel, *Kritische Ausgabe (KA)*, ed., Ernst Behler (Paderborn: Schöningh, 1958 ff.). *KA* XVIII: 418. Nr. 1168; p. 420, Nr. 1200.

56. *NS* II: 668, pp. 26 ff.

57. See, Manfred Frank, "Auf der Suche nach einem Grund: Über den Umschlag von Erkenntniskritik—Mythologie bei Musil," *Mythos und Moderne*, ed., Karl-Heinz Bohrer (Frankfurt/M: Suhrkamp, 1983), 318–362.

58. *PhJ* VI/5 (1797): 66 ff.

Lecture 3: On the Unknowability of the Absolute

1. Immanuel Kant, *Der Einzig mögliche Beweisgrund zu einer Demonstration des Daseins Gottes*. This publication is available in English translation by Gordon Treasch (Lincoln, NE: University of Nebraska Press, 1994). References are to this edition.

2. Ernst Tugendhat and Ursula Wolf, eds., *Logisch-semantische Propädeutik* (Stuttgart: Reclam, 1983), 215. Even more decisively negative in the prologue to, *Philosophische Aufsätze* (Frankfurt/M: Suhrkamp, 1992), 14, and in the lecture, "Heideggers Seinsfrage," (121,2), which is reprinted there.

3. Bertrand Russell, *Logic and Knowledge* (London: G. Allen and Unwin, 1956), 252.

4. Kant, *One Possible Basis*, 73; Treash translation p. 59.

5. Ibid., 72; Treash translation p. 57.

6. Ibid., 72 ff; Treash translation pp. 58–59.

7. I. Kant, *Kritik der reinen Vernuft*, translated by Norman Kemp Smith as *Critique of Pure Reason* (CPR) (New York: Modern Library, 1958). CPR A143 /B182 and A597f./ B 625 f.

8. Kant, *One Possible Basis*, p. 73; Treash translation p. 59.

9. Jean-Jacques Rousseau, *Emile* in *Œuvres completes, edition sous la direcion de Bernard Gagnebin et Marcel Raymond*, Book IV of *Emile*, volume IV (Paris: Bibliothèque de la Pléiade, 1969), 565–635.

10. D. Henrich, *Der Grund im Bewußtsein: Untersuchungen zu Hölderlin's Denken* (1794–1795) (Stuttgart: Klett-Cotta, 1992), pp. 48 ff.

11. Christian August Crusius, l.c., 161. Kant is certainly not in agreement with the conclusion of Crusius' argument. See Kant, *AA* II, 76, bottom.

12. D. Henrich, *Grund im Bewusstsein*. See esp. pp. 58 ff.

13. I have presented and analyzed these connections in detail in my epilogue to the collection, *Selbstbewußttheorien von Fichte bis Sartre* (Frankfurt am Main: Suhrkamp, 1991), 416–432, esp. pp. 422 ff.

14. Henrich, *Grund im Bewußtsein*, pp. 60 f.

15. See F. H. Jacobi, *Über die Lehre des Spinoza in Briefen an den Herrn Moses Mendelssohn*. 2d ed. (Leipzig: Löwe, 1789). In this context, Jacobi comes to the concept of the natural through the simple consideration (taken from Kant), that, "nature" is that to which the laws of the understanding make reference, "so we are in no position to form concepts as concepts of the merely natural, and what cannot be actual in nature, is also not possible in representation" (Spin. 2, 431).

Lecture 4: On the Search for the Unconditioned

1. This text has been translated by Fritz Marti, *The Unconditioned in Human Knowledge: Four Early Essays. 1794–96* (Lewisburg, PA: Bucknell University Press, 1980). I have consulted this translation and made slight amendments.

2. This has already been shown in Birgit Sandkaulen-Bock's doctoral dissertation, *Ausgang vom Undbedingten: Über den Anfang in der Philosophie Schellings* (Departure from the Unconditioned. On the Beginning in Schelling's Philosophy) (Göttingen: Vandenhoeck & Ruprecht, 1990), esp. 13 ff and 37 ff.

3. Cf. F. W. J. Schelling, *Über das Unbedingte im menschliehen Wissen* (Frankfurt: Suhrkamp, 1975), "The highest service of philosophical investigation is not to display abstract concepts and from these to spin out systems. The final purpose of philosophical investigation is pure, absolute Being; its greatest service is to uncover and to reveal that which can never be brought to a concept, which cannot be clarified or developed—in short, its final task is to uncover and reveal the Unresolvable, the Unmediated, the Simple." (p. 186) See also, 216; "[. . .] I wish for Plato's language or that of his kindred spirit, Jacobi, in order to be able to distinguish absolute and unchangeable Being from conditioned, changeable existence.

4. Translator's note: The German term for judgment is composed of a root, 'teilen' which means to divide, with the prefix, 'ur' which means original—in English, one would not be led to play with the term as Hölderlin, Hegel, and others had and to produce such a creative and thought-provoking misinterpretation of the etymology of 'judgment.'

5. Cf. Michael Franz, "Hölderlin's Logik: Zum Grundriß von 'Sein,' Urtheil und Möglichkeit." *Hölderlin Jahrbuch* 25 (1986–87): 93–124, here, p. 97, note 9. Bardilis *Grundriß der Ersten Logik* first appeared in 1800. Cf. Schelling's later and angry polemic against Reinhold and Bardili: *Über das absolute Identitäts-System und sein Verhältniß zu dem neuesten (Reinholdischen) Dualismus* (*SW* I: 5, 18–77).

6. Violetta Waibel, "*Spuren Fichtes in der Textgenese der Werke Hölderlin*" (masters thesis, University München, 1986), 54. See also, *Hölderlin Texturen 2: Das 'Jenaische Projekt': Wintersemester 1794–95*, eds., Ulrich Gaier, Valérie Lawitschka, Wolfgang Rapp, and Violetta Waibel (Marback, 1995), 114 ff.

7. Peter Strawson, *Introduction to Logical Theory* (London: Routledge Kegan and Paul, 1952), 5. Strawson's theory of judgment is very clearly reported in lecture Four of Ernst Tudgendhat's and Ursula Wolf's *Logisch-semantischer Propädeutik* (Stuttgart: Reclam, 1983), esp. pp. 57 ff.

8. Strawson, *Introduction to Logical Theory*, p. 6.

9. For more on the implicit conception of logic, which underlies such speculations, cf., some interesting, though unfortunately not detailed enough, suggestions in the study Andeas Graeser, "Hölderlin über Urtheil und Seyn," *Freiburger Zeitschrift für Philosophie und Theologie* Heft 1–2 (1991): 111–127.

10. Wolfram Hogrebe, *Prädikation als Genesis* (Frankfurt/M: Suhrkamp, 1989), stw 772, esp., pp. 81 ff.

11. *Die Weltalter*, ed., Manfred Schröter, ed. from 1811 and 1813 (München: C. H. Beckische Verlags-buchhandlung, 1946), 28. This has been translated by Wolfe Bolman as *The Ages of the World* (New York: Columbia University Press, 1942), 99.

See also Jason Wirth's recent translation, *The Ages of the World* (New York: State University of New York Press, 2000).

12. Friedrich Wilhelm Joseph Schelling, *System of Transcendental Idealism*, trans., Peter Heath, with an introduction by Michael Vater (Charlottesville, VA: University Press of Virginia, 1978). I have consulted this translation and made adjustments as I deemed suitable.

13. Schelling, *System of Transcendental Idealism*, SW I: 3, 508 top/Heath translation, p.136.

14. In this context, Schelling refers to his early *Form-Schrift* (l.c., 224, note: the reference is to SWI/1: 108 ff). There "the Rheinholdian deduction of these forms" (of modality) was " with regard to its formal aspects [recognized] as a masterpiece of philosophical art" (l.c. 110, comment), even when it also held for this deduction that it took something as a given (as a fact of consciousness) . . . p. 712 footnote. Cf. on this issue, Birgit Sandkaulen, "Für das absolute Ich gibt es keine Möglichkeit" Zum Problem der Modalität beim frühen Schelling, *Schellingiana* (Stuttgart, 1998).

15. Cf. Manfred Frank's earlier work, *Der uendliche Mangel an Sein: Schellings Hegelkritik und die Anfänge der Marxschen Dialektik* (Frankfurt/M: Suhrkamp, 1975; 2d rev. ed., Frankfurt/M: Suhrkamp, 1991). Frank claims that in this work, he underestimated the realistic character of Schelling's early writings and their proximity to Hölderlin's metaphilosophical considerations.

16. E.g., SW I: 6, p. 147: "the entire and absolute independence of identity or sameness in itself from the subjective and objective" as their relata; cf. 162, and esp. 163, bottom: "If the opposite of subjective and objective were the point of departure, the Absolute only the product, which subsequently only first after the eradication of the opposition would be posited, then the Absolute would indeed be merely a negation, namely, the negation of a difference, of which one does not know the origin or why precisely it is the negation of this difference that serves to demonstrate the Absolute. The Absolute would then be no position, but merely a negative idea, a product of synthesizing thinking [. . .]." The talk of the Absolute as the "self affirming" or "assenting" appears to go back to the old Kantian language rule of Being as Absolute or, as the case may be, relative positing.

Lecture 5: On Hölderlin's Disagreement with Schelling's *Ich-Schrift*

1. F. W. J. Schelling, "Timaeus" (1794), in *Schellingiana*, ed., Hartmut Buchner, *Schellingiana*, vol. 4 (1994).

2. Of course, the discussion was already carried out in the *Philosophisches Journal* before the publication of the text at hand. In this journal, the discussion had its most mature expression and most journalistic expression.

3. For more on the following, cf., Dieter Henrich, *Der Grund im Bewußtsein*, pp. 29 f.

4. Cf. Dieter Henrich, "*Hölderlin über Urtheil und Seyn: Eine Studie zur Entstehungsgeschichte des Idealismus*," *Konstellationen* (Stuttgart: Klett-Cotta, 1992), 63.

5. For more on this discussion, see Violetta Waibel, "*Spuren Fichtes in der Textgenese der Werke Hölderlins*" (Textual Traces of Fichte in Hölderlin's Work) (masters thesis, Munich, 1986), 54.

6. Martin Bondeli, *Das Anfangsproblem bei Karl Leonhard Reinhold* (Frankfurt: v. Klostermann, 1994), 96. Martin Bondeli has shown how Reinhold could, from this fundamental understanding of judgment, explain, "the relation of analytic with synthetic judgment [. . .] as a kind of two-tiered process of judgment: that which is brought together in the subject can be dissolved again in the presentation of its parts (predicates).

7. Reinhold, *Versuch* (op. cit), p. 438.

8. Cf. the parallel formulation in Reinhold, Beyträge I: 222 "to become aware of oneself as the representing in particular" (*sich / seiner selbst als des Vorstellenden insbesondere bewußt [. . .] werden*).

9. Ernst Mach, *Beiträge zur Analyse der Empfindungen* (Jena: G. Fischer, 1886), 34.

10. There is a similar example in Perry, "The Problem of the Essential Indexical," *Nous* 13 (1979): 3.

11. Jacques Lacan, "Le stade du miroir [. . .]," *Écrits* (Paris, 1966), 93–100.

12. Cf. Jürgen Stolzenberg, "Selbstbewußtsein: Ein Problem der Philosophie nach Kant. Reinhold-Hölderlin-Fichte," *Le premier romantisme allemand (1796)*, ed., Manfred Frank of *Revue internationale de philosophie*, Nr. 3 (1996): 461–482, special vol.

13. Similar formulations are to be found in Reinhold's, *Neuer Darstellung [. . .]*: "Here, too, [namely in self-consciousness] the object is distinguished from the subject; indeed self-consciousness can only be thought insofar as the I distinguishes itself through a special representation from both the subject qua representing property and from the object qua represented property (Reinhold, Beyträge I: 181 f.). Cf. l. c., 197: "Also by that kind of consciousness, which is called self-consciousness [. . .] the representing (*das Vorstellende*) is distinguished as subject and as object, as that which is thinking and as that which is thought." Also, cf., l. c., 222.

14. Jacob Sigismund Beck, *Einzig-möglicher Standpunkt aus welchem die kritische Philosophie beurtheilt werden muß*, (Riga: Hartknoch, 1796), 104 f.

15. Hans-Georg Gadamer, "Rhetorik, Hermeneutik und Ideologiekritik," *Kleine Schriften*, vol. I (Tübingen: Mohr, 1967), 127.

16. Cf. Manfred Frank, *Einführung in Schellings Philosophie* (Frankfurt/M: Suhrkamp, 1985, 1995), 68 f.

17. He summarized his excursus on Schelling in a somewhat cloudy way as follows: "Hölderlin knew that this expression [from the Ich-Schrift] would meet with Niethammer's approval [but this writing comes from a much later period!]. Even he himself could agree with Schelling to a certain degree, without this agreement having had to entail that he had to have been able to speak with him in full "accordance" (*StA* VI: 1, 203). For Schelling sought at this time and on this side of a philosophy based on first principles[?] to further develop that other notion of Fichte's which Hölderlin had claimed was untenable. He wanted to see in consciousness the I itself as something unconditioned [no, the unconditioned was deprived of all consciousness, not only intellectual intuition!]. And he wanted to join this unconditioned

(from early considerations which he had probably already discussed in the *Tübingen Stift* with Hölderlin) to Jacobi's certainty regarding 'Being,' which cannot be provided via any result of inferences. Hölderlin, however, must have noticed that this happened in such a way that the basic difference between that which is thought is the proposition 'I am' and in Being, which is the ground of its possibility which must be presupposed and not taken into account as a measured and consistent result. Even if Schelling's way was the better one, it was still deserving of a fundamental critique. And Hölderlin expected Niethammer to understand the content of his critique even without further explanation and to agree somewhat with it (Dieter Henrich, *Grund im Bewußtsein*, p. 130).

18. "The Absolute [. . .] must precede all thinking and representing" (SW I/1, 167); "Have you even considered that the I, insofar as it comes before consciousness, is no longer the pure, absolute I, that for the absolute I absolutely no object can be given, and so even less it can itself become an object?—self-consiousness presupposes the danger of losing the I. It is no free act of the unchangeable, but rather an extorted striving of the changeable I, which, conditioned by the Non-I, strives to save its identity and in the flowing current of change to grasp itself again" (l.c., 180); "The infinite I, however, does not know any object at all, and so no consciousness or unity of consciousness, personality" (l. c., p. 200).

19. Manfred Frank, *Der unendliche Mangel an Sein: Schellings Hegel-Kritik und die Anfänge der Marxschen Dialektik* (Frankfurt/M: Suhrkamp, 1975), expanded, new version, Frankfurt/M: Suhrkamp, 1991.

Lecture 6: On Hölderlin's Critique of Ficthe

1. A reminder: As a student, Hölderlin would have been able to attend the second (practical) part of Fichte's first Jena Lecture on the *Wissenschaftslehre*. The first letter to his friends Schelling and Hegel give evidence of this. Towards the end of January 1795, Hegel writes to Schelling: "Hölderlin writes to me now and then from Jena [. . .]. He is attending Fichte's lectures and speaks enthusiastically of him as a titan, who battles for humanity and whose circle of influence will certainly not remain limited to those within the walls of the lecture room." And on January 19, 1795, Hölderlin wrote the following lines to Neuffer: "I work the entire day. Only in the evenings do I attend Fichte's lectures."

2. F. D. E. Schleiermacher, *Sämtliche Werke*, sec. III, vol. 4, part 2 (Berlin: Realschulbuchhandlung 1839), esp., pp. 422 ff. Earlier we saw that in Beitr. II, 1, Reinhold also speaks of a transcendent ground in contrast to a transcendental one. And Schleiermacher would have it from this (even if, of course, for Reinhold there is absolutely no application to the transcendence of the ground of consciousness).

3. Cf. Violetta Waibel's report on this entire context in, Ulrich Gaier, Valérie Lawitschka, Wolfgang Rapp, and Violetta Waibel, *Hölderlin Texturen 2: Das "Jenaische Project" Wintersemester 1794–95*, ed. Hölderlin-Gesellschaft in Tübingen in collaboration with the German Schillergesellschaft (Marbach, Tübingen: Mohr, 1995), 100

ff. esp., pp. 107 ff. ("Hölderlin im Gespräch mit Fichte") and 114 ff. ("Urtheilung"—"ursprünglich theilen").

4. Friedrich Wilhelm Joseph Schelling, "*Epikurisch Glaubensbekenntnis Heinz Widerporstens*," in M. Frank *Materialien zu Schellings philosohisches Anfängen*, eds. M. Frank and G. Kurz (Frankfurt/Main: Suhrkamp, 1975), 151). "Vom ersten Ringen dunkler Kräfte / Bis zum Erguß der ersten Lebenssäfte, / Wo Kraft in Kraft, und Stoff in Stoff verquillt, / Die erste Blüt', die erste Knospe schwillt, / Zum ersten Strahl von neu gebornem Licht, / Das durch die Nacht wie zweite Schöpfung bricht / Und aus den tausend Augen der Welt / Den Himmel so Tag wie Nacht erhellt. / Hinauf zu des Gedankens Jugendkraft, / Wodurch Natur verjüngt sich wieder schafft, / Ist Eine Kraft, Ein Pulsschlag nur, Ein Leben, / Ein Wechselspiel von Hemmen und von Streben."

5. Friedrich Schiller, dtv-Gesamtausgabe, Munich vol. 18 (1966): 46.

6. Hölderlin, "Der Abschied" ("Ach! wir kennen uns wenig, / Denn es waltet ein Gott in uns").

7. "Die Liebe allein [. . .] ist das absolut Große selbst, was in der Anmuth und Schönheit sich nachgeahmt und in der Sittlichkeit sich befriedigt findet, es ist der Gesetzgeber selbst, der Gott in uns, der mit seinem eigenen Bilde in der Sinnenwelt spielt" (Schiller, L. c., Vol. 18, pp. 49 f.).

8. Manfred Frank has given a more precise account of the relation between virtual and actual identity, or, as the case may be, the difference in moments of the Absolute in Schelling in his, *Die Grenzen der Verständigung. Ein Geistergespräch zwischen Lyotard und Habermas* (Frankfurt/M: Suhrkamp, 1988), 85 ff.

9. Cf. Hector-Neri Castañeda, " 'He': A Study in the Logic of Self-Consciousness," *Ratio* 8 (1966): 130–157.

10. For a more detailed account, see Manfred Frank, *Eine Einführung in Schellings Philosophie* (Frankfurt/Main: Suhrkamp, 1985), 61 ff.

Lecture 7: On Isaac von Sinclair

1. Quoted according to Berthold Dirnfellner's, "Isaac von Sinclair: Zur Edition seiner Jugendbriefe," *Le pauvre Holterling*, nos. 4/5, Frankfurt Edition (92–140): 138.

2. Cf. Ursula Brauer's comprehensive and thoroughly researched life history of Sinclair, *Isaac von Sinclair: Eine Biographie* (Stuttgart: Klett-Cotta, 1993). See also the shorter report of Sinclair's stay in Jena in, "Das "Jenaische Project": Wintersemester 1795/5," *Hölderlin Texturen* 2, eds., Ulrich Gaier, Valérie Lawitschka, Wolfgang Rapp, and Violetta Waibel (Tübingen: Mohr, 1995), pp. 178 ff.

3. Dirnfellner, "Isaac von Sinclair," pp. 122 ff.

4. See the literary remains of Kirchner, Hölderlin Archive of the Württemberg State Library, cod. Hist 4, 668, Beilage Bl. 11r–13 v (quoted by Ursula Brauer, 108 and 359, note 67).

5. From Wilhelm Fabricius, *Die deutschen Corps: Eine Historische Darstellung mit besonderer Berücksichtigung des Mensurwesens* (Berlin, 1898). Cited in Ursula Brauer, *Isaac von Sinclair: Eine Biographie*, p. 96.

6. Ibid., p. 95.

7. Ursula Brauer gives a much more refined and sympathetic portrayal of Sinclair's last days, *Isaac von Sinclair: Eine Biographie*, pp. 283–306.

8. Cf. Christoph Jamme, *Isaac von Sinclair: Politiker, Philosoph und Dichter zwischen Revolution und Restauration* (Bonn: Bouvier, 1988), 9 ff, 48 ff; Ibid., "Isaac von Sinclairs *Philosophische Raisonnements*: Zur Wiederfindung ihrer Originale," *Hegel Studien* 18 (1983): 240–44. The "Raisonnements" themselves are presented in print in the appendix of a doctoral thesis by Hannelore Hegel, "Issak von Sinclair zwischen Fichte, Hölderlin und Hegel: Ein Beitrag zur Enstehungsgeschichte der idealistischen Philosophie" (Ph.D. diss., Frankfurt/M: Klostermann, 1971), 289–91 (the page numbers referred to above are to this edition). For the most penetrating account of Zwilling's contribution to the Jena and Homburg discussions, see Dieter Henrich and Christoph Jamme, "Jakob Zwillings Nachlass: Eine Rekonstruktion," *Hegel Studien*, Beiheft 28 (1986): 9–99.

Lecture 8: On Jakob Zwilling's *Über das Alles*

1. For more on the following cf., Ludwig Strauß, *Jacob Zwilling und sein Nachlaß*, *Euphorion* 29 (1928): 368–396. This report by the important Hölderlin researcher still offers (almost) the only information and scarce sources that we have on Zwilling. Strauß was able to work on two batches of Zwilling's entire literary remains, which have since, for unknown reasons, have become lost. Unfortunately, nothing new has been found in Strauß's literary remains which are located in the Jewish National and Unversity Library (where Christoph Jamme did thorough research). So, we remain dependent upon, the report and the excerpts provided by Ludwig Strauß. For more on Strauß's literary remains, see Chr. Jamme's report in *Jakob Zwillings Nachlaß in Rekonstruktion*, (op. cit), 13 f.)

2. Zwilling's spelling and punctuation are chaotic. Justifiably, Ludwig Strauß writes: "The nineteen-year-old philosophizes with passion and is decisively independent. But he is no writer: surprising, pithy expressions are mixed with completely muddled ones; the expression is, with all its liveliness, one that is not epoch-making, but rather that of a constitutive messiness, so to speak. The ordering and capturing of the rich and swelling thoughts in the written word seem to be tedious and almost painful for the writer. In one of his notes he writes: "Excuse my spelling and my bad, bad style and unreadable handwriting" (Strauß, *Jacob Zwillig und sein Nachlaß*, 371).

3. Dieter Henrich, *Jacob Zwillings Nachlaß* in *Konstellationen*, 81/3–100, first in more comprehensive form and with the subtitle, *Gedanken, Nachrichten und Dokumente aus Anlaß seines Verlustes*, printed in *Homburg vor der Höhe in der Deutschen Geistesgeschichte*, eds., Christoph Jamme and O. Pöggeler (Stuttgart: Klett-Cotta, 1981), 245–266.

4. Manfred Frank, *Der unendliche Mangel an Sein: Schellings Hegelkritik und die Anfänge der marxschen Dialektik*, (Frankfurt/M: Suhrkamp, 1975, expanded, new edition Frankfurt/M: Suhrkamp, 1991), I have shown that this is precisely what Schelling's critique of Hegel's "Logic of Reflection" will be.

Lecture 9: On Novalis' Pivotal Role in Early German Romanticism

1. *Konstellationen*, p. 228.

2. Julius Wilhelm von Oppel (1765–1832) was the privy finance councillor in the department of the privy (*Geheimen*) Saxon Finance Kollegium and a consultant for the organization of salt mines (*Salinenwesen*), and like Novalis a student of Abraham Gottlob Werner (whom Novalis knew from Freiberg), and since his inspection of the mines of Dürrenberg, Artern, and Kösen in May–June 1799, Novalis' friend and patron.

3. Because of the range of the first group, Hans-Joachim Mähl finds September to be a more likely date than November (the date of the letter to Erasmus—this letter also reports on work habits that must have begun before November [NS II: 43, 1]).

4. I have not personally undertaken any direct research of the handwriting, but nevertheless see no reason to dispute the results that Havenstein, Riter, or Mähl have come to on the basis of a comparison of the handwritten manuscripts.

5. Cf. the catalogue of the Berlin Auction Houses, Hellmut Meyer and Ernst, and J. A. Stargardt: Novalis (Friedrich Freiherr von Hardenberg), *Der handschriftliche Nachlaß des Dichters*, available for viewing in the rooms of the German Lyceum Club, Berlin W. Lützowplatz 15, Sunday, December 20, 1930 from 9:00 A.M. to 1:00 P.M.; Auction in the German Lyceum Club, Berlin W. Lützowplatz 15, Sunday, December 20, *only* at 4:00 P.M.

6. It has been claimed that Novalis' father took on the guardianship and financial support of Fichte after Miltitz's death. Such a hypothesis is somewhat supported through a formulation in a name registry cited in *NS* V: 845: "Ernst Hauboldt v. Miltitz (Father of Dietrich) was his [Fichte's] guardian, after his death in 1774 Novalis' father, Heinrich Ulrich Erasmus v. Hardenberg was Johann Gottlieb Fichte's guardian." This is not supported by any evidence. Later, the independent thinker Fichte was in no need of a guardian, but rather was since May, 23, 1794 a well-positioned, when not a highly decorated professor *ordinarius supernumerarius* in Jena. (Cf. the complete, referenced report of Herbert Uerling, in *Friedrich von Hardenberg, genannt Novalis* (Stuttgart: Klett-Cotta, 1991), 115. Uerling does claim that the elder Hardenberg supported Fichte.

7. Cf. *Zeitschrift für Religions—und Geistesgeschichte* I (1948): 7. Reprinted in *NS* IV: p. 588, cf. p. 997.

8. Caroline "persuaded" Fichte into doing this. At the same time, she asked Charlotte Ernst (Schlegel's sister), to send Novalis a copy; cf. l.c. 850. In the atheism controversy, Novalis stood firmly on Fichte's side. To Dietrich, who was early on excited about the French Revolution and democracy, Novalis wrote: "Fichte's *Apellation* [*sic*] to the public [. . .] is an excellent work and makes you familiar with such unusual spirits and plans of our government and clergy, with some parts of the conceived plans of the repression of public opinion—that it demands the attention of every reasonable person to follow these steps to draw a meaningful conclusion from these premises" (l.c., p. 277; cf. also p. 517, p. 519, p. 522; III, 470 and 997 ff.; cf. also Gerhard Schulz, *Novalis: In Selbstzeugnissen und Bilddokumenten* (Reinbeck bei Hamburg: Rowohlt, 1969), 109 ff.

9. In the biography that Ludwig Tieck presented as the preface to the third edition of Novalis' writings, Tieck speaks of a "perhaps exaggerated diligence" (*NS* IV: 552, line 20). Cf. Tieck's report to the *Hofrat* Friedrich Wilhelm Riemer in Weimar from July 3, 1843: "He [Novalis] was the most healthy, cheerful person, the most daring rider, tireless mountain climber and hiker, hardly slept, for he was always writing or doing something practical—but, of course, he died, and unexpectedly, of consumption" (*TS*, p. 560, lines 30–33). In the introduction to the volume of letters, Richard Samuel writes:

> Tieck's comments can be substantiated; fighting duels at the university, mountain climbing, most of the countless trips were covered on horseback, the 14-day geological trip in June 1800 was, however, covered on foot, with 16 hours of daily work from 4 A.M. onwards. Mines were worked [,] and writing and practical activity, from the beginning of 1796 onwards is continuous" (*TS*, p. 45).

10. The following passage from a letter to Caroline Just, the niece of the district magistrate (*Amtmann*) written on April 10 is puzzling: "Tell your good uncle that I will not write to him before the conference [the Easter Conference in Leipzig began on April 17, 1796]. A deplorable accident, of the prompt/ printing of the Fichtean *Naturrechts*, has delayed the printing of the commentary. I send you three sample pages" (*NS*, pp. 180 f.). It is not clear what Novalis means here. Did he know from Dietrich, his father or Fichte himself of the unexpected and prompt printing of Fichte's *Grundlage des Naturrechts* (in April 1796)—a work that Novalis thought of using in his *Fichte-Studien*? Or had Novalis been planning, as Mähl suspects, to print his own work and because of Fichte's new work, was forced to wait so that he could incorporate Fichte's new work into his own (cf. Mähl's commentary II, p. 32)? The latter is completely unlikely, when one looks at the chaotic state of the written copy. In any case, the pages have not been conserved. It could be that Novalis is making reference, when he speaks of the delayed printing of his commentary, to the book of an unknown author, which he had promised to send to the uncle in mid-March.

11. This appeared in Friedrich Schlichtegroll's "Nekrolog der Teutschen für das neunzehnte Jahrhundet," *Gotha* 4 (April 1805): 187–241. (Also as a separate printing, "Andenken an Friedrich von Hardenberg," *Gotha* 1805: 75).

12. Without exception, Novalis defends the view that error arises when one mistakes the part for the whole (cf., above all, Nr. 234, 176 ff., esp. 180: "for illusion (*Schein*) is everywhere the half—half of a whole alone is illusion" [lines 18 f.]; "Hence, illusion arises [. . .] from the elevation of the part to the whole [. . .]" (lines 25 f. and passim.).

13. In his commentary to this passage, Hans-Joachim Mähl refers to a passage from Fichte's *Begriffsschrift* (*WW* I, sec. 7, pp. 70 f.). In the passage from Fichte, the 'what' is defined as the object of that "which is present in the human spirit independently of science (*Wissenschaft*)," namely, as its actions (*Handlungen*). Fichte does not put forth an etymological reference that would be completely misleading. 'Wissen' is derived from 'wizzan,' *to have seen* (cf. Latin *videre*).

14. This corresponds to the definition of the I as Ec-stasis: "It finds itself, out of itself" (150, Nr. 98, lines 29 f.). This ecstatic self-finding (*Selbstfindung*) is explained by Novalis as sensation (*Empfindung*) (and this again following Fichte [cf. *WW* I: 339] as "an inner-finding of actuality" (lines 30 f., whereby 'actuality' is, since Kant, the essential companion of sensation [*CPR* B 272 f.]).

15. In these considerations, Novalis joins two Fichtean theoretical lines (indeed, most freely), we could also say that these considerations are influenced by Novalis's excitement with two readings he undertook. He relies upon a passage from the *Grundriß des Eigentümlichen der Wissenschaftslehre in Rücksicht auf das theoretische Vermögen* (Jena 1795; *WW* I, sec. 3, pp. 374 ff.), a work that, in early 1795, gave him a new opening for his reflections (cf. *NS* II: 345 ff., 356–359). Another time, in his notes, he toyed with a theory of signs that came from Fichte's short essay on the origin of language that was published in the *Philosophisches Journal* (I, Nos. 3 and 4 (1795): 255–273; 287–326; also *WW* VIII: 301–341.

16. Joahnn Cristoph Hoffbauer was a professor of philosophy in Halle and author of a book on logic entitled, *Anfangsgründe der Logik*.

17. *Reflectirt das Subject aufs reine Ich—hat es nichts—indem es was für sich hat—reflectirt es hingegen nicht darauf—so hat es für sich nichts, indem es was hat.*

18. "The real separated from the ideal is the objective. The content considered alone, is therefore the object. Feeling would be a relation to the object. Reflection is a relation to the subject. The subject is however the mediated I. The middle must be that through which the subject stops being a subject—this is content and form, feeling and reflection, subject and object in a reciprocal relation. Here the roles change—the object becomes the subject, the subject the object. For the subject this is a total contradiction—it dissolves itself—therewith is nothing—from here the absolute I is postulated—now everything is settled. If the subject does not postulate the absolute I, then it must lose itself here in an abyss of error—this can only happen for reflection—that is for only a part of the subject, the reflecting part. This losing is an illusion, like every elevation of a part to the whole is an illusion, the subject remains what it is—divided, absolute, and identical I (130 f., Nr. 31).

19. Cf. Ficthe's *WW* I: 295 ff., 305. Fichte openly warns philosophers about, "postulating the being present (*Vorhandseyn*) of a certain feeling, to do such a thing means to proceed superficially" (296). Fichte also speaks of "how the I can feel itself as driven toward something unfamiliar" (296 ff.) Cf. also the talk of the I as "itself and its only power in feeling itself" merely as determined, that is, as feeling itself, is feeling itself as all a characteristic of the I (299). With such formulations the true *praxis*-philosophical context of self-feeling is given up, as we will soon see. (Almost synonymous with the term 'sensation,' the term 'self-feeling' shows up in the *Grundriß* [*WW* I: 360(1), 366 (3), 3960 (0); cf. 372 0]).

20. This use of language can also be found in Fichte. Cf. for example Fichte's essay on the origin of language in the third and fourth numbers of volume 1 of the *Philosophisches Journal*, 289, footnote or the following passage from the *Grundlage der gesammten Wissenschaftslehre*: "In reality generally, there is belief not only in the I but also in the Non-I" (*WW* I: 301).

21. Later, this consideration will find a precise yet perplexing echo in Schelling's so-called Erlangen inaugural lecture of January 1821, *Über die Natur der Philosophie als*

Wissenschaft (*SW* I: 9, 209–246; esp. 234: "it is not the case that my knowledge is re-shaped, but rather it becomes shaped; its prevailing form is only the reflex (or the inverse, hence reflexion!) of it in eternal freedom"). Novalis had already made the same claim a quarter of a century earlier.

22. Parsifal, *Die Wunde heilt der Speer nur: der sie schlug.*

23. Novalis, *NS*, II: 226.

24. Ibid., p. 116.

25. Ibid., pp. 172, 174.

26. Ibid., p. 114.

27. Cf. Ibid., pp. 259, 528 ff.

28. Ibid., p. 196.

29. Ibid., p. 199.

30. Ibid., p. 226.

31. G. W. F. Hegel, *Enzyklopädie der Philosophischen Wissenschaften im Grundrisse*, ed. F. Nicolin and O. Pöggeler (1830; reprint, Hamburg: F. Meiner, 1959), sec. 256.

32. *NS* II: 177, lines 10/11.

33. Ibid., p. 179, lines 17 ff.; cf. p. 247.

34. Ibid., pp. 247 f.

35. Ibid., pp. 248 f.

36. The decisive passages can be found in ibid., pp. 250 ff. But they are prepared by the doctrine of drives and striving which first emerges in No. 32 ("On the Empirical I," pp. 126 ff.), from where it runs like a leitmotiv through the developments of the oppositional pairs. Certainly, these reflections presuppose a reading of part 3 of the *Wissenschaftslehre*. But they radicalize Fichte's talk of "striving" in a manner that can no longer be reconciled with the notion of an ultimate justification from an evident principle.

37. Cf. *NS* II: 269: "Noteworthy Passages and Remarks on Reading the *Wissenschaftslehre*."

38. *NS* II: 269. Cf. pp. 268 f.: "Golden Ages may appear—but they do not bring the end of things—the end of the human being is not the golden age—it is destined to exist forever, and be and remain a beautifully ordered individual."

39. Ibid., pp. 269 f.

40. Ibid., p. 270.

41. Ibid.

42. Ibid.

43. Ibid., p. 252, cf. p. 254.

44. Ibid., p. 179.

45. Ibid., p. 255.

46. *CPR*, B417 note.

47. Ibid., A358.

Lecture 10: On Friedrich Schlegel's Place in the Jena Constellation

1. Cf. *KA* XVIII: 512, Nr. 71: "The Absolute itself is indemonstrable, but the *philosophical assumption* of it must be justified and proven analytically" <This is not

anything absolute—mysticism rises and falls with this *misunderstanding.>"* Cf. *KA* II: 179, Nr. 95: "Philosophy has to provisionally and eternally presuppose something, and it may because it must."

2. The following consideration underlies both of these central propositions: "Nicht das Gebot: *Wissenschaft soll seyn*—kann der Philosophie zum Grunde gelegt werden. Denn diese kann nur *synthetisch* aus dem: *Das Ich soll seyn*—abgeleitet und also von dem Gegner in Anspruch genommen werden.—Dies *schlechthin* ohne Rücksicht / auf den Gegner postuliren und den Gegner nicht widerlegen, sondern ihm nur beweisen, daß er sich selbst widerspreche, daß er ein Sophist sey—ist noch nicht hinreichend. Es ist dann gewiß, daß der Gegner Unrecht habe, aber nicht, ob der Philosoph Recht habe." It is unlikely that Schlegel is referring to this remark that Fichte makes in the *Wissenschaftslehre nova methodo*: "Übrigens ist es richtig[,] daß man in der Philosophie von einem Postulate ausgehen müße; auch die Wißenschaftslehre thut dieß, und drückt es durch Thathandlung aus" (*Krause-Nachschrift*, ed., Erich Fuchs (Hamburg: Meiner, 1982), 28. In the first place because this is a citation from a postscript from the winter semester 1798–99 and we don't have any postscript from the first courses, which began on October 18, 1796; secondly, Schlegel's note, in the case that he actually attended the course, was written earlier, for he had already used the notion of a 'Wechselerweis' in his Woldemar review, that is, at the latest, by the beginning of August (Ernst Behler claimed that the Woldemar Review was written shortly before Schlegel's arrival in Jena, that is, during his visit to Novalis in Dürrenberg and Weißenfels between July 29 and August 6, 1796 (Ernst Behler, "Friedrich Schlegel's Theory of an Alternating Principle Prior to his Arrival in Jena (6. August 1796)," *Revue internationale de philosophie*, special volume entitled, *Le premier romatisme allemand (1796)*, Manfred Frank, ed., vol. 50, Nʳ. 197, 3 (1996): 383–402, esp., p. 386). This early date for the writing of the note has been disputed by Guido Naschert in his master's thesis (Eberhard-Karls Universität, Tübingen, 1995). He sees a terminological dependency between Schlegel's notes in the Beilage II and Fichte's *Wissenschaftslehre nova methodo*.) What is similar in Fichte and Schlegel's view of philosophy is their emphasis on the beginning as a decision of will, as a demand which must necessarily lie somewhere between the point of departure and the end point (cf. *WW* I: 73 and *Krause-Nachschrift*, p. 138: there the will is described as the "Midpoint" of his new method.)

3. In this phase, Schlegel associates, rather irreverently, the pretension of knowledge of the transcendent with that which is "mystical" or as "theology/mythology." Two examples of this: "Die Lehre von *Einem* obersten Grundsatz, *Fundament d[es] menschlichen Wissens* gehört zur systemat [ischen] *Theologie*" (*KA* XVIII: 101, Nr. 868; the term 'theology' is still used pejoratively; cf. Ibid., p. 103, Nr. 886: "Theologie ist ein widersprechender Begriff—es giebt keine Wissenschaft von Gott"). "Das absolute Setzen und das Setzen des Absoluten ist Charakter der [Mythologie]" (Ibid., p. 108, Nr. 945). Even in the postscript to the Jena *Transzendentalphilosophie* from winter 1800–01, Schlegel writes: "*Der Begriff des Unendlichen ist transcendent*" (*KA* XIII: 28, 8).

4. The entire fragment reads as follows: "Postulirt man Wissenschaft und sucht nur d.[i.e.] Bedingung ihrer Möglichkeit, so geräth man in d[en] Mysticism und d.[i.e.] consequenteste[,] von diesem Standpunkte einzig mögliche Auflösung d.[er]

Aufgabe ist—*das Setzen eines absoluten Ich*—wodurch Form und Inhalt d.[er] absoluten Wissenschaftsl[ehre] zugleich gegeben wird."

5. The idea of infinite progress is already to be found in the "Versuch über den Begriff des Republikanismus, veranlaßt durch die Kantische Schrift zum ewigen Frieden" (*KA* VII: 11–25, esp., pp.: 12, 16 ff., and 20 ff.). This has been translated by Frederick Beiser as *Essay on the Concept of Republicanism occasioned by the Kantian tract 'Perpetual Peace'* in *The Early Political Writings of the German Romantics*, ed., Frederick Beiser, (Cambridge: Cambridge University Press, 1996), 93–112. The first version of this essay was already completed in spring 1796 (that is to say, *before* Schlegel's move to Jena).

6. Without an application of the term 'analytic,' this passage from the Cologne private lectures points to the same insight: "Insofar as I strive toward something, the object of the striving is external to me, and yet it must at the same time be in me; I must possess it mentally, otherwise no striving at all would be possible, for it must have a definite direction" (*KA* XII: 336).

7. Here is the complete citation: "Das *Gegebne* womit d[er] [Philosoph] anfängt, ist: *Ich strebe nach Allheit d[es] Wissens.*—Wer dieß nicht thut d[er] ist nicht nur kein [Philosoph] sondern er philosophiert auch gar nicht mehr.—" Cf. also p. 519, Nr. 19: "Bei der Untersuchung, was vorausgesetzt werden darf, darf ich gar nichts voraussetzen als das Denken selbst.—'Ich will alles wissen wo möglich; wo nicht, so viel ich kann und auch warum ich nicht mehr wissen kann—;'—das ist der Punkt, von dem jeder ausgeht. [. . .] Der unbestimmte *Wissenstrieb*—um seiner selbst willen—ist also der Grund und elastische Punkt der Wissenschaftslehre."

8. Cf. the many parallel formulations in the private lectures that Schlegel delivered in Cologne, esp., *KA* XII: 337, 343, 348, 353, 380 ff., and 393.

9. In an earlier work (*Das Problem 'Zeit' in der deutschen Romantik*), I showed how Schlegel, through the adoption of the position that the I could only be grasped as something "dismembered, ripped, derivative" (and, that is, could only relate to its original form through a memory of its lost totality), could, in the horizon of thought of his time, develop a highly original theory of time. Cf. *KA* XII: 348 ff.

Lecture 11: On the Origins of Schlegel Talk of a *Wechselerweis* and His Move Away from a Philosophy of First Principles

1. In their attack on a philosophy based on first principles, Johann Benjamin Erhard and Friedrich Carl Forberg, used these terms. For more on this see, Manfred Frank, *Unendliche Annäherung*, lectures 17, 23, and 24.

2. Cf. The subject index for the following related terms: 'progress,' 'progression,' 'progressive,' etc. in *KA* XIX: 749 f. Cf. l.c., 42, Nr. 11: "Infinite progress leads to absolute unknowability." That was the result of Niethammer's skepticism regarding the proof of the unavoidability of a justification regress. But Schlegel seems to deduce the infinite progress directly from the notion of the "unknowability of the Absolute" (*KA* XVIII: 511, Nr. 64; cf. 512, Nr. 71). The overhang of the Absolute vis-à-vis any possible (finite) expression of it leads directly to the idea of an infinite approximation to the Absolute (infinite because the Absolute cannot be reached).

3. Cf. *KA* XIX under key words, 'Annäherung' (616), 'Approximation' (619), and 'unendlich' (786f.).

4. Schlegel makes this claim in several places. For example, *KA* XVIII: 7, Nr. 36: "Philosophy, in its true sense, has neither a first principle, object, nor a specific task." 518, Nr. 13: "There is no first principle, which would be the all purpose companion and guide to truth."

5. Cf. *KA* XVIII: 26, Nr. 93: Philosophy must not begin with one, but rather with 'infinitely many' principles." Cf. l.c., 505, Nr. 2, where, in view of "deduced systems of knowledge" Schlegel speaks of a plurality of *Wechselerweise* and of a system of the "totality of *Wechselerweise*."

6. To be sure, in the essays on the ancients from the period of 1794–95, that is, before the publication of Fichte's *Naturrecht*—there was frequent talk of *Wechselbestimmung* or *Wechselwirkung* (between freedom and nature (*KA* I: 229 f, 232; 631). The circularity of the ancients and the infinite progression of the moderns were dealt with as *vollendete Wechselbegriffe* [perfect alternating concepts], which "each correspond reciprocally to the most perfect."

7. These terms also had a generally familiar prehistory. In the *Groundwork of the Metaphysics of Morals* (1785), Kant spoke of "freedom and the will's own law-giving" as "reciprocal concepts (*Wechselbegriffe*)" (*AA* IV: 450). The "circle" of reciprocal presupposition is resolved in that Kant determines the moral law as the ground of our knowledge of freedom and freedom as the real ground of the moral law (cf. l.c., 448 f., 453).

8. Fichte even put forth a "Principle of *Wechselbestimmung*" (*WW* I: 149): "Durch Wechsel-Thun und Leiden (das durch Wechselbestimmung sich gegenseitig bestimmende Thun und Leiden) wird die unabhängige Thätigkeit; und durch die unabhängige Thätigkeit wird umgekehrt Wechsel-Thun und Leiden bestimmt"(150). Violetta Waibel has attempted to show how important this Fichtean theorem could have been for Hölderlin's and Schelling's aesthetic thought: "Wechselbestimmung. Zum Verhältnis von Hölderlin, Schiller und Fichte in Jena," *Fichte-Studien* 12 (1997), 43–69. Ernst Behler has provided much evidence for how important Schlegel's pre-Jena study of Fichte's notion of *Wechselbestimmung* or *Wechselwirkung* could have been: "Friedrich Schlegel's Theory of an Alternating Principle Prior to his Arrival in Jena (6 August 1796)," l.c., 394 f. While one must admit that Schlegel's preference for thinking in terms of the expression '*Wechsel*' played an important role in his pre-Jena period, I cannot see how one can make full sense of Schlegel's talk of '*Wechselerweis*' only by reference to this period.

9. "Here reflection becomes what feeling is—feeling becomes what reflection is—they switch roles" (*NS* II: 127, line 31). Cf. the detailed account given in my doctoral thesis, which was published as "Das Problem 'Zeit' in der deutschen Romantik."

10. Letter to Novalis from January 2, 1797 (*KA* XXIII: 340). The reference could also be related to a conversation with Novalis during his visit to Jena on December 3 and 4 (cf. *Kommentar-Anm.* 2, p. 517, and *NS* II:, 301 f.).

11. Behler himself conjectures that it might have been "the beginning of the notes," "which later received the title, 'Philosophische Lehrjahre' " (*KA* XVIII: 3–23). But already in the *Philosophische Lehrjahre* we find talk of a "*Wechselgrund*" (alternating ground) rather than a monadic "principle" (e.g., *KA* XVIII: 7, Nr. 36).

12. D. Henrich to M. Frank, letter of November 20, 1996.

13. Some notes in the *Fichte-Studien* are directly inspired by Schelling, namely, those concerning the '*wechselweise Begründung*' [reciprocal foundation] of form and content (*NS* II: 171, lines 20 ff.; p. 175, line 30).

14. Johann Georg Rist, *Lebenserinnerungen*, ed., G. Poel, part I (Gotha: 1880), 57.

15. Cf. Walter Asmus, *Johann Friedrich Herbart: Eine pädagogische Biographie*, vol. I: *Der Denker 1776–1809* (Heidelberg, 1968), 88 ff.

16. Cf. the entries in the book of minutes kept by the Brotherhood in Paul Raabe, "Das Protokollbuch der Gesellschaft der freien Männer in Jena 1794–1799," pp. 351 ff. in *Festgabe für Eduard Berend zum 75. Geburtstag am 5. Dezember 1958* (Weimar, 1959), 336–383.

17. Herbart was the first to discover and to most clearly present the infinite regress involved in the definition of the 'I' as that which consists of the 'presentation of oneself.' Cf. the new edition of his critique from 1824 in Manfred Frank, ed., *Selbstbewußtseinstheorien von Fichte bis Sartre* (Frankfurt/M: Suhrkamp, 1991), 70–84; cf. the commentary of the editor on pp. 482 ff.

18. Cf. his letter to Johann Smidt from July 1, 1796. Karl Kehrback and Otto Flügel, eds., *Sämtliche Werke I* (Langensalza, 1912; new ed. Aalen: Scientia, 1964), vol. 16. This volume contains the letters from and to Herbart during the years 1776–1807), p. 28. Letters provided in chronological order.

19. Herbart's *Sämtliche Werke*, pp. 16, 28.

20. Cf. Guido Naschert, "Friedrich Schlegels philosophischer Grundgedanke: Ein Versuch über die Genese des frühromantischen Ironiebegriffs" (*Jena 1796–97*) (master's thesis, Tübingen, unpublished, 1995), 37. A shortened and revised version of the thesis has been published in two parts as "*Friedrich Schlegel über Wechselerweis und Ironie*," part I appeared in *Äthenäum: Jahrbuch für Romantik*, vol. 6 (1996): 47–90; part II appeared in Ibid., vol. 7.

21. Herbart's, *Sämtliche Werke*, vol. I: 12–16, and 17–33.

22. Especially his review of the *Ich-Schrift*; cf. the letters of Herbart and his friend, Smidt in *Sämtliche Werke*, vol. 16: 16, 40, 42. Fichte's critique is printed with Herbart's defense in Herbart's *Sämtliche Werke*, vol. I: 17–33. Guido Naschert has provided evidence for the claim that Schlegel's conception of *Wechselerweis* could very well be related to the critique that Herbart directed against Fichte and Schelling. Cf. Naschert's, "Friedrich Schlegels."

23. Herbart, "Hier kommt ein jenem ganz ähnliches Räsonnement wieder vor," (*Sämtliche Werke*, vol. 1: 14).

24. Johann Heinrich Abicht, "On the Freedom of the Will, *Neues philosophisches Magazin*, eds., J. H. Abicht and F. G. Born, vol. I, Nr. 1 (1790): 64–85. (The individual issue in which Abicht's essay was first published had already appeared in 1789.) Reprinted in Rüdiger Bittner and Konrad Cramer, eds., *Materialien zu Kants 'Kritik der praktischen Vernunft'* (Frankfurt/M: Suhrkamp, 1975), 229–240.

25. Johann August Heinrich, Ulrich's, *Eleutheriologie oder über Freiheit und Nothwendigkeit* was published in Jena, 1788.

26. J. H. Abicht, "On the Freedom of the Will," p. 230.

Lecture 12: On Schlegel's Role in the Genesis of Early German Romantic Theory of Art

1. In his commentary to Friedrich Schlegel's "Studien zur Philosophie und Theologie," Ernst Behler speaks of Schlegel's "rejection of a first principle for philosophy" (KA VIII: 42, cf. 43). Cf. the context provided there of the relation between the rejection of philosophy based on first principles and Schlegel's characterization of philosophy as an "infinite progression" ("Schelling und die Frage nach der Form der Philosophie" [l.c., pp. 37 ff.]).

2. In his master's thesis, Guido Naschert has shown that in his talk of "beginning in the middle," Schlegel was thinking of Homer in the Ars Poetica of Horace. The corresponding reference is found in Schlegel's essay, "Über die Homerische Poesie" (KA I: 124 f, with a footnote that leads to the citation from Horace). Similar formulations of the epic-like beginning of philosophy in the middle are found in KA XVIII: 82, Nr. 626, and KA II: 178, Nr. 84.

3. Der Begriff der Kunstkritik in der deutschen Romantik, Walter Benjamin, Gesammelte Schriften, eds., Rolf Tiedemann and Hermann Schweppenhäuser (Frankfurt/M: Suhrkamp, 1974), I: 38 ff., 62 ff. This has been translated as The Concept of Criticism in German Romanticism eds., Marcus Bullock and Michael W. Jennings, Walter Benjamin: Selected Writings, Volume 1, 1913–1926 (Cambridge, MA: Harvard University Press, 1996), 116–200.

4. "The first, original Belief is therefore a belief in ourselves" (332). For more on this belief, cf. the following pages (332 ff.). Schlegel draws a connection between belief and probability: "Belief also always presupposes a probability [. . .]" (332, top). "It is this belief in ourselves that is merely an intensification of the objective and necessary probability of the I [. . .]."

5. Cf. Evidence of Schlegel's enthusiastic reception of Jacobi in Hans Eichner's introduction (p. XVIII): "Schlegel's work on Jacobi can be traced to the year 1792 and continues throughout the rest of his life" (Ernst Behler in commentary to vol. 20: 371). Cf. the even better supported and researched introduction to vol. 8: 30 ff., for example, 31: "Jean Paul reports to Herder and later to Jacobi that Novalis had told him of the enthusiasm with which Schlegel had studied Jacobi's work during his stay with him in Weißenfels (1796) (cf. Jean Paul, Sämtliche Werke, ed. Eduard Berend (Berlin, 1959), 287. Historical-Critical edition. vol. III, Letters 1797–1800). For more on the Woldemar-Rezension, see 33 ff.

6. The review, as Schlegel's letter to Körner of September 30, 1796 makes clear, was written in the few weeks between his arrival in Jena (August 6) and September 30 (KA XXIII: 332). Behler, however, places the date (perhaps of the writing of the original draft), somewhere between July 29 and August 6, 1796, which was the period that Schlegel spent with Novalis in Dürrenberg and Weißenfels before his trip to Jena ("Friedrich Schlegel's Theory of an Alternating Principle [. . .]," l.c., p. 386).

7. Yet, it is the case that during his stay in Weißenfels, Schlegel did write a "short provisional letter," which has since been lost (Letter to Körner, September 21, 1796 [KA XXIII: 332]). In that letter, some remarks could have been made (as we can

gather from the continuation of the exchange on September 30) that I shall now cite. There Schlegel says that he has spoken of "philosophical projects," which can "really" only be "realized" in Jena this winter. It would be truly sensational if this lost letter to Körner really did contain references to Schlegel's notion of the 'Wechselerweis'— but nothing we have now allows us to support this.

8. Cf. *partem pro toto* the letter from December 1, 1796 (*KA* XXIII: 339 f.): "I have occupied myself almost exclusively with speculative philosophy, and have to lock everything within me here. I think it would interest you very much. If I am not here, I will leave you the package (the beginning of my *Philosophischen Lehrjahre*) with my sister-in-law Caroline." Cf. the very similar tenor of the letter to Körner from September 30, 1796 (l.c., 332: "It seems that the critical air here has infected me, and finally some of my philosophical projects will be realized this winter, projects about which I have already spoke to you once before.") and from January 30, 1797: "I have fallen most powerfully into speculation this winter. I have come to my own view of the main issues and of Fichte's system" (l.c., 343).

9. Cf. *KA* XVIII: 36, Nr. 193: "The *I posits itself* and *the I should posit itself* are not propositions that can be deduced from a higher one; one is as high as the other, they are two first principles, not one, *Wechselgrundsatz.*"

10. With the famous formulation: "*Woldemar* is really an invitation to an acquaintance with God, and this theological work of art ends, as all moral *Debauches* end, with a *salto mortale* into the abyss of divine mercy" (*KA* II: 77). Cf. also the *Athenäum*-Fragment Nr. 346, l.c., pp. 226 f./Firchow translation, p. 70: "The renowned *salto mortale* of the philosophers is often only a false alarm. In their thoughts they take a frightfully long approach run and then congratulate themselves on having braved the danger; but if one only looks a little more closely, they're still sitting on the same old spot. It's like Don Quixote's flight on the wooden horse. Jacobi too seems to me someone who, though he can never stop moving, always stays where he is: caught in a squeeze between two kinds of philosophy, the systematic and the absolute, between Spinoza and Leibniz, where his delicate spirit has gotten to be rather pinched and sore"(Cf. *KA* XVIII: 115, Nr. 1047; *KA* XVIII: 3, Nr. 3, and *KA* XIX: 371 f.)

11. This has been translated by George di Giovanni in *The Main Philosophical Writings and the Novel Allwill* (Montreal and Kingston: McGill-Queen's University Press, 1994), 230. The translation of the passage above is mine, though I have consulted Di Giovanni's translation.

12. Manfred Frank, ed., *Phantasus* (Frankfurt/M: Suhrkamp, 1986), 81, lines 21 f.

13. Ludwig Tieck, *Erinnerungen aus dem Leben des Dichters* (Leipzig: Brockhaus, 1855), 2: 250.

14. It is in this sense that Schlegel must have read the forty-seventh anthropological fragment from Forberg's, *Fragmente aus meinen Papieren* (p. 45): "For most philosophers, their philosophy marks the end of their philosophizing. //From a philosopher, who is done creating his system, there is usually nothing more to expect, except polemics and reminiscences." Cf. fragment Nr. 19 (p. 27): "And isn't the path almost as valuable as that which we find by following it?"

15. In Karl Konrad Pohlheim, *Die Arabeske: Ansichten und ideen aus Friedrich Schlegels Poetik* (Paderbron: Schöningh, 1966), 59.

Glossary

Ahnung—premonition
Allheit—totality
Annäherung—approximation
Antrieb—impulse
Aufhebung—dissolution, abolishment
Auflösung—dissolution
Befindliches—something existent
Beglaubigung—verification
Begründung—justification, foundation
Begründungsaufgabe—task of justification
Begründungsregreß—regress
Bestehen—existence
Bestimmungsunbezogenheit—non-referential determination
Bewußtnahme—conscious apprehension
Beziehung—relation
Beziehungslosigkeit—relationlessness
Bezug—reference
Binnenartikuliert—internally articulated
Darstellbarkeit—presentability
Darstellen—to present
Darstellung—presentation
Das Absolute—the Absolute
Empfindung—sensation or feeling
Einerleiheit—sameness
Einheit—unity (in text contrasted to manifoldness)
Einigkeit—union, oneness (in text contrasted to the term 'Einheit')
Entgegensetzung—counterpositing

Erscheinung—appearance
Erweis—proof
Frühromantik—early Romanticism
fugenlos—seamless
Fülle—plenitude
Ganzheit, die—wholeness, completeness
Gattung—genus
Gefühl—feeling
Gegensatz—counterproposition (when opposed to the term 'Satz' proposition),
    or opposition
Gegenwirkung—reaction
Gespaltenheit—cleaving
Grund—reason, foundation
Grundsatz—first principle
Grundsatzphilosophie—philosophy based on first principles
Hemmung—inhibition
Höchste, das—the highest
letzbegründet—absolutely justified
Letztbegründung—ultimate foundation
Nichtendgültigkeit—nonconclusiveness
Sachverhalt—state of affairs
Satz des Bewusstseins—principle of consciousness
Satz von Grunde—principle of sufficient reason
Schein—illusion
Schluß—inference
Schließen—to infer
Schweben—hovering, to hover
Sehnen—longing, to long
Sehnsucht—longing
Seiend—being
Sein, das—Being
Sein schlechthin—Being pure and simple
Selbstbezug—self-reference
Selbstgefühl—self-feeling
Selbsthätigkeit—self-activity
Setzen, das—positing
Sog—aspiration
Täuschung—illusion
Trieb—drive
Unbedingte, das—the unconditioned
Unbezüglichkeit—non-referentiality
Undarstellbaren—the unpresentable

Undarstellbarkeit—unpresentability
unendliche—infinite
ungegenständlich—nonobjective
Unendgültigkeit—inconclusiveness
unhintergehbar—insurmountable
unmittelbar—immediate, unmediated
Unvollendung—imperfection, incompletion
Ur-Ich—Original I
Urseyn—original Being
Urspünglich—original
urteilsmäßige—judgment-like
Vollendung—perfection, completion
vorstellen—to represent
Vorstellung—representation
Wechselbegründung—reciprocal establishment, foundation
wechselseitige—reciprocal
Wechselvernichtung—reciprocal annihilation, extermination
Wesen—essence, being
Wirken—effect
Wirklichkeit—actuality
Wißbegierde—hunger for knowledge
Witz—wit
Zusammenbestand—thoroughgoing connection

Bibliography

Primary Sources

General Collections in English

Behler, Ernst, ed. *The Philosophy of German Idealism: Fichte, Jacobi, and Schelling*. New York: Continuum, 1987.

Beiser, Frederick, trans. and ed. *The Early Political Writings of the German Romantics*. Cambridge, England: Cambridge University Press, 1996.

Breazeale, Daniel. "English Translations of Fichte, Schelling, and Hegel: An Annotated Bibliography." *Idealistic Studies* 6 (1976): 279–97.

Ibid., with Kenley R. Dove, Michael Vater, David Wood, and Arnuif Zweig, trans. *New Translations of German Classics: Kant, Fichte, Novalis, Schelling, Hegel. The Philosophical Forum* 32, No. 4 (Winter 2001).

Chamberlain, Timothy, ed. *Eighteenth Century German Criticism*. New York: Continuum, 1992.

Di Giovanni, Georg and H. S. Harris, trans. and eds. *Between Kant and Hegel: Texts in the Development of German Idealism*. 2d ed. Indianapolis, IN: Hackett Publishing, 2000.

Furst, Lilian R., comp. *European Romanticism: Self-Definition*. London: Methuen, 1980.

Nisbet, H. B., ed. *German Aesthetics and Literary Criticism*. Cambridge, England: Cambridge University Press, 1985.

Reiss, Hans, ed. *The Political Thought of the German Romantics (1793–1815)*. Oxford: Blackwell, 1955.

Schmidt, James, ed. *What is Enlightenment? Eighteenth Century Answers and Twentieth Century Questions*. Berkeley, CA: University of California Press, 1996.

Schulte-Sasse, Jochen, Haynes Horne, Andreas, Michel, Elizabeth Mittman, Assenke Oksiloff, Lisa C. Roetzel, Mary R. Strand, trans. and eds. *Theory as Practice. A Critical Anthology of Early German Romantic Writings*. Minneapolis, MN: University of Minnesota Press, 1997.

Simpson, David, ed. *The Origins of Modern Critical Thought: German Aesthetic and Literary Criticism from Lessing to Hegel*. Cambridge, England: Cambridge University Press, 1988

Taylor, Ronald, ed. *The Romantic Tradition in Germany: An Anthology with Critical Essays and Commentaries*. London: Methuen, 1970.

By Author

The authors and works listed here are those that had some influence on the development of early German Romantic Philosophy. Hence, for those figures who cannot properly be considered early German Romantic philosophers, the works cited are limited to those which shaped the thought of the major figures of the movement. For example, in the case of Schelling, a figure often associated with the Romantic movement, the works listed are those that can be said to have contributed to the development of Romantic philosophy. Sadly, some of the texts by Schelling that are most relevant for a full understanding of the evolution of Romantic thought have not yet been translated. The case with Fichte is quite different, almost all of his work has been translated, yet I have only included those works most relevant to the Romantics.

JOHANN GOTTLIEB FICHTE

Fichte, Johann Gottlieb. *Gesamtausgabe der Bayerischen Akademie der Wissenshaften*, ed. Reinhard Lauth and Hans Jacob (Sttugart-Bad Canstatt: Fromann, 1962 ff.).

―――. *Attempt at a Critique of All Revelation*. Translated by Garrett Green. New York: Cambridge University Press, 1978.

―――. *Fichte im Gespräch: Johann Gottlieb Fichte im Gespräch*. Bericht der Zeitgenossen, ed. Erich Fuchs (Stuttgart-Bad Canstatt: Fromann, 1978 ff).

―――. *Science of Knowledge* (with the first and second introductions). Translated by Peter Heath and John Lachs. New York: Appleton-Century-Crofts, 1970. Reissued, with minor corrections, Cambridge: Cambridge University Press, 1982.

―――. *The Vocation of Man*. Translated by Peter Preuss. Indianapolis, IN: Hackett Publishing, 1987.

―――. *Early Philosophical Writings*. Translated by Daniel Breazeale. Ithaca, New York: Cornell University Press, 1988.

―――. *Introductions to the Wissenschaftslehre and Other Writings*. Translated by Daniel Breazeale. Indianapolis, IN: Hackett Publishing, 1994.

Friedrich von Hardenberg or Novalis

Novalis, Friedrich von. *Hymms to the Night and Other Selected Writings*. Translated by Charles E. Passage. Indianapolis, IN: Bobbs-Merrill, 1960.

———. *Schriften: Die Werke Friedrich von Hardenbergs*. Edited by Paul Kluckholm and Richard Samuel. Stuttgart, 1960.

———. *Spiritual Saturnalia: Fragments of Existence*. Translated by John N. Ritter. New York: Exposition Press, 1971.

———. "Aphorisms and Fragments." Translated by Alexander Gelley. In *German Romantic Criticism*. Edited by A. Leslie Willson, 62–83. New York: Continuum, 1982.

———. "From Miscellaneous Writings," "Monologue," "Dialogues," "On Goethe," "Studies in the Visual Arts." In *German Aesthetic and Literary Criticism: The Romantic Ironists and Goethe*. Translated by Joyce Crick. Edited by Kathleen M. Wheeler. Cambridge, England: Cambridge University Press, 1984.

———. *Pollen and Fragments: Selected Poetry and Prose of Novalis*. Translated by Arthur Versluis. Grand Rapids, MI: Phanes Press, 1989.

———. *Henry von Ofterdingen*. Translated by Palmer Hilty. Prospect Heights, IL: Waveland Press, 1990.

———. "Miscellaneous Remarks." Translated by Alexander Gelley. *New Literary History* 22 (1991): 383–406.

———. *Philosophical Writings*. Translated by Margaret Mahony Stoljar. Albany, New York: State University of New York Press, 1997.

Friedrich Hölderlin

Hölderlin, Friedrich. *Sämtliche Werke. Grosse Stuttgarter Ausgabe*. Edited by F. Beißner and A. Beck. Stuttgart: Cottanachfolger, 1943–1985.

———. *Hymns and Fragments*. Translated by Richard Sieburth. Princeton, NJ: Princeton University Press, 1984.

———. *Selected Verse*. Translated by Michael Hamburger. London: Anvil Press Poetry, 1986.

———. *Essays and Letters on Theory*. Translated by Thomas Pfau. Albany, New York: State University of New York Press, 1987.

———. *Hyperion and Selected Poems*. Edited by Eric L. Santner. New York: Continuum, 1990.

———. *Selected Poems*. Translated by David Constantine. Newcastle upon Tyne: Bloodaxe, 1990.

———. *Poems and Fragments*. Translated by Michael Hamburger. London: Anvil Poetry Press, 1994.

FRIEDRICH WILHELM JOSEPH SCHELLING

Schelling, Friedrich Wilhelm Josef. *Sämtliche Werke*. Edited by K. F. A. Schelling. Stuttgart: Cotta, 1858–61.

———. *Of Human Freedom*. Translated by J. Gutman. Chicago: Open Court Press, 1936.

———. *The Ages of the World*. Translated by Frederick de World Bolman. New York: Columbia University Press, 1942.

———. "Concerning the Relation of the Plastic Arts to Nature." Translated by Michael Bullock. Appendix to Herbert Read, *The True Voice of Feeling*. New York: Pantheon Books, 1953.

———. *On University Studies*. Translated by E. S. Morgan and Norbert Gutterman. Athens, Ohio: Ohio University Press, 1966.

———. "Epikurisch Glaubensbekenntnis." In *Materialien zu Schellings philosophisches Anfängen*. Edited by M. Frank. Frankfurt/Main: Suhrkamp, 1975.

———. *System of Transcendental Idealism*. Translated by Peter Heath. Charlottesville, VA: University Press of Virginia, 1978.

———. "On the Possibility of a Form of Philosophy in General, 1794." Translated by F. Marti. In *The Unconditioned in Human Knowledge: Four Early Essays. 1794–96*. Lewisburg, PA: Bucknell University Press, 1980.

———. *Bruno or on the Natural and Divine Principle of Things*. Translated by Michael G. Vater. Albany, New York: State University of New York Press, 1984.

———. "Schelling's Aphorisms of 1805." *Idealistic Studies* 14 (1984): 237–58.

———. *Ideas for a Philosophy of Nature*. Translated by E. Harris and P. Heath. Cambridge, England: Cambridge University Press, 1988.

———. *Philosophy of Art*. Translated by Douglas W. Stott. Minneapolis, MN: University of Minnesota Press, 1989.

———. *Idealism and the Endgame of Theory: Three Essays*. Translated by Thomas Pfau. Albany, New York: State University of New York Press, 1994.

———. *On the History of Modern Philosophy*. Translated by Andrew Bowie. Cambridge, England: Cambridge University Press, 1994.

———. "Timaeus." In *Schellingiana*. Edited by Hartmut Buchner. Vol. 4. Stuttgart: Fromann, 1994.

————. *The Ages of the World.* Translated by Jason Wirth. Albany, New York: State University of New York Press, 2000.

Friedrich Schiller

Schiller, Friedrich. *Werke. Nationalausgabe.* Edited by J. Peterson, L. Blumenthal, and B. von Weise. Weimar: Böhlau, 1943 ff.

————. *Aesthetic Letters.* Translated by Reginald Snell. New Haven: Yale University Press, 1954.

————. *On the Aesthetic Education of Man.* Translated by Elizabeth Wilkinson and L. A. Willoughby. Oxford: Oxford University Press, 1982.

————. *Essays.* Translated by Walter Hinderer and Daniel Dahlstrom. New York: Continuum, 1993.

August Wilhelm von Schlegel

Schlegel, A. W. *A Course of Lectures on Dramatic Art and Literature.* Translated by John Black. 2d ed. London: H. G. Bohn, 1846.

————. *A. W. Schlegel's Lectures on German Literature from Gottsched to Goethe.* Oxford: Blackwell, 1944.

Dorothea Mendelssohn Schlegel

Schlegel, Dorothea. *Florentin: A Novel.* Translated by Edwina Lawler and Ruth Richardson. New York: Mellen Press, 1988.

————. *Camilla: A Novel.* Translated by Edwina Lawler. Lewiston: Edwin Mellen Press, 1990.

Friedrich von Schlegel

Schlegel, Friedrich. *Lectures on the History of Literature, Ancient and Modern.* Edinburgh: W. Blackwood, 1818.

————. *Lectures on the History of Literature, Ancient and Modern,* 2d ed. Philadelphia, PA: Moss, 1848.

————. *The Philosophy of Life and Philosophy of Language.* Translated by A. J. W. Morrison. New York: Harper, 1848.

————. *A Course of Lectures on Modern History: to Which Are Added Historical Essays on the Beginning of Our History and on Caeser and Alexander.* Translated by Lyndsey Purcell and R. H. Whitelock. London, 1886.

———. *The Aesthetic and Miscellaneous Works of Friedrich von Schlegel*. Translated by E. J. Millington. London: G. Bell and Sons, 1900.

———. *Kritische Ausgabe*. Edited by Ernst Behler. Paderborn: Schoenigh, 1958 ff.

———. *Dialogue on Poetry and Literary Aphorisms*. Translated by Ernst Behler and Roman Struc. University Park, PA: Pennsylvania State University Press, 1968.

———. *Friedrich Schlegel's Lucinde and the Fragments*. Translated by Peter Firchow. Minneapolis, MN: University of Minnesota Press, 1971.

———. *The Philosophy of History: In a Course of Lectures Delivered at Vienna, with a Memoir by the Author*. Translated by J. B. Robertson. London: G. Bell and Sons, 1893. Reprint, New York: Harper, 1976.

———. *Philosophical Fragments*. Translated by Peter Firchow. Foreword by Rodolphe Gasché. Minneapolis, MN: University of Minnesota Press, 1991.

———. *On Incomprehensibility*. In *Theory as Practice: A Critical Anthology of Early German Romantic Writings*. Edited and translated by Jochen Schulte-Sasse, et al. Minneapolis, MN: University of Minnesota Press, 1997.

———. *On the Study of Greek Poetry*. Translated by Stuart Barnett. Albany, NY: State University of New York Press, 2001.

CAROLINE SCHLEGEL-SCHELLING

Schlegel-Schelling, Caroline (with Dorothea Schlegel). *Bitter Healing: German Women Writers 1700–1830*. Selected letters, in Jeannine Blackwell and Susanne Zantop. Lincoln, NE: University of Nebraska Press, 1990.

FRIEDRICH DANIEL ERNST SCHLEIERMACHER

Schleiermacher, F. D. E. *Hermeneutics: The Handwritten Manuscripts*. Translated by James Duke and Jack Forstman. Missoula, MT: Scholars Press for the American Academy of Religion, 1977.

———. *On Religion: Speeches to its Cultured Despisers*. Translated by Richard Crouter. Cambridge: Cambridge University Press, 1996.

———. *"Hermeneutics and Criticism" and Other Writings*. Translated by Andrew Bowie. Cambridge: Cambridge University Press, 1998.

———. *Lectures on Philosophical Ethics*. Edited by Robert B. Louden. Translated by Louise Adey Huish. Cambridge: Cambridge University Press, 2002.

LUDWIG TIECK

Tieck, Ludwig. *Schriften*. Berlin, 1828–1854.

———. *Erennerungen aus den Leben des Dichters*. Vol. 2. Leipzig, 1855.

———. *Letters of Ludwig Tieck: Hitherto Unpublished, 1792–1853*. Oxford: Oxford University Press, 1937.

———. *Letters to and from Ludwig Tieck and His Circle: Letters from the Period of German Romanticism, Including the Unpublished Correspondence of Sophie and Ludwig Tieck*. Collected and edited by Percy Matenko, Edwin H. Zeydel, and Bertha M. Masche. Chapel Hill, NC: University of North Carolina Press, 1967.

———. *A Weimar Correspondence: the Letters of Friedrich and Sophie Tieck to Amalie von Voight, 1804–1837*. Translated by James Trainer. South Carolina: Camden House, 1995.

Secondary Sources

Alford, Steven E. *Irony and the Logic of the Romantic Imagination*. New York: Lang, 1984.

Alexander, W. M. *Johann Georg Hamann, Philosophy of Faith*. The Hague: Nijhoff, 1966.

Allison, Henry E. *Lessing and the Enlightenment*. Ann Arbor, MI: University of Michigan Press, 1966.

———. *The Kant-Eberhard Controversy*. Baltimore, MD: Johns Hopkins, 1973.

Altmann, Alexander. *Moses Mendelssohn: A Biographical Study*. Alabama: University of Alabama Press, 1973.

Ameriks, Karl. "Reinhold and the Short Arguments to Idealism." *Proceedings of the Sixth International Kant Congress*. Edited by G. Funke and T. M. Seebohm, 1985, pp. 441–53.

———. "Kant, Fichte, and Short Arguments to Idealism." *Archiv für Geschichte der Philosophie* 72 (1990): 63–85.

———, ed. *The Modern Subject: Conceptions of the Self in Classical German Philosophy*. Albany, New York: State University of New York Press, 1995.

———, ed. *The Cambridge Companion to German Idealism*. Cambridge, England: Cambridge University Press, 2000.

———. *Kant and the Fate of Autonomy: Problems in the Appropriation of the Critical Philosophy*. Cambridge, England: Cambridge University Press, 2000.

———, ed. *Cambridge Companion to German Idealism*. Cambridge, England: Cambridge University Press, 2000.

Aris, R. *History of Political Thought in Germany: from 1789 to 1815*. New York: Russell and Russell, 1965.

Asmus, Walter. *Johann Friedrich Herbart: Eine pädagogische Biographie*. Vol. 1: *Der Denker 1776–1809* (Heidelberg, 1968).

Atlas, Samuel. *From Critical to Speculative Idealism: The Philosophy of Salomon Maimon*. The Hague: Martinus Nijhoff, 1964.

Bansen, Jan. *The Antimony of Thought: Maimonian Skepticism and the Relation between Thoughts and Objects*. Dordrecht: Kluwer, 1991.

Baum, Wilhelm. "Staats polizeyund Känntner Geistegleben." *Forum* 36, No. 432 (1989): 20–23.

———. "Die Aufklärung und die Jakobinerin Österreich: Der Klagenfurter Herbert-Kreis. In *Verdrängter Humanismus—verzögerte aufklärung: Österreichische Philosophie zur Zeit der Revolution und Restauration (1750–1829)*. Edited by Wilhelm Baum, Michael Benedikt, and Reinhard Knoll. Vienna: Turia and Kent, 1992.

Beck, Jacob Sigismund. *Einzig-möglicher Standpunct aus welchem die critische Philosophie beurtheilt werden muß*. Riga: Hartknoch, 1796.

Beck, Lewis White. *Early German Philosophy, Kant and his Predecessors*. Cambridge, MA: Harvard University Press, 1969.

Behler, Ernst. "Der Wendepunkt Fr. Schlegels." *Philosophische Jahrbuch der Görresgesellschaft* (1956): 256 ff.

———. trans. *Friedrich Schlegel's Dialogue on Poetry and Literary Aphorisms*. University Park, PA: Pennsylvania State University Press, 1966.

———. ed. *Die Europäische Romantik*. Frankfurt a.Main: Suhrkamp, 1972.

———. *German Romantic Criticism: Novalis, Schlegel, Schleiermacher and others*. Foreword. New York: Continuum, 1982.

———. *Die Zeitschriften der Brüder Schlegel*. Darmstadt: Wissenschaftliche Buchgesellschaft, 1983.

———. ed. *Die Aktualität der Frühromantik*. Paderborn: Schöningh, 1987.

———. "Friedrich Schlegel's Theorie des Verstehens Hermeneutik oder Dekonstruktion" in Ernst Behler, ed. *Die Aktvalitat der Frühromantik*. Paderborn: Ferdinand Schöningh, 1987, 141–160.

———. ed. *Fichte, Jacobi and Schelling: Philosophy of German Idealism*. New York: Continuum, 1987.

———. *Frühromantik*. Berlin: Walter de Gruyter, 1992.

———. *German Romantic Literary Theory*. Cambridge, England: Cambridge University Press, 1993.

———. "Friedrich Schlegel's Theory of an Alternating Principle Prior to his Arrival in Jena (6. August 1796)." *Revue internationale de philosophie*. Edited by Manfred Frank. Vol. 50, Nr. 197, 3 (1996): 383–402, esp. 386.

Behrens, Klaus. *Fr. Schlegels Geschichtsphilosophie (1794–1808)*. Tübingen: Niemayer, 1984.

Beierwaltes, Werner, ed. *Schelling: Texte zur Philosophie der Kunst*. Stuttgart: Reclam, 1982.

Beiser, Frederick C. *The Fate of Reason: German Philosophy from Kant to Fichte*. Cambridge, MA: Harvard University Press, 1987.

———. *Enlightenment, Revolution, and Romanticism: The Genesis of Modern German Political Thought, 1790–1800*. Cambridge, MA: Harvard University Press, 1992.

———. *The Early Political Writings of the German Romantics*. Edited and translated by Frederick C. Beiser. Cambridge: Cambridge University Press, 1996.

———, ed. *The Early Political Writings of The German Romantics*. Cambridge, England: Cambridge University Press, 1996.

———. *German Idealism: The Struggle against Subjectivism, 1781–1801*. Cambridge, MA: Cambridge University Press, 2002.

Bell, Stephen. *Spinoza in Germany from 1670 to the Age of Goethe*. London: Institute of Germanic Studies, 1984.

Benjamin, Walter. *Der Begriff der Kunstkritik in der deutschen Romantik. Band 1 Gesammelte Schriften*. Frankfurt a.Main: Suhrkamp, 1974. English Translation: *The Concept of Criticism in German Romanticism*. In *Walter Benjamin: Selected Writings*. Volume 1—1913–1926. Edited by Marcus Bullock and Michael W. Jennings, 116–200. Cambridge, MA: Harvard University Press, 1996.

Benz, Ernst. *The Mystical Sources of German Romantic Philosophy*. Allison Park, PA: Pickwick Publications, 1983.

Bergman, Samuel Hugo. *The Autobiography of Salomon Maimon with an Essay on Maimon's Philosophy*. London: The East and West Library, 1954.

———. *The Philosophy of Solomon Maimon*. Translated from the Hebrew by Noah J. Jacobs. Jerusalem: Magnes Press, The Hebrew University, 1967.

Berman, Antoine. *The Experience of the Foreign: Culture and Translation in Romantic Germany*. Translated by S. Heyvaert. Albany, New York: State University of New York Press, 1992.

Berlin, Isaiah. *Vico and Herder: Two Studies in the History of Ideas*. London: Hogarth, 1976.

———. *The Magus of the North: J. G. Hamann and the Origins of Modern Irrationalism*, ed. Henry Hardy. New York: Farrar, Straus and Giroux, 1993.

———. *The Roots of Romanticism*. Edited by Henry Hardy. Princeton, NJ: Princeton University Press, 1999.

Bittner, Rüdiger and Konrad Cramer, eds. *Materialien zu Kants 'Kritik der praktischen Vernunft.'* Frankfurt/M: Suhrkamp, 1975.

Bondeli, Martin. *Das Anfangsproblem bei Karl Leonhard Reinhold: eine systematische und entwicklungs-geschichtliche Utersuchung zur Philosophie Reinholds in der Zeit von 1789 bis 1803.* Frankfurt: V. Klostermann, 1994.

Bowie, Andrew. *Schelling and Modern European Philosophy: An Introduction.* London: Routledge and Kegan Paul, 1993.

————. *Aesthetics and Subjectivity: From Kant to Nietzsche.* Manchester, 1993.

————. "John McDowell's *Mind and World* and Early Romantic Epistemology," in *Revue Internationale de Philosophie* 3 (1996): 515–554.

————. *From Romanticism to Critical Theory: The Philosophy of German Literary Theory.* London: Routledge and Kegan Paul, 1997.

————. "German Philosophy Today Between Idealism, Romanticism and Pragmatism." In *German Philosophy Since Kant: Royal Institute of Philosophy Lectures.* Edited by Anthony O'Hear. Cambridge, England: Cambridge University Press, 1999.

Brauer, Ursula. *Isaac von Sinclair: Eine Biographie.* Stuttgart: Klett-Cotta, 1993.

Breazeale, Daniel. "Fichte's Aenesidemus Review and the Transformation of German Idealism." *Review of Metaphysics* 34 (March 1981): 545–568.

————. "Between Kant and Fichte: Karl Leonard Reinhold's Elementary Philosophy." *Review of Metaphysics* 35, Nr. 4 (1982): 785–822.

————. "How to Make an Idealist: Fichte's 'Refutation of Dogmatism' and the Problem of the Starting Point of the *Wissenschaftslehre*." *The Philosophical Forum* 19, No. 2–3 (W-S, 1987–88): 97–123. This is a special issue devoted to a discussion of Fichte's thought an includes articles by Walter E. Wright, Robert B. Pippin, Alexis Philonenko, Stanley Rosen, Tom Rockmore, John Lachs, Luc Ferry and A. J. Mandt.

————, trans., ed. *Fichte, early philosophical writings.* Ithaca: Cornell University Press, 1988.

————. " 'The Standpoint of Life' and the 'Standpoint of Philosophy' in the Context of the Jena Wissenschaftslhehre." *Transzendentalphilosophie als System: Die Auseinandersetzung zwischen 1794 und 1806.* Edited by A Müs, 81–104. Hamburg: Felix Meiner, 1989.

————. "Fichte on Skepticism." *Journal of the History of Philosophy* 88 (1991): 524–31.

————, trans., ed. *Fichte, Foundations of Transcendental Philosophy, Wissenschaftslehre nova methodo (1796/99).* Ithaca, New York: Cornell University Press, 1992.

————, trans., ed. *Introduction to the Wissenschaftslehre and other writings 1797–1800.* Indianapolis, IN: Hackett Publishing, 1994.

Breazeale, Daniel and Tom Rockmore, eds. *Fichte: Historical Contexts/Contemporary Controversies*. NJ: Humanities Press, 1994.

Brown, Marshall. *The Shape of German Romanticism*. Ithaca: Cornell University Press, 1979.

Bubner, Rüdiger. "Kant, Transcendental Argument and the Problem of Deduction." *Review of Metaphysics* 28, No. 3 (1975): 453–467.

Bullock, Marcus. *Romanticism and Marxism*. New York: Peter Lang, 1987.

Bullock, Marcus and Michael W. Jennings, eds. *Walter Benjamin: Selected Writings, Volume 1, 1913–1926*. Cambridge, MA: Cambridge University Press, 1996.

Capen, Samuel Paul. *Friedrich Schlegel's Relations with Reichhart and his Contributions to Deutschland*. Publications of the University of Pennsylvania: Series in Philology and Literature. Vol. 9, No. 2. Boston: Ginn and Co., 1903.

Cassirer, Ernst. *Das Erkenntnisproblem in der Philosophie und Wissenschaft der neueren Zeit. Dritter Band, Die Nachkantischen Systeme*. 3d ed. Darmstadt: Wissenschaftliche Buchgesellschaft, 1991.

Castañeda, Hector-Neri. " 'He': A Study in the Logic of Self-Consciousness." *Ratio* 8 (1966): 130–157.

Cavell, Stanley. *In Quest of the Ordinary: Lines of Skepticism and Romanticism*. Chicago: University of Chicago Press, 1988.

―――. *This New Yet Unapproachable America: Lectures after Emerson and Wittgenstein*. Albuquerque, NM: Living Batch Press, 1989.

Cragg, Gerald R. *Reason and Authority in the Eighteenth Century*. Cambridge, MA: Harvard University Press, 1964.

Cunningham, Andrew and Nicholas Jardine, eds. *Romanticism and the Sciences*. Cambridge, England: Cambridge University Press, 1990.

DeMan, Paul. *The Rhetoric of Romantics*. New York: Columbia University Press, 1984.

―――. *The Romantic School and Other Essays*. Edited by Joat Hermond and Robert Holub. New York: Continuum, 1985.

―――. *Romanticism and Contemporary Criticism: the Gauss Seminar and Other Papers*. Baltimore, MD: Johns Hopkins University Press, 1993.

Di Giovanni, George. "Kant's Metaphysics of Nature and Schelling's Ideas for a Philosophy of Nature." *Journal of the History of Philosophy* 18 (1979): 197–215.

―――. "From Jacobi's Novel to Fichte's Idealism: Some Comments on the 1798–99 Atheism Dispute." *Journal of the History of Philosophy* 27, Nr. 1 (1989): .

―――. "The first twenty years of criitque: The Spinoza Connection." *The Cambridge Companion to Kant*. Edited by Paul Guyer, 417–448. Cambridge, England: Cambridge University Press, 1992.

———. trans., with introductory study. *The Main Philosophical Writings and the Novel Allwill of Fr. Heinrich Jacobi.* Montreal: McGill-Queen's University Press, 1994.

———. "The Jacobi-Fichte-Reinhold Dialogue and Analytical Philosophy." *Fichte-Studien* 14 (1999): 63–86.

di Giovanni, G., and H. S. Harris, eds. *Between Kant and Hegel: Texts in the Development of Post-Kantian Idealism.* Albany: State University of New York Press, 1985; 2d ed. Indianapolis, IN: Hackett Publishing, 2000.

Dieckmann, L. "Fr. Schlegel and Romantic Concepts of the Symbol." *Germanic Review* 34 (1959): 276–283.

Dilthey, Wilhelm. *Die Entstehung der Hermeneutik.* Göttingen: Vandenhoeck & Ruprecht, 1961.

———. *Das Leben Scheiermachers.* Vol. 1, Book 2. Berlin: Walter de Gruyter, 1970.

Dirnfellner, Berthold. "Isaac von Sinclair: Zur Edition Seiner Jugendbriefe." *Le pauvre Holterling,* Nos. 4 and 5 (92–140): 138; Frankfurt edition.

Eichner, Hans. "Romantisch-Romantik-Romantiker." In *'Romantic' and Its Cognates—The European History of a Word.* Edited by Hans Eichner, 98–156. Toronto: University of Toronto Press, 1972.

Eldridge, Richard. "A Continuing Task: Cavell and the Truth of Skepticism." In *The Sense of Stanley Cavell.* Edited by Richard Fleming and Michael Payne, 76. Lewisburg: Bucknell University Press, 1989.

———. "Some Remarks on Logical Truth: Human Nature and Romanticism." *Midwest Studies in Philosophy* 19 (1994): 220–242.

———, ed. *Beyond Representation: Philosophy and Poetic Imagination.* Cambridge, England: Cambridge University Press, 1996.

———. *The Persistence of Romanticism. Essays in Philosophy and Literature.* Cambridge: Cambridge University Press, 2001.

Fabricius, Wilhelm. *Die deutschen Corps: Eine Historische Darstellung mit besonderer Berücksichtigung des Mensurwe sens.* Berlin, 1898.

Ferris, David, ed. Walter Benjamin on Romanticism, special volume of *Studies in Romanticism* 31:4 (Winter 1992).

Feuerbach, Paul Johann Anselm. "Über die Unmöglichheit eines ersten absoluten Grundsatzes der Philosophie." *Philosophisches Journal* 2, No. 4 (1795): 306–322.

Fischer, Michael. "Accepting the Romantics as Philosophers." *Philosophy and Literature* 12 (October 1988): 179–89.

Forberg, Friedrich Karl. *Fragmenten aus meinen Papieren.* Jena: bey. J. C. Voigt, 1796.

Frank, Manfred. *Das Problem "Zeit" in der deutschen Romantik: Zeitbewußtsein und Bewußtsein von Zeitlichkeit in der frühromantischen Philosophie und in Tiecks Dichtung.* München: Winkler, 1972.

————. *Der kommende Gott: Vorlesungen über die Neue Mythologie.* Frankfurt a.Main: Suhrkamp, 1982.

————. *Eine Einführung in Schellings Philosophie.* Frankfurt a.Main: Suhrkamp, 1985.

————. "Auf der Suche nach einem Grund: Über den Umschlag von Erkenntnis Kritik—Mythologie bei Musil." In *Mythos und Moderne.* Edited by Karl-Heinz Bohrer. Frankfurt/M: Suhrkamp, 1983.

————. *Die Grenzen der Verständiging: Ein Geistesgespräch zwischen Lyotard und Habermas.* Frankfurt/M: Suhrkamp, 1988.

————. *Das Sagbare und das Unsagbare.* Frankfurt a.Main: Suhrkamp, 1988.

————. *Einführung in die Frühromantische Ästhetik: Vorlesungen.* Frankfurt a.Main: Suhrkamp, 1989.

————. *Selbstbewußtseinstheorie von Fichte bis Sartre.* Frankfurt a.Main: Suhrkamp, 1991.

————. "Two Centuries of Philosophical Critique of Reason and its 'Postmodern' Radicalization." In *Reason and Its Other: Rationality in Modern German Philosophy and Culture.* Edited by Dieter Freundlieb and Wayne Hudson, 67–86. Berg European Studies Series. Rhode Island: Berg, 1993.

————. "Philosophische Grundlage der Frühromantik." *Athenäum, Jahrbuch für Romantik* (1994): 37–130.

————. "The Philosophical Foundations of Early Romanticism. In *The Modern Subject: Conceptions of the Self in Classical German Philosophy.* Edited by K. Ameriks and D. Sturma, 65–85. Albany: State University of New York Press, 1995.

————. "Hölderlin's Philosophische Grundlagen," In *Hölderlin und die Moderne: Eine Bestandsaufnahme.* Edited by G. Kurz, V. Lawitschka, and J. Wertheimer, 174–194. Tübingen: Attempto, 1995.

————. "Les fondements philosophiques du premier romantisme allemande." Vol. 50, No. 197 (1996).

————. "Wechselgrundsatz: Friedrich Schlegels philosophischer Ausgangspunkt." *Zeitschrift für philosophische Forschung* 50 (1996): 26–50.

————. "*Alle Wahrheit ist relativ, alles Wissen symbolisch*—Motive der Grundsatz-Skepsis in der frühen Jenaer Romantik (1796)." *Revue internationale de Philosophie. Numero special: Fondements philosophiques du premier romantisme allemand (Jena 1796).* (September 1996).

————. *The Subject and the Text: Essays on Literary Theory and Philosophy.* Translated by Helen Atkins and edited by Andrew Bowie. Cambridge: Cambridge University Press, 1997.

————. *Unendliche Annaehuerung: Die Anfaenge der philosophischen Fruehromantik.* Frankfurt/M: Suhrkamp, 1997.

―――. "Wie reaktionär war eigentlich die Frühromantik?" In *Athenäum Jahrbuch für Romantik*. Paderborn: Ferdinand Schöningh, 1997.

Franz, Michael. "Hölderlin's Logik: Zum grundriß von 'Sein,' Urtheil und Möglichkeit." *Hölderlin Jahrbuch* 25 (1986–87): 93–124.

Friedrichsmeyer, Sara. *The Androgyne in Early German Romanticism: Friedrich Schlegel, Novalis, and the Meyaphysics of Love*. Bern: Lang, 1983.

Gadamer, Hans Georg. *Die Aktualität des Schönen*. Stuttgart: Reclam, 1977.

―――. *Truth and Method*. Translated from the German by Joel Weinsheimer and Donald G. Marshall. New York: Crossroad, 1991.

Gaier, Ulrich, Valérie Lawitschka, Wolfgang Rapp, and Violetta Waibel, eds. *Hölderlin Texturen 2: Das "Jenaische Projekt": Wintersemester 1794–95*. Edited by Hölderlin-Gesellschaft in Tübingen in collaboration with the German Schillergesellschaft. Marbach, Tübingen: Mohr, 1995.

Gardiner, Patrick L. *Nineteenth Century Philosophy*. London: The Free Press, 1969.

Gasché, Rodolphe. "Ideality in Fragmentation." Foreword to *Philosophical Fragments Friedrich Schlegel*. Translated by Peter Firchow. Minneapolis, MN: University of Minnesota Press, 1991.

―――. "Comparatively Theoretical." In *Germanistik und Komparistik*. Edited by H. Birus, 417–432. Stuttgart: J. B. Metzler Verlag, 1995.

Goldinger, Walter. "Kant und die österreichischen Jakobiner." In *Beiträge zur neueren Geschichte Österreichs*. Edited by Heinrich Fichtenau and Erich Zöllner. Vienna-Cologne-Graz: Hermann Böhlaus Nachfo, 1974.

Goodman, Russell B. *American Philosophy and the Romantic Tradition*. New York: Cambridge University Press, 1991.

Graeser, Andreas. "Hölderlin über Urtheil and Seyn." *Freiburger Zeitschrift für Philosophie und Theologie*. Heft 1–2 (1991): 111–127.

Griswold, Charles. "Fichte's Modification of Kant's Transcendental Idealism in the *Wissenschaftslehre* of 1794 and Introductions of 1797." *Auslegung* 4, Nr. 2: 132–151.

Grondin, Jean. *Sources of Hermeneutics*. Albany, New York: State University of New York Press, 1995.

―――. *Introduction to Philosophical Hermeneutics*. New Haven, CT: Yale University Press, 1994.

Grugan, Arthur A., ed. Special issue on Hölderlin. *Philosophy Today* 37. No. 4 (Winter 1993).

Hannah, Richard W. *The Fichtean Dynamic of Novalis' Poetics*. Bern: Peter Lang, 1981.

Hanssen, Beatrice and Andrew Benjamin, eds. *Walter Benjamin and Romanticism*. New York: Continuum, 2002.

Haym, Rudolf. *Die Romantische Schule*, 5th ed. 1870. Reprint, Berlin: Weidmann, 1928.

Hegel, G. W. F. *Enzyklopädie du Philosophischen Wissenschaften in Grundrisse*. Edited by F. Nicolin and O. Pöggeler, sec. 256. 1830 Reprint, Hamburg: F. Meiner, 1959.

———. *Hegel's Theologische Jugendschriften*, H. Nohl, ed. Tübingen, 1907. Reprint. Frankfurt/M: Suhrkamp, 1966.

Hegel, Hannelore. *Issak von Sinclair zwischen Fichte, Hölderlin und Hegel. Ein Beitrag zur Entstehungsgeschichte der idealistischen Philosophie*. Frankfurt a.Main: Klostermann, 1971.

Helfer, Martha B. *The Retreat of Representation: The Concept of Darstellung in German Critical Discourse*. Albany, New York: State University of New York Press, 1996.

Heinrich, Dieter. "The Proof-Structure of Kant's Transcendental Dialectic." *The Review of Metaphysics* 22 (1969): 640–59.

———. *Identität und Objektivität: eine Untersuchung über Kants transzendentale Deduktion*. Heidelberg: C. Winter, 1976.

———. "Gedanken, Nachrichten und Dokumente aus Anlaß seiner Verlustes." In *Homburg vor der Höhe in der Deutschen Geistesgeschichte*. Edited by Christoph Jamme and O. Pöggeler. Stuttgart: Klett-Cotta, 1981.

———. "Fichte's Original Insight." Translated by David Lachterman. *Contemporary German Philosophy* 1 (1982): 15–51.

———. *Selbstverhältnisse: Gedanken und Auslegungen zu den Grundlagen der klassischen deutschen Philosophie*. Stuttgart: Reclam, 1982.

——— and Christoph Jamme. "Jakob Zwillings Nachlass: Eine Rekonstruktion." *Hegel Studien*, Beiheft 28 (1986): 9–99.

———. with Christoph Jamme, eds. *Jakob Zwillings Nachlass: Eine Rekonstruktion; mit Beiträge zur Geschichte des spekulativen Denkens*. Hegel-Studien, 28. Bonn: Bouvier, 1986.

———. *Konstellationen: Probleme und Debatten am Ursprung der idealistischen Philosophie (1789–1795)*. Stuttgart: Klett-Cotta, 1991.

———. *Aesthetic Judgment and the Moral Image of the World: Studies in Kant*. Stanford, CA: Stanford University Press, 1992.

———. *Der Grund im Bewußtsein: Untersuchungen zu Hölderlins Denken (1794–1795)*. Stuttgart: Klett-Cotta, 1992.

———. "Hölderlin über *Urtheil und Seyn*: Eine Studie zur Entstehungsge-schichte des Idealismus." In *Konstellationen*. Stuttgart: Klett-Cotta, 1992.

———. "The Origins of the Theory of the Subject." In *Philosophical Interventions in the Unfinished Project of the Enlightenment*. Edited by Axel Honneth, Thomas McCarthy, Claus Offe, and Albrecht Wellmer. Cambridge, MA: MIT Press, 1992.

————, ed. Fr. Heinrich Jacobi. Präsident der Akademie, *Philosoph*, Theoretiker der Sprache. München, 1993.

————. *The Unity of Reason: Essays on Kant's Philosophy*. Edited by Richard L. Velkey. Cambridge, MA: Harvard University Press, 1994.

————, ed. *Immanuel Carl Dietz, Briefwechsel und Kantische Schriften: Wissensbegründung in der Glaubenskrise Tübingen-Jena (1790–1792)*. Stuttgart: Klett-Cotta, 1997.

————. *The Course of Remembrance and Other Essays of Holderlin*. California: Stanford University Press, 1997.

Hoffbauer, Johann Cristoph. *Anfangsgründe der logik*. Berlin, 1810.

Hogrebe, Wolfram. *Prädikation als Genesis*. Frankfurt/M: Suhrkamp, 1989.

Horstmann, Rolf-Peter. "Maimon's Criticism of Reinhold's 'Satz des Bewußtseins.'" *Proceedings of the 3rd International Kant Congress*. Edited by L. W. Beck, 331–38. Dordrecht: Reidel, 1972.

Huch, Richarda. *Die Blützeint der Romantik—Ausbreitung, Blützeit und Verfall der Romantik*. Tübingen: Rainer Wunderlich, 1951.

Immerwahr, Raymond. "The Word Romantisch and its History." *The Romantic Period in Germany. Essays by Members of the London University Institute of Germanic Studies*. Edited by Siegbert Prawer, 34–63. London: Weidenfeld and Nicolson, 1970.

Jacobi, Friedrich Heinrich. *Über die Lehre des Spinoza in Briefen an den Herrn Moses Mendelssohn, Neue vermehrte Ausgabe*. Breslau: Löwe, 1789.

Jamme, Christoph. *Isaac von Sinclair: Politiker, Philsoph und Dichter zwischen Revolution und Restauration*. Bonn: Bouvier, 1988.

————. "Isaac von Sinclairs *Philosophische Raisonnements:* Zur Wiederfindung ihrer Originale." *Hegel Studien* 18 (1983): 240–44.

Katzoff, Charlotte. "Salomon Maimon's Critique of Kant's Theory of Consciousness." *Zeitschrift für philosophische Forschung* 35 (1981): 185–95.

————. "Salomon Maimon's Interpretation of Kant's Copernican Revolution." *Kant-Studien* 66 (1975): 342–56.

Kaufmann, Walter. "Goethe and the History of Ideas." *Journal of the History of Ideas* 10 (October 1949): 503–516.

Kant, Immanuel. *Critique of Pure Reason*. Translated by Norman Kemp Smith. New York: Modern Library, 1958.

————. *Critique of Judgment*. Translated by Werner S. Pluhar. Indianapolis, IN: Hackett Publishing Company, 1987.

————. *Der Einzig mögliche Beweisgrund zu einer Demonstration des Daseins Gottes*. Translated by Gordon Treasch. Lincoln, NE: University of Nebraska Press, 1994.

Kehrback, Karl and Otto Flügel, eds. *Sämtliche Werke*. Langensalza, 1912; new ed. Aalen: Scientia, 1964.

Klemm, David and Günter Zöller, eds. *Figuring the Self: Subject, Absolute, and Others in Classical German Philosophy*. Albany, New York: State University of New York Press, 1997.

Kluckhohn, Paul. *Das Ideengut der deutschen Romantik*, 3d ed. Tübingen: Niemayer, 1953.

Krausz, Michael. "Relativism and Foundationalism." *The Monist* 67, No. 3 (July 1984): 395–404.

Krell, David F. "The Crisis of Reason in the Nineteenth Century: Schelling's Treatise on Human Freedom." In *The Collegium Phaenomenlogicum*. Edited by John Sallis, 13–32. Dordrecht and Boston: Kluwer, 1988.

———. *Contagion: Sexuality, Disease, and Death in German Idealism and Romanticism*. Bloomington: Indiana University Press, 1998.

Kuehn, Manfred. "The Early Reception of Reid, Oswarld and Beattie in Germany 1768–1800." *Journal of the History of Philosophy* 21 (1983): 479–97.

———. *Scottish Commonsense in Germany, 1768–1800: A Contribution to the History of Critical Philosophy*. Kingston, Canada: McGill-Queen, 1987.

Kuzniar, Alice. *Delayed Endings: Nonclosure in Novalis and Hölderlin*. Athens, GA: University of Georgia Press, 1987.

———. "Reassessing Romantic Reflexivity—The Case of Novalis." *The Germanic Review* 63 (1988): 77–86.

Kroner, Richard. *Von Kant bis Hegel*. Tübingen: J. C. B. Mohr, 1921.

Lacan, Jacques. "Le stade du miroir [. . .]." In *Ecrits*. Paris: Seuil, 1966.

Lachs, John. "Fichte's Idealism." *American Philosophical Quarterly* 9 (1972): 311–318.

Lacoue-Labarthe, Philippe and Jean-Luc Nancy. *The Literary Absolute: The Theory of Literature in German Romanticism*. Translated from the French by Phillip Barnard and Cheryl Lester. Albany: State University of New York Press, 1988.

Larmore, Charles. *The Romantic Legacy*. New York: Columbia University Press, 1996.

Lovejoy, A. O. "The Meaning of 'Romantic' in Early-German Romanticism." In *Essays in the History of Ideas*, 183–206. Baltimore, MD: The Johns Hopkins Press, 1948.

———. "Schiller and the Genesis of German Romanticism." Baltimore, MD: The John Hopkins Press, 1948. 207–227.

Lukács, Georg. *Die Seele und die Formen*. Soul and Form, Anna Bostock, trans. Cambridge, MA: MIT Press, 1974.

————. *The Destruction of Reason*. Translated by Peter Palmer. Atlantic Highlands, NJ: Humanities Press, 1981.

Mach, Ernst. *Beiträge zur Analyse der Empfindungen*. Jena: G. Fischer, 1886.

Mandt, A. J. "Fichte's Idealism in Theory and Practice." *Idealistic Studies* 14 (1984): 127–147.

Margolis, J. *Pragmatism without Foundations: Reconciling Realism and Reflection*. Oxford: Blackwell, 1986.

Marti, Fritz, trans. *The Unconditioned in Human Knowledge: Four Early Essay. 1794–96*. Lewisburg, PA: Bucknell University Press, 1980.

Menninghaus, Winfried, ed. *Fr. Schlegel. Theorie der Weiblichkeit*. Frankfurt a.Main: Insel, 1983.

————. *Unendliche Verdopplung: die frühromantische Grundlegung der kunsttheorie im Begriff absoluter Selbstreflexion*. Frankfurt a.Main: Suhrkampt, 1987.

Molnár, Géza von. *Novalis' "Fichte-Studies": The Foundation of His Aesthetics*. The Hague: Mouton, 1970.

————. *Novalis*. Boston: Twayne, 1980.

————. *Romantic Vision, Ethical Context. Novalis and Artistic Autonomy*. Minneapolis. MN: University of Minnesota Press, 1987.

Naschert, Guido. "Friedrich Schlegels philosophischer Grundgedanke: Ein Versuch über die genese des frühromantischen Ironiebegriffs." Master's thesis, Tübingen, 1995.

Nauen, Franz Gabriel. *Revolution, Idealism, and Human Freedom: Schelling, Holderlin, Hegel and the Crisis of Early German Idealism*. The Hague: Nijhoff, 1971.

Niethammer, Friedrich I. "Concerning the Demands of Common Sense on Philosophy." *Philosophisches Journal* 1 (May 1795): 1–45.

Norton, Robert E. *The Beautiful Soul: Aesthetic Morality in the Eighteenth Century*. Ithaca, New York: Cornell University Press, 1995.

O'Brien, William. Arctander. *Novalis. Signs of Revolution*. Durham, NC: Duke University Press, 1995.

Perry, John. "The Problem of the Essential Indexical." *Nous* 13 (1979): 3.

Peter, Klaus. "Friedrich Schlegel und Adorno: Die Dialektik der Aufklärung in der Romantik und heute" in Ernst Behler, ed. *Die Aktualität der Frühromantik*. Paderborn: Ferdinand Schöningh, 1987: 219–235.

Petzhold, Emil. *Hölderlins Brot und Wein: Ein theoretisches Versuch*. Sambor: Schwarz and Trojan, 1896, New ed., Darmstadt: Wissenschaftliche Buchgesellschaft, 1967.

Pfefferkorn, Kristin. *Novalis. A Romantic's Theory of Language*. New Haven: Yale University Press, 1988.

Pinkard, Terry. *German Philosophy 1760–1860. The Legacy of Idealism*. Cambridge, England: Cambridge University Press, 2002.

Pohlheim, Karl Konrad. *Die Arabeske: Ansichten und ideen aus Friedrich Schlegels Poetik*. München-Paderbron-Wien: Schöningh, 1966.

Prickett, Stephen. *Origins of Narrative: The Romantic Appropriation of the Bible*. Cambridge: Cambridge University Press, 1996.

Raabe, Paul. "Das Protokollbuch der Gesellschaft der freien Männer in Jena 1794–1799." In *Festgabe für Eduard Berend zum 75. Geburtstag am 5. Dezember 1958*. Weimar, 1959.

Rajan, Tilottama. *The Supplement of Reading: Figures of Understanding in Romantic Theory and Practice*. Ithaca, New York: Cornell University Press, 1990.

Reardon, Bernard G. *Religion in the Age of Romanticism: Studies in Early Nineteenth Century Thought*. Cambridge: Cambridge University Press, 1985.

Reill, Peter. *The German Enlightenment and the Rise of Historicism*. Berkeley, CA: University of California Press, 1975.

Reinhold, Karl Leonhard. *Versuch einer neuen Theorie des menschlichen Vorstellungsvermögens*. Prague and Jena: Widtmann and Mauke, 1789.

Reiss, Hans, ed. *The Political Thought of the German Romantics, 1793–1815*. Oxford: Basil Blackwell, 1955.

Richards, Robert J. *The Romantic Conception of Life: Science and Philosophy in the Age of Goethe*. Chicago: Chicago University Press, 2002.

Rist, Johann Georg. *Lebenserinnerungen*. Edited by G. Peol, Part I. Gotha, 1880.

Röhr, Sabine. *A Primer on German Enlightenment: With a Translation of K. L. Reinhold's 'The Fundamental Concepts and Principles of Ethics.'* Columbia: University of Missouri Press, 1985.

Rosen, Charles. *Romantic Poets, Critics, and Other Madmen*. Cambridge, MA: Harvard University Press, 1988.

Rotenstreich, Nathan. "On the Position of Maimon's Philosophy." *The Review of Metaphysics* 21 (1967): 534–45.

Roubiczek, Paul. "Some aspects of German Philosophy in the Romantic Period." In *The Romantic Period in Germany: Essays by members of the London University Institute of Germanic Studies*. Edited by Siegbert Prawer, 305–326. London: Weidenfeld and Nicolson, 1970.

Rousseau, Jean Jacques. *Oevres Complétes, edition sous la direccion de Bernard Gagnebin et Marcel Raymond*. Paris: Bibliothèque de le Plèiade, 1969.

Russell, Bertrand. *Logic and Knowledge*. London: G. Allen and Unwin, 1956.

Sandkaulen-Bock, Birgit. *Ausgang vom Unbedingten. Über den Anfang in der Philosophie: Schellings*. Göttingen: Vandenhoeck and Ruprecht, 1990.

Sassen, Brigitte, trans. and ed. *Kant's Early Critics: The Empiricist Critique of the Theoretical Philosophy*. Cambridge, England: Cambridge University Press, 2000.

Schaber, Steven. "Novalis' Theory of the Work of Art as Hieroglyph." *The Germanic Review* 48 (1973): 35–43.

Schlichtegroll, Friedrich. "Nekrolog der Teutschen für das neunzehnte Jahrhundert." *Gotha* 4 (April 1805): 187–241.

Schmid, Carl Christian Erhard. *Empirische Psychologie,* 7th ed. Jena, 1791.

Schulz, Gerhard. *Novalis: In Selbstzeugnisse und Bilddokumenten*. Reinbeck bei Hamburg: Rowohlt, 1969.

Schulze, Gottlob E. *Aenesidemus oder über die Fundamente der von Herrn Professor Reinhold in Jena gelie ferten Elemental Philosophie*. Frankfurt: Meiner Verlag, 1996.

Sedgwick, Sally, ed. *The Reception of Kant's Critical Philosophy: Fichte,Schelling, and Hegel*. Cambridge: Cambridge University Press, 2000.

Seidel, George J. *Activity and Ground: Fichte, Schelling and Hegel*. New York: Olms, 1976

———. *Fichte's Wissenschaftslehre of 1794: A Commentary on Part I*. West Lafayette: Purdue University Press, 1993.

Seth, Andrew. *The Development from Kant to Hegel*. New York: Garland, 1976.

Seyhan, Azade. *Representation and Its Discontents: The Critical Legacy of German Romanticism*. Berkeley, CA: University of California Press, 1992.

Simon, W. M. "The Historical and Social Background of the Romantic Period in Germany." *The Romantic Period in Germany: Essays by members of the London University Institute of Germanic Studies*. Edited by Siegbert Prawer, 17–33. London: Weidenfeld and Nicolson, 1970.

Snow, Dale E. "F. H. Jacobi and the Development of German Idealism." *Journal of the History of Philosophy* 25 (1987): 397–415.

———. *Schelling and the End of Idealism*. Albany, New York: State University of New York Press, 1996.

Solomon, Robert C., and Kathleen M. Higgens, eds. *The Age of German Idealism*. New York: Routledge and Kegan Paul, 1993.

Sprigge, T. L. S. *The Vindication of Absolute Idealism*. Edinburgh: Edinburgh University Press, 1983.

Stamm, Marcelo. *Die Reorganisation der Philosophie aus einem Prinzip*. Stuttgart: Klett-Cotta, forthcoming.

————. "Mit der Überzeugung von der Entbehrlichkeit eines höchsten und einzigen Grundsatzes . . ." *Ein Konstellationsporträt um Fr.I. Niethammers 'Philosophisches Journal einer Gesellschaft teutscher Gelehrten.'* Munich, 1992.

Stoljar, Margaret. *Athenäum: A Critical Commentary.* Bern: Lang, 1973.

Stolzenberg, Jürgen. "Selbsthewußtsein: Ein Problem der Philosophie nach Kant: Reinhold-Hölderlin-Fichte." In *Le premier romantisme allemand (1796).* Edited by Manfred Frank. *Revue internationale de philosophie,* Nr. 3 (1996): 361–482; special volume.

Straub, Ludwig. *Jacob Zwilling und sein Nachlaß.* Euphorion 29 (1928): 368–396.

Strawson, Peter. *Introduction to Logical Theory.* London: Routledge and Kegan Paul, 1952.

Surber, Jere Paul. *Language and German Idealism: Fichte's Linguistic Philosophy.* New Jersey: Humanities Press, 1996.

Thalmann, Marianne. *The Literary Sign Language of German Romanticism.* Translated by Harold A. Basilius. Detroit: Wayne State University Press, 1972.

Tugendhat, Ernst and Ursula Wolf, eds. *Logisch-semantische Popädeutik.* Stuttgart: Reclam, 1983.

Ulrich, Johann August Heinrich. *Eleutheriologie oder über Freiheit und Nothwendigkeit.* Jena, 1788.

Vallée, G. *The Spinoza Conversations between Lessing and Jacobi: Text with Excerpts from the Ensuing Controversy.* Introduction and translation with J. B. Lawson and C. G. Chapple. Lanham, MD: University Press of America, 1988.

Verweyen, Hans J. "New Perspectives on J. G. Fichte." *Idealistic Studies* 6, No. 2 (1976): 117–159.

Viereck, Peter. *Metapolitics: The Roots of the Nazi Mind.* New York: Capricorn Books, 1965.

Waibel, Violetta. "Spuren Fichtes in der Textgenese der Werke Hölderlins." Master's thesis, University München, 1986.

Wallner, Ingrid. "J. S. Beck and Husserl: The New Episteme in the Kantian Tradition." *Journal of the History of Philosophy* 23 (1985): 195–220.

————. "A New Look at J. S. Beck's 'Doctrine of the Standpoint.' " *Kant-Studien* 75 (1984): 294–316.

Walzel, Oskar. *German Romanticism.* Translated by Alma Elsie Lussky. New York: Capricorn Books, 1966.

Weiss, Hermann F. "Eine Reise nach Thüringen im Jahre 1791: Zueiner unbeachteten Begegnung Karl Wilhelm Justis und Joseph Friedrich Engelschalls mit Schiller und Novalis." In *Zeitschrift für hessische Geschichte und Landeskunde* 101 (191): 43–56.

Welleck, René. "The Concept of Romanticism in Literary History." In *Concepts of Criticism*, 128–198. New Haven: Yale University Press, 1963.

———. "Between Kant and Fichte: Karl Leonhard Reinhold." *Journal of the History of Ideas* 45 (1984): 323–327.

Wheeler, Kathleen M. "Kant and Romanticism." *Philosophy and Literature* 13 (April, 1989): 42–56.

Wilson, A. Leslie. *German Romantic Criticism*. New York: Continuum, 1982.

Wittgenstein, Ludwig. *Werkausgabe*. Frankfurt/M, 1984.

Zammito, John H. *The Genesis of Kant's Critique of Judgment*. Chicago: University of Chicago Press, 1992.

Ziolkowski, Theodore. *German Romanticism and Its Institutions*. Princeton, NJ: Princeton University Press, 1990.

———. *Das Wunderjahr in Jena: Geist und Gesellschaft 1794–95*. Stuttgart: Klett-Cotta, 1998.

Zöller, Günter. *Fichte's Transcendental Philosophy. The Original Duplicity of Intelligence and Will*. Cambridge: Cambridge University Press, 1998.

Index

Abel, Jakob Friedrich, 128
Abicht, Johann Heinrich, 20, 198, 199, 200
Absolute, the, 8, 16, 18, 19, 20, 24, 32, 34, 36, 44, 47, 50, 54, 55, 56, 66, 68, 80, 81, 88, 89, 90, 91, 92, 93, 95, 96, 97, 98, 103, 105, 108, 110, 116, 119, 120, 122, 123, 127, 137, 149, 163, 164, 165, 167, 172, 173, 174, 175, 177, 180, 181, 182, 183, 184, 187, 193, 194, 201, 205, 206, 207, 209, 211, 214, 215, 216, 218, 235n. 16, 237n. 18, 238n. 8, 243n. 1; knowledge of, 178; representation of, 179; unknowability of, 56, 180
absolute foundation, 24, 32, 34, 39, 50, 52, 174, 215
absolute I, 30, 32, 82, 84, 96, 98, 110, 115, 169, 185
absolute idealism, 16, 18, 19, 25, 33, 51, 56, 150, 169, 171, 178; refutation of, 180
Adorno, Theodor, 53, 222n. 10

Aenesidemus issue, 14, 29, 35, 47, 196, 198
Aenesidemus-Schulze, 29, 47
aesthetic: consequences, 18, 19, 127; experience, 12, 17, 18, 19, 20; ideal, 12, 136
allegorical, 208, 209, 212
allegory, 19, 20, 53, 178, 206, 207, 208, 209, 210, 216, 217
Allgemeine Literatur-Zeitung, 45, 231n. 34
Ameriks, Karl, 222n. 7, 223n. 16
anti-foundationalism, 3, 7, 11
apperception, 70, 83, 94; transcendental, 64
Aristotelian tradition, 59
Arnim, Achim von, 2
art, 3, 4, 5, 9, 12, 19, 20, 21, 28, 49, 52, 53, 144, 162, 167, 186, 206, 207, 208, 212, 214, 219; completion of philosophy in, 178; and divination, 232n. 42; and music, 213; theological work of, 249n. 10
atheism controversy, 240n. 8

Baader, Franz, 2
Baggesens, Jens Immanuel, 65
Bardili, C.G., 85
Baum, Wilhelm, 7, 227n. 9
Behler, Ernst, 12, 13, 181, 194, 195,
　　200, 203, 222n 6, 223n. 18, 225nn.
　　37, 39, 43, 226n. 49, 233n. 55,
　　244n. 2, 246n. 8, 248n. 1
Being, 15–19, 30, 56–78, 84–116, 122–
　　26, 133–38, 145–50, 163–76; absolute,
　　66–69, 77, 93–95, 96, 105, 138,
　　146; existential and predicative,
　　63, 83; of the I, 179; Jacobi on
　　transrelexivity of, 178; original,
　　57, 173; pure, 93; as a real
　　predicate, 69; relative, 93, 95,
　　138; as revealed, 73, 104, 167;
　　singularity of, 67; unity of, 84
Beiser, Frederick, 6, 7, 15, 222nn. 7,
　　11, 226n. 50, 245n. 5
Beißner, Frederick, 102
belief, 12, 30–36, 40, 49, 57, 79, 168,
　　170, 203–5, 232, 242, 248
Benjamin, Walter, 222n. 9, 248n. 3;
　　and medium of reflection, 202; *The
　　Concept of the Critique of Art in
　　German Romanticism*, 202
Berlin, 2, 3, 25, 27, 41, 103
Berlin salons, 25
Berlin, Isaiah, 221n. 3
Beuys, Joseph, 53
Böhlendorff, Casimir Ulrich, 28, 129,
　　130, 197
Boisserée brothers, 32
BonJour, Lawrence, 40
Bowie, Andrew, 6, 223n. 12
Brauer, Ursula, 238nn. 2, 5, 239n. 7
Brechtel, Jakob, 129
Brentano, Bettine, 131
Brentano, Clemens, 2
Bülow, Eduard von, 156
Bund der Geister, 130, 142

Castañeda, Hector-Neri, 238n. 9
Catholic, 132, 206, 207
Catholicism, 25

Cavell, Stanley, 7, 8, 222n. 7,
　　224n. 22
censors, 25, 39, 41
Cervantes, Miguel de, 12
Chisholm, Roderick, 40
classical poetry, 12
cogito, 61, 64–65, 70, 125, 135; as
　　empirical proposition, 71
coherence theory of truth, 7, 19, 137
Cologne, 10, 20, 32, 179, 185;
　　Cathedral of, 207
concept of representation, 16, 41, 44
conditioned, 34, 49, 56, 69, 72–75, 78,
　　80–82, 96, 104, 105, 116, 198, 204,
　　216; I as, 183; knowledge, 59,
　　180; relation, 87
consciousness, 133, 165; mediated, 73;
　　moral, 101; objective, 81, 135, 176;
　　unmediated, 82
constellation portrait, 7, 16, 141
Creuzer, Christoph Andreas Leonhard,
　　158
Critique of Pure Reason, 15, 16, 37, 59
Crusius, Christian August, 16, 68, 77,
　　230n. 12, 233n. 11

Danto, Arthur C., 53
Das Athenäum, 8, 13, 27, 221n. 6
Dasein, 61–65, 68–77, 83, 94, 104,
　　137, 199, 209
deduction: from a highest principle, 31,
　　33; transcendental, 14, 35
deductive method, 8, 13, 56, 138
Descartes, René, 10, 117, 173
Devitt, Michael, 29
di Giovanni, George, 226n. 47, 227nn.
　　7, 8, 249n. 11
Diez, Carl Immanuel, 27, 31, 47, 51,
　　151, 228n. 13, 232n. 38; critique of
　　Reinhold, 45, 147,182
Dilthey, Wilhelm, 5, 222n. 8
Döderlein, Johann Christoph, 197
Döderlein, Johann Ludwig, 153
dogmatism, 78, 113–14, 180
Dürrenberg, 194, 240n. 3, 248n. 6

Earliest Program for a System of German Idealism, 145

Ebel, Johann Gottfried, 130

Eberhard, Johann August, 14, 23, 45, 196

Eichendorff, Johann von, 2

Eldridge, Richard, 6, 7, 8, 223n. 13, 224n. 22

epistemological realism, 28, 56

Erhard, Johann Benjamin, 7, 16, 25, 31, 37, 41–52, 97–99, 109, 119–20, 158, 177, 199, 227n. 9, 228n. 11, 230n. 10, 245n. 1; criticism of Schelling, 47; critique of Reinhold and Fichte, 163; and Novalis, 153; objections to Reinhold, 47

feeling, 21, 34, 48, 49, 57, 64, 70–78, 104, 126, 131, 136, 144, 165–73, 178, 184–89, 194, 203, 216; of limitation, 187; puzzle of self-feeling, 186

Feuerbach, Paul Johann Anselm, 14, 35, 36, 50, 55, 97, 100, 101, 102, 128, 136, 186, 197

Fichte, Johann Gottlieb, 2, 3, 5, 7–11, 13–20, 57, 61, 63–66, 74, 84, 86–91, 94–111, 142–46, 152, 155, 161–71, 174, 178, 181; and *Act of Annihilation*, 37; arrival and teaching activities in Jena, 55, 85, 115–16, 128–29, 141, 155, 182, 198; association with Schelling, 109; early education of, 158; *Eigene Meditationen*, 65, 121; and feeling, 168–70; financial support of, 240; *Grundlage des Naturrechts nach Principien der Wissenschaftslehre*, 192, 196; and Hölderlin's critique, 113–26; and imagination, 193, 215; on language, 166; lectures on *Wissenschaftslehre*, 132; *Logic and Metaphysics*, 103, 115; and Novalis, 23–54, 162; and philosophy of first principles, 101, 109, 155, 183, 193; Platner-Lectures,

85; and Reinhold, 26; relation with Hardenberg family, 158; on relative identity, 125; and Schelling, 91, 179, 205; and Schlegel, 180, 185, 188, 192–97, 205–7; and self-consciousness as principle of philosophy, 107; on *setzen*, 65; and Spinoza, 120; theory of judgment, 85–87; *Wissenschaftslehre*, 20, 25, 30, 98, 102–3, 108, 113, 119–20, 127, 141, 143, 144, 154, 159, 165, 167, 181, 182, 185, 193, 195, 197, 215; *Wissenschaftslehre nova methodo*, 135, 197; writings on the revolution, 114

fichtesize, 161

Fichte-Studien, 16, 18, 41–42, 48, 52, 139, 153–58, 160–64, 169, 171, 193, 241

finite I, 179, 200, 218

Firchow, Peter, 222n. 6

first principles, 3, 15,–20, 24, 26, 33, 35, 43, 51, 56, 58, 100, 101, 107, 153, 155, 161, 177, 181, 183, 192, 195, 197, 203, 205; critique of, 119, 195; philosophy of, 154

Forberg, Friedrich Carl, 7, 14, 16, 23, 36, 41, 45, 50, 54, 97, 120, 186, 199, 228n. 15, 231n. 29, 245n. 1, 249n. 14

foundations, 1, 7, 10, 18–20, 23, 24, 26, 31, 34, 49, 51, 55, 68, 72, 79, 145, 192, 221; search for, 53, 205

fragment, 4, 6, 11, 13, 20, 34, 77, 131, 156, 179, 210, 211, 213, 214, 218; philosophical place of, 210–11

Frank, Manfred, 1, 2, 3, 5, 6, 7, 8, 11, 14, 15, 16, 17, 18, 19, 20, 21, 148, 152, 222n. 7, 223n. 16, 224n. 18, 226n. 23, 232n. 38, 233n. 13, 235n. 15, 236n. 16, 237n. 19, 238n. 4, 244n. 2, 245n. 9, 249n. 12; *Einführung in die frühromantische Ästhetik*, 152, 223n. 16; *Selbstbewußtseinstheorien von Fichte bis Sartre*, 152

Freemasonry, 128

Frege, Gottlob, 123

French Revolution, 128, 240n. 8
Friedrich, Caspar David, 2

Gadamer, Hans-Georg, 30, 108, 222n. 8, 236n. 15
German Idealism, 11, 16, 24, 28, 56, 75, 109, 130, 144, 145, 222n. 7
Goethe, Johann Wolfgang von, 2, 3, 130, 131, 211
Gontard, Susette, 130
Günther, Anton, 194

Hamann, Johann Georg, 65
Hardenberg, Erasmus von, 155, 159, 163, 240n. 6
von Hardenberg, Sophie, 156
Hardenberg, Friedrich von. *See* Novalis
Hardenberg, Karl August von, 25
von Hardenberg, Karoline, 156
Harris, H.S., 226n. 47
Haubold, Ernst, 157
Haym, Rudolf, 211, 221n. 5, 225n. 35
Hegel, Georg Friedrich Wilhelm, 2, 17, 19, 24, 27–29, 55, 56, 78–79 84, 85, 95, 97, 100–1, 113, 115, 117, 123, 130–33, 135, 142, 145–50, 171, 173–74, 182, 193, 208, 211, 225n. 43, 237n. 1, 243n. 31; and absolute idealism, 178; and absolute knowledge, 187; Berlin Encyclopedia, 84; on idealism, 178; *Phenomenology of Spirit*, 132; relation of finitude to infinitude, 178; and Issac Sinclair, 128; and Jacob Zwilling, 141
Hegel, Hannelore, 133
Heidegger, Martin, 53, 58
Heilborn, Ernst, 156
Hemsterhuis, Franz 64, 161
Henrich, Dieter, 7, 15, 16, 18, 26–27, 30–31, 50–51, 67, 70–71, 73, 100, 107–10, 113, 132–33, 143, 146–49, 151–55, 195–96, 223n. 15, 227n. 11, 228n. 13, 229n. 16, 232n. 38, 235n. 3, 237n. 17, 239n. 3; and constellation research, 26; *Grund im Bewußtsein*,

70–73, 100, 152, 155; *Jakob Zwillings Nachlaß*, 132, 143, 146; *Konstellationen*, 148, 151, 239n. 3, 240, n. 1
Herbart, Johann Friedrich, 20, 102, 128, 154, 197–98, 247nn. 21, 22, 23; and critique of Schelling, 197; and Schlegel, 197–98; and Sinclair, 128
Herbert, Franz Paul von, 7, 14, 16, 23, 25, 31, 41, 97, 99, 227n. 9, 228n. 11; and Novalis, 153
Herder, Johann Gottfried, 58
Heydenreich, Karl Heinrich, 42, 43, 45, 230n. 13, 231n. 30
Hoffbauer, Johann Christoph, 52, 166, 232nn. 43, 46, 50, 242n. 16
Hogrebe, Wolfgang, 90, 234n. 10
Hölderlin, Friedrich, 3, 5, 7, 14–18, 25–31, 36–37, 56–57, 63–68, 74, 75, 77–96, 127, 129, 130, 131, 132, 133, 134, 135, 137, 138, 141, 142, 143, 144, 145, 146, 147, 149, 150, 151, 152, 163; and absolute idealism, 150; and aesthetic intuition, 100; early thought, 16, 17, 26; and feeling, 170; and Fichte, 91, 104, 113–26, 158, 237; and Herbart, 197; Hölderlin circle, 27, 131; Hölderlin Tower, 131; *Hyperion*, 66, 100, 116–18, 121, 124, 144; and intellectual intuition, 64, 74, 89, 104, 105, 134; and Jacobi, 27–30, 57, 78, 107; in Jena, 114; and judgment, 88, 90, 101–4, 125, 138, 152, 164; and Kant, 62, 119; on love, 123, 161; and Niethammer, 98, 100, 101, 113; and Novalis, 153, 154, 155, 162; and Reinhold, 103, 106, 115; and Schelling, 97–111, 113; and schizophrenia, 130, 131; and self-consciousness, 105, 106; and Sinclair, 127–30, 150; and skepticism, 100, 182; and Society of Free Men, 128; and Susette Gontard, 130; *Über die Verfahrungsweise des poetischen Geistes*, 107, 126–27; *Urtheil und Seyn*, 16, 17, 68, 74, 78, 79, 83, 87–88, 92–93, 98–102,

109, 110, 113, 116, 122, 124, 133, 146, 156, 173; and *Wechselwirkung*, 193; and *Zwilling*, 139–44, 147
Homburg Circle, 7, 15, 28, 146 , 152, 197, 239n. 8
Homburg, 108, 123, 127, 130, 131, 141
Horn, Friedrich, 128, 130, 142, 197
Humboldt, Wilhelm von, 166
Hume, David, 69, 71, 117

idealism, 5, 15, 16, 18, 19, 24, 29, 41, 55, 107, 150, 171, 207; and accessibility of absolute principle, 177; consciousness immanent, 117; criticism of, 41, 78; in contrast to *Frühromantik*, 178; speculative, 97; transcendental, 56
identity theory of predication, 90
imagination, 1, 40, 48, 84, 132, 144, 145, 147, 148, 207, 210, 215; and hovering, 207, 215
infinite, 16–21, 29, 32, 34, 36, 39, 40, 44, 49, 51, 54, 56, 72, 73, 80, 101, 120, 138, 144, 146, 148, 149, 161, 174, 181, 184, 186, 193, 198, 202, 203, 207–11, 213, 214–15, 217–19; challenge posed by, 137; knowledge of, 185; meaning of, 67; presentation of, 206; striving towards, 118, 119; transition to finite, 69; unity of the self, 126
infinite approximation, 30, 99, 121, 133, 135, 137, 163, 180, 184, 187, 192, 245n. 2
infinite progress, 99, 100, 179, 245n. 2
infinite progression, 17, 34, 36, 56, 107, 138, 177, 187, 192, 248n. 1
infinite regress, 57, 205
infinite striving, 122
intuition: aesthetic, 56, 100, 133, 163; antimony of, 187; in Hölderlin, Fichte and Schelling, 78; in Hölderlin, and Schelling, 82, 89; immediate, 105; intellectual, 48, 49,

64, 71, 78, 92, 94, 95, 98, 104, 105, 107, 110, 125, 133–36, 171, 184–85, 187–88, 236; of self, 185, 186, 188; as starting point, 185; unmediated, 79
invention, 51–53, 232
irony, 19–21, 25, 179, 181, 205, 215–18; romantic, 214

Jacobi, Friedrich Heinrich, 14–16, 29–30, 33, 34, 36, 40, 56–64, 65, 67, 68, 69–74, 152; on Being, 59, 165; on feeling 77–96, 104, 203, 205; and Hölderlin, 78, 88, 99–100, 108, 125; and judgment, 87; and Kant, 59–72, 203; and Novalis, 57, 64, 164, 170–71, 176; on revelation, 70–73; and Schelling, 78, 79, 82, 83, 204; and Schlegel, 178, 200–6; and search for knowledge, 74, 186; and Sinclair, 132, 136; *Spinoza-Büchlein*, 34, 40, 58, 72, 113, 200–5; and unknowability of the Absolute, 178–80; *Woldemar*, 200–3
Jacobin, 25, 31, 41
Jamme, Christoph, 132, 239n. 3
Jena, 2, 3, 7, 15, 17, 20, 23, 25, 26, 27, 28, 30, 31, 32, 33, 37, 39, 41, 45, 50, 54, 89, 101, 109, 114, 127, 128, 129, 130, 132, 141, 142, 143, 152, 154, 155, 158, 161, 170, 178, 181, 182, 183, 197, 198, 199, 203, 207, 240n. 6, 244n. 2, 245n. 5, 246n. 10, 248n. 6, 249n. 7
Jena Circle, 15, 19, 27, 28, 30, 35, 37, 55, 177
Jewish, 25, 239n. 1
judgment, 24, 59, 78, 83–87, 99, 107, 115, 133, 146, 147, 152, 165, 171, 172, 174, 197, 207, 234n. 4, 236n. 6; Hölderlin on, 88, 90, 101–4, 125, 138, 152, 164; Kant on, 61–64, 66, 83, 94, 103, 124–25, 164; Novalis on, 164; as original division, 85, 88, 103, 115, 124, 125, 146, 164; predicative 77, 84, 92, 164; Schelling on, 88–96; Sinclair on, 135–39; synthetic, 126; thetical, 61, 65, 78, 92, 105, 108

Jung, Franz Wilhelm, 128, 130
Just, Caroline, 241

Kamnitzer, Ernst, 156
Kant, Immanuel, 2, 5, 6, 12, 13, 14, 15,
    16, 24, 29, 31, 35, 37, 42–52, 71–72,
    77–78, 83–84, 89–90, 101, 117, 122,
    124, 138, 146, 159, 169, 176, 196; and
    British empiricists, 70; and Christian
    August Crusius, 68, 70; and dualism,
    198; and freedom of will, 199, 246;
    and Hölderlin, 62, 119; and imagina-
    tion, 207; and Jacobi, 59–72, 203; and
    judgment, 61–64, 66, 83, 94, 103,
    124–25, 164; and Novalis, 62, 158,
    171; on positing and position, 62, 67;
    pre-critical writings, 58; regulative
    idea, 179; self-consciousness, 173; table
    of categories, 95
Kantian tradition, 65, 90
Kepler, Johannes, 27
Kierkegaard, Søren, 211
Kluckhohn, Paul, 18, 156, 157, 221n.
    5, 226n. 43, 229n. 1
knowledge, search for, 7, 17, 21, 39, 186
Kondylis, Panajotis, 152
Krausz, Michael, 224n. 26
Kühn, Sophie von, 2, 27, 155, 161

Lacan, Jacques, 106, 236n. 11
Lacoue-Labarthe, Phillipe, 8
Late Romanticism, 2, 224n. 31, 226n. 43
Leibniz, Gottfried Wilhelm, 67, 199
Leibnizian tradition, 126
Leibnizians, 29, 42, 199
Leipzig, 42, 145, 159
Leutwein, Ph.J., 130
longing, 4, 19, 21, 29, 49, 54, 100,
    168, 192, 218, 223n. 13; for the
    infinite, 4, 21, 29, 100, 174, 177,
    184, 192; for knowledge, 184
love, 12, 25, 116, 117, 123, 130, 132,
    161; Schelling's formulation of, 122
Lovejoy, A.O., 12, 224n. 35
Lukács, Georg, 25, 221n. 2, 226n. 43

Mach, Ernst, 106, 236n. 9
Mähl, Hans-Joachim, 18, 157, 160,
    163, 240n. 3, 241n. 10
Maimon, Salomon, 14, 29, 47, 226n. 47
Marti, Fritz, 234n. 1
Marx, Karl, 55, 107
Meistersinger, 52
Mendelssohn, Moses, 15, 204, 207
Middle Romanticism, 2, 226n. 43
Miltitz, Baron Ernst Haubold von, 157
Miltitz, Dietrich Freiherr von, 157
modern thought, 24, 117
Molitor, Joseph Franz, 130
Moritz, Karl Philipp, 28
Muhrbeck, Friedrich, 129, 130, 142, 197
Müller, Adam, 2
Musil, Robert, 54, 233n. 57
mysticism, 180

Nancy, Jean-Luc, 8
Napoleon Bonaparte, 142, 143
Naschert, Guido, 244n. 2, 247n. 20,
    248n. 2
naturalism, 6, 7
Nazis, 25
Nazism, 1
Neuffer, Christian Ludwig, 114
Newton, Issac, 54
Niethammer, Friedrich Phillip 7, 14,
    16, 23, 27, 31, 33–37, 41, 49, 51,
    97, 98, 99, 100, 108–10, 119–20,
    132, 136, 143, 151, 154, 159, 164, 175,
    197, 204; and anti-foundationalism,
    108; and *Concerning the Demands of
    Common Sense on Philosophy*, 35;
    critique of Fichte, 101; critique of
    Reinhold and Fichte, 163; coherence
    theory of truth, 137; Hölderlin, 98,
    100, 101, 113; host to Fichte, Schlegel,
    and Novalis, 158; literary remains,
    160; and Novalis, 153; and search for
    knowledge, 186; and skepticism, 245
Nietzsche, Friedrich, 4
nonsense, realm of, 24, 30, 36, 44, 51,
    56, 97

Index

Novalis, 2, 3, 5, 7, 12, 14, 15, 16, 18, 19, 20, 23, 24, 25, 26, 27, 28, 30, 31, 32, 33, 34, 35, 36, 37, 55, 56, 57, 63, 75, 77, 78, 80, 84, 95, 97, 99, 102, 139, 150, 174, 177, 186, 200, 205, 215, 228n. 15, 229n. 3, 241n. 9, 243n. 21; and Abicht, 200; on the Absolute, 122; and coherence theory of truth, 49–50; critical edition of his work, 18, 156, 157; and Erhard, 48, 101; and feeling, 167, 168, 170, 171, 184, 205; and Fichte, 39–54, 155, 158, 159, 161, 194; and Herbert, F.P. von, 101; and Hölderlin, 151, 153, 154, 155, 162, 163; on the I, 169; on intellectual intuition, 64; and Jacobi, 57, 64, 164; on judgment, 164; and Kant, 62, 158, 164, 171; on language, 166; and Niethammer, 98, 101, 153; and *Philosophisches Journal*, 160; philosophy as infinite activity, 174, 175; and philosophy of first principles, 45, 54, 154, 194; and pivotal role in early German Romanticism, 151–76; on reflection, 167, 171, 172, 173; and Reinhold, 101, 154; and Schelling, 48; and Schlegel, 64, 153, 159 161, 177, 188, 194, 195, 203; and Schmid, 153, 158, 169–70; and self-feeling, 186; and Sinclair, 135; and skepticism, 175; and *Wechselbestimmung*, 193; and *Wechselerweis*, 194. See *Fichte-Studien*
ontological: argument, 95; monism, 56; proof of substance, 67; realism, 28, 169
von Oppel, Julius Wilhelm, 154, 155, 158, 159
Orthmann, Johann Joachim, 129

Pantheism Controversy, 15
Perry, John, 236n. 10
Peter, Klaus, 222n. 10
Petzold, Emil, 28
philosopher's stone, 33, 175

philosophical method, 13, 181, 185
Philosophisches Journal, 7, 33–35, 37, 43, 50, 98–101, 119–20, 153–54, 157, 160, 175, 226n. 49, 229n. 18, 235n. 2, 242n. 20
philosophy: as an infinite task, 18, 19, 174–75, 177; based on first principles, 5, 8, 20, 26, 35, 46, 55, 135, 137, 153, 154, 155, 175, 191, 193, 194, 196, 203, 204, 245n. 1, 248n. 1; completed in and as art, 19; of reflection, 15, 18, 151
Plato, 4, 100, 145, 234n. 3
poetic saying, 20, 207
poetry, 3, 6, 8, 9, 11, 12, 13, 21, 177, 207–8, 211, 213, 214; and philosophy, 219
Popper, Karl, 54
post-Kantian, 10, 23
premonition [*Ahnung*], 142, 179, 187
presentation, 20, 65; of the unpresentable, 53, 208
principle: of consciousnes, 14, 31, 40, 45, 46, 47, 49, 58, 196, 203; of approximation, 97

Rastatt Congress, 130
realism, 28, 29, 55, 75, 171, 172; in Romanticism, 68
reflection, 18, 19, 21, 33, 48, 56, 71, 87, 89, 117, 121, 123, 125–26, 188, 192, 193, 194, 205, 208, 210; I as object of, 179; medium of, 202; in Novalis, 164–67, 170–73; philosophizing, 137; principle of, 121; self, 192; in Sinclair, 127–39; in Zwilling, 141–50
Regensburg Congress, 130
regulative: concept, 44, 51; idea, 32, 44, 51, 149, 179
Rehberg, August Wilhelm, 14, 42, 45, 196
Reimarus, Hermann Samuel, 51, 52
Reinhold, Karl Leonhard, 2, 7, 14, 15, 16, 24, 28, 29, 30, 31, 32, 33, 35,

Reinhold, Karl Leonhard (*continued*)
36, 37, 40, 42, 43, 44, 45, 46, 47,
49, 50, 54, 58, 65, 68, 74, 84, 99,
104, 106, 115, 119, 120, 128, 129,
154, 155, 163, 176, 188, 196;
*Attempt at a New Theory of the
Human Faculty of Representation*, 44;
and *Elementarphilosophie*, 26, 31, 39,
68, 204; and Fichte, 26; and
Hölderlin, 103, 106; lectures and
students in Jena, 23, 26, 27, 41, 47,
98, 101, 120, 128, 132, 153, 154,
158; and Novalis, 101, 154; and
philosophy of first principles, 55,
147; and principle of consciousness,
203; and Schlegel, 203; and Schmid,
45, 50, 182; and self-consciousness as
principle of philosophy, 107; turn of
1792, 97
Re-Kantianization of philosophy, 97,
101, 175
relationship between the finite and the
infinite, 72
representation: concept of, 42, 46;
conditions of, 46; representing, 65,
89, 106, 171
revolutionaries, 132
Richards, Robert J., 6. 222n. 7
Rist, Johann Georg, 128
romantic poetry, 12, 13
Romanticism, opposition to absolute
idealism, 75, 178
Rousseau, Jean-Jacques, 64, 70, 124,
170, 233n. 9; Savoyard Vicar, 124
Russell, Bertrand, 59, 62, 233n. 3

Sachs, Hans, 52
salto mortale, 82, 88, 203, 249
Sandkaulen, Birgit, 234n. 2, 235n. 14
Sartre, Jean-Paul, 152, 170, 233, 247
Schelling, Friedrich Wilhelm Joseph, 2,
6, 14, 16, 20, 24, 25, 27, 28, 29, 48,
49, 50, 55, 64, 66, 71, 77, 80, 83,
92, 93, 95, 100, 110, 111, 113, 121,
131, 143, 145, 150, 152, 161, 178,
181, 197; and the Absolute, 122;
and absolute I, 81, 84, 94, 96, 110;
absolute idealism, 178; and absolute
knowledge, 175; and allegory, 206;
and art, 208; and feeling, 168; and
Fichte, 91, 179, 205; *Form-Schrift*,
196, 197; and Hölderlin, 97–111,
113; *Ich-Schrift*, 89, 92, 95, 97, 188,
197, 200; and intellectual intuition,
64, 82, 89, 134; and Jacobi, 78, 79,
82, 83, 204; and judgment, 88–96;
Letters on Dogmatism and Criticism,
110; *On the Possibility of a Form of
Philosophy*, 109, 195; *Philosophical
Letters on Dogmatism and Criticism*,
109; philosophy of identity, 56, 78,
79, 93, 123; philosophy of nature,
55, 143; and Schlegel, 178, 182, 195,
196, 200; and self-consciousness, 81–
82; and Sinclair, 127; *System of
Transcendental Idealism*, 56, 91; *Vom
Ich*, 17, 47, 78, 97, 98, 102, 105,
108, 109, 110, 195; writings: early,
82; and Zwilling, 141, 144
Schiller, Friedrich, 2, 99, 100, 109,
114, 118, 128, 133, 145, 146, 153,
154, 193, 211, 246n. 8; *Aesthetic
Letters*, 118; on love, 122; teacher of
Novalis, 158
Schlegel, August Wilhelm, 2, 221
Schlegel, Caroline, 2, 27, 203
Schlegel Dorothea, 27, 207
Schlegel, Friedrich, 2, 3, 5, 8, 9, 10,
11, 12, 13, 14, 16, 18, 19, 20, 21,
23, 26, 27, 28, 30, 32, 33, 34, 36,
46, 55, 57, 102, 119, 131, 132, 151,
152, 153, 156, 160, 161, 177, 181,
187, 191, 196, 200, 202, 204, 205,
207, 208, 210, 213; and Abicht, 200;
and the Absolute, 122, 178, 206,
207; and aesthetic consequences,
177; and allegory, 206, 208, 209; and
alternating principle, 182–84; and
analytic path, 191; and art, 214; and
beginning in *media res*, 188, 189,
202; and break with philosophy of
first principles, 177, 185, 188; and

coherence theory of truth, 137, 177; and Cologne Lectures, 185, 189, 202, 207; and conversion to Catholicism, 206, 207; and feeling, 184, 186; and Fichte, 185, 188, 192–97, 205–7; and first principles, 182, 183, 191, 192, 193, 194, 197, 200; and fragment, 179, 210, 211, 214; and *Gräkomanie*, 12; on hearing, 213; on the I, 179, 213, 218; and infinite approximation, 180; and infinite becoming, 212; and intuition, 187; and irony, 216; and Jacobi, 178, 200–6; and lectures on transcendental philosophy, 20, 183, 207; and longing for the infinite, 100; modes of consciousness, 179; and music, 212; and mysticism, 180; and Novalis, 64, 153, 159 161, 177, 188, 194, 195, 203; on philosophy and poetry, 219; references to the infinite, 192; refutation of absolute idealism, 180; and relation of art and philosophy, 178; and review of *Woldemar*, 200, 204; and Schelling, 178, 182, 195, 196, 200; and search for knowledge, 186; and skepticism, 177; and Spinoza, 184; and theory of time, 245; and *Wech-selerweis*, 193, 195, 196, 202; and *Wechselbestimmung*, 193

Schleiermacher, Friedrich Daniel Ernst, 2, 6, 12, 27, 28, 72, 117, 237; on feeling, 205

Schmid, Carl Christian Erhard, 16, 17, 31, 37, 41–50, 97, 119, 143, 170, 175, 198, 199, 228n. 13, 230n. 11, 231n. 30; *Empirische Psychologie*, 37, 41, 42, 43, 169, 170; and Kant Dictionary, 153; lectures in Jena, 127–128; and Novalis, 153, 158, 169–170; and Reinhold, 45, 50, 182

Schmid, Siegfried, 130

Schocken, Salman, 156

Schokken Library in Jerusalem, 102

Schulte-Sasse, Jochen, 222n. 6

Schulz, Gerhard, 240n. 8

Schwab, Johann Christoph, 14, 45, 102, 196, 199

self-consciousness, 16, 17, 36, 43, 57, 58, 63, 65, 71, 73, 75, 81, 82, 88, 89, 97, 98, 105–8, 110, 125, 134–37, 146, 150, 167, 170–76, 178, 179, 186; fact of, 47; problem of, 62

sensation, 64, 68, 94, 105, 145, 169, 170, 198

Shakespeare, William, 12, 225n. 35

Sinclair, Issac von, 14, 16, 17, 18, 57, 93, 102, 103, 123, 124, 127–39, 141, 142, 143, 144, 145, 146, 148, 152, 154, 163, 170, 186; and coherence theory of truth, 137; on consciousness, 135; death of, 131; dependence on Fichte, 91; and Hölderlin, 127–30, 150; and intellectual intuition, 135; and Jacobi, 132, 136; and judgment, 135–39, 164; literary remains, 156; and Novalis, 135; *Philosophische Raisonnements*, 93, 124, 127, 133, 141, 145, 146; on self-consciousness, 146; and treason, 131; *Wahrheit und Gewissheit*, 132; and Zwilling, 139, 141

skepticism: as basis for philosophizing, 56; regarding first principles, 3, 5, 8, 15, 20, 33, 34, 50, 69, 154, 155, 161, 163, 175, 177, 228n. 11

Smidt, Johann, 128, 197

Spinoza, Baruch de, 30, 34, 43, 57, 58, 59, 66, 67, 69, 70, 71, 114, 120, 125, 152, 161, 164, 197; and atheism, 72; *Ethics*, 67; and rationalism, 72; and Schlegel, 184; on substance, 114, 120

Spinozism, 73

spirit, 1, 47, 49, 58, 97, 98, 117, 128, 165, 170, 172, 173, 181, 208, 209, 213, 216; of Kantian criticism, 115

Staiger, Emil, 50

Stamm, Marcelo, 7, 232n. 38
State Library of Württemberg, 102
Stolzenberg, Jürgen, 7, 106, 236n. 12
Stolzing, W. von, 52
Strauß, Ludwig, 27, 142, 143, 144, 145, 146, 147, 148, 149, 239n. 1
Strawson, Peter, 86, 234n. 8
Sturma, Dieter, 223
Summerer, Stefan, 152
symbol, 146, 208
symbolic, 98, 178
symbolically represent, 208
Symbolists, 53

Tennstedt, 39, 153, 155, 159, 160, 162
Teplitz, 25, 41
the highest, 32, 33, 40, 42, 43, 44, 48, 49, 53, 65, 80, 88, 90, 100, 124, 126, 146, 170, 198, 200, 202, 206, 207, 208, 209, 211
thing in itself, 28, 29, 45, 46
Tieck, Ludwig, 2, 27, 131, 153, 156, 207, 211, 212, 216; *Der Aufruhr in den Cevennen*, 131; *Prince Zerbino*, 207; *Sternbald*, 212
Tieck, Sophie, 2
Timm, Hermann, 152
Tübingen, 17, 31, 45, 47, 85, 98, 111, 128, 130, 131, 143, 148, 178
Tübingen Stift, 27, 31, 237
Tudgendhat, Ernst, 58, 233n. 2, 234n. 7

Ulrich, Johann August Heinrich, 199
unconditioned, the, 24, 31, 34, 36, 50, 57, 69, 72, 73, 74, 77, 78, 79, 81, 82, 87, 88, 116, 178, 185, 216, 236; I, 193; search for, 204
understanding, as infinite task, 108

Vater, Michael, 235n. 12
Vienna, 31, 106, 132

Wackenroder, 27, 132
Waibel, Violetta, 7, 85, 103, 120, 234n. 6, 236n. 5, 237n. 3, 238n. 2
Walzel, Oskar, 221n. 5, 226n. 43
Wechselbegriff, 193, 197, 201
Wechselbestimmung, 193, 246; of I and Non-I, 166
Wechselerweis, 20, 36, 46, 181, 182, 184, 191, 193, 195, 196, 198, 200, 202, 203, 204, 231n. 32, 244n. 2, 246n. 5, 247n. 20, 249n. 7
Wechselgrundsatz, 36, 181, 182, 183, 198, 200, 229n. 20
Weißenfels, 155, 159, 160, 188, 194, 244n. 2, 248nn. 5, 6
Weißhuhn, Friedrich August, 14, 99, 101, 136, 197
Welleck, René, 225n. 36
Wirth, Jason, 235n. 11
Wissenschaftslehre, 11, 15, 17, 33, 37, 43, 65, 87, 102, 115, 157, 174, 180, 194
wit, 4, 19, 20, 181, 206, 209–11, 216–17
Wittgenstein, Ludwig, 4, 7, 51, 53, 232n. 40
Wolff, Christian, 29, 43, 52, 67, 199
Wolff School, 29
Wolffian school, 49

Zinzendorf, Nikolaus Ludwig, 161
Ziolkowski, Theodor, 221n. 4
Zwilling, Jakob, 14, 16, 17, 18, 102, 103, 128, 130, 132, 134, 139, 141, 142, 143, 144, 145, 146, 147, 148, 149, 150, 155, 163, 239; death of, 142; literary remains, 156, 239n. 1; and reflection, 141–50; and Sinclair, 139, 141; *Über das Alles*, 139–47

Made in the USA
Lexington, KY
14 August 2013